THE LAW OF INSURANCE WARRANTIES

LLOYD'S INSURANCE LAW LIBRARY

Series Editors: Robert Merkin and Malcolm A. Clarke

Directors' and Officers' Liability Insurance
Adolfo Paolini and Deepak Nambisan

Insurance Law and the Financial Services Ombudsman Service
Judith P. Summer

Reinsuring Clauses
Ozlem Gurses

Insurance Disputes
Third Edition
The Right Honourable Lord Mance, Iain Goldrein QC and Robert Merkin

The Law of Liability Insurance
Malcolm A. Clarke

Lloyd's
Law and Practice
Julian Burling

Systemic Risk and the Future of Insurance Regulation
Edited by Andromachi Georgosouli and Miriam Goldby

Chinese Insurance Contracts
Law and Practice
Zhen Jing

The Law of Liability Insurance
Second Edition
Malcolm A. Clarke

Good Faith and Insurance Contracts
Fourth Edition
Peter MacDonald Eggers QC, Simon Picken and Patrick Foss

The Law of Compulsory Motor Vehicle Insurance
Özlem Gürses

Directors' and Officers' Liability Insurance
Adolfo Paolini and Deepak Nambisan

The Law of Insurance Warranties
Alastair Owen

For more information about this series, please visit:
www.routledge.com/Lloyds-Insurance-Law-Library/book-series/LILL

THE LAW OF INSURANCE WARRANTIES

FLAWED REFORM AND A NEW PERSPECTIVE

ALASTAIR OWEN

informa law
from Routledge

First published 2021
by Informa Law from Routledge
2 Park Square, Milton Park, Abingdon, Oxon OX14 4RN

and by Informa Law from Routledge
605 Third Avenue, New York, NY 10017

Routledge is an imprint of the Taylor & Francis Group, an informa business

British Library Cataloguing-in-Publication Data
A catalogue record for this book is available from the British Library

Library of Congress Cataloging-in-Publication Data
Names: Owen, Alastair, author. Title: The law of insurance warranties : an insoluble problem? / Alastair Owen.
Description: Milton Park, Abingdon, Oxon ; New York, NY : Routledge, 2021. | Series: Lloyd's insurance law library | Includes bibliographical references and index.
Identifiers: LCCN 2021005116 (print) | LCCN 2021005117 (ebook) | ISBN 9780367468828 (hardback) | ISBN 9781003031734 (ebook)
Subjects: LCSH: Insurance law. | Marine insurance—Law and legislation. | Warranty. | Insurance law—Great Britain. | Warranty—Great Britain. | Great Britain. Insurance Act 2015.
Classification: LCC K1241 .O94 2021 (print) | LCC K1241 (ebook) | DDC 346/.086—dc23
LC record available at https://lccn.loc.gov/2021005116
LC ebook record available at https://lccn.loc.gov/2021005117

ISBN 13: 978-0-367-46882-8 (hbk)
ISBN 13: 978-1-03-201736-5 (pbk)

DOI: 10.4324/9781003031734

For Matt

CONTENTS

DETAILED CONTENTS

ACKNOWLEDGEMENTS

It remains a great surprise to me, and no doubt a number (if not all) of my friends and family, that I should be the author of a book on insurance law. There is no doubt in my mind whatsoever that it would never have come to pass without the support and encouragement of Professor Rob Merkin QC. It was Rob who first encouraged me to attend his class on marine insurance when I was studying for a master's degree at the University of Exeter, and it was he who first suggested I should follow this up with a PhD. His advice, guidance and support in the preparation of the book has been fundamental to its evolution. Any expression of appreciation must inevitably fall short of what is merited.

I am also grateful for the assistance provided to me in relation to s54 of the Australian Insurance Contracts Act by Peter Mann, author of Mann's Annotated Insurance Contracts Act and the guru on the ICA. Similarly Fred Hawke also provided me with his time and invaluable insights into the operation of s54.

I am, of course, also indebted to an array of learned authors on insurance law whose work precedes this book. Of these I have relied most heavily on the work of Professor Bariş Soyer and in particular successive editions of his work, *Warranties in Marine Insurance*. Special mention should also be given to the work of Ozlem Gurses.

On a personal level I will forever be grateful to my son Matt for being such a huge part of my life and for tolerating his father's gradual re-acquaintance with law after a 35-year gap.

FOREWORD

Warranties made their first appearance in marine policies well over 300 years ago. The warranty was in essence an unconditional promise by the policyholder that he would act or not act in a given way, and his failure to adhere to the promise would discharge the underwriters from liability. The early warranties were largely concerned with subject matter security in time of war, and the absence of speedy communications and the all too common lack of evidence as to the circumstances of a loss required wording that allowed the underwriters to walk away from liability without being required to prove that the breach had caused the loss. Proof of breach sufficed. In the eighteenth century the courts recognised an implied obligation in both insurance contracts and charterparties – with the consequences of a breach of warranty – for a vessel to be seaworthy.

The initial justification for the use of warranties had largely disappeared by the middle of the nineteenth century. Economic warfare at sea had largely come to an end, the telegraph made communication much speedier, and iron steam vessels were less likely than wooden sail vessels to disappear without trace. However, warranties continued to be used, the insurance market extended them to the many new forms of insurance in the nineteenth century, and Chalmers in his codification of the law in the Marine Insurance Act 1906 rather confusingly converted settled legal principles relating to legality into warranties.

With the rise of consumerism, warranties were increasingly criticised by courts, academics and practitioners. However, they survived a Law Reform Commission Report in 1957 and a Law Commission Report in 1980. In the meantime, New Zealand in 1977 and Australia in 1984 legislated to impose a causation requirement as between breach and loss.

All of this came to an end with the Insurance Act 2015, the product of a decade of consultation by the English and Scottish Law Commissions. Under the Act warranties can no longer be used against consumers, and the default rule is that they cannot be used against businesses: there has to be some relationship between breach and loss.

This background makes Dr Alastair Owen's text both timely and invaluable. There is as yet no guidance, although much speculation, on the meaning of sections 9, 10 and 11 of the 2015 Act and their impact on warranties. This book examines the pre-existing law (which will still be relevant when the parties have contracted out of the 2015 Act as well as in the 70 or so jurisdictions that have retained English common law principles) and then considers whether the 2015 Act operates in the same way as the Australian and New Zealand legislation.

The same issues arise under all three Acts, but each is differently expressed and the outcomes are not necessarily the same in any one case. By discussing the Australian and

New Zealand measures, and the copious case law that they have spawned, Dr Owen has been able to identify the problem areas and to show how they have been addressed. That is not to say that the rather unique formulations adopted in the 2015 Act – which were the product of much discussion and redrafting, a process traced in the work – will be construed in the same way, but it is at least possible to demonstrate a range of possibilities. A key feature of the book is indeed the use of scenarios to explore those matters.

England, unlike Australia and, seemingly, New Zealand, has chosen to extend the new regime to marine warranties, thereby raising a series of additional problems of compatibility with the implied warranties set out in the Marine Insurance Act 1906. Dr Owen expertly addresses these issues.

Dr Owen's book, like many monographs, began its life as a PhD thesis, but it has been greatly expanded. With so much unresolved, Dr Owen has provided lawyers, insurance professionals and academics with a detailed and analytical study of the changes to English law. Nothing equivalent to it has been written, and this book will deservedly become the key reference point for those seeking answers to the various conundrums posed by the 2015 Act.

Professor Rob Merkin QC

TABLE OF CASES

TABLE OF LEGISLATION

CHAPTER 1

Introduction

1.1 The treatment of breaches of insurance warranties in England and Wales has long been recognised as a source of injustice and a potentially damaging slight on the reputation of the London insurance market and the English legal system. Any breach, however minor, historically resulted in automatic termination of the policy, regardless of the absence of a causal link between breach and loss. The playing field was tilted firmly in favour of the insurer. A number of overseas jurisdictions have introduced legislative change in order to seek to redress this imbalance. It was not until the Insurance Act 2015, which became law in August 2016, that similar change was introduced in England and Wales.

1.2 In critically reviewing the reform initiatives implemented to date, the objective of this volume is to examine whether it is possible to develop a 'one size fits all' approach that provides a simple and clear pathway for addressing breaches of insurance warranties (and other provisions giving the insurer the ability to escape liability), while at the same time delivering outcomes that provide an equitable balance between the interests of the insured and insurer.

1.3 This book is confined to the law of insurance warranties in commercial insurance; it does not address the law in relation to consumers. This author is of the view that it is on the area of commercial insurance that the reputation of the London market most relies and that it is the impact of the Insurance Act 2015 on the commercial insurance market that will most affect that reputation.

1.4 While in some jurisdictions, such as Australia, marine insurance is subject to a separate regime from other commercial insurance, this is not the case in the UK. Nevertheless, there are aspects of marine insurance, notably the regime of implied warranties, that are unique to that sphere. Implied warranties were not abolished by the Insurance Act 2015; accordingly this book examines implied warranties in marine insurance and considers whether a separate regime for marine insurance warranties can be justified in the UK. The Insurance Act (s10 and s11) specifically applies to implied warranties, and the view of this author is that a failure to reform implied warranties represents an omission, not least because in the modern era they are an increasing source of controversy. Accordingly the proposals for reform set out in this volume include specific recommendations in relation to implied warranties.

1.5 The history of insurance warranties is reviewed, both in terms of statutory provision under the Marine Insurance Act 1906 and the common law, highlighting the historic imbalance in favour of the insurer. Attempts by the courts and the market to address the shortcomings of the law are assessed with the conclusion that ultimately they were no substitute for statutory reform. The evolving position of the Law Commission regarding

DOI: 10.4324/9781003031734-1

reform of the law in this area, culminating in its latest report in 2014 which led directly to the measures now incorporated in the Insurance Act 2015, is critiqued.

1.6 The approach adopted in England and Wales in the Insurance Act 2015 is compared with reform initiatives in Australia and New Zealand; prior to the enactment of the Insurance Act, these were the two common law jurisdictions that had already reformed the law of insurance warranties. As a result these jurisdictions provide an excellent basis for examining both the challenges and pitfalls of reforming this sphere of the law. In the view of this author, while the approaches in both Australia and New Zealand have their (different) merits, neither is successful in providing a comprehensive solution to the historic problems and ongoing challenges with the law of warranties. In examining the approach adopted in each of these jurisdictions, this volume analyses both the merits and shortcomings of the particular mechanisms; this analysis is then supported by comprehensive 'stress testing' of the approaches in which each jurisdiction's regime is hypothetically applied to the facts of a range of key historic cases. This analysis demonstrates that, while in both New Zealand and Australia, reform has undoubtedly improved the position of the insured, the approaches in each jurisdiction have their own, separate, shortcomings, confirming that, in the view of this author, neither can be seen as offering a template for a long-term comprehensive solution.

1.7 In critically reviewing the provisions of the Insurance Act 2015, a number of the reforms in the Act are welcomed, but analysis demonstrates several shortcomings and potential problems posed by the legislation. In particular, this author argues that the final form of s11 of the Act is likely to create an unwelcome degree of uncertainty and consequential litigation. This volume demonstrates that the 'risk as a whole' formula, incorporated within s11, is likely to be especially problematic. It is suggested that the purported absence of a causal linkage mechanism is a further missed opportunity and analysis shows that it is unclear to what extent s11 addresses exclusion clauses and conditions precedent. It is further argued that the inability to take account of any prejudice suffered by the insurer and the lack of a right for the insurer to terminate in the event of a breach will hinder the ability of the legislation to deliver balanced outcomes.

1.8 In order to test and compare the approach in the Insurance Act with those in New Zealand and Australia, the provisions in the Act are 'stress tested' by applying the new legislation to the facts of past cases. This 'stress testing' demonstrates that the framework offered by the Act, and in particular s11, is likely to be fraught with issues and uncertainties and falls short of providing a comprehensive solution; at best, it represents a case of two steps forward and one step back.

1.9 Drawing on its evaluation of the approach adopted in the three jurisdictions reviewed, the book summarises the key challenges encountered in seeking to find an equitable and workable solution to the issue of insurance warranties. This provides a picture of the complexity that any alternate solution would need to address and represents a matrix for testing the likely effectiveness of any new approach.

1.10 Building on the experience of all the jurisdictions examined, the author proposes a new and unique solution to the issue of breaches of insurance warranties and similar provisions. Although based firmly on a causal linkage approach, the proposed solution also combines features drawn from the approaches adopted in Australia and New Zealand, as well as elements from the Insurance Act; however, it also introduces new and innovative features proposed for the first time. By 'stress testing' this new approach against historic cases, the book demonstrates that the recommended structure provides a more equitable, straightforward and malleable solution than that offered either by the Insurance Act, or the approaches adopted in Australia and New Zealand.

1.11 Concluding on a note of caution, the book recognises that the many years the Law Commission spent examining this issue, combined with the realities of practical politics and the impacts of the COVID-19 pandemic, means that it is unfortunately very unlikely there will be any appetite to revisit the issue of insurance warranties for several years in England and Wales. The solution offered by s54 of the Insurance Contracts Act in Australia is, despite its flaws, now well accepted by the market and accordingly it is again unlikely that there would be much appetite for radical reform in that jurisdiction, although improvements to the operation of aspects of s54 of the Insurance Contracts Act and the separation of the marine insurance regime remain possible areas of legislative action. While some reform to s11 of the New Zealand Insurance Law Reform Act has been recommended and is again under consideration, this is likely to take the form of tinkering with the existing regime, rather than radical reform.

1.12 Nevertheless, a number of other common law jurisdictions, for example Singapore and possibly Hong Kong, recognise the need to introduce reform in relation to insurance warranties, but have yet to take steps to do so. In those jurisdictions, the solution set out in this book potentially offers a reform package with significant advantages over the approaches adopted in England and Wales, Australia and New Zealand.

CHAPTER 2

The origin and history of warranties

Early marine insurance

2.1 The concept of marine insurance first appears to have been introduced to England in the thirteenth century by Lombardian merchants. This early form of insurance was based on the marine insurance that had been developed in Europe in the early part of the twelfth century. The Royal Exchange in Lombard Street was established under a Royal Charter in 1570; at this stage merchants themselves were the main providers of insurance. Despite its common heritage with insurance law in Europe, from the sixteenth century onwards the law in England began to diverge significantly from that on the continent. The Chamber of Assurances at the Royal Exchange, established in 1577, doubled as both an underwriting and arbitration centre and a register for marine policies.[1] One of the earliest recorded London policies was issued in 1547 on the cargo of the vessel *Santa Maria Venetia*;[2] the policy was written in Italian, but subscribed to by London merchants. The earliest known insurance claim was filed in the Court of Admiralty in 1524,[3] and in the second half of the sixteenth century most insurance cases were decided in Admiralty courts. The first reported English judicial ruling upon a marine policy in the King's Bench was in 1588. By the end of the sixteenth century the concept of Bottomry Bonds was well established; under such bonds the shipowner received a loan in advance of the voyage, on security of the vessel, to be repaid with interest if the vessel arrived safely within the agreed period; however, the assured would retain the benefit of the loan if the vessel was lost or repairs were required to complete the voyage.[4] The Merchant Assurances Act 1601 established a special Court on Policies of Assurance. The Act, under which the Lord Chancellor was to appoint a standing commission, failed to work as intended and was amended in 1662, but judgements could be enforced against vessels and cargos. The Act lapsed and was replaced by a system of arbitration established under the Arbitration Act 1698.

2.2 The cost of the War of the Spanish Succession (the end of which was marked by the 1713 Treaty of Utrecht) was to some extent met by the South Sea Company which had been formed in 1711 with a charter from Queen Anne and which assumed a substantial proportion of the national debt. As part of the arrangements, the company was given exclusive trading

1 Rossi, *Insurance in Elizabethan England,* The London Code, 2016.

2 R Merkin, *Foundations of Marine Insurance: Law, War and Trade,* draft: not yet published; extract kindly provided to the author.

3 *Cavalicant v Maynard* in 1550 is the first known case where the parties are named.

4 *Franchiottie v Schroder* ((1593), SS XI, pg 175) provides an example of such a bond.

DOI: 10.4324/9781003031734-2

rights in the Americas. The initial success of the company led to a number of attempts to raise capital on speculative, and often fraudulent, overseas ventures. Many of these were based around forms of insurance. The Bubble Act of 1720 was introduced in order to reduce these speculative ventures and funnel investment to the South Sea Company. In order to curb gambling, the Marine Insurance Act of 1746 effectively outlawed insurance where the policyholder held no interest in the subject of the insurance (an 'insurable interest').

2.3 Several provisions in the Bubble Act were directed at marine insurance. Royal Charters were issued to two corporations, the Royal Exchange Assurance and London Assurance, and conferred upon them the right to effect loans by way of bottomry. Until 1824, they remained the only joint-stock firms with such a charter.[5] Legislation introduced in 1725 led to the chartered companies being able to plead partial loss only and face liability only for that sum. The Bubble Act was eventually repealed in 1825. There was nothing in the Act which prevented individuals from offering marine insurance, and indeed the Act included a specific allowance for 'private or particular persons.' In any event there remained a need for additional insurance capacity. This capacity was provided by shipowners forming associations or 'Mutuals'; the owners contributed sums towards a common fund which would be used to pay any losses suffered by individual members: if the fund was insufficient, it could be supplemented by 'calls' on members for additional payments. Easily the most important of these associations was Lloyd's, and Lloyd's coffee shop became a focus for these underwriters. Although unintended, one of the consequences of the Bubble Act was to cement the dominance of Lloyd's as the provider of marine insurance. By 1740 most of the marine underwriting in England was effected at Lloyd's; in 1771 there were 79 subscribers at the coffee house, but by 1810 this had mushroomed to approximately 1500, of whom two-thirds were underwriters.

The origin of insurance warranties

2.4 Particularly in marine insurance policies, warranties were used extensively as risk control measures throughout the seventeenth, eighteenth and nineteenth centuries. The initial purpose of a warranty was to define the risk run by the insurers:[6] if the risk was not as described, the insurers could avoid liability. Early litigation relating to warranties was nearly all marine related. A warranty in an insurance policy became recognised as an unconditional promise, breach of which discharged the insurer from all future liability. Some of the earliest examples of marine insurance warranties are found in cases arising from the War of Spanish Succession, utilising the phrase 'warranted to depart with convoy.'[7] The judgements in a number of instances were seemingly based on the assumption that compliance with the warranty was a condition precedent to recovery. In *Jefferies v Legandra*,[8] the ship *The Olive Branch* was insured on a voyage from London to Naples and subject to a warranty that it would sail in convoy. The vessel set sail in convoy, but became separated in bad weather and was captured by a French warship. The court found that, while the warranty was intended

5 R Merkin, *Foundations of Marine Insurance: Law, War and Trade,* draft: not yet published; extract kindly provided to the author.

6 R Merkin, *Foundations of Marine Insurance: Law, War and Trade,* draft: not yet published; extract kindly provided to the author.

7 For example *Jeffries v Legandra* (1690) 2 Salk 443.

8 (1690) 2 Salk 443.

for the entire voyage, if, as on the facts of the case, the insured vessel became separated from the convoy without the fault of the assured, then there was no breach of the warranty and the assured could recover. Merkin argues that the legal effect of a breach of warranty is not clear from the early cases, and suggests that the draconian effect of insurance warranties had not been established by the time of *Jefferies v Legandra* and did not become evident until the middle of the eighteenth century.[9] In *Jefferies*, while the court accepted that, had the insured deliberately broken with the convoy, the insurers would not have been on risk, the court did not discuss whether the removal of cover would have applied to all risks, or only those likely to be mitigated by sailing in convoy.

2.5 In 1779 Lloyd's adopted a standard form of wording for marine insurance which became known as the Lloyd's SG Policy. This cumbersome policy, which remained in use until 1982, has been the butt of much judicial and practitioner criticism. The policy defined the insured perils, delineated the duration of cover and was supplemented by specific clauses, often in the form of warranties, restricting cover in various respects. The guiding principles of marine insurance evolved in the period 1756 to 1815, and Lloyd's played a crucial role in this evolution. Reportedly, Lloyd's underwriters accounted for a 96% market share in the period between 1720 and 1825.[10] Over time, the insurer's exposure was mitigated in a number of ways. The assured's duty of utmost good faith encompassed the duty to disclose and not misstate material facts, but immaterial misstatement gave no actionable rights to the insurer. As a result the habit grew of the assured being required to warrant statements which, if breached, gave the insurer the right to treat the policy as discharged. The lack of effective communications and the resultant inability to prove cause led to assumption of an approach of strict liability under which proof of breach was sufficient to discharge the insurer. Absent specific provision, if the risk increased after the inception of the policy, underwriters were required to bear that risk. This in turn led to the introduction of both present warranties requiring, at the commencement to risk, strict compliance with statements made in the policy and future warranties, with which the assured was obliged to comply throughout the policy term.

2.6 The principle underpinning warranties was stated by Buller J in *Blackhurst v Cockell*; 'It is a matter of indifference whether the thing warranted be or be not material; but it must be literally complied with; and if it be so, that is sufficient.'[11] The warranty had to appear on the face of the policy: *Pawson v Watson*.[12] In this case a representation was made concerning the number of guns with which a ship would be armed. This was not reflected on the face of the policy and the insurer was obliged to meet the claim, notwithstanding that the ship was not in fact armed in accordance with the representation. A warranty could be incorporated into the policy by reference in another document: *Worsley v Wood*.[13] Ambiguity was, however, construed in favour of the assured: *Le Mesurier v Vaughan*.[14] In the eighteenth century the strict nature of a warranty was re-enforced by a series of judgements; for example in *Hore v Whitmore*,[15] where the sailing warranty required departure on or before 26 July, however

9 R Merkin, *Foundations of Marine Insurance: Law, War and Trade,* draft: not yet published.
10 R Merkin and O Gurses, 'Insurance Contracts after the Insurance Act 2015' (2016) 132(3) LQR 445.
11 (1789) 3 TR 360.
12 (1778) 2 Cowp 785.
13 (1795) 6 TR 710.
14 (1805) 6 East 382.
15 (1778) 2 Cowp 784.

sailing was delayed and the vessel was subsequently taken by a privateer, a risk expressly covered by the policy; nevertheless, because of the late departure, the insurer escaped liability.

2.7 Against a backcloth in which the nation was often in a state of war, convoy warranties, requiring vessels to sail in convoy, were commonplace. A key question was whether the warranty only related to the situation where initial compliance was required, or whether it imposed a continuing obligation. In *Lilly v Ewer*[16] 'sailing with convoy' was held to constitute a continuing obligation. This case also confirmed that a vessel separated from the convoy by an insured peril was not in breach of the warranty to sail with convoy. The need for a convoy warranty was partially superseded by the Convoy Act 1798, designed to protect British shipping and their cargoes against capture. The Act in effect established a presumption that vessels should travel in convoy. A licence to sail without convoy could be granted by the Lord High Admiral, but if a licence was available, but was for some reason invalid, then the voyage was illegal and insurance coverage was lost: *Ingham v Agnew.*[17] Insurers sought to protect themselves as far as possible by imposing a warranty of neutrality on the vessels of a nation not at war, usually using the formulation 'warranted neutral ship and property.' It is evident from *Woolmer v Muilman*[18] that non-neutral status from the outset meant that the risk did not attach. It was held in *Lothian v Henderson*[19] that a statement as to the nationality of a vessel was to be construed as a warranty and thus took effect as an implied warranty of neutrality where that nation was neutral. In *Rich v Parker*,[20] at the time of sailing the insured vessel did not have papers to support a warranty that she was American. The necessary papers were subsequently obtained and the vessel was seized after the papers had been secured; however, the initial breach was sufficient to release the insurer from liability as the breach of warranty terminated the risk with effect from the date of sailing and could not be cured. In *Eden v Parkinson*,[21] however, it was held that the words 'warranted a neutral ship and neutral property' did not have a continuing effect. In this case the policy was entered into on 28 November 1780. On the commencement of the policy both the ship and her cargo, being Dutch, were neutral property. This remained the case when the vessel sailed and continued to be so until 20 December, when war broke out between Britain and Holland. At that point as the vessel and its cargo were Dutch, both ceased to be neutral property. The vessel was captured on 25 December and subsequently condemned as a lawful prize. In the words of Lord Mansfield the warranty was 'that things stand so at the time; not that they shall continue.' In *Garrels v Kensington*[22] it was held that, although the loss of neutrality did not, of itself, release the underwriters, misconduct by the master and crew, leading to a loss of neutrality, provided a defence to a claim under the policy. When in 1807 America introduced an embargo on trade with England and France, the market responded by introducing provisions stating that relevant vessels, and/or cargo, were 'warranted free from American condemnation.'[23] War

16 (1779) 1 Doug 72.
17 (1812) 15 East 517.
18 (1763) 3 Burr 1419.
19 (1803) 3 B&P 499.
20 (1798) 7 TR 705.
21 (1782) 2 Doug 732.
22 (1799) 8 TR 230.
23 *Livie v Janson* (1810) 12 East. 648; 104 ER 253 cited in R Merkin and O Gurses, 'Insurance Contracts after the Insurance Act 2015' (2016) 132(3) LQR 445.

risks were essentially excluded from standard policies following the introduction of The Free from Capture and Seizure warranty in 1883.

2.8 In *Bean v Stupart*[24] Lord Mansfield held that a warranty in the margin of a policy must be strictly adhered to, as if it had been written into the body of the document. In this case the insured warranted that the insured ship would carry 'Eight nine-pounders with close quarters, six six-pounders on her upper decks, thirty seamen, besides passengers.' The court held that 30 persons belonging to the ship's company, including cook, surgeon, boys etc. were in this instance sufficient to meet the terms of the warranty in relation to manning levels. In *Hibbert v Pigou*[25] a warranty required the insured vessel to sail in convoy. The ship missed the departure of the designated convoy, but met another navy vessel and sailed under its protection; however, this did not constitute a 'convoy' and accordingly the warranty was breached and the insurer escaped liability. Buller J observed:

> It is immaterial whether the captain of the "Arundel" did all he could to procure a convoy or not; the warranty must still be complied with. Whether it was complied with or not is a question of fact, and the facts show that the ship departed without convoy.[26]

2.9 The courts increasingly interpreted warranties according to what was customary amongst merchants, holding that warranties were not breached by minor discrepancies, thus allowing the assured to recover; see for example *Gordon v Morley*[27] and *Lethulier's Case*.[28] In *Gordon v Morley* the vessel was warranted 'to depart with convoy,' but missed its initial rendezvous point and so proceeded to another, but was seized by the French en route. The court held that it was common practice for the wording to be interpreted as referencing 'a place of general rendezvous,' rather than one specific point; as a result the insurers remained liable. If the parties had intended a meaning that was different from that which was commonly understood, they should have specified the specific departure point.

Implied warranty of seaworthiness

2.10 The concept of an implied warranty of seaworthiness seems to have emerged in the eighteenth century. In *Eden v Parkinson* Lord Mansfield held that

> by implied warranty, every ship insured must be tight, staunch, and strong; but it is sufficient if she is so at the time of her sailing. She may cease to be so in twenty-four hours after her departure, and yet the underwriter will continue liable.[29]

In *Law v Hollingsworth*, where, on the homeward voyage, a failure to take on a pilot prior to mooring in accordance with a statutory requirement was held to be a breach of the implied warranty, Lord Kenyon said:

24 (1778) 99 ER 9.
25 (1783) 3 Douglas 224, 99 ER 624.
26 (1783) 3 Douglas 228.
27 93 Eng Rep 1171.
28 (1692) 91 Eng Rep 384.
29 (1782) 2 Doug 732.

> The principle on which this case must be determined seems to be admitted on all sides, namely, that the assured cannot recover on a policy of assurance, unless they equip the ship with everything necessary to her navigation during the voyage; the ship herself must be seaworthy.[30]

This author agrees, however, with Soyer that on the facts, this case was wrongly decided.[31] In *Wedderburn v Bell*, an implied warranty of seaworthiness was held to act as a condition precedent to the policy attaching.[32] In this case the court also held that for a ship to be seaworthy, it must be rendered as secure as possible from capture, as well as from the perils of the sea. Lord Ellenborough observed that

> It is not enough that a ship is supplied with such sails as are essential to her safety from the perils of the sea, and which might enable her, if not intercepted, from at some period or other completing her voyage. ... [In addition the insurer could also expect] that she may be able to keep up with the convoy, and get to her port of destination with reasonable expedition. She must be rendered as secure as possible from capture by the enemy, as well as from the dangers of the winds and waves.[33]

2.11 In *Watson v Clark*, Lord Eldon stated that where the vessel was seaworthy at the start of the voyage, if she became unseaworthy an hour later, the insurer would be unable to avoid liability; however, if it became evident a short time after the commencement of the voyage that the vessel was unseaworthy, the presumption was that this arose from a pre-existing cause that was present at the time the vessel sailed. In these circumstances the onus would be on the assured to show otherwise.[34] The standard required to meet the implied warranty varied from case to case: in *Hucks v Thornton* the court held that a vessel was seaworthy if she was fit for any of the purposes of her voyage. The fact that she may not have been equipped for some of the purposes of her voyage did not mean she was unseaworthy.[35]

Early instances of illegality

2.12 There are a number of early instances of prohibition on particular forms of insurance. For example insurance on goods smuggled into England without the payment of customs duties was banned in 1693. In *Parkin v Dick*, insurers were held not to be liable for the loss of a vessel seized and condemned by the French when at the time she was carrying naval stores, the export of which had been prohibited.[36] The common law also gave effect to public policy, so that insuring a neutral vessel on a voyage to break a British embargo was void: *Delmada v Motteux*.[37]

---

30 (1797) 7 TR 160.
31 B Soyer, *Warranties in Marine Insurance,* Routledge, London, 3rd Edition, 2017, page 85.
32 (1807) 1 Camp 1.
33 (1807) 170 ER 855 at 856.
34 (1813) 1 Dow 336.
35 (1815) Holt 30.
36 (1809) 11 East 502.
37 (1785) 1 TR 85n.

Causation

2.13 In *Hadkinson v Robinson*, Lord Alvaney opined that the assured could not recover 'unless the article be totally lost by a peril within the policy; and such peril must, as I think, act directly and not collaterally upon the thing insured.'[38] The loss had to be immediately caused by the insured peril and not by anything more remote: *Green v Elmslie.*[39] In *Powell v Gudgeon* Bayley J held that the proximate cause was the 'immediate cause of loss.'[40]

Role of Lord Mansfield

2.14 In the second half of the eighteenth century Lord Mansfield was responsible for refining marine insurance law and introducing a more modern perspective. He sought first to ascertain the customary practice from merchants and then to seek to assimilate those customs into general principles of English Law, paying due regard to the Continental Codes and especially the Marine Ordinance of 1681.[41] Many of the properties of marine insurance law prior to the Marine Insurance Act 1906 were developed by Lord Mansfield.[42] In *Kenyon v Berthou*, for example, he held that there was no need for a connection of materiality between the breach and the loss in order for the insurer to employ a warranty defence.[43] In *De Hahn v Hartley* he held that the validity of the insurance contract depended upon exact (literal) compliance with the warranty.[44] In this case a warranty specified specific manning levels on a vessel. The ship departed Liverpool with six crew short of the specified level. Docking soon afterwards at Beaumaris, the shortfall was made up, but the vessel was subsequently lost as a result of enemy action. Lord Mansfield held:

> A warranty in a policy of insurance is a condition or a contingency, and unless that be performed, there is no contract. It is perfectly immaterial for what purpose a warranty is introduced; but, being inserted, the contract does not exist unless it be literally complied with. Now in the present case, the condition was the sailing of the ship with a certain number of men; which not being complied with, the policy is void.[45]

Marine Insurance Act 1906

2.15 Almost all the rules developed by Lord Mansfield regarding marine warranties were codified and incorporated into the Marine Insurance Act by Sir Mackenzie Chalmers: the intention being to codify the existing law, rather than to make changes.[46] The Act remained the governing legislation for insurance warranties until the Insurance Act 2015.

38 (1803) 2 B & P 388.
39 (1792) Parke NP 212.
40 (1816) 5 M & S 431.
41 HB Hurd, *Marine Insurance,* Effingham Wilson, London, 1922, at pg 15.
42 B Soyer, *Warranties in Marine Insurance,* Routledge, London, 3rd Edition, 2017, page 7.
43 (1778) [1 Doug 12 (n)].
44 (1786) 1 TR 343.
45 (1786) KB 1 Term Reports 343 at 346.
46 B Soyer, *Warranties in Marine Insurance,* Routledge, London, 3rd Edition, 2017, page 7.

2.16 Much of the Marine Insurance Act was based on cases decided on Lloyd's policies and practices, and as a result set in stone principles that were already to a greater or lesser extent out of date. This impediment was further compounded as the courts subsequently applied the Act to all forms of insurance. This reality constrained the development of the law. In 2012 the Law Commission observed:

> In many ways it is unfortunate that primary legislation was used to codify the commercial practices of a relatively small and specialist market in London. It was doubly unfortunate that the courts applied these rules to all forms of insurance. It has made it difficult for the law to develop as the market has expanded the types of risks insured. Although recent cases have glossed the law to accommodate contemporary conditions, the clear words of the 1906 Act continue to exert a strong gravitational pull. There are still many instances where the courts are prepared to interpret the words of the Act strictly, even if those words embody social and economic attitudes from a previous era.[47]

47 Law Commission Joint Consultation Report 204 Insurance Contract Law: The Business Insured's Duty of Disclosure and the Law of Warranties, the Law Commission of England and Wales 2012, para 1.13.

CHAPTER 3

The law relating to warranties prior to the Insurance Act 2015

Definition of a warranty

3.1 As originally conceived, warranties were designed to describe and delimit the risk that insurers were prepared to run.[1] Soyer argues that warranties in insurance law serve two main functions.[2] On the one hand, they are intended to protect the insurer against an alteration, by the assured, of the risk during the term of the policy. On the other hand, a warranty can assist the underwriter in assessing the scope of the proposed risk. As we have seen, prior to the Insurance Act 2015 (which took effect in August 2016), the law relating to warranties was set out in the Marine Insurance Act 1906. Warranties are the only legal term to be defined and regulated by the Marine Insurance Act 1906.[3] S33(1) provides a partial definition of a warranty as follows:

> A warranty, in the following sections relating to warranties, means a promissory warranty, that is to say, a warranty by which the assured undertakes that some particular thing shall or shall not be done, or that some condition shall be fulfilled, or whereby he affirms or negatives the existence of a particular state of facts.[4]

3.2 The courts have long been clear that the principles applicable to warranties under the Marine Insurance Act apply equally to non-marine as well as marine insurance.[5] As we will see, the exception to this is implied warranties, which are only applicable to marine insurance. In general contract law, 'warranties' are considered to be relatively minor contractual terms: if breached, they give rise to a right to damages and not a right to rescind. A warranty in an insurance contract is however a critical term which, if not strictly adhered to, results in severe consequences for the assured. Much of the 1906 Act, insofar as it relates to warranties, remains valid today, notwithstanding the Insurance Act 2015.

3.3 At common law, warranties had a number of features that distinguished them from other policy terms:

---

1 R Merkin, Reforming Insurance Law: Is There a Case for Reverse Transportation?; A Report for the English and Scottish Law Commissioners on the Australian Experience of Insurance Law Reform; available at http://www.lawcom.gov.uk/app/uploads/2015/03/ICL_Merkin_report.pdf or at https://eprints.soton.ac.uk/27860/.

2 B Soyer, *Warranties in Marine Insurance*, Routledge, London, 3rd Edition, 2017, pages 3 and 4.

3 Ss33–41 Marine Insurance Act 1906.

4 S33(1) Marine Insurance Act 1906.

5 'In my opinion, as regards the effect of breach of warranty, the same principles apply whether the insurance be marine or not.' Lord Blackburn *Thomas v Weems* (1884) 9 App Cas 671 at 684.

DOI: 10.4324/9781003031734-3

(1) By a warranty the assured guaranteed the truth of his statement. Thus, if the assured's statement as to existing facts was untrue, or, in the case of a continuing warranty, ceased to be true, there was breach of warranty.
(2) Exact compliance was required.
(3) The insurer was not required to show that the warranty was material to the risk.
(4) The insurer did not need to show that the breach of warranty contributed to the assured's loss.
(5) Breach of warranty automatically terminated the risk.[6]

3.4 A present warranty comprises a promise made by the assured concerning a factual situation or state of affairs at the time the policy is entered into which, if not complied with, results in the risk never attaching. A continuing, or future, warranty regulates the future conduct of the assured. If a continuing or future warranty is breached after the risk has attached, the insurer has the right to refuse liability under the policy.

3.5 Section 33(3) of the Marine Insurance Act[7] states that a warranty 'must be exactly complied with, whether material to the risk or not.' Prior to the Insurance Act 2015, a breach of a continuing warranty also meant that the future possibility of recovery under the policy was ended from the date of the breach: s33(3) of the Marine Insurance Act 1906 stated that the 'insurer is discharged from liability from the date of the breach of warranty.'[8] Before the Insurance Act, remedying the breach of a warranty (be it present or continuing) made no difference: the consequences of breach continued.[9] Under s34(2), once a warranty was breached the policyholder could not 'avail himself of the defence that the breach has been remedied, and the warranty complied with, before loss.'[10] Thus, if the assured had breached a warranty, even unknowingly, the insurer could avoid liability under the policy from the date of the breach, even if the assured had subsequently remedied the breach and even if the breach of warranty had no linkage with the loss the assured subsequently suffered. Insurance warranties must be expressly stated, save in respect of the implied warranties specified in the Marine Insurance Act (the latter are discussed in detail Chapter 4[11]). A warranty was capable of binding the assured even though he was unaware of its existence or contents, as long as the obligation was contained in the policy.[12]

3.6 Whether questions contained in proposal forms can be taken to import warranties as to the future is a question of construction. Although expressly stated to be a warranty, if the court is of the view that the provision in question is not, by its nature, capable of constituting a warranty, it will not be held to be a warranty. In *Marina Offshore Pte Ltd v China Insurance Co (Singapore) Pte Ltd*[13] the policy contained a 'warranty' obliging the assured to comply with surveyor's recommendations prior to sailing. One of the surveyor's recommendations related to the route to be taken. The Singapore Court of Appeal held that the recommendation could not be a warranty because it could not be met prior to sailing. However, in *Royal &*

6 *Colinvaux's Law of Insurance,* ed Prof RM Merkin, 11th Edition, Sweet and Maxwell, London, 2016.
7 S33(3) Marine Insurance Act 1906.
8 Repealed by s10(7)(a) of the Insurance Act 2015.
9 R Merkin, 'Australia: Still a Nation of Chalmers?' (2011) 30(2) *University of Queensland Law Journal,* University of Queensland 189–224.
10 S34(2) Marine Insurance Act 1906: repealed by s10(7)(b) of the Insurance Act 2015.
11 See Chapter 4.
12 *Bennett v Axa Insurance Plc* [2004] Lloyd's Rep IR 615.
13 [2007] 1 Lloyd's Rep 66.

Sun Alliance Insurance (Singapore) Ltd v Metico Marine Pte,[14] the court held that a warranty should attach to a recommendation not to start the voyage in unfavourable weather.

3.7 In determining whether a breach has occurred, the court must determine whether the warranty operates at inception only, or whether it imposes continuing obligations. This will be a question determined by the individual facts of each case. In *Hussain v Brown (No 1)*[15] the proposal form, which purported to be drafted as the basis of the contract, (see the following for a discussion of basis clauses), contained a statement that the premises were to be fitted with an intruder alarm. While true at the time of the contract, the assured subsequently failed to pay charges and the alarm service was suspended. The Court of Appeal held there was no breach of warranty as the proposal form related only to present facts and did not make a promise about the future. However, on a number of occasions the courts have interpreted warranties as imposing ongoing obligations on the assured. In *Agapitos v Agnew (The Aegeon) (No. 2)*[16] at the time of contract, the assured warranted that the insured vessel had London Salvage Association approval of location, firefighting and mooring arrangements. The vessel had approval at the date of the policy, but it lapsed shortly thereafter. Moore-Bick J held this was a continuing warranty: there was no sense in underwriters securing such protection only to relinquish it days later.

3.8 Where the assured has 'warranted' that it is his intention that an existing state of affairs is not to be altered during the currency of the policy, the courts have refused to treat this wording as amounting to a promise that no change will be made, presumably on the basis that the statement only relates to the insured's present state of mind. For example in *Kirkbride v Donner*[17] the court applied this approach to a statement by an assured in a motor policy that no person aged under 25 years would drive the vehicle, other than himself. Accordingly, it would appear that for a warranty to impose ongoing obligations, the intent to do so must normally be expressly stated in the policy.[18] In *De Maurier (Jewels) Ltd v Bastion Insurance Co,*[19] the court held that a clause under which the assured warranted that his vehicle was fitted with locks and alarms was merely suspensory during any period of non-compliance. In *Farr v Motor Traders Mutual Insurance Society,*[20] the assured warranted that the insured taxi would be driven for only one shift each day. However, for a short time it was driven for two shifts. An accident happened after this practice ceased. It was held that the term was merely descriptive of the risk, so that the insured was entitled to recover for an accident happening at a time when the vehicle was being operated in accordance with the policy.

3.9 S35(2)[21] of the Marine Insurance Act requires a warranty to be included in, or written upon, the policy, or contained in some document incorporated by reference into the policy. Section 35(1) states that 'an express warranty may be in any form of words from which the intention to warrant is to be inferred.'[22] In *Thomas v Weems* it was held that the words

14 [2006] 3 S.L.R. 333.
15 [1996] 1 Lloyd's Rep 627.
16 [2002] EWHC 1558; [2003] Lloyd's Rep IR 154.
17 [1974] 1 Lloyd's Rep 549.
18 *Colinvaux's Law of Insurance,* ed Prof RM Merkin, 11th Edition, Sweet and Maxwell, London, 2016, Chapter 7, Terms of Insurance Policies.
19 [1967] 2 Lloyd's Rep 550.
20 [1920] 3 KB 669.
21 S35(2) Marine Insurance Act 1906.
22 S35(1) Marine Insurance Act 1906.

used in a warranty should be construed in 'their plain, ordinary and popular sense.'[23] The construction should take into account the commercial object or function in which the warranty is formulated[24] and the policy should be construed as a whole to establish the meaning of the warranty.[25]

3.10 In *HIH Casualty and General Insurance Ltd v New Hampshire Insurance Co.*, in a case concerning a commitment to make a specified number of films, Rix LJ outlined three tests for a warranty:

(a) Did the term go to the root of the contract?
(b) Was it descriptive of the risk or did it bear materially on the risk?
(c) Would damages be an inadequate or unsatisfactory remedy for breach?[26]

These criteria are now generally applied by the courts in assessing whether a clause amounts to a warranty on behalf of the assured.

3.11 Prior to the Insurance Act 2015, warranties could also be created through 'basis of the contract clauses.' If a prospective policyholder signed a statement on a proposal form stating that the answers given formed the 'basis of the contract,' this had the effect of converting all the answers into warranties.[27] Accordingly, 'basis clauses' permitted representations (including minor ones) made by the assured to be converted into warranties, absolving the insurer from liability if they were, or became, untrue.

3.12 Unlike a failure to disclose information or a misrepresentation, the insurer is not required to show that warranted matters are material or that they induced it to enter into the contract.[28] A basis of the contract clause allowed the insurer to avoid liability for any inaccuracy, however immaterial. In *Dawsons Ltd v Bonnin*[29] an inaccurate statement about the normal location at which a lorry was parked was converted into a warranty by a basis of contract clause. The House of Lords held that it did not matter whether the mistake was material: the fact that the statement made in a basis of contract clause did not add to the risk and arguably reduced it, did not matter; the insurer was entitled to avoid all liability under the policy. Prior to the reform of this area of the law an insurer could, referencing a basis clause, use any mistake on the form to refuse all claims under the policy.

3.13 Although still widely used prior to the Insurance Act 2015, generally the courts had a low opinion of use of basis clauses. In *Zurich General Accident & Liability Insurance Co v Morrison*, Lord Greene MR described basis clauses as 'traps,' as they allowed the insurer to refuse claims because of minor and irrelevant mistakes.[30] As long ago as 1927, the use of basis of contract clauses was described by Lord Westbury as 'contemptible.'[31] Following the Consumer Insurance (Disclosure and Representations) Act 2012 (CIDRA), representations made in connection with a proposed consumer insurance contract (or variation thereto) are no longer capable of being converted into a warranty by any provision of the relevant

23 (1884) 9 App Cas 671 at pg 687.
24 *The Milasan* [2000] 2 Lloyd's Rep 458.
25 *Sirus International Insurance Co (Publ) v FAI General Insurance Ltd* [2005] EWCA Civ 294.
26 [2001] Lloyd's Rep IR 596.
27 Law Commission and Scottish Law Commission, Insurance Contract Law: The Business Insured's Duty of Disclosure and the Law of Warranties (LCCP No 204; ScLCDP No 155: 2012).
28 Hertzell and Burgoyne, 'The Law Commissions and Insurance Contract Law Reform' 114 (2013) 19 JIML.
29 [1922] 2 AC 413, 1922 SC (HL) 156.
30 [1942] 2 KB 53, Lord Greene MR at 58.
31 *Glicksman v Lancashire and General Assurance Co* [1927] AC 139 at pp 144–145.

consumer insurance contract (or the terms of the variation) or any other contract.[32] Section 9 of the Insurance Act 2015 abolishes the use of basis clauses in commercial insurance policies.[33]

3.14 The Law Commission described the law on warranties as 'extremely harsh.'[34] In *Wasa International Insurance Co Ltd v Lexington Insurance Co*, Lord Mance described the law of warranties as 'an area where English law has long been recognised as unduly stringent and in need of review.'[35] The severity of the law as it stood prior to the Insurance Act is well illustrated by *De Hahn v Hartley*,[36] where, as we have seen, a vessel was warranted as sailing 'with 50 hands or upwards,' but in fact sailed with only 44 hands. Soon afterwards the vessel docked and the requisite additional hands were taken on board, but the vessel was subsequently lost. The court held that the insurer was not liable: it was irrelevant that the breach of warranty had been addressed long before the loss occurred; a breach of warranty could not be 'remedied.' As Lord Mansfield opined: 'a warranty must be strictly complied with ... it is perfectly immaterial for what purpose a warranty is introduced.'[37] At the same time the requirement for exact compliance had been tempered to some extent by the complementary rule that the assured's duty did not extend beyond exact compliance. This could produce bizarre results: in *Hide v Bruce*,[38] a warranty that a vessel had 20 guns was held not to require that there be sufficient hands available to operate those guns.

3.15 In *Hibbert v Pigou*,[39] it was held that it did not matter that there is no causal link between the breach of warranty and the loss. *Yorkshire Insurance Co v Campbell* involved insurance on a horse covering marine perils and risks of mortality during a sea voyage.[40] The proposal included a statement that the horse was of a certain pedigree. The horse was however not of the stated pedigree. The Privy Council held that the description of the horse was converted to a warranty by a basis clause. The horse died during the course of the voyage. There was no evidence that the horse's actual pedigree had any bearing on the circumstances of the loss, but the breach of warranty was sufficient to discharge the insurer from liability. The burden of proving that a warranty had been broken lay upon the insurers: *Stebbing v Liverpool and London and Globe*.[41] It was accepted in *Overseas Commodities Ltd v Style*[42] that a measure of relief from the severity of the principle could be provided by the application of the *de minimis non curat lex* rule. However, the application of the rule is

---

32 S6 Consumer Insurance (Disclosure and Representations) Act 2012.

33 S9 Insurance Act 2015.

34 Law Commission and Scottish Law Commission, Insurance Contract Law: Business Disclosure; Warranties; Insurers' Remedies for Fraudulent Claims; and Late Payment Law Com No 353 / Scot Law Com No 238 Cm 8898 SG/2014/131 July 2014 para 13.39.

35 [2010] 1 AC 180 HL. The severity of the law can sometimes apply against the insurer: in *Amlin Corporate Member Ltd v Oriental Assurance Corporation* [2012] EWCA Civ 1341 the reinsurer was able to secure a judgement that he was not obliged to pay under a follow the settlement clause, despite the fact that the underlying case was still the subject of litigation in the Philippines, resulting in the insurer having to argue in an English court the opposite to that which he argued in the Philippines, as well as being potentially exposed to a different outcome in the foreign court.

36 (1786) 1 TR 343.

37 (1786) 1 TR at 345.

38 [1773] 3 Doug KB 213.

39 [1783] 3 Doug KB 213.

40 [1917] AC 218.

41 [1917] 2 KB 433. See also *Bond Air Services v Hill* [1955] 2 QB 417.

42 [1958] 1 Lloyd's Rep 546. The case recognised the possibility of the rule applying, though on the facts was held not to apply.

limited: in *Boon & Cheah Steel Pipes SDN BDH v Asia Insurance Co Ltd*,[43] the assured sought to establish a total loss as only 12 out of 668 pipes were delivered undamaged, but the court held this was too many to be *de minimis* in that context.

3.16 Nevertheless, it remained possible for the parties to limit by agreement the circumstances in which a breach of warranty would apply. In *Printpak v AGF Insurance Ltd*[44] it was held that the wording of the policy – 'Failure to comply with any Warranty shall invalidate any claim for loss, destruction, damage or liability which is wholly or partly due to or affected by such failure to comply' – had the effect of limiting the impact of a breach of warranty to circumstances where there was a causal link between the breach and the loss.[45] Prior to the Insurance Act was there therefore a case for suggesting that the parties' existing freedom of contract provided sufficient flexibility to ensure that equitable outcomes were achieved, notwithstanding the harshness of the statutory provisions? On the contrary, as will be discussed later in this chapter, this author argues that the scope for abuse and inadvertent injustice was such as to outweigh the merits of this argument and that the case for reform was compelling, even before considering the wider implications of the English market offering assureds a less attractive proposition than that available in competing jurisdictions.

3.17 In most instances it mattered not what caused the breach of warranty. In *Hore v Whitmore*[46] we have seen that a warranty regarding the date of sailing was breached as a result of an embargo, a risk expressly covered in the policy, but the court held that it was the breach that mattered, not its cause. It was irrelevant that the assured played no part in the breach of warranty: *Douglas v Scougall*.[47] However an intention to breach a warranty was insufficient: *Simpson SS Co Ltd v Premier Underwriting Assoc Ltd*.[48] Under s34(1) of the Marine Insurance Act, where a warranty had been incorporated for a particular reason, the assured would be excused from non-compliance if that rationale ceased to exist after the attachment of the policy.[49] Arnould argues that where there was uncertainty regarding the meaning and scope of a warranty, a *contra proferentem* approach would often be appropriate.[50] This would at least provide a crumb of protection for the assured.

The legal effect of a breach of warranty: *The Good Luck* case

3.18 In *Bank of Nova Scotia v Hellenic Mutual War Risks, The Good Luck*[51] the House of Lords held that the effect of a breach of warranty was to *automatically* discharge the insurer from liability under the policy from the time of the breach. Lord Goff indicated that a

---

43 [1975] 1 Lloyd's Rep 452.

44 [1999] 1 Lloyd's Rep IR 542.

45 Thus diluting the application of s33(3).

46 [1778] 2 Cowp 784.

47 [1816] 4 Dow 269.

48 [1905] 10 Comm Cas 198.

49 S34(1) Marine Insurance Act 1906 reads, 'Non-compliance with a warranty is excused when, by reason of a change of circumstances, the warranty ceases to be applicable to the circumstances the contract, or when compliance with the warranty is rendered unlawful by any subsequent law.' Section 34 of the Marine Insurance Act was repealed by s10(7)(b) of the Insurance Act 2015.

50 *Arnould, Law of Marine Insurance and Average,* eds J Gilman, Prof R Merkin, C Blanchard QC and M Templeman QC, Sweet and Maxwell, London, 18th Edition, 2013.

51 [1991] 3 All ER 1, 2 Lloyd's Rep 191 (HL).

breach of warranty did not avoid the contract *ab initio*, nor strictly speaking did it have the effect of bringing the contract to an end: the assured may have continuing obligations (e.g. to pay premium) and the breach could be waived.[52] While it is not suggested that the decision in *The Good Luck* necessarily represented a change in the law, the decision served to reinforce the way in which the playing field was stacked against the assured. As Clark has pointed out, automatic discharge could be particularly problematic for the assured:[53] the policyholder may well be unaware that it must either negotiate with the insurer to restore cover, or take steps to find alternative cover.[54] Furthermore, the loss of insurance cover may also have serious consequences for third parties, such as assignees or mortgagees. They may be left without cover, even if they did not cause or contribute to the breach.[55]

3.19 Although section 84(3)(a) of the Marine Insurance Act 1906 states that where the policy is avoided by the insurer from the commencement of the risk, the premium is returnable provided that there has been no fraud or illegality on the part of the assured, one of the impacts of automatic discharge was that the insurer was entitled to retain the total premium unless the risk was divisible.[56] This is a further illustration of the inequity of the position under English law: one that has not been addressed by the Insurance Act 2015.

Waiver of breach

3.20 S34(3)[57] of the Marine Insurance Act provided that a breach of warranty may be waived by the insurer. However, as we have seen,[58] it is clear that no election was necessary from the insurer in relation to the effect of a breach of warranty. Consequently, the only scope for waiver in terms of s34(3) was waiver by estoppel or promissory estoppel: *HIH Casualty and General Insurance Ltd v Axa Corporate Solutions*.[59] For the waiver to be effective there had to be a clear and unequivocal representation that the insurer would forgo his right and the insured must have relied upon such a representation.[60] Mere inactivity by the insurers once they had become aware of the circumstances constituting the breach would not, of itself, constitute a waiver.[61] Instead, it appears that a waiver had to consist of some distinct and intentional act.[62] Once again, the tables were stacked in the insurer's favour. Whether

52 [1991] 3 All ER 1 at 262–3.

53 M A Clarke, 'Insurance Warranties: The Absolute End?' (2007) LMCLQ 474.

54 As pointed out by the Association of British Insurers in a submission to the Law Commission, cited in Law Commission and Scottish Law Commission, Insurance Contract Law: The Business Insured's Duty of Disclosure and the Law of Warranties (LCCP No 204; ScLCDP No 155: 2012).

55 See for example *Scottish Equitable Life Assurance Society v Buist & Ors* (1877) 4 R 1076.

56 B Soyer, *Warranties in Marine Insurance,* Cavendish Publishing, London, 2nd Edition, 2006, page 149. See for example *A Chapman & Co Ltd v Kadirga Denizcilik ve Ticaret* [1998] Lloyd's Rep IR 377.

57 S34(3) Marine Insurance Act 1906, omitted by s10(7)(b) of the Insurance Act 2015.

58 *The Good Luck* [1991] 3 All ER 1, [1991] 2 Lloyd's Rep 191 (HL), earlier.

59 *HIH Casualty and General Ins Ltd v Axa Corporate Solutions (2003)* Chris Nicholl, LQR 2003 119 (Oct) 572.

60 *Motor Oil Hellas (Corinth) Refineries S.A. v Shipping Corporation of India (The Kanchenjunga)* per Lord Goff: [1990] 1 Lloyd's Rep 391.

61 *Argo Systems FZE v Liberty Insurance (Pte)* [2011] EWCA Civ 1572. See also *Brownsville Holdings Ltd v Adamjee Insurance Co Ltd, The Milasan* [2000] 2 Lloyd's Rep 458; *Bhopal v Sphere Drake Insurance* [2002] Lloyd's Rep IR 413; *HIH Casualty and General Insurance Ltd v Axa Corporate Solutions* [2003] Lloyd's Rep IR 1; *Phillips & Co v Whatley (Gilbraltar)* [2008] Lloyd's Rep IR 111.

62 *Bolton v New Zealand Insurance Co Ltd* [1995] 1 NZLR 224 at 236.

the representation was unequivocal was a question of fact.[63] The assured had to show that he acted, or desisted from acting, in reliance of that representation and the court had to be satisfied that it would be inequitable to allow the insurer to go back on its representation and treat the breach of warranty as discharging their liability.[64]

Non-statutory attempts to address the shortcomings in the warranty regime

The courts' response: a reason to avoid reform?

3.21 In a commercial context, if, as might be expected, the parties are aware of the consequences of a breach of warranty, was there any justification for statutory intervention? Consistent with the parties' freedom to contract, Thomas LJ has argued that if a term was important to the insurer or reinsurer, the parties could seek to make the term an express warranty. In such circumstances, the parties should know where they stood: a breach could discharge the insurer. A court should, where there was no express agreement, 'approach the issue of construction with these considerations in mind.'[65] Unfortunately the reality of the courts' interpretation of warranties has been different. Davey argued, and this author would agree, that the judiciary had destroyed much of the single advantage of the insurance warranty – 'legal certainty' – by adopting a range of creative, but inconsistent, approaches to the enforcement of such terms.[66]

3.22 On several occasions the courts recognised the harshness of the law[67] and sought to mitigate some of its defects. One approach was for the courts to interpret terms that appeared to be warranties to be instead 'suspensive conditions,' with suspension applied only for the duration of the breach. *Bluebon Ltd v Ageas (UK) Ltd & Ors*[68] can be seen as a more recent example of this approach. In this case the policy contained an 'electrical inspection warranty' which required that the electrics of a hotel be inspected on a five-year basis. Following the loss of the hotel through fire, the case turned on the wording of the inspection provision. The policy also contained a provision that read:

> The due observance and fulfilment of the terms of this Policy, insofar as they relate to anything to be done or complied with by the Insured shall be conditions precedent to any liability of the Insurers to make any payment under this Policy.

The court held that, using the test of what 'a reasonable person, having all the background knowledge which would have been available to the parties, would have understood' the clause to mean, the inspection requirement was not a 'true insurance warranty.' The court defined the latter as a term of the policy 'which takes effect as a condition precedent to the existence of any cover under it, rather than in relation to any particular risk, or claim or class

63 *Sleigh v Tyser* [1900] 2 QB 333 in this case an inspection of the vessel by the insurer did not prevent him relying on a breach of the implied warranty of seaworthiness. See also *Samuel & Co Ltd v Dumas* [1924] AC 431.

64 *HIH Casualty and General Insurance Ltd v Axa Corporate Solutions (2003)* Chris Nicholl, LQR 2003 119 (Oct) 572.

65 *Toomey v Banco Vitalicio de Espana SA de Seguros y Reasseguros* [2004] EWCA Civ 622; [2005] Lloyd's Rep IR 423, [42].

66 J Davey, 'Remedying the Remedies: the Shifting Shape of Insurance Contract Law' (2013) LMCLQ 478.

67 See for example Lord Griffiths in *Forsakringsaktielselskapet Vesta v Butcher* [1989] 1 Lloyd's Rep 331, where his Lordship is particularly critical of the absence of any causal link between the breach and the loss.

68 [2017] EWHC 3301 (Comm) (15 December 2017).

of claims arising from that risk.' The court held the inspection requirement to be a suspensive condition. As the inspection had not been carried out in the previous five years, the court held that it was required to be conducted immediately and that cover was suspended until the assured had complied with the condition. Interestingly, the court held that the whole policy should be suspended, but in obiter comments observed that as a minimum fire risk would be suspended. As a result the insurer was not liable to meet the loss. The court further stressed that there was 'no requirement that there be any causal link between the breach of the suspensory condition and the loss.'

3.23 Davey describes interventions by the courts in interpreting warranties as follows:

(i) Interpretation: in such instances, although there appears to be a breach, when judicially interpreted, the clause is held to impose a much less onerous obligation on the insured. Davey describes this approach as 'reclassification.'[69] In *Provincial Insurance Company Ltd v Morgan & Foxton*[70] coal merchants declared that their lorry would be used for the transport of coal, a statement that became the basis of the contract. On the day of the accident, the lorry had also been used to carry timber, but at the time of the accident only coal was on board. The House of Lords held that on 'a strict but reasonable construction,' the clause meant only that transporting coal was to be the normal use, and that accordingly transporting other goods would not terminate liability under the policy.

(ii) Waiver/estoppel: here, even though there had been a breach of a clause that would normally discharge prospective liability, the insurer was held to have acted inconsistently with this right, and the right had been lost.[71] For this to be the case the insurer must have 'communicated his election to the other party in clear and unequivocal terms.'[72]

3.24 Other attempts by the courts to ameliorate the harsh effects of the law on warranties included the following:

(1) Construing an ambiguous warranty against the insurer: *Pratt v Aigion Insurance Company SA (The Resolute)*[73];
(2) Narrow construction of the term: *Hide v Bruce*[74];
(3) Holding that if the underwriters wish a warranty to have draconian consequences, they must stipulate this in clear terms: *AC Ward & Sons Ltd v Catlin (Five) Ltd*[75];
(4) Determining that the draconian effect of a warranty is relevant to considering whether the literal words are consistent with a reasonable and businesslike interpretation: *AC Ward & Sons v Catlin (Five) Ltd*[76];

69 J Davey, 'Remedying the Remedies: the Shifting Shape of Insurance Contract Law' (2013) LMCLQ 478.

70 [1933] AC 240.

71 *Motor Oil Hellas (Corinth) Refineries S.A. v Shipping Corporation of India (The Kanchenjunga)* [1990] 1 Lloyd's Rep 391.

72 *Motor Oil Hellas (Corinth) Refineries S.A. v Shipping Corporation of India (The Kanchenjunga)* per Lord Goff: [1990] 1 Lloyd's Rep 391, at 398.

73 [2008] EWCA Civ 1314 at [14], [2009] 2 All ER (Comm) 387.

74 (1783) 3 Doug 213: as we have seen, a warranty requiring 20 guns on the insured vessel was held to be satisfied even though, although the guns were installed, there were insufficient crew to operate them.

75 [2009] EWCA Civ 1098 at [28].

76 [2008] EWHC 3585 (Comm) at [29].

(5) Deciding that the more unreasonable the result, the more unlikely it is that the parties can have intended it, and if they did intend it, the more necessary it is that they should make the meaning clear: *Wickman Machine Tools Sales Ltd v Shuler AG*[77];
(6) Construing the warranty as being relevant to only some risks covered in the policy: *Printpak v AGF Insurance Ltd*[78];
(7) Arguing that a literal interpretation of a warranty must not be inconsistent with other terms in the policy: *AC Ward & Son Ltd v Catlin (Five) Ltd*[79];
(8) Finding that the term is not a warranty, but some other contractual term, such as one descriptive of the risk: *Farr v Motor Traders Mutual Insurance*.[80]

3.25 Could it be argued that the courts' interpretative approach means that reform is unnecessary? In *Bamcell II*[81] the policy 'warranted' that a watchman would be stationed on board each night from 8pm to 6am. No watchman was on duty the night before the loss, but there was no linkage between breach and loss. Despite the apparently clear wording of the policy, the court interpreted the clause as one delimiting risk, with the result that cover was only suspended while the breach continued. It has been suggested that, in the light of this case, in Canada it is only in rare circumstances that a court will find that a policy contains a true warranty: essentially only where the warranty is material to the risk and the breach has a causal linkage with the loss.[82]

3.26 In *Kler Knitwear Ltd v Lombard General Insurance Co Ltd*[83] the policy stated that the assured's sprinkler system would be inspected within 30 days of renewal. This provision was stated to be a warranty and that non-compliance would bar any claim 'whether it increases the risk or not.' However, the court held that the clause was only a suspensive condition limiting risk, notwithstanding that on the facts it did appear that the parties intended the clause to be a warranty. The court's interpretation in *Kler Knitwear* has been criticised by Bird, who felt it was difficult for the parties to be clearer about their intention that the clause should be a warranty.[84] This case is to be contrasted with *Sugar Hut v Great Lakes Reinsurance (UK) Plc*,[85] where the policy required installation of a burglar alarm that rang through to a central monitoring station. Although an alarm was installed, it only rang through to an employee. The premises were damaged by fire, but the court held that failure to comply with the burglar alarm provision was sufficient to release the insurers from liability under the policy. In *Hussain v Brown*, however, Saville LJ suggested that if the insurers wanted the protection of automatic discharge for breach of a warranty, it 'was up to them to stipulate it in clear terms.'[86]

77 [1974] AC 2325, cited in *AC Ward & Sons v Catlin (Five) Ltd* [2009] EWCA Civ 1098 at [29].
78 [1999] Lloyd's Rep IR 542.
79 *AC Ward & Son Ltd v Catlin (Five) Ltd* [2009] EWHC 3122 (Comm).
80 [1920] 3 KB 669, the term that a taxi was to be driven for only one shift a day was held to be descriptive of the risk and cover was suspended when it was used for two shifts a day. The case was approved in *Provincial Insurance v Morgan* [1933] AC 240.
81 *Case Existological Laboratories Ltd v Foremost Insurance Co et al (the Bamcell II)* [1983] 2 SCR 47.
82 C Giaschi, Warranties in Marine Insurance, a paper to the Association of Marine Underwriters of British Columbia Vancouver, 10 April 1997.
83 [2000] Lloyd's Rep IR 47.
84 *Birds' Modern Insurance Law*, Sweet and Maxwell, 8th Edition, 2010, is particularly critical of the decision at para 9.8.
85 [2010] EWHC 2636.
86 [1996] 1 Lloyd's Rep 627 at 630.

3.27 In *Printpack v AGF Insurance*[87] insurance for a business premises was split into a number of sections, each providing for different cover in separate schedules. A burglar alarm had not been switched on in breach of a warranty under the section covering theft. The assured suffered a loss as a result of fire. The court held the policy was divisible and that the breach of warranty did not apply to the fire risk provided under a different section. While one may be comfortable with the outcome in this case, in practice it is surely simply another illustration of the shortcomings of the law as it then stood: how could the assured be expected to know and assess whether, in his particular case, the policy was divisible or not?

3.28 It could be said that inconsistency was the one constant in the courts' approach to interpreting warranties. This inconsistency is starkly illustrated by comparing *GE Frankona Reinsurance Ltd v CMM Trust No 1400 (The Newfoundland Explorer)*[88] and *Pratt v Aigion Insurance (The Resolute)*.[89] In the former case, the policyholder warranted the vessel would be 'fully crewed at all times,' while in the latter the policy stated that the owner, or the skipper in charge and one crew member would be on board 'at all times.' In *The Newfoundland Explorer*, the court interpreted the warranty literally, finding that the provision meant 'the whole time, not some of the time.' While in *The Resolute*, the Court of Appeal held that the warranty should be given a reasonable and businesslike interpretation in the light of its context and purpose. The provision was held to refer only to when the vessel was being navigated.

3.29 These decisions demonstrate that, as the Law Commission has pointed out, where the outcome of a case was dependent on the courts' interpretation, inconsistencies crept in.[90] In the Law Commission's words it made the law in the UK 'appear unfair and unprincipled in the international market.'[91] The Commissioners have observed that very few legal systems would consider it just to permit an insurer to refuse a claim for fire damage because the wrong sort of burglar alarm was installed.[92] Although, given the apparent harshness of the statute, judicial interpretation of the kind referenced earlier may be understandable and engender sympathy, the resultant uncertainties can only be unhelpful to all parties. In line with the Law Commission's findings, it is surely the case that judicial interventions of this kind are not a rationale for avoiding statutory reform. Indeed, if anything, they strengthen the case for reform. To leave the matter for interpretation by the courts, while retaining the potential for severe sanctions on the assured, would be to leave the law in the uncertain, perilous and inconsistent position that existed prior to the Insurance Act 2015. However, although the need for statutory reform was clear, it will be argued that the Insurance Act fails to meet that need and that it represents, at best, a missed opportunity.

---

87 [1999] 1 Lloyd's Rep IR 542.

88 [2006] EWHC 429.

89 [2008] EWCA Civ 1314.

90 Law Commission Consultation Paper No. 204, Insurance Contract Law: The Business Insured's Duty of Disclosure and the Law of Warranties, (2012) at para 12.55.

91 Law Commission Consultation Paper No. 204, Insurance Contract Law: The Business Insured's Duty of Disclosure and the Law of Warranties, (2012) at para 12.83.

92 Law Commission and Scottish Law Commission, Insurance Contract Law: The Business Insured's Duty of Disclosure and the Law of Warranties (LCCP No 204; ScLCDP No 155: 2012) para 12.54.

CHAPTER 4

Implied warranties and the case for a separate regime for marine insurance

Implied warranties

4.1 The Marine Insurance Act 1906 provides for implied warranties in relation to seaworthiness and legality. Perhaps surprisingly, the Insurance Act 2015 did not abolish implied warranties: sections 10 and 11 of the Insurance Act 2015 confirm that the provisions of the Act applying to breaches of warranty (and in the case of s11 other provisions) apply to implied, as well as express, warranties.[1] Accordingly under s10 of the Act, breaches of implied warranties also result in suspension of liability, rather than a full discharge from liability for the insurer. Because implied warranties have not been abolished by the Insurance Act, it is necessary to address them in some detail.

Implied warranty of seaworthiness

4.2 S39(1) of the Marine Insurance Act[2] provides that in a voyage policy 'there is an implied warranty that at the commencement of the voyage the ship shall be seaworthy for the purpose of the particular adventure insured.' S39(3) provides that where a voyage will be conducted in stages, with differing requirements for each stage, there is an implied warranty of seaworthiness for each stage.[3] Soyer argues that the reason the warranty of seaworthiness is implied in voyage policies is because the assured is usually in control/possession of the vessel before she embarks on a voyage and, in this respect, is capable of rendering her seaworthy.[4]

4.3 Note that the implied seaworthy warranty applies only at the commencement of the risk and the start of each stage of the voyage: s39(1) and (3).[5] Seaworthiness is defined by s39(4): 'A ship is deemed to be seaworthy when she is reasonably fit in all respects to encounter the ordinary perils of the seas of the adventure insured.'[6] The definition of seaworthiness in Black's Law Dictionary is 'an ability to withstand ordinary stress of wind,

---

1 S10(1) and s11(1) Insurance Act 2015.

2 S39(1) Marine Insurance Act 1906.

3 In *Bouillon v Lupton*, (1863) 33 LJ PC 37, the insured vessel undertook a voyage that involved both river and sea stages. The fact that for the river stage the vessel was without masts or heavy tackle did not render her unseaworthy as she was properly equipped when at sea.

4 B Soyer, *Warranties in Marine Insurance*, Routledge, London, 3rd Edition, 2017, page 115.

5 S39(1) and (3) Marine Insurance Act 1906.

6 S39(4) Marine Insurance Act 1906.

DOI: 10.4324/9781003031734-4

waves and other weather which the vessel might normally be expected to encounter.'[7] S40(2) of the Act provides that in voyage policies on goods, there is an implied warranty that at the commencement of the voyage the ship is reasonably fit to carry the goods to the contemplated destination. Mustill J in *JJ Lloyd's Instrument Ltd v Northern Star Insurance Co (The Jay Jay)*[8] categorised weather conditions under three headings: (i) 'abnormal bad weather': where the weather lies outside the range of conditions which the assured could reasonably foresee that the vessel might encounter; (ii) 'adverse' weather: weather at the unfavourable end of what might be foreseen; (iii) 'favourable weather': within the foreseeable range, but not bad enough to be 'adverse.' To be seaworthy, Mustill J opined that a vessel must be able to cope with both 'favourable' and 'adverse' weather. In *McFadden v Blue Star Line*,[9] Channel J suggested that for a vessel to be seaworthy it must 'have that degree of fitness which an ordinary, careful and prudent owner would require his vessel to have at the commencement of her voyage, having regard to all the probable circumstances of it.'

4.4 The scope of the implied warranty is wide: while some breaches will go directly to the integrity of the vessel, others can be more technical in nature and yet fall foul of the implied warranty: in *Woolf v Clagett* it was held that leaving port with insufficient medicines may amount to a breach of the implied warranty.[10] In *Garnat Trading & Shipping (Singapore) Pte Ltd v Baominh Insurance Corp.*[11] it was held that seaworthiness is relative to the nature of the ship: the vessel should be in a condition to encounter whatever perils of the sea a ship of that kind and laden in that way may be fairly expected to encounter. Once again, prior to the Insurance Act 2015, it was immaterial that a defect was remedied prior to a loss, or that there was no linkage between the breach and the cause of loss. In *Quebec Marine Insurance Co v Commercial Bank of Canada*,[12] a defective boiler was repaired prior to the loss of the vessel, however, as there had been a breach of the implied warranty of seaworthiness (the vessel having sailed with the defective boiler), the underwriters were able to escape liability. It is clear that seaworthiness means the same in an insurance policy as it does in a contract for carriage by sea: *The Fireman's Fund Insurance Company v Western Australia Insurance Co Ltd and Atlantic Insurance Co Ltd.*[13]

4.5 The implied warranty does not suggest that the vessel will be free from the suspicion of unseaworthiness, only that she is, in fact, seaworthy.[14] Seaworthiness is a question of fact; the issue is, having regard to all the circumstances of the particular voyage, was the vessel at the time she set sail, able to encounter the ordinary perils that might reasonably be expected on that particular voyage: *Steel v State Line SS Co.*[15] Accordingly the definition of seaworthiness varies according to the voyage to be undertaken and the nature of the seaworthiness obligation may differ for the same voyage if undertaken in different seasons: a voyage in winter may well require a higher bar to meet the implied warranty than the

---

7 T West, *Black's Law Dictionary* (10th Edition), 2014 as cited in B Soyer, *Warranties in Marine Insurance*, Routledge, London, 3rd Edition, 2017, page 63.

8 [1985] 1 Lloyd's Rep 264, at 271.

9 [1905] 1 KB 697.

10 (1806) 3 Esp 257.

11 [2012] 1 All ER (Comm) 790.

12 [1870] LR 3 PC 234.

13 (1927) 28 LIL Rep 243.

14 *Towse v Handerson* (1850) 4 Exch 890.

15 (1877) LR 3 App Cas 72.

same voyage conducted in summer.[16] Similarly the nature of the cargo can be a factor in determining whether or not a vessel is seaworthy: *Stanton v Richardson*.[17] Inevitably and sensibly the definition of seaworthiness also develops over time to reflect evolving technologies, international conventions etc. Perhaps surprisingly, a vessel will be judged seaworthy for the purposes of the implied warranty if all reasonably practicable steps have been taken to make her seaworthy: *Burges v Wickham*;[18] accordingly it seems the implied warranty is not the same as an objective assessment of safety or security. It is also important to note that the implied warranty is absolute in nature: a breach can occur regardless of whether the assured has acted honestly or whether he was aware of the defect. In *Lee v Beach*,[19] the owner of a vessel had it surveyed and (he thought) had fully repaired it, but the vessel proved unseaworthy as a result of a latent defect; the court held that the underwriter was able to escape liability. The competence of the crew is relevant to the implied warranty of seaworthiness: in *Wedderburn v Bell*[20] it was held that 'seaworthiness' includes a crew sufficient generally in number and skill for the proper navigation of the vessel. A ship will be considered unseaworthy if her crew is incompetent, but not if they are merely negligent.[21] The absence of relevant equipment, not necessarily attached to the vessel can be sufficient to render it unseaworthy: *The Eurasian Dream*;[22] in this case the lack of walkie-talkies to provide adequate means of communication between master and crew was sufficient to breach the implied warranty. On the other hand a temporary defect which could be easily remedied by the crew does not constitute a breach of the implied warranty[23] and it does not matter that in practice the defect has not been addressed: *Steel v State Line SS Co*.[24] A temporary defect that is not capable of ready remedy would constitute a breach: *Dobell v Rosemore*.[25] Insufficient fuel to enable the vessel to complete the voyage renders the vessel unseaworthy: *Thin v Richards & Co*.[26] Soyer argues, and this author concurs, while a failure to provide a pilot at the commencement of a voyage where one is required as a result of custom or statute would constitute a breach of the implied warranty, the lack of a pilot at the end of the voyage or at an intermediate stage, should not render the vessel unseaworthy.[27] Note that the implied warranty of seaworthiness does not extend to vessels used to transfer the cargo from the quay to vessel prior to the commencement of the relevant voyage. Clause 5.1 of the Institute Cargo Clauses (ICC) 2009 version (type A, B and C) does however exclude liability of the insurer for loss caused by the unfitness of such vessels.

4.6 An express warranty does not exclude an implied warranty unless it is inconsistent with the latter; in order to have such an effect the wording must be 'be express, pertinent

16 B Soyer, *Warranties in Marine Insurance*, Routledge, London, 3rd Edition, 2017, pages 65–66.
17 (1873–74) LR 9 CP 390.
18 (1863) 3 B & S 669.
19 [1795] 91 ER 858.
20 (1807) 1 Camp 1.
21 B Soyer, *Warranties in Marine Insurance*, Routledge, London, 3rd Edition, 2017, page 79.
22 [2002] EWCH 118 Comm.
23 See for example *Leonard v Leyland* (1902) 18 TLR 727.
24 (1877) LR 3 App Cas 72 see the obiter remarks of Lord Blackburn at 90–91.
25 [1895] 2 QB 408.
26 [1892] 2 QB 141.
27 B Soyer, *Warranties in Marine Insurance*, Routledge, London, 3rd Edition, 2017, page 85.

and apposite.'[28] Stipulations in the policy may, in practice, not have the effect of excluding the implied warranty or mitigating the consequences of it: in *Quebec Marine Insurance Co v Commercial Bank of Canada*,[29] the policy contained an exception of losses from rottenness, inherent defects and other seaworthiness, but the Privy Council held that implied warranty was not thereby excluded.

4.7 S39(1) applies at the commencement of the voyage; there is no implied warranty that the vessel will continue to be seaworthy: *Holdsworth v Wise*.[30] What is the meaning of 'commencement of the voyage'? Soyer argues[31] and this author would concur, that 'commencement of the voyage' means the same as 'at the time of sailing' and that it comprises leaving the vessel's moorings ready for sea, though not leaving port, so long as it was possible to demonstrate a motive to commence the voyage.[32]

4.8 A recent case, *Alize 1954 & another v Allianz Elementar Versicherung AG & Others (The CMA CGM LIBRA)*,[33] heard in the Court of Appeal, but subject to appeal to the Supreme Court, may have extended the definition of seaworthiness further, potentially blurring the boundary between seaworthiness and navigational issues. The decision will raise concerns for carriers and shipowners.

4.9 In May 2011, the container vessel *CMA CGM LIBRA* (the 'Vessel') grounded while leaving the port of Xiamen, China. Some of the cargo interests refused to pay the owners' claim for general average contributions, alleging fault on the part of the owners. There were defects in the passage plan and the relevant working chart. Neither document had recorded a warning, contained within a Notice to Mariners, that charted depths were unreliable, and that waters were shallower than recorded on the chart. At first instance, it was held that the defective passage plan and chart rendered the vessel unseaworthy. Given that the master and second officer could, by exercising reasonable care and skill, have prepared a proper passage plan, the court further held that the owners had not exercised due diligence.

4.10 The Court of Appeal held that a vessel may be rendered unseaworthy by negligence in the navigation or the management of the vessel. The court further held that once the owners had assumed responsibility for the cargo as carriers, all the acts of the master and crew in preparing for the voyage were performed qua carrier, and the obligation to exercise due diligence to make the ship seaworthy was an overriding obligation.

4.11 The court recognised that the 'conclusion that the vessel was unseaworthy due to having a defective passage plan appears to have been novel,' but stressed that 'a properly prepared passage plan is an essential document which the vessel must carry at the beginning of any voyage. There is no reason why the absence of such a document should not render a vessel unseaworthy, just as in the case of any other essential document.'[34]

4.12 The appeal to the Supreme Court will be significant in terms of potentially further refining the definition of seaworthiness. The owners are appealing the Court of

28 Bigham J in *Sleigh v Tyser* [1900] 2 QB 333.

29 [1870] LR 3 PC 234.

30 [1882] 7 B&C 794.

31 B Soyer, *Warranties in Marine Insurance*, Routledge, London, 3rd Edition, 2017, page 89.

32 *Sea Insurance Co. v Blogg* [1898] 2 QB 398.

33 *Alize 1954 & another v Allianz Elementar Versicherung AG & Others (The CMA CGM LIBRA)* [2020] EWCA Civ 293.

34 *Alize 1954 & another v Allianz Elementar Versicherung AG & Others (The CMA CGM LIBRA)* [2020] EWCA Civ 293, Males LJ at 85–87.

Appeal's decision on the ground that passage planning constitutes a navigational decision, rather than an 'attribute of the vessel,' and therefore the failure to record the warning was a type of error in navigation that could not render the vessel unseaworthy. One issue that will likely be addressed in the appeal is the contention by the owners that the obligation to exercise due diligence was limited to acts by third parties qua carrier, and the failure by the master and crew to navigate carefully was outside of the 'orbit of responsibility' of the owners.[35]

4.13 As it stands the ruling suggests that a carrier or owner will be liable for mistakes made by its employees if those mistakes lead to a subsequent loss during the voyage, notwithstanding that those mistakes are navigational in nature and are made before the commencement of the voyage. It is currently anticipated that the Supreme Court hearing will be held in late 2021.

4.14 S40(1) of the MIA provides that in a policy on goods there is no implied warranty that the goods are seaworthy.[36] Because s40(2)[37] provides that the vessel should not only be seaworthy as a ship, but also be reasonably fit to carry the goods contemplated (the implied warranty of cargoworthiness), it is possible in the same voyage to satisfy the implied warranty in relation to (say) the ship, but not the cargo. S40(2) reads as follows:

> In a voyage policy on goods or other moveables there is an implied warranty that at the commencement of the voyage the ship is not only seaworthy as a ship, but also that she is reasonably fit to carry the goods or other moveables to the destination contemplated by the policy.

4.15 In *Almojil (M) Establishment v Malayan Most and General Underwriters (Private) Ltd (The Al-Jubail IV)*, the Court of Appeal held that the warranty of seaworthiness was implied in mixed policies in respect of the voyage part of the cover, even though this is not explicitly stated in the Marine Insurance Act.[38] The key under s40(2) is not so much the capability of the vessel to carry the relevant cargo, but whether the vessel is in a fit state to receive the cargo. In *Tattersall v National SS Co*, failure properly to cleanse the hold prior to receiving a cargo of cattle, after having previously carried cattle with foot and mouth disease, was a breach of the implied warranty of cargoworthiness.[39] The vessel must be fit to carry the particular cargo she is contracted to receive.[40] As with the implied warranty of seaworthiness, it will be a question of fact whether or not a vessel is cargoworthy. Given that an assured may well have no way of knowing whether a vessel was cargoworthy, in practice almost all cargo policies waive the implied warranty of cargoworthiness, provided the assured or his servants were not privy to any such defect.[41] The scope of the implied warranty of cargoworthiness is confined by s40(2) to voyage policies on goods

35 CMA CGM LIBRA – Supreme Court to consider shipowners' seaworthiness and due diligence obligations, A Chamberlain, C Wormersly and R Allan De Maldonado, HFW, August 2020, available at https://www.lexology.com/library/detail.aspx?g=22601bb8-be8a-4305-94be-f2fd82bc5a7d

36 S40(1) Marine Insurance Act 1906.

37 S40(2) Marine Insurance Act 1906.

38 [1982] 2 Lloyd's Rep 637.

39 (1884) 12 QBD 297.

40 *Stanton v Richardson* (1872) LR 7 CP 421.

41 See for example cl 5.2 of ICC 2009 (type A, B and C).

or other moveables.[42] The implied warranty is by its nature relative, and the nature of the voyage being undertaken will be an important factor in determining whether the vessel is cargoworthy. While s40(2) requires a vessel to be cargoworthy at the commencement of the voyage, the decision in *McFadden v Blue Star Line*[43] makes it clear that there is no continuing duty to keep the vessel cargoworthy. Accordingly if a refrigerator, which is working when the goods are loaded, subsequently breaks down, there is no breach of the implied warranty of cargoworthiness.

4.16 S39(2) of the Marine Insurance Act states that:

> Where the policy attaches while the ship is in port, there is also an implied warranty that she shall, at the commencement of the risk, be reasonably fit to encounter the ordinary perils of the port.

Hodges has coined this as an implied warranty of 'portworthiness';[44] others see it as a subset of the implied warranty of seaworthiness. Whether a particular vessel is 'portworthy' or not will be a question of fact and can vary significantly with different circumstances. The implied warranty of 'portworthiness' does not apply where the policy applies 'from' a given port, as the policy does not attach while the vessel remains in that port, but only on departure. The application of the 'portworthiness' implied warranty has been significantly reduced by the wording of standard insurance clauses.[45] As s39(2) is worded in the same way as s39(1) (which contains the implied warranty of seaworthiness), stating that the implied warranty (of portworthiness) shall apply 'at the commencement of the risk,'[46] it seems likely that Soyer is correct in arguing that there is therefore no continuing implied warranty of portworthiness.[47]

Time policies

4.17 S39(5) provides that there is no implied warranty of seaworthiness in a time policy, but where, with the privity of the assured, the vessel is sent to sea in an unseaworthy state, the insurer is not liable for any loss attributable to unseaworthiness.[48] Historically there was perceived to be a problem in determining when the warranty would bite if there were an implied warranty of seaworthiness in time policies.[49] In addition it has been argued that determining the different standards of seaworthiness required for the different voyages undertaken in a time policy could be difficult. In reality, as argued by Mustill, the increased level of homogeneity in sea transport has surely rendered these argumentslargely redundant.[50] As we will see in Chapter 9, the situation remains unaltered by the Insurance Act 2015.

---

42 Rule 17 of the Rules for the Construction of the policy provides 'the term goods means goods in the nature of merchandise, and does not include personal effects or provisions or stores for use on board.'

43 [1905] 1 KB 697.

44 S Hodges, *Law of Marine Insurance,* Cavendish Publishing, London, 1996, pages 122–3.

45 See for example clause 8 of ICC 2009 (type A, B and C) where there is no implied warranty of port worthiness as the policy attaches from the time the goods leave the warehouse and not while the ship is in port.

46 S39(2) Marine Insurance Act 1906.

47 B Soyer, *Warranties in Marine Insurance,* Routledge, London, 3rd Edition, 2017, page 136.

48 S39(5) Marine Insurance Act 1906.

49 B Soyer, *Warranties in Marine Insurance,* Routledge, London, 3rd Edition, 2017, page 96.

50 MJ Mustill, 'Fault and Marine Losses' (1988) LMCLQ 310.

4.18 In terms of the application of s39(5), it is clear that an assured can be privy without being guilty of wilful misconduct. Privity means 'with the knowledge and consent' of the assured, but it can include turning a blind eye in order to avoid confirming the truth: *Compania Maritime San Basilio SA v Oceanus Mutual Undertaking Assoc (Bermuda) Ltd (The Eurysthenes)*.[51] Geoffrey Lane LJ described the situation as follows:

> The assured only loses his cover if he consented or concurred in the ship going to sea when he knew, or believed, that it was in an unseaworthy condition. I add the word 'believed' to cover the man who deliberately turns a blind eye to what he believes to be true, in order to avoid obtaining certain knowledge of the truth.[52]

4.19 This is not an objective test: actual knowledge that there might be a problem is the key.[53] It does not matter that the reason the assured does not have the actual knowledge was because he was negligent: *The Gloria*.[54] In *The Sea Star*, the House of Lords held that it had to be shown that, subjectively, the assured had to have at least a suspicion of the relevant unseaworthiness, coupled with a decision not to check.[55] In the words of Lord Scott: 'in order for there to be blind eye knowledge, the suspicion must be firmly grounded and targeted on specific facts.'[56] In a corporate situation the knowledge must be in mind of the directing mind and will of company.[57] This concept has now been developed somewhat in the context of s39(5), such that in the case of a corporate entity, it is necessary to identify the person or persons within the company who are involved in the decision making process required for sending the ship to sea.[58] This will be a question of fact in each case.

4.20 If unseaworthiness is found to be one of one or more proximate causes of the loss, the assured will be precluded from recovery if he was privy to this specific unseaworthiness when the vessel was sent to sea.[59] But if the assured was not privy to unseaworthiness, the insurer will be unable to rely on a s39(5) defence; the normal principles of causation will determine whether the assured can be indemnified or not: *The Miss Jay Jay*.[60] But does the defence offered to the insurer (in s39(5)) in instances where the assured was privy to the unseaworthiness, mean that the insurer is always liable where there was no such privity? Soyer argues that this surely cannot be the case and that if unseaworthiness is the sole proximate cause of the loss then the insurer is not liable as unseaworthiness is not an insured peril.[61] He cites s55(1) of the Marine Insurance Act in support of this argument. S55 states, 'Subject to the provisions of this Act, and unless the policy otherwise provides, the insurer is liable for any loss proximately caused by a peril insured against.' Accordingly, absent specific provision to the contrary, the insurer is not liable for any loss that is proximately caused by an uninsured peril. This author would concur with Soyer. Any other outcome would have

51 [1977] 1 QB 49.

52 Ibid [1977] 1 QB 49 at 81.

53 Ibid [1977] 1 QB 49, L Scott at page 116.

54 (1935) 54 LIL Rep 34.

55 [2001] 1 UKHL 1; [2003] 1 AC 469; [2001] 1 Lloyd's Rep 389.

56 Ibid at 116.

57 *Lennards Carrying Co Ltd v Asiatic Petroleum Co Ltd.* [1915] AC 705.

58 B Soyer, *Warranties in Marine Insurance,* Routledge, London, 3rd Edition, 2017, page 105, citing *Meridian Global Funds Management Asia Ltd v The Securities Commission* [1995] 2 AC 500.

59 B Soyer, *Warranties in Marine Insurance,* Routledge, London, 3rd Edition, 2017, page 111.

60 [1987] 1 Lloyd's Rep 32 (CA).

61 B Soyer, *Warranties in Marine Insurance,* Routledge, London, 3rd Edition, 2017, page 112.

the effect of expanding the scope of cover beyond that agreed by the parties. As we will see, because under s39(5) there is no implied warranty in a time policy, s11 of the Insurance Act 2015 potentially applies to it, but s10 does not.[62]

4.21 An insurer can deny liability where unseaworthiness is a proximate cause together with another proximate cause of equal or almost equal efficiency and the other proximate cause is explicitly excluded under the policy.[63] If unseaworthiness is a proximate cause of the loss with another proximate cause of equal or almost equal efficiency, then the insurer must indemnify the assured where the other proximate cause comes within the terms of the policy: *The Miss Jay Jay*.[64] In *Global Process Systems Inc v Berhad, The Cendor Mopu* in a case concerning inherent vice, the Supreme Court ruled that if there has been a peril of the seas affecting an unseaworthy vessel, then the assured was entitled to recover.[65] (If unseaworthiness were the dominant cause of loss, the assured would not recover as it is an uninsured peril.) The effect is arguably to at least partially erode the implied warranty.

The burden of proof

4.22 Generally the burden of proof in establishing unseaworthiness lies with the insurer. The exception is where, soon after sailing, a ship starts leaking or sinks without apparent cause: in the absence of another possible explanation such as a violent storm, there is a presumption that the problem arose from unseaworthiness at the start of the voyage. The courts tend, however, to be reluctant to invoke such presumption and will not do so if there is any other possible explanation: *Pickup v Thames & Mersey Marine Insurance Co.*[66]

Contemporary relevance of the implied warranty of seaworthiness

4.23 What is the practical relevance of the implied warranty of seaworthiness in modern marine insurance practice? In recent years international agreements governing shipping have introduced a raft of additional requirements for shippers; failure to comply with such regulations will likely result in the vessel being deemed unseaworthy.[67] For example, following the 9/11 attacks in the US, a new chapter was added to The International Convention for the Safety of Life at Sea (SOLAS), introducing the International Ship and Port Facility Security Code (ISPSC), comprising a series of legally binding obligations on behalf of the vessel, her owners and operators, as well as on the relevant governments, flag state administrations and port operators. The provisions of the ISPSC will determine the minimum standards required for vessels and failure to hold an International Ship Security Certificate will likely be regarded as meaning that the relevant ship is unseaworthy.[68] Of course possession of a valid certificate would not, of itself, establish seaworthiness.

---

62 See Chapter 9. S10 of the Insurance Act only applies to warranties.

63 *Board of Trade v Hain SS Co Ltd* [1929] AC 554. The House of Lords opined that if a loss is a 'product of two causes, joint and simultaneous,' and one of the causes is expressly excluded by an exclusion clause, the insurers are not liable.

64 [1987] 1 Lloyd's Rep 32 (CA).

65 [2011] UKSC 5, albeit the case focused on proximate cause not warranties.

66 (1878) 3 QBD 594.

67 Questions also arise as to whether breaches of safety regulations result in a breach of the implied warranty of legality: see later in this chapter.

68 B Soyer, *Warranties in Marine Insurance,* Routledge, London, 3rd Edition, 2017, page 129.

4.24 In the aftermath of *The Exxon Valdez* disaster the International Maritime Organisation (IMO) introduced the International Safety Management (ISM) Code, focussing on the management of shipping companies and requiring the development of standard management systems. The provisions of the ISM Code have been implemented into English Law by the Merchant Shipping (International Safety Management (ISM)) Code Regulations 2014.[69] The ISM Code imposes requirements on shipowners to produce and maintain documents and data relevant to the Safety Management System. These requirements make it easier for underwriters to meet the burden of establishing unseaworthiness. Again compliance with the ISM Code does not establish that a vessel is seaworthy; for example the vessel may be unseaworthy due to a latent defect in its hull. On the other hand failure to comply may well result in a court finding the vessel to be unseaworthy.[70] Soyer suggests that, following the introduction of the ISM Code, there is likely to be an increase in the use of the defence available to insurers of time policies under s39(5) of the Marine Insurance Act 1906.[71]

4.25 The provisions of the Maritime Labour Convention, setting out minimum standards for conditions of work, employment and health and welfare for seafarers have been introduced into English law by the Merchant Shipping (Maritime Labour Convention (MLC)) (Minimum Requirements for Seafarers etc.) Regulations 2014. Soyer asserts, and this author agrees, that it is very likely that failure to possess the correct MLC documentation would render a vessel unseaworthy.[72] Soyer suggests that even a failure to comply with the rest requirements for crew as specified in the MLC could, in the case of a time policy, trigger a s39(5) defence for the insurer if the relevant management in the company owning the vessel were privy to regular breaches of the MLC.

4.26 Does this mean that the implied warranty of seaworthiness still plays a vital role in modern maritime insurance? On the contrary, the importance of the implied seaworthy warranty is greatly diminished in the modern environment. It is true that the standard Institute voyage policies on hull and freight do not expressly waive the breach of the implied warranty of seaworthiness. However, most policies on hulls, machinery and freight are now written on a time basis and cargo is nearly always written on the basis of the London Institute of Cargo Clauses, in which breach of the implied warranty of seaworthiness is waived, providing the insured was not privy to any unseaworthiness. Specifically clause 5.2 of the Institute Cargo Clauses provides: 'The Underwriters waive any breach of the implied warranties of seaworthiness of the ship and fitness of the ship to carry the subject matter insured to the destination, unless the insured or their servants are privy to such unseaworthiness or unfitness.'[73] Nevertheless, under clause 13 of the International Hull Clauses,[74] the insured is likely to lose his insurance cover if the assured or the insured vessel is not ISM Code compliant. Clause 13 provides that unless the underwriters agree to the contrary, in the event of non-compliance (i.e. amongst other

69 Statutory Instrument 2014/1512.

70 B Soyer, *Warranties in Marine Insurance,* Routledge, London, 3rd Edition, 2017, page 121, citing Cresswell J in *The Eurasian Dream* ([2002] EWCH 118 (Comm) at 143) to support this assertion.

71 That the insured was privy to the unseaworthiness: B Soyer, *Warranties in Marine Insurance,* Routledge, London, 3rd Edition, 2017, page 123.

72 B Soyer, *Warranties in Marine Insurance,* Routledge, London, 3rd Edition, 2017, page 134.

73 Clause 5.2 of the London Institute of Cargo Clauses 1982 and 2009 (type A, B and C).

74 Clause 13 International Hull Clauses 1 November 2003.

things failure to hold a valid Document of Compliance in respect of the vessel and a valid Safety Management Certificate, both as required by SOLAS), the insurance will terminate automatically at the time of the breach. Importantly, the IHC 2003 introduced a new management clause, clause 14.4, which creates a contractual duty on the part of the individuals in charge of the insured vessel to ensure that all statutory requirements relating to construction, adaption, condition, fitment, equipment operation and manning of the vessel are complied with. Failure to comply will ensure the insurer is not liable for *any loss causally linked to the breach*.[75] The fact that the IHC adopts a causal linkage approach is significant and reflects the market's familiarity with, and acceptance of, the concept. However, in the view of this author, neither the requirements of the ISM Code/Clause 13 of the International Hull Clauses, nor clause 14.4 of the IHC represents a substantive reason for retaining the implied warranty of seaworthiness.

4.27 Finally use of the *'Inchmaree'* clause[76] which provides cover for, amongst other perils, loss of, or damage to, the insured property caused by a latent defect in machinery or hull, significantly expands the hull insurer's undertaking and arguably also reduces the impact of the implied warranty of seaworthiness. Soyer suggests it is arguable that as far as unseaworthiness is concerned, the express provision contained in the *Inchmaree* clause prevails over the implied warranty, such that the insurer should not be able to rely on a latent defect being a breach of the implied warranty of seaworthiness.[77] The decision in *The Lydia Flag*[78] arguably supports the proposition that the *Inchmaree* clause has the ability to waive a breach of warranty in many cases.[79]

4.28 The earlier analysis demonstrates that in modern commercial maritime practice, the importance of the implied warranty of seaworthiness has been greatly eroded. Nevertheless, the implied warranty was not abolished by the Insurance Act 2015. Sections 10 and 11 of the Insurance Act 2015 are explicitly stated to apply to both express or implied warranties (s10) and 'terms' (s11). The implications of this are considered in detail in Chapter 9. As detailed in Chapter 12, it is argued by this author that implied warranties (including the implied warranties of legality, portworthiness and cargoworthiness, in addition to seaworthiness)[80] are now largely redundant and should be abolished.

---

75 Emphasis added. Clause 14.4 of the IHC 2003 states:

> It is the duty of the Assured, Owners and Managers at the inception of and throughout the period of this insurance and any extension thereof to comply with all statutory requirements of the vessel's flag state relating to the construction, adaption, condition, fitment, equipment operation and manning of the vessel ... in the event of any breach of any of the duties of this clause ... the Underwriters shall not be liable for any loss, damage, liability or expense attributable to such a breach.

76 Named after the vessel of this name in *Thames and Mersey Marine Insurance Co v Hamilton Fraser and Co (The Inchmaree)* (1887) 12 AC 484.

77 B Soyer, *Warranties in Marine Insurance,* Routledge, London, 3rd Edition, 2017, page 204; Arnould agrees, suggesting that where damage is caused by a latent defect that would otherwise amount to a breach of the implied warranty of seaworthiness, the insurer cannot rely on a breach of warranty to deny liability. *Arnould, Law of Marine Insurance and Average,* eds J Gilman, Prof R Merkin, C Blanchard QC and M Templeman QC, Sweet and Maxwell, London, 18th Edition, 2013, page 710.

78 *Martin Maritime Ltd v Provident Capital Indemnity Fund Ltd (The Lydia Flag)* [1998] 2 Lloyd's Rep 652.

79 B Soyer, *Warranties in Marine Insurance,* Cavendish Publishing, London, 2nd Edition, 2006, at page 169.

80 See Chapter 12.

Other warranty-like provisions relating to marine insurance

4.29 The Marine Insurance Act contains a number of other provisions which are pertinent only to marine insurance and which operate in a similar way to warranties. For the purposes of this volume the relevant provisions are the following:

S43 Alteration of port of departure

S44 Sailing for different destination

S45 Change of voyage

S46 Deviation

4.30 S43 reads as follows: 'Where the place of departure is specified in the policy, and the ship instead of sailing from that place sails from any other place, the risk does not attach.' In *Molinos Nacionales v Pohjola Insurance Company Ltd*,[81] the insured vessel was meant to sail from Tallinn, but instead sailed from Muuga, an adjacent port, managed by the same port authority and separated from Tallinn only by a narrow headland. The difference in port had no bearing on the risk. The presiding judge described the insurer's argument that the risk did not attach as having 'no merit whatsoever,' but was nevertheless obliged to allow it as the Act and previous precedent allowed insurers to avoid the policy in such circumstances for 'trivial, entirely immaterial, deviations.' S44 provides that the policy does not attach if the ship sails for another destination, rather than the one specified in the policy. Under sections 45 and 46, if the destination is changed or there is a deviation, the insurer is discharged. Sections 43 and 44 are conditions precedent to the attachment of risk. Amongst those who, during the consultative phase, urged the Law Commission to recommend the removal of all these provisions were Professor Merkin and The City of London Law Society. This author agrees that the repeal, or at least reform, of these provisions would have been beneficial and would have contributed to a more equitable balance between the interests of insured and insurer, as well as being broadly consistent with the approach taken by the Commission to the reform of warranties generally: the failure to do so represents a missed opportunity.[82] Soyer argues that sections 45 and 46 (and s48, delay in voyage) resemble continuing warranties. As such he suggests that all three sections would be subject to s11 of the Insurance Act. If this were correct, the insured may have the opportunity to argue that a deviation for example could not have increased the loss that actually occurred in the circumstances in which it occurred.[83] This would provide some potential assistance to insureds. The interpretation of s11 of the Insurance Act is discussed in more detail in Chapter 9.

81 (Unreported) High Court, 5 May 1998.

82 See Chapter 12 for this author's recommendations for reform.

83 B Soyer, *Warranties in Marine Insurance,* Routledge, London, 3rd Edition, 2017, page 230.

The implied warranty of legality

4.31 There is an established legal principle that a person cannot profit from his illegal act or criminal conduct.[84] S41[85] of the Marine Insurance Act imposes an implied warranty of legality. Specifically s41 states:

> There is an implied warranty that the adventure insured is a lawful one, and that, so far as the assured can control the matter, the adventure shall also be carried out in a lawful manner.

4.32 If the adventure is unlawful from the outset the warranty acts as a condition precedent and the risk never attaches. Merkin argues that the implied warranty comprises two separate warranties: the first a present warranty that the insured adventure is lawful in its formation and the second, a future warranty that the insured adventure will be carried out lawfully so far as the assured can control the matter.[86] Merkin suggests that there was not a well-established common law concept of an implied warranty of legality prior to the statute. He argues that the New Zealand equivalent of s41[87] was a statement of the circumstances in which the policy is of no effect, and that, in turn, can only be the position if the general law recognises the illegality of the underlying risk or the illegality of the performance of an otherwise lawful risk.[88] This interpretation sits uncomfortably with where the section is positioned in the Act, in a part of the Act dealing with implied warranties. If Merkin's interpretation were correct it would suggest s42 should not operate as a contractual warranty by terminating the risk as soon as the assured commits an illegal act. In Merkin's words, his interpretation would mean that the section 'should be construed as no more than a statement that there is an implied limitation in a policy of marine insurance that an adventure or performance rendered unlawful by the ordinary law is not covered by the policy.' For Merkin it would accordingly follow that the warranty of legality stands or falls with ordinary principles of illegality affecting contracts.[89] With respect to Merkin, this author believes this is a step too far. The wording of the statute and the positioning of the section in the Act are surely not consistent with this interpretation. Absent s41, Soyer argues that there can be no doubt that marine insurance contracts that insure unlawful acts or adventures that are performed illegally would be regarded at common law as void on the grounds of public policy.[90] However, at common law the assured would be unable to recover only if there was a sufficient connection between the illegal conduct and the loss if the illegality arose during the performance of the contract.[91] Under s41 the assured would be denied recovery if he has control over the matter and illegality arises during performance of the contract, regardless of whether there is any causal linkage between the illegal act and the loss. Conversely at common law, if the illegality is committed by the assured's employees, he would still be

84 *Baresford v Royal Insurance Co.* [1938] AC 586.

85 S41 Marine Insurance Act 1906.

86 NZILA Lecture Series 2018, Can the Assured's Conduct Defeat a Claim? *Dougal v BoatsRUs* 2018, Unreported, Professor Rob Merkin QC.

87 S42 of the NZ Marine Insurance Act, essentially identical to s41 of the Marine Insurance Act 1906.

88 NZILA Lecture Series 2018, Can the Assured's Conduct Defeat a Claim? *Dougal v BoatsRUs* 2018, Unreported, Professor Rob Merkin QC.

89 NZILA Lecture Series 2018, Can the Assured's Conduct Defeat a Claim? *Dougal v BoatsRUs* 2018, Unreported, Professor Rob Merkin QC.

90 B Soyer, *Warranties in Marine Insurance,* Routledge, London, 3rd Edition, 2017, page 140.

91 *Madoff Securities International Ltd v Raven* [2013] EWHC 3147 (Comm); [2014] Lloyd's Rep 95.

deemed responsible for the illegality. Under s41, if the illegal act was performed without the knowledge of the assured he would not be held responsible for the illegal act and thus would prima facie have a defence.[92]

4.33 While in some instances illegality will be clear, in others it may be difficult to judge whether, for example, the contravention of a statute or regulation, renders an adventure illegal. In relation to a statute, it will be a question of construction to determine if the intention of Parliament was to ban such contracts, or merely impose fines for those in breach.[93] The implied warranty will also be breached where the adventure is lawful, but the assured commits an illegal act during its performance; for example where the vessel on an otherwise legal voyage, is used for smuggling: *Pipon v Cope*.[94]

4.34 At what point does s41 kick in to render a contract illegal? In *St John Shipping Corporation v Joseph Rank Ltd*, Devlin J held that illegality in the course of performance did not generally render a contract illegal.[95] He urged that caution was required at a time when 'so much of commercial life is governed by regulations of one sort or another, which may easily be broken without wicked intent.' Soyer argues that the principles in *St John Shipping*[96] also apply to section 41. This would mean that a violation of shipping safety legislation would not render the performance of the adventure illegal for the purposes of s41. This seems sensible.

4.35 In relation to safety regulations, the key question is whether the act prohibited by statute is incidental to the insurance contract, or whether it forms an essential part of that contract. Soyer argues that it is unlikely that an act prohibited by a safety regulation would be viewed as an essential part of a marine insurance contract.[97] As a result, if a vessel fails to hold either an ISM (International Safety Management) or ISPS (International Ship and Port Facility Security) certificate, it is unlikely to be regarded as in breach of the implied warranty of legality under English law. In Australia however breach of shipping safety regulation has often been held to be a factor in rendering the performance of a contract illegal.[98] Soyer's view, that the approach adopted in England and Wales is to be preferred, is more sensible: from a purely practicable perspective a large number of insurance policies would be rendered inadvertently invalid if a simple violation of a safety regulation constituted illegality. It would surely be completely impractical for any accidental breach to be the trigger for illegality. Nevertheless, this would not prevent clearly flagrant and deliberate breaches acting as a tipping point.

4.36 As far as the continuing implied warranty of legality is concerned, the assured is provided with some protection as the warranty is qualified by the words 'so far as the assured can control the matter.' So if the ship's master were responsible for the illegality without the assured's knowledge, there would be no breach of the implied warranty.[99] A further issue arises over whether the illegality referenced by s41 should apply to acts that are illegal in a

92 B Soyer, *Warranties in Marine Insurance,* Routledge, London, 3rd Edition, 2017, page 141.

93 See Devlin J's analysis in *St John Shipping Corp v Joseph Rank Ltd* [1957] 1 QB at 287.

94 (1888) 1 Camp 434.

95 [1957] 1 QB 267.

96 B Soyer, *Warranties in Marine Insurance,* Routledge, London, 3rd Edition, 2017, page 154.

97 B Soyer, *Warranties in Marine Insurance*, Routledge, London, 3rd Edition, 2017, page 147, citing *Archbolds (Freightage) Ltd v Sparglett (S) Ltd, Rendell Third Party* [1961] 1 QB 374 and *St John Shipping Corp v Joseph Rank Ltd.* [1957] 1 QB 267.

98 For example *Doak v Weeks and Commercial Union Assurance Co plc* [1986] 82 FLR 334.

99 *Wilson v Rankin* (1865) LR 1 QB 162.

foreign jurisdiction, but not in England and Wales. Soyer is surely correct in suggesting that,[100] when introduced, it was improbable that the statute was intended to cover illegalities in foreign jurisdictions and that any other interpretation could have bizarre consequences. The Law Commission cautioned that the parties may not be able to contract out of the effect of s41 if it does not suit their needs, although the Commission acknowledged that there was no authority on the point.[101] Again, it has been argued that, as the warranty has notions of public policy, it should not be possible to waive a breach of the implied warranty of legality.[102] While there is merit in this rationale, this author argues that a better solution would be to do away with the implied warranty of legality entirely.

4.37 While the Insurance Act 2015 preserves implied warranties, it seems clear that s11 of the Act does not apply to the implied warranty of legality, as s11 does not apply to terms that define the risk as a whole.[103] Although, as described in Chapter 9, there are a number of issues arising from section 11 of the Insurance Act,[104] it is appropriate that the section should have no application in this instance as, if the contract has an illegal act at its heart, the basis of the insurer's whole risk assessment will have been undermined. Whether a similar argument can be made in relation to the implied warranty of seaworthiness applying to the risk as a whole, and therefore not being subject to s11 of the Insurance Act, is more debatable. This is also discussed further in Chapter 9.

4.38 There is no implied warranty of legality in non-marine insurance. The rational for this was explained by Staughton J at first instance in *Euro-Diam Ltd v Bathurst*: 'Suppose that a motor car is insured for a calendar year, and is driven in January in excess of the speed limit. Would that be an answer to a claim for loss by theft or fire or a road accident in June?'[105] From a strictly logical perspective, a similar argument could surely be applied to a marine policy where a vessel is used briefly for smuggling and is subsequently lost; nevertheless, the position was affirmed by the Court of Appeal, which indicated that a policy could have business efficacy without implying a term of this nature.[106] The absence of an implied warranty of legality in non-marine insurance policies further strengthens the case for its abolition in marine insurance. The case for abolition is considered in more detail below.[107]

Commercial practice in the London marine insurance market: is a separate regime for marine insurance justified?

4.39 Although the law as it stood prior to the Insurance Act 2015 was difficult to support and reform was clearly necessary in relation to general commercial insurance, was there a similar imperative in the context of marine insurance? Had the market not adjusted to alleviate most of the damaging implications of the law, such that there were

---

100 B Soyer, *Warranties in Marine Insurance,* Routledge, London, 3rd Edition, 2017, page 152.

101 Law Commission Insurance Contract Law Issues Paper 2 Warranties, November 2006, para A 23.

102 *Gedge and Others v Royal Exchange Assurance Corp* [1900] 2 QB 214. See also B Soyer, *Warranties in Marine Insurance,* Cavendish Publishing, London, 2nd Edition, 2006, page 219.

103 S11(1) Insurance Act 2015. See also B Soyer, *Warranties in Marine Insurance,* Routledge, London, 3rd Edition, 2017, page 154.

104 See Chapter 9.

105 [1987] 1 Lloyd's Rep 178, at 186.

106 [1990] 1QB1.

107 See Chapter 11 Issues: Problems with the Law on Warranties and Potential Solutions for Resolving Them.

few practical adverse consequences? If the case for reform is to be robust, there must surely be a practical, as well as a theoretical, rationale for change: if in the marine context the adverse impacts of the law on warranties are easily overcome, is the argument for reform significantly weakened? Does this in turn argue for a separate regime for marine insurance?

4.40 Prior to the Insurance Act, in the case of marine insurance, held covered clauses were widely used in the London market to alleviate the harshness of the warranties regime.[108] Such clauses had been in use since the late nineteenth century[109] to keep the insurance relationship on foot, notwithstanding a breach of warranty by the assured. A held covered clause initially creates an irrevocable unilateral obligation on the part of the insurer to provide the specified additional cover if demanded by the assured.[110] The obligation requires performance once notice is given by the assured: absent notice, it never becomes an active obligation.[111] The assured must pay the additional premium and accept the amended terms of cover. In *Thames & Mersey Marine Insurance Co Ltd v HT Van Laun & Co.* the court held that, even in the absence of an express provision to provide notice, the assured must nevertheless provide notice within a reasonable time of learning of the breach: this was implied as a condition of the assured's right to be held covered.[112] It seems notice can be given even after a loss has been incurred if there was no way the assured could have learnt about the breach earlier,[113] and in *Overseas Commodities Ltd v Style* it was suggested in an obiter observation from McNair J, that a held covered clause could also be invoked after the policy period had expired.[114]

4.41 In practice, held covered clauses usually take one of two forms: (i) held covered at a rateable premium,[115] where automatic coverage is provided for on a pro rata premium in circumstances where the policy would otherwise lapse before the insured vessel has reached its destination because the vessel is missing or in distress; or (ii) held covered with premium to be agreed. For example the Institute Time Clauses (Hulls) contract terms contain a held covered clause that holds the insured covered for a breach of warranty as to cargo, trade, locality, towage, salvage services or date of sailing if notice is given to the insurer immediately and any amended terms of cover and additional premiums are agreed.[116] We have seen elsewhere that the use of the *Inchmaree* clause significantly expands the hull insurer's undertaking and arguably reduces the impact of the implied warranty of seaworthiness.[117]

108 In addition to alleviating the consequences of breaches of warranty, held covered clauses normally afford protection against the risk of deviation or change in voyage, for example clause 8.3 in the ICC 1982 (type A, B and C).

109 See for example *Simon Israel & Co v Sedgwick* [1893] 1 QB 303.

110 *United Dominions Trust (Commercial) Ltd v Eagle Aircraft Services Ltd* [1968] 1 WLR 74 at page 86 per Diplock LJ.

111 B Soyer, *Warranties in Marine Insurance,* Routledge, London, 3rd Edition, 2017, page 197; see also DR Thomas, in *Modern Law of Marine Insurance,* Vol. 2, (2002), LLP at 1.141–1.152.

112 [1917] 2 KB 48.

113 B Soyer, *Warranties in Marine Insurance,* Routledge, London, 3rd Edition, 2017, page 198, citing Hamilton J in *Mentz Decker & Co v Maritime Insurance Co* [1910] 1 KB 132 at 134.

114 [1958] 1 Lloyd's Rep 546 at 559.

115 For example Institute Time Clauses (Hull) (ITCH) 83 cl 2 and International Hull Clauses (IHC) 2003 cl 12.

116 Clause 3 ITCH 1983 Similar provisions are contained in the ITC Freight Contract, cl 4.

117 See earlier in this chapter.

4.42 Prior to the Insurance Act 2015, reflecting the general unease with the law on warranties, commercial terms used in the London marine market had increasingly avoided reference to warranties in marine insurance. The position in the International Hull Clauses 2003 represented a firm move away from the use of warranties: the only warranty is the disbursements warranty,[118] restricting double insurance. Even classification[119] and navigation[120] provisions are expressed as suspensory clauses, so that recovery is prevented only where the vessel is unclassified or off route at the time of loss. Premium payment obligations are set out as conditions that cannot be invoked without an extension of time followed by notice.[121] In the Institute of Cargo Clauses (ICC) 2009 the word 'warranty' does not appear at all. Clause 10.1 dispenses with the traditional held cover approach, but with the objective of achieving the same outcome:

> Where after attachment of this insurance the destination is changed by the assured, this must be promptly notified to the insurer for rates and terms to be agreed. Should a loss occur prior to such agreement being obtained, cover may be provided, but only if cover would have been available at a reasonable commercial market rate on reasonable market terms.[122]

4.43 It is the view of this author that the development of marine market practice to diminish the harsher impacts of the law of warranties is not a reason to exempt marine insurance from statutory reform of the law. A separate regime for marine insurance is maintained in Australia and this is examined in Chapter 6. Stress testing of the Australian regime in Chapter 10 highlights the potential disadvantages of maintaining two regimes that follow divergent reform programmes.[123] Introducing a separate regime for marine insurance in the UK would be unnecessary and would risk an unwelcome element of confusion. Marine insurance will, assuming it wishes to do so, continue to be able to maintain its own individual elements of market practice, notwithstanding the reforms introduced in the Insurance Act.

4.44 Indeed, the fact that the marine insurance market, where there is often greater balance between the respective negotiating positions of the insured and insurer, had taken steps to mitigate the impact of the law was evidence of the need for reform. The case for reform was stronger still in the wider, non-marine, commercial insurance market where, given their lack of knowledge of the insurance market, many insureds were inevitably in a weaker bargaining position. The reputation of the English legal system, with its core principles of equality before the law, offering a platform that is demonstrably fair to all, demanded reform. The question is whether the steps taken in the Insurance Act 2015 to redress the balance between insured and insurer present an optimal solution, or whether, instead, they represent a missed opportunity.

118 International Hull Clauses (IHC) 2003, cl 24.
119 IHC 2003, cll 13–14.
120 IHC 2003, cll 10–11 and 32–33.
121 IHC 2003, cl 35.
122 Institute of Cargo Clauses cl 10.1.
123 See Chapter 10.

CHAPTER 5

The Law Commission's previous reports and recommendations on warranties

The Commission's 1980 report

5.1 As long ago as 1957 the Law Commission recommended the abolition of warranties,[1] but this recommendation was never pursued. In 1980 the Commission observed 'it seemed quite wrong that an insurer should be entitled to demand strict compliance with a warranty which was immaterial to the risk.'[2] The Law Commission's 1980 report, Insurance Law: Non-Disclosure and Breach of Warranty, adopted a complex approach under which a breach of warranty could not be relied upon if, inter alia, it could not have increased the risk that the event which gave rise to the claim would occur in the way that it did in fact occur.[3] The Commission recommended that basis clauses should be abolished and that insurers be required to provide policyholders with written documents containing any warranties. The Commission observed that its proposals would not prevent specific facts from constituting a warranty, provided this was incorporated into the policy itself.[4] Clause 8(2) of the draft Bill accompanying the Commission's report stated that an insurer would not be entitled to rely on a breach of warranty unless the insured was supplied with 'a written statement of the provision which constitutes the warranty.' This statement was to be supplied to the insured at or before the time the contract was entered into, or 'as soon thereafter as was practical in the circumstances of the case.' The Commission's subsequent reports acknowledged that the problem with clause 8(2) was that an insurer could comply with it even if it buried the warranty in a mass of small print.[5]

5.2 Although in its initial consultation paper, the Commission proposed that for a warranty to be effective, an insurer would have to show it was material to the risk, in its final report the Commission withdrew this requirement. Instead, it proposed that a warranty should be assumed to be material, unless the insured showed that it would not have influenced a prudent underwriter. The Commission's draft Bill envisaged that an insured would be able to challenge an insurer's decision not to indemnify for breach of warranty on three grounds:

(1) The warranty did not relate to a matter which was material;[6]
(2) The warranty was intended to safeguard against a risk of a description 'which does not include the event which gave rise to the claim';[7] or

1 Fifth Report of the Law Reform Committee (1957) Cmnd 62.
2 Insurance Law: Non-Disclosure and Breach of Warranty (1980) Law Com No 104, para 6.9(a).
3 Law Commission Report Insurance Law, Non-Disclosure and Breach of Warranty (1980) Law Com No 104.
4 Insurance Law, Non-Disclosure and Breach of Warranty (1980) Law Com No 104, para 7.10.
5 Law Commission Insurance Contract Law Issues Paper 2 Warranties, November 2006, para 3.9.
6 Law Commission draft Bill, clause 8(1).
7 Law Commission draft Bill, clause 10(5)(a).

DOI: 10.4324/9781003031734-5

(3) The breach of warranty could not have increased the risk that the event which gave rise to the claim would occur in the way in which it did in fact occur.[8]

5.3 A key criticism of the Commission's proposals was that the defence available to a policyholder only applied if the term was classified as a warranty. Birds and Hird suggested that as a result, the Commission's recommendations might have been easily evaded by insurers resorting to the use of other conditions and exceptions.[9] The Commission later acknowledged the flaw in its 1980 proposals, commenting in its subsequent Issues Paper on Warranties that 'the same answer should apply to both warranties and descriptions of the risk. It should not depend on formalities about how the term has been written.'[10] This is clearly sensible; as will be discussed later, for reform of this area of the law to be effective it is essential that it should not be confined solely to warranties.

Law Commission Insurance contract law issues paper 2 warranties, November 2006

5.4 The Law Commission returned to the subject of insurance warranties in 2006. At this juncture the Commission indicated that in its view the principal problems with the law of warranties were that insurers could refuse to pay a claim for actions or omissions that:

(i) Were immaterial to the risk;
(ii) Were only relevant to other risks;
(iii) Had already been remedied.[11]

5.5 The Commission observed that these problems were exacerbated by the ability to use basis clauses. However, in the Commission's view, 'The greatest and most obvious problem with the law on warranties is that it permits the insurer to escape liability for technical breaches that have nothing to do with the loss in question.'[12] The Commission recommended that all express warranties should be in writing and included or referred to in the main contract document. The Commission was of the view that the law should afford policyholders some protection against claims being denied for reasons unconnected with the loss. The Commission concluded that a policyholder should be entitled to be paid a claim if he could prove, on the balance of probability, that the event or circumstances constituting the breach of warranty did not contribute to the loss:[13] a clear causal linkage test. Further, the Commission tentatively proposed that the law should provide that if a breach contributed to only part of a loss, the insurer may not refuse to pay the part not related to the breach.[14] Moving away from their previous approach, the Commission also tentatively recommended that, as in New Zealand, the recommended approach should extend beyond warranties and apply to all terms that enabled the insurer to refuse to pay a claim for events

8 Law Commission draft Bill, clause 10(5)(b).
9 J Birds and NJ Hird, *Birds' Modern Insurance Law*, Sweet and Maxwell, London, 6th Edition, 2004, page 166, note 36.
10 Law Commission Insurance Contract Law Issues Paper 2 Warranties, November 2006, para 3.24.
11 Law Commission Insurance Contract Law Issues Paper 2 Warranties, November 2006, para 5.3.
12 Law Commission Insurance Contract Law Issues Paper 2 Warranties, November 2006, para 7.66.
13 Law Commission Insurance Contract Law Issues Paper 2 Warranties, November 2006, para 7.76.
14 Law Commission Insurance Contract Law Issues Paper 2 Warranties, November 2006, para 7.81.

or circumstances that add to the risk of loss.[15] The Commission acknowledged that if the reform were confined to warranties, it would simply encourage insurers to draft around the constraint.

5.6 In order to overcome their concerns regarding the potential for expanding the scope of the cover agreed between the parties to the prejudice of the insurer, the Commission proposed that the causal connection test should not apply where the insurance related to one purpose, activity or place, and the loss arose from an entirely different purpose or activity or in another place.[16] The approach recommended by the Commission was that a court would need to ask whether the difference in use was such that a reasonable insured could have expected the loss to be covered and the objective should be to distinguish between occasional and regular misuse. In order to apply such an approach, the courts would need to assess what it was reasonable for the insured to expect.[17] The Commission recommended that its proposed causal connection test should also apply to marine insurance[18] and that it should apply equally to both express and implied warranties.[19]

5.7 While in 1980 the Law Commission recommended against extending the reforms to reinsurance contracts generally, in its 2006 report, it proposed to reverse its position such that its recommended reforms *would* apply to the re-insurance market.[20] Importantly the Commission also indicated that it was tentatively in favour of granting a right of termination to the insurer where the insured had breached a warranty.[21]

Law Commission Consultation Paper No. 182 Insurance Contract Law: misrepresentation, non-disclosure and breach of warranty by the insured, November 2007

5.8 The Commission observed that the existing law on warranties 'defies logic and normal expectations, is inconsistent with good practice as recognised by the industry's own Statements of Practice and risks bringing the UK insurance industry into disrepute.'[22]

5.9 The Commission reiterated its principal concerns regarding the existing law on warranties.[23] Crucially however on this occasion the Commission's proposals sought to distinguish between current fact warranties and future conduct warranties.

15 Law Commission Insurance Contract Law Issues Paper 2 Warranties, November 2006, para 7.88.

16 Law Commission Insurance Contract Law Issues Paper 2 Warranties, November 2006, para 7.94.

17 Law Commission Insurance Contract Law Issues Paper 2 Warranties, November 2006, paras 7.94–6.

18 Law Commission Insurance Contract Law Issues Paper 2 Warranties, November 2006, para 7.108.

19 Law Commission Insurance Contract Law Issues Paper 2 Warranties, November 2006, para 7.118.

20 Law Commission Insurance Contract Law Issues Paper 2 Warranties, November 2006, para 7.129.

21 Law Commission Insurance Contract Law Issues Paper 2 Warranties, November 2006, para 7.137.

22 Law Commission Consultation Paper No. 182 Insurance Contract Law: Misrepresentation, Non-Disclosure and Breach of Warranty by the Insured, November 2007 para 8.22.

23 As reflected in its 2006 Report, the Commission's principal concerns were that a breach of warranty automatically discharged the insurer from liability and insurers could refuse to pay a claim because of actions or omissions that:

(1) Were immaterial to the risk.
(2) Were irrelevant to the loss that had occurred.
(3) Had already been remedied.

5.10 The key elements of the Commission's 2007 proposals in respect of business insurance were as follows:

(1) In the absence of an agreement to the contrary, a specific fact warranty would entitle the insurer to refuse the claim following a breach of the warranty, provided that:

(a) the breach of warranty was material. For example, the insurer could not refuse a claim where the breach related to a failure to disclose a minor conviction (such as speeding) that would not have influenced the insurer's decision to provide cover;

(b) the breach had some connection to the loss. For example, a manager's conviction for dangerous driving would be unconnected to a flood damage claim.[24]

(2) Where a warranty concerned future conduct:

(a) It should be set out in writing.[25]

(b) A business should be entitled to be paid a claim if it could prove on the balance of probabilities that the event or circumstances constituting the breach did not contribute to the loss.[26] This would be a default rule and amounted to a causal linkage test. The parties could agree other consequences if they wished (subject to controls on standard term contracts).[27] The Commission's report left it unclear whether (as the burden of proving a breach was not causative was on the assured) the insurer would be 'off risk' until the insured had satisfied the burden of proof? If so, in this author's view, this would surely have been unreasonable.

(c) Proportionality would apply: if the insured could prove that a breach contributed only to part of the loss, the insurer would not be able to refuse to pay for that element of the loss that was unrelated to the breach.[28]

(d) A breach of warranty would not automatically discharge the insurer from liability, but would instead give the insurer the right to terminate cover for the future,[29] but (unless otherwise agreed) only if the breach had sufficiently serious consequences to justify termination under the general law of contract.[30] The Commission further recommended that if the

---

24 Law Commission Consultation Paper No. 182 Insurance Contract Law: Misrepresentation, Non-Disclosure and Breach of Warranty by the Insured, November 2007 para 5.132.

25 Law Commission Consultation Paper No. 182 Insurance Contract Law: Misrepresentation, Non-Disclosure and Breach of Warranty by the Insured, November 2007 para 8.8–8.12.

26 Law Commission Consultation Paper No. 182 Insurance Contract Law: Misrepresentation, Non-Disclosure and Breach of Warranty by the Insured, November 2007 para 8.45.

27 Law Commission Consultation Paper No. 182 Insurance Contract Law: Misrepresentation, Non-Disclosure and Breach of Warranty by the Insured, November 2007 para 8.51–8.53.

28 Law Commission Consultation Paper No. 182 Insurance Contract Law: Misrepresentation, Non-Disclosure and Breach of Warranty by the Insured, November 2007 para 8.48.

29 Law Commission Consultation Paper No. 182 Insurance Contract Law: Misrepresentation, Non-Disclosure and Breach of Warranty by the Insured, November 2007 para 8.81–8.100.

30 Law Commission Consultation Paper No. 182 Insurance Contract Law: Misrepresentation, Non-Disclosure and Breach of Warranty by the Insured, November 2007 para 8.89.

insurer chose to terminate in such circumstances, the insured should cease to be liable for any future premiums, as yet unpaid.[31]

(3) Where the parties contracted on the insurer's written standard terms of business, the insurer should not be permitted to rely on a warranty, exception or definition of the risk if this would render the cover substantially different from that which the insured reasonably expected.[32] The Commission explained: 'The idea was that it would catch situations where, for example, a clause was put into the small print of a contract with a small business, saying that the consequence of all misrepresentations was avoidance, no matter whether they were material or honest.'[33] The Commission saw three main arguments in favour of its reasonable expectations proposals;[34]

   (i) The protection only applied to standard policy terms. It did not interfere with the freedom of large businesses to negotiate contracts on an individual basis.
   (ii) It applied to any term that defined cover in a way that policyholders would not reasonably expect, whether it was a warranty, a condition precedent to liability or to cover, an exception, or a narrow definition of the risk.[35]
   (iii) The proposal would apply only if the effect of the term were to render the cover substantially different from what the insured reasonably expected. The objective was to provide a strong incentive to insurers to re-write their contractual documents in a way that their policyholders could understand.

5.11 The Commission rejected the argument that a harsh warranties regime was necessary as a protection against fraud on the grounds that the use of technical defences was counter-productive and likely to bring both the law and the insurance industry into disrepute.[36] The Commission identified three reasons to reform business insurance law: to protect businesses that were not expert in insurance; to provide a default regime that corresponded to legitimate expectations; and to ensure that UK insurance law remained competitive with that of other jurisdictions.[37]

5.12 The Commission also observed that it was unfortunate that the insured might simply not realise that the policy imposed a warranty obligation on him. Contrary to the position set out in their second Issues Paper, the Commission recommended that a causal connection test

31 Law Commission Consultation Paper No. 182 Insurance Contract Law: Misrepresentation, Non-Disclosure and Breach of Warranty by the Insured, November 2007 para 8.96.

32 Law Commission Consultation Paper No. 182 Insurance Contract Law: Misrepresentation, Non-Disclosure and Breach of Warranty by the Insured, November 2007 para 8.54–8.80.

33 Reforming Insurance Contract Law: A Summary of Responses to Consultation published on 13 October 2008.

34 Law Commission Consultation Paper No. 182 Insurance Contract Law: Misrepresentation, Non-Disclosure and Breach of Warranty by the Insured, November 2007 para 8.72.

35 Law Commission Consultation Paper No. 182 Insurance Contract Law: Misrepresentation, Non-Disclosure and Breach of Warranty by the Insured, November 2007 para 8.72 (2) page 200.

36 Law Commission Consultation Paper No. 182 Insurance Contract Law: Misrepresentation, Non-Disclosure and Breach of Warranty by the Insured, November 2007 para 1.67.

37 Law Commission Consultation Paper No. 182 Insurance Contract Law: Misrepresentation, Non-Disclosure and Breach of Warranty by the Insured, November 2007 para 1.78.

should be confined to warranties in the narrow sense.[38] It seems the Commission reached this conclusion on the grounds that their original proposal would be too complex and would need several exceptions to cover: the Commission felt the causal connection test should not, for example, apply to terms which limited the age of a driver or the geographical coverage of the policy.[39] The Commission re-affirmed its belief that insurers should not be entitled to rely on a breach of warranty unless the insured was supplied with a written statement of the warranty either before the contract was made, or as soon as possible thereafter.[40] As will be argued in more detail later, this author proposes that, for it to be properly comprehensive, any reform of the law in this area must apply to all clauses that purport to provide the insurer with a right to avoid liability. It will be demonstrated that the issue of whether proposals for reform cover exclusion clauses, or are able to impact on questions of scope are central to the effectiveness or otherwise of any attempt to overhaul the law.[41]

5.13 The Commission indicated that in relation to warranties of fact, it did not think that it accorded with the expectation of any class of insured that the insurer should be discharged by an immaterial breach of warranty, or a breach that had been cured before any claim arose.[42] Nor in the Commission's view would an insured reasonably expect a claim to be rejected on the grounds of a breach of warranty of fact that had no connection to the loss.[43] Crucially the Commission felt that it was not sufficient to leave it to the courts to construe a term in a fashion that gave it an equitable meaning. Furthermore, the Commission concluded that the UK was out of touch with global developments in this regard and that the UK concept of warranties no longer accorded with international conceptions of fairness.[44] The Commission was concerned that this could lead prospective insureds to reject the UK market in favour of jurisdictions that were less harsh, or at least that required the position to be made more transparent.

5.14 The Commission was initially attracted to the New Zealand approach to the reform of warranties,[45] but backed away from this position in the light of concerns from consultees. On the other hand, the Commission felt (perhaps surprisingly: see Chapter 6) that the Australian approach was too generous to the insured.[46] The Commission suggested that an

---

38 Law Commission Consultation Paper No. 182 Insurance Contract Law: Misrepresentation, Non-Disclosure and Breach of Warranty by the Insured, November 2007 para 8.39. In Issues Paper No. 2 the Commission recommended following the New Zealand approach which applied a causal connection test not just to warranties, but to any term that excludes liability because of events or circumstances likely to increase the risk of a loss occurring.

39 Law Commission Consultation Paper No. 182 Insurance Contract Law: Misrepresentation, Non-Disclosure and Breach of Warranty by the Insured, November 2007 para 8.3.

40 While the 1906 Act already requires that, in marine policies, express warranties must be in writing, this requirement is met by a reference in the policy to a written proposal, even if the insured was not supplied with a copy.

41 See Chapter 11 Issues: Problems with the Law on Warranties and Potential Solutions for Resolving Them and Chapter 12: A Proposed Solution.

42 Law Commission Consultation Paper No. 182 Insurance Contract Law: Misrepresentation, Non-Disclosure and Breach of Warranty by the Insured, November 2007 para 5.132.

43 Law Commission Consultation Paper No. 182 Insurance Contract Law: Misrepresentation, Non-Disclosure and Breach of Warranty by the Insured, November 2007 para 7.47.

44 Law Commission Consultation Paper No. 182 Insurance Contract Law: Misrepresentation, Non-Disclosure and Breach of Warranty by the Insured, November 2007 para 7.51.

45 See Chapter 7.

46 Law Commission Consultation Paper No. 182 Insurance Contract Law: Misrepresentation, Non-Disclosure and Breach of Warranty by the Insured, November 2007 para 8.43. See Chapter 6 for detailed consideration of the Australian approach.

insurer should be entitled to reject a claim if the breach had been a contributor to the cause of loss, albeit not the dominant cause.

5.15 Importantly the Commission intended that its proposed reasonable expectations approach should be an alternate to a wide causal connections test.[47] In the Commission's view, the law should 'give potential policyholders confidence in the insurance by ensuring that it meets their reasonable expectations, while protecting the legitimate interests of insurers and not imposing undue costs or unnecessary restrictions'; further it should also be coherent, clear and readily understandable.[48] The Commission suggested that, as it stood, 'the law imposes a default regime that undercuts, rather than supports, accepted market practice. In so doing, it risks defeating the reasonable expectations of the insured.'[49]

5.16 It seems that under the Commission's proposals the relevant consideration would be whether the assured appreciated the existence of the term before entering into the contract. In this context a significant factor would be whether the insurer had done enough to bring the relevant clause and its impact to the assured's attention. If the assured was aware of a provision, a court would not be able to declare a provision invalid because the assured lacked the negotiating power to resist it.[50] One obvious definitional question likely to arise would be what constituted 'standard terms': in some cases this would be clear, but at what stage in a negotiation would 'standard' become 'non-standard'? The Commission proposed that the test would look only at procedural issues: did the insured appreciate the existence of the term, or did it undermine its reasonable expectation? If the insurer showed that the insured knew about the term and its implications before entering the contract, the term would stand, even if the insured only agreed to the term because it had no alternative.[51]

5.17 The Commission proposed that its recommendations in relation to warranties should apply equally to marine insurance as to other forms of insurance[52] and that the causal connection test should apply to implied warranties. Interestingly, the Commission suggested that the courts had tended to construe warranties more strictly in marine cases than in other forms of insurance.[53] Under the Commission's proposals, in a voyage policy, the insured would only be paid if it could show, on the balance of probabilities, that the breach did not contribute to the loss.[54] Under the Commission's proposals for time policies, the insurer would have to prove that the breach was a real or dominant cause of the loss. The Commission suggested that if an insured could prevent the ship from being

47 Law Commission Consultation Paper No. 182 Insurance Contract Law: Misrepresentation, Non-Disclosure and Breach of Warranty by the Insured, November 2007 para 8.54, page 197.

48 Law Commission Consultation Paper No. 182 Insurance Contract Law: Misrepresentation, Non-Disclosure and Breach of Warranty by the Insured, November 2007 para 1.38.

49 Law Commission Consultation Paper No. 182 Insurance Contract Law: Misrepresentation, Non-Disclosure and Breach of Warranty by the Insured, November 2007 para 1.49.

50 B Soyer, Reforming Insurance Warranties: Are We Finally Moving Forward? in *Reforming Marine and Commercial Insurance Law,* General Editor Dr Bariş Soyer, Informa, London, 2008.

51 Law Commission Consultation Paper No. 182 Insurance Contract Law: Misrepresentation, Non-Disclosure and Breach of Warranty by the Insured, November 2007 para 5.145.

52 Law Commission Consultation Paper No. 182 Insurance Contract Law: Misrepresentation, Non-Disclosure and Breach of Warranty by the Insured, November 2007 para 8.115.

53 Law Commission Consultation Paper No. 182 Insurance Contract Law: Misrepresentation, Non-Disclosure and Breach of Warranty by the Insured, November 2007 para 8.113.

54 Law Commission Consultation Paper No. 182 Insurance Contract Law: Misrepresentation, Non-Disclosure and Breach of Warranty by the Insured, November 2007 para 8.119.

overloaded and failed to do so, it was possible that this might constitute a breach of the implied warranty that 'the adventure shall be carried out in a lawful manner' under s41 of the MIA. Under the Commission's proposals it would be open to the insured to argue that the overloading was not intended at the outset, but was only a subsequent illegality. If the insured could prove that the overloading did not contribute to the loss, the insurer would remain liable.[55] Although the Commission indicated that a number of representations had been made to them suggesting that implied warranties should be abolished,[56] (as had been recommended (albeit not implemented) in Australia[57]), it stopped short of making such a recommendation.

5.18 Confusingly, the Commission's recommendations could be interpreted as proposing an end to implied warranties, as under the Commission's proposals, in order to defeat a claim on a policy, the warranty would have to be set out in writing in the main contract document or some other document at or before the time the contract was made or as soon as possible thereafter.[58] However the Commission did not make such an explicit recommendation and it is probable that no such implication was intended. The Commission doubted the merit of retaining the implied voyage provisions set out in s43–46 of the MIA, but if they were retained, recommended that they should be subject to a causal linkage test as recommended elsewhere.[59]

5.19 Subsequently the Chairman of the Law Commission, Lord Hertzell, indicated that while consultees of the Commission's proposals had expressed concern about the detail of the proposals, most supported a requirement for causal connection in order for the insurer to have a remedy.[60] The Commission noted that the need for reform had been endorsed by the British Insurance Law Association.[61] In the past the Association of British Insurers and its predecessor had argued that any changes were best dealt with as a matter of self-regulation or ombudsman discretion, rather than by a change in the law itself.

Criticism of the reasonable expectations approach

5.20 Although the distinction made by the Commission between current fact warranties and future conduct warranties received much adverse comment (which in this author's view was in the main justifiable), the most controversial aspect of the Commission's proposals were those elements relating to the insured's 'reasonable expectations.' These came in for

55 Law Commission Consultation Paper No. 182 Insurance Contract Law: Misrepresentation, Non-Disclosure and Breach of Warranty by the Insured, November 2007 para 8.123.

56 Law Commission Consultation Paper No. 182 Insurance Contract Law: Misrepresentation, Non-Disclosure and Breach of Warranty by the Insured, November 2007 para 8.124.

57 ALRC, Review of the Marine Insurance Act 1909 (2001) No 91.

58 Law Commission Consultation Paper No. 182 Insurance Contract Law: Misrepresentation, Non-Disclosure and Breach of Warranty by the Insured, November 2007 para 8.12, cited in Sir R Aikens, The Law Commission's Proposed Reforms of the Law of Warranties in Marine and Commercial Insurance: Will the Cure Be Better than the Disease? in *Reforming Marine and Commercial Insurance Law,* General Editor Dr Bariş Soyer, Informa, London 2008.

59 Law Commission Consultation Paper No. 182 Insurance Contract Law: Misrepresentation, Non-Disclosure and Breach of Warranty by the Insured, November 2007 para 8.129.

60 D Hertzell, Insurance Contract Law Reform in England Wales and Scotland, in *Reforming Marine and Commercial Insurance Law,* General Editor Dr Baris Soyer, Informa, London 2008, page 5.

61 British Insurance Law Association, Insurance Contract Law Reform – Recommendations to the Law Commissions (2002).

considerable criticism, much of which, it is suggested, had some merit. Bennett argued that businesses would prefer a clear rule that might operate harshly against their interests in particular circumstances, rather than an unclear rule designed to produce fair and equitable results, but which might require a lengthy and costly process to apply.[62] Soyer had sympathy with arguments suggesting that the reasonable expectations approach was inherently vague and not appropriate to commercial insurance; he suggested that commercial insurers would seek to draft around it and pass the cost of doing so on to insured's.[63] He urged the Law Commission to re-consider. Rather than applying the reasonable expectations test to SMEs, Soyer suggested it might be better to treat SMEs as if they were consumers; although this could lead to definitional issues in terms of what constituted an SME, he argued that was preferable to the uncertainty of the reasonable expectations approach.[64] However, notwithstanding his reservations regarding the Commission's proposals in relation to 'reasonable expectations,' Soyer saw the Commission's recommendations as a step in the right direction.[65] Merkin observed that the meaning of the reasonable expectations test would remain unclear until tested by courts.[66] Aikens was sceptical that it was a good argument to suggest that, because one party did not understand the law or its effect, the effect should therefore be changed in the hope that in the future that party would understand the law and that it would therefore meet their expectations. He suggested that it was more likely that the aggrieved party would continue to argue that the law did not meet their expectations. As a result, such an approach was likely to result in a slippery slope that tilted the playing field dramatically in favour of one party. He argued it was up to business parties to make themselves aware of the consequences of their actions.[67] Aikens further suggested that there was some danger of parties' freedom to contract being constrained in circumstances where standard terms used provisions other than a standard default regime and the assured argued that the outcome failed to match its reasonable expectations.[68] This could be exacerbated by uncertainty over the definition of reasonable expectations. It did not follow in Aiken's view that the law was 'wrong and unjust,'[69] simply because it did not meet with the assured's reasonable expectations.[70] In Aiken's view a better solution would be for warranties to be

62 H Bennett, 'Reflections on Values: The Law Commissions' Proposals with Respect to Remedies for Breach of Promissory Warranty and Pre-Formation Non-Disclosure and Misrepresentation in Commercial Insurance' in *Reforming Marine and Commercial Insurance Law,* General Editor Dr Bariş Soyer, Informa, London, 2008, page 159.

63 B Soyer, 'Reforming Insurance Warranties: Are We Finally Moving Forward?' in *Reforming Marine and Commercial Insurance Law,* General Editor Dr Baris Soyer, Informa, London, 2008.

64 B Soyer, 'Reforming Insurance Warranties: Are We Finally Moving Forward?' in *Reforming Marine and Commercial Insurance Law,* General Editor Dr Baris Soyer, Informa, London, 2008, page 153.

65 B Soyer, 'Reforming Insurance Warranties: Are We Finally Moving Forward?' in *Reforming Marine and Commercial Insurance Law,* General Editor Dr Baris Soyer, Informa, London, 2008, page 154.

66 R Merkin and J Lowry, 'Reconstructing Insurance Law: The Law Commissions' Consultation Paper' (2008) 71 *Modern Law Review* 95, 111.

67 Sir R Aikens, 'The Law Commission's Proposed Reforms of the Law of Warranties in Marine and Commercial Insurance: Will the Cure Be Better than the Disease?' in *Reforming Marine and Commercial Insurance Law,* General Editor Dr Bariş Soyer, Informa, London 2008.

68 Sir R Aikens, 'The Law Commission's Proposed Reforms of the Law of Warranties in Marine and Commercial Insurance: Will the Cure Be Better than the Disease?' in *Reforming Marine and Commercial Insurance Law,* General Editor Dr Bariş Soyer, Informa, London 2008, page 122.

69 Law Commission Consultation Paper No. 182 Insurance Contract Law: Misrepresentation, Non-Disclosure and Breach of Warranty by the Insured, November 2007 para 7.39.

70 Sir R Aikens, 'The Law Commission's Proposed Reforms of the Law of Warranties in Marine and Commercial Insurance: Will the Cure Be Better than the Disease?' in *Reforming Marine and Commercial Insurance Law,* General Editor Dr Bariş Soyer, Informa, London 2008, page 122.

specific, specifically agreed and, rather than appearing in standard terms, to be included in a separate document.[71]

5.21 In the round, the reasonable expectations elements of the Commission's proposals raised too many issues and uncertainties and did not represent a robust approach to reforming the law of insurance warranties. An approach rooted in causal connection is, in this author's view, to be preferred. What was welcome however was the Commission's recommendation that a breach of warranty or other term should give the insurer the right to terminate the contract (rather than automatically discharging it from liability), provided (unless otherwise agreed) the breach was sufficiently serious to justify termination under the general law of contract. It will be argued that a right to terminate has a key role to play in the reform of the law in this area.[72] Finally this author rejects the Commission's proposal that a causal connection test should be confined only to breaches of warranties.

Law Commission Consultation Paper No. 204 Insurance Contract Law: the business insured's duty of disclosure and the law of warranties, a joint consultation paper, June 2012

5.22 No progress was made on the Commission's 2007 proposals and the Commission again returned to the subject in 2012.

5.23 The Commission acknowledged that many thought that the Commission's 2007 proposals were too complicated, particularly in their distinction between current fact warranties and future conduct warranties. It also acknowledged that concern had been expressed about causation proposals and its proposed approach based on the insured's reasonable expectations.

5.24 Echoing its earlier reports, the Commission identified four main problems with the existing law on warranties:

(i) Under section 33(3) of the 1906 Act, a warranty 'must be exactly complied with, whether it be material to the risk or not.' This meant that an insurer could refuse a claim as a result of a trivial mistake that had no bearing on the risk.
(ii) Under section 34(2), once a warranty had been broken, the policyholder could not use the defence that the breach had been remedied.
(iii) The breach of warranty discharged the insurer from all liability under the contract, not just for liability for the type of risk in question.
(iv) A statement could be converted into a warranty using obscure words that most policyholders did not understand.

5.25 The Commission argued that the result was that the existing law brought 'the law in the UK into disrepute in the international market place.'[73] As a consequence, outcomes lacked 'logical reason' and could not be explained in terms of either legal fairness or

71 Sir R Aikens, 'The Law Commission's Proposed Reforms of the Law of Warranties in Marine and Commercial Insurance: Will the Cure Be Better than the Disease?' in *Reforming Marine and Commercial Insurance Law,* General Editor Dr Bariş Soyer, Informa, London 2008.

72 See Chapter 12.

73 LC Consultation Paper 204 para 14.2.

economic efficiency.[74] Attempts by the courts to ameliorate the situation had introduced inconsistency and uncertainty.[75]

5.26 The Commission's consultations did however demonstrate widespread support for reform.[76] The Forum of Insurance Lawyers concluded that reform was 'long overdue,' while the Bar Council observed that reform 'would be in keeping with most people's sense of justice.' Although many insurers welcomed the prospect of reform, the Association of British Insurers felt that the existing regime 'works well for consumers and the industry,' while for business customers 'the guiding principle should be freedom to contract.' Nevertheless, representations from industry made it clear that commercial buyers of insurance were strongly in favour of reform.[77] A report from Mactavish suggested that mid-sized firms, turning over between £50 million and £5 billion, were particularly vulnerable[78] to adverse outcomes under the existing law.

5.27 Submissions to the Commission included criticisms of the Commission's earlier proposals for a causal connection test: that it would be difficult to apply in practice; that it would lead to an increase in costs; that it was not appropriate for all warranties; and it might increase moral hazard.[79] Some suggested that there would be difficulties in applying the test where the breach increased the risk, or the loss incurred, but could not be shown to have directly caused either.[80] Nevertheless, the Commission acknowledged that the causal link approach did receive wide-ranging support from both legal practitioners, and representatives of both insurers and insureds.

5.28 The Commission accepted that its proposals had gone too far and dropped the reasonable expectations element of their 2007 recommendations. The Commission also observed that the causal connection test was unsuited to many terms, and that it would be unduly confusing to apply the test to warranties and not to suspensive conditions.[81] The Commission retained its view that its proposals should represent a default position for business insurance: business parties should be free to contract out, provided that both sides understood and agreed to a term.[82]

5.29 The key elements of the Commission's revised proposals were as follows[83]:

(i) Abolish basis clauses;

(ii) A breach of a warranty should trigger suspension of the insurer's liability for the duration of the breach. The insurer's liability would be restored once the breach was cured;

(iii) For any term (not just warranties) designed to reduce the risk of a particular type of loss, a breach of that term should only suspend liability in respect of that type of loss. Thus, according to the Commission, a requirement to install a mortice lock

74 Professor Wilhelmsen Duty of Disclosure, Duty of Good Faith, Alternation of Risk and Warranties: An Analysis of the Replies to the CMI Questionnaire, CMI Yearbook 2000 pp 392 and 409.

75 LC Consultation Paper 204 para 14.3.

76 LC Consultation Paper 204 para 14.4.

77 LC Consultation Paper 204 para 14.4–9.

78 Corporate Risk & Insurance – The Case for Placement Reform. The Mactavish Protocols (2011).

79 LC Consultation Paper 204 para 14.36.

80 The British Maritime Law Association argued this: LC Consultation Paper 204 para 14.42.

81 LC Consultation Paper 204 para 14.50.

82 LC Consultation Paper 204 para 14.55.

83 LC Consultation Paper 204 paras 15.1.

would suspend liability for theft loss, but not for fire loss. The same approach would apply where a term was designed to reduce the risk of loss at a particular time or at a particular location.

5.30 Reversing the position it took in 2007, the Commission, while continuing to support a right to terminate, felt that this was best left to the terms of the contract.[84] While being of the view that business parties should be free to contract out of its proposals, the Commission recommended that any variation should be spelled out in clear and unambiguous terms, and specifically brought to the attention of the insured before the contract was formed.[85] Unlike the position it had previously adopted, the Commission decided against recommending that warranties should always be in writing (although in practice business insurers do put warranties in writing).

5.31 The Commission recommended that its proposals apply to marine insurance, as well as to other forms of commercial insurance. The Commission suggested that the distinction between marine and other forms of insurance was unhelpful and had caused particular definitional problems in Australia.[86] However in the light of submissions from insurers recommending the maintenance of the status quo, the Commission recommended the retention of implied warranties.[87] Further the Commission recommended that the consequences of breach of an implied warranty should be consistent with breach of an express warranty and should thus suspend liability.[88] The Commission recommended that the default regime for breach of warranty should apply to reinsurance in the same way as it applied to direct business insurance.

5.32 In seeking to illustrate the application of its proposals, the Commission suggested that in *Forsikringsaktieselskapet Vesta v Butcher*[89] a warranty that the insured should keep a 24-hour watch at the farm would be interpreted as being aimed at the particular risk of loss through theft or vandalism.[90] As a result, the Commission argued that liability would be suspended only in respect of theft or vandalism and that accordingly the insurer would be liable for storm damage. This interpretation is however open to challenge: nowhere in the policy did it indicate that the posting of a watch related only to those specific risks. The example in fact illustrates the difficulty in determining when a given provision relates to a specific risk or risks and when it relates to the risk more generally.[91]

The Commission's 2014 report and the Insurance Act 2015

5.33 The Commission's reports over the period 1957 to 2012 illustrate the evolving nature of the Commission's thinking and the difficulties in crafting a set of proposals

84 LC Consultation Paper 204 para 15.33.
85 LC Consultation Paper 204 para 15.55.
86 LC Consultation Paper 204 para 16.4 citing *Gibbs v Mercantile Mutual Insurance (Australia) Limited* [2003] HCA 39.
87 LC Consultation Paper 204 para 16.9.
88 LC Consultation Paper 204 para 16.18.
89 [1989] AC 852.
90 LC Consultation Paper 204 para 15.42.
91 As we will see, this issue is particularly relevant in relation to s11 of the Insurance Act 2015.

that deal effectively with the range of complex issues presented by the law in this area. The Commission returned to the subject once more in 2014, with their proposals finally leading to the enactment of the Insurance Act 2015. Given their importance and the very close linkage between the Commission's 2014 proposals and the Act, these two items are considered in Chapters 8 and 9. However, before considering the UK reforms we will first, as a basis for comparison, critically examine reform initiatives taken in Australia and New Zealand.

CHAPTER 6

The law on insurance warranties in Australia

Non-marine insurance: s54 of the Insurance Contracts Act 1984

Background

6.1 In *Deaves v CML Fire & General Insurance Co Limited*[1] Murphy J, describing the law as it stood prior to the enactment of the Insurance Contracts Act, said:

> The existing state of insurance law is so favourable to insurers that any insurance company can easily frame its proposal forms and policy in such a way that only an extremely weary proponent will be able to recover. This has been tolerable only because, in general, insurers have not taken advantage of their superior position.

6.2 Assessing the post-ICA scene, Greg Pynt has observed

> The Insurance Contracts Act has been very beneficial. It has almost rid us of those two unpleasant contractual terms, the "warranty" and the "condition precedent," that haunted insureds for hundreds of years, and it has replaced them with the attractive s54, which has so far given us no trouble that we couldn't handle.[2]

6.3 While acknowledging that the approach in the Insurance Contracts Act offers a number of benefits over the law as it previously existed, this author does not believe the Act offers an optimal solution to the challenges inherent in seeking a balanced approach to breaches of insurance warranties and other provisions.

6.4 In Australian law s54 of the Insurance Contracts Act 1984 (ICA) provides relief for non-compliance with contractual requirements (including warranties) of an insurance policy, where the non-compliance did not cause or contribute to the loss. If the non-compliance did contribute, however, the section gives insurers the ability to reduce the payout to the extent that their interests were adversely affected.

6.5 Under s54 there is no entitlement to cancel the insurance for breach, or automatic termination for non-compliance. When it applies, the section abolishes the distinction between a warranty and a representation. Sutton argues that s54 cannot apply to a term which defines or describes the scope of risk and thus would not apply to a warranty of this

1 (1979) 143 CLR 24.

2 G Pynt, *Australian Insurance Law: A First Reference,* 3rd Edition at page 382. The quote is based on an original observation from Lord Denning in *Roles v Nathan* [1963] 2 All ER 908, commenting on the Occupiers Liability Act.

DOI: 10.4324/9781003031734-6

nature (this is discussed further later in this chapter).[3] Meanwhile a representational warranty, given prior to entering into the insurance contract is subject to the ICA s24 (see later in this chapter) and Pt IV. Section 24 provides that any pre-contractual statement has to be treated as a representation, rather than a warranty, so that it is subject to the usual materiality and inducement tests. Once the contract has been entered into, s54 applies.

6.6 In its report ALRC 20, 'Insurance Contracts,'[4] the Australian Law Reform Commission (ALRC) indicated that it felt there should be a fairer balance between the interests of the insurer and the insured. The ALRC expressed concern about cases where 'the insured is deprived of indemnity for conduct which is totally unrelated to the loss which has actually been suffered.'[5] The ALRC suggested that the parties' rights in the event of a breach of, or non-compliance with, a contractual term should depend on 'matters of substance,' emphasising the effect of terms, rather than whether a term was characterised as a warranty or a condition. The ALRC stressed its recommendations should be unaffected by the form in which policies were drafted.[6]

6.7 This objective was reiterated in the Explanatory Memorandum that accompanied the Insurance Contracts Bill. Paragraph 182 of the Memorandum stated

> The existing law is unsatisfactory in that the parties' rights are determined by the form in which the contract is drafted, rather than by reference to the harm caused. The present law ... may lead to termination of the contract regardless of whether or not the insurer suffered any prejudice as a result of the insured's breach. The proposed law will concentrate on the substance and effect of the term and ensure that a more equitable result is achieved.[7]

As pointed out by Sutton, the potential downside to this lack of definition, the 'hollowness at its core,' is uncertainty about the precise ambit of the provision and the possibility that it may apply to provisions that define the risk accepted by the underwriter.[8]

6.8 S24 of the ICA essentially abolishes present warranties (and thus basis of contract clauses) by treating every statement 'made in or in connection with a contract of insurance ... by or attributable to the insured' as a representation 'made to the insurer by the insured during the negotiations for the contract but before it was entered into,' rather than as a warranty.[9] Accordingly a breach does not have automatic consequences, but rather triggers the ordinary rules governing misrepresentation as set out in s23 and s28 of the ICA.[10] Under these rules the insurer's remedy for breach is limited to that offered by s28. S28(1) provides that an insurer has no remedy for pre-contractual non-disclosure if it would have entered into the contract on the same terms if the misrepresentation had not been made. S28(3) provides that an insurer cannot avoid a contract for an insured's innocent or negligent pre-contractual non-disclosure or misrepresentation.[11] In these circumstances the insurer's

3 *Sutton on Insurance Law,* eds Merkin, Kirby and Enright, 4th Edition, Lawbook Co., 2015, at 3.1180 page 235.

4 Australian Law Reform Commission Report No. 20 1982 at page 224.

5 Australian Law Reform Commission Report No. 20 1982 at page 220.

6 Australian Law Reform Commission Report No. 20 1982 at page 229.

7 Explanatory Memorandum to the Insurance Contracts Bill 1984, para 182, available at www5.austlii.edu.au/au/legis/cth/bill_em/icb1984230/memo_0.html.

8 *Sutton on Insurance Law,* eds Merkin, Kirby and Enright, 4th Edition, Lawbook Co., 2015, page 200.

9 S24 Insurance Contracts Act 1984.

10 S23 and s28 of the Insurance Contracts Act 1984.

11 S28(3) Insurance Contracts Act 1984.

liability for a claim is limited to an amount that would put the insurer in the position it would have been in if the non-disclosure had not occurred or the misrepresentation had not been made. The focus is on compensating the insurer, not penalising the insured.[12] If the insurer would have inserted a term that would have excluded his liability for the claim, the insurer's liability will be reduced to zero.[13] If the insurer can show he would not have entered into the contract at all if there had been no misrepresentation, his liability will again be reduced to zero. The onus is on the insurer to establish his position on the balance of possibilities.[14] Subject to s28(1), an insurer is entitled to avoid an insurance contract for fraudulent non-disclosure/misrepresentation.

6.9 In ALRC 20 the ALRC argued that where the conduct of the insured might in principle have caused or contributed to the loss, a causal connection test should be adopted.[15] The Commission recommended that the burden of proof should rest on the insured where his conduct *could* have contributed to the loss.[16] Where it is shown that the conduct of the insured could not in principle have contributed to the damage, the insurer's redress should be limited to damages. Such damages should be measured by reference to the prejudice the insurer suffered as a consequence of insured's conduct.

6.10 The High Court has described the primary objective of s54 as follows: to strike a fair balance between the interests of an insurer and an insured with respect to a contractual term designed to protect the insurer from an increase in risk during the period of insurance cover.[17] S54 represents a combination of proportionality and causal connection test,[18] such that the insured should only suffer penalties in proportion to the harm caused by his conduct. As s54 focuses on effect and not form, it represents a much more broad reaching provision than sections 10 and 11 of the Insurance Act 2015, its closest UK equivalents.

6.11 Merkin has aptly described s54 as being based on the need for a causal link between the assured's breach of contract and the loss and, if there is such a link, reduction of the claim on a proportionate, rather than absolute, basis.[19]

S54 Insurance Contracts Act

6.12 S54(1)[20] of the ICA denies the insurer the right to avoid liability by simply relying on a breach of warranty or some other condition: the insurer's redress is confined to a reduction in liability by an amount reflecting the extent to which his interests were prejudiced. Specifically s54(1) states

> where the effect of a contract of insurance would, but for this section, be that the insurer may refuse to pay a claim, either in whole or in part, by reason of some act of the insured

12 G Pynt, *Australian Insurance Law: A First Reference,* Butterworths, Chatswood, Australia, 3rd Edition, 2015.

13 *Ferrcom Pty Ltd v Commercial Union Insurance Co of Australia Ltd* [1993] 176 CLR 332 at 14–15.

14 *Prepaid Services Pty Ltd v Atradius Credit Insurance NV* [2013] NSWCA 252.

15 Australian Law Reform Commission Report No. 20, 1982 at para 228.

16 Emphasis added.

17 *Maxwell v Highway Hauliers* [2014] HCA 33, 10 September 2014, P12/2014, at 20.

18 P Mann, *Mann's Annotated Insurance Contracts Act,* Thompson Reuters, Sydney, 7th Edition, 2016, page 409.

19 R Merkin, Reforming Insurance Law: Is There a Case for Reverse Transportation? A Report for the English and Scottish Law Commissions on the Australian Experience of Insurance Law Reform; available at http://www.lawcom.gov.uk/app/uploads/2015/03/ICL_Merkin_report.pdf or at https://eprints.soton.ac.uk/27860/.

20 S54 is set out in full in Appendix 1.

or some other person, being an act that occurred after the contract was entered into but not being an act in respect of which subsection 2 applies, the insurer may not refuse to pay the claim by reason only of that act but the insurer's liability in respect of the claim is reduced by the amount that fairly represents the extent to which the insurer's interests were prejudiced as a result of that act.

6.13 S54(2) permits the insurer to refuse to pay a claim where the act or omission could reasonably be regarded as being capable of causing or contributing to a loss in respect of which insurance cover is provided by the contract. However, this is subject to four qualifications: if the assured proves that no part of the loss was caused by the breach, the insurer may not refuse to pay the claim by reason only of that act (ICA, s54(3)): i.e. in such circumstances s54(1) applies; if the assured proves that some part of the loss was not caused by the breach, the insurers must pay that part (ICA, s54(4)); steps taken to preserve life or property are to be disregarded (ICA, s54(5)(a)); and an act which could not have been reasonably avoided is to be disregarded (ICA, s54(5)(b)). By virtue of s54(6) an 'act' in s54(1) includes an omission.[21] Contracting out of s54 is prohibited: under s52 of the ICA any term that purports to limit or exclude the operation of s54 to the prejudice of a person other than the insurer is void.[22]

6.14 Reflecting the ALRC's recommendations, s54 makes no distinction between warranties and other contractual terms. The effect of s54 is to treat all policy obligations or restrictions affecting the assured's conduct, in whatever form they appear, in exactly the same way because they can have the effect of entitling the insurer to refuse to pay a claim.[23] Specifically the ALRC argued that in particular, no difference should be drawn between a term framed: (a) as an obligation of the insured (e.g. 'the insured is under an obligation to keep the motor vehicle in a roadworthy condition'); (b) as a continuing warranty of the insured (e.g. 'the insured warrants he will keep the motor vehicle in a roadworthy condition'); (c) as a temporal exclusion from cover (e.g. 'this cover will not apply while the motor vehicle is unroadworthy'); or (d) as a limitation on the defined risk (e.g. 'this contract provides cover for the motor vehicle while it is roadworthy.')[24] Consequently continuing warranties no longer exist as a separate category attracting particular treatment. As we have seen, insurers are entitled to damages under s54(1), but only to the extent that they can demonstrate prejudice. Crucially whatever the nature of the insured's breach, the insurer has the right to cancel the policy under s60.[25]

6.15 The Explanatory Notes to the Draft Insurance Contracts Bill 1982 contained a number of examples that sought to illustrate the intended operation of s54.

---

21 See Appendix 1 for s54 of the Insurance Contracts Act in full.

22 S52 Insurance Contracts Act 1984.

23 R Merkin, Reforming Insurance Law: Is There a Case for Reverse Transportation?; A Report for the English and Scottish Law Commissioners on the Australian Experience of Insurance Law Reform; available at http://www.lawcom.gov.uk/app/uploads/2015/03/ICL_Merkin_report.pdf or at https://eprints.soton.ac.uk/27860/.

24 Australian Law Reform Commission, Insurance Contracts, Report No 20, (1982). See also Australia, House of Representatives, Insurance Contracts Bill 1984, Explanatory Memorandum at 78–80.

25 Section 60(1)(d) of the Insurance Contracts Act provides that the insurer may cancel the contract where the insured has failed to comply with a provision of the contract. S60(2)(b) provides the insurer may cancel the contract where he has the right to refuse to pay a claim as a result of an act or omission by the insured or some other person.

(i) A motor vehicle policy contains a warranty that the vehicle will be maintained in a roadworthy condition. The brakes fail (as a result of lack of maintenance) and the vehicle collides with another, but the other driver is 50% to blame. The Notes suggest that s54(2) applies because the failure to maintain the vehicle in a roadworthy condition could reasonably have been supposed to cause or contribute to the loss. However, the insured is able to prove that he was at most 50% to blame and so the insurer is only able to deduct 50% from his liability for the claim (s54(4)).

(ii) If the vehicle was damaged while parked then, according to the Explanatory Notes, the insured would be able to recover the full amount of his loss (less of course any deductible). This is presumably because, although the breach could be reasonably regarded as being *capable of causing or contributing to a loss in respect of which cover was provided*[26] (the vehicle could, for example have rolled down hill as a result of having defective brakes) (s54(2)), the assured is able to establish that no part of the loss was caused by his breach (s54(3)).

(iii) A motor policy includes a term that excludes liability if the driver is unlicensed. A has an accident whilst driving the car and is unlicensed, having forgotten to renew his license which had expired two weeks earlier. The Explanatory Note argues that, as A's conduct (in not renewing the licence) could not reasonably have been considered capable of contributing to the accident (and thus s54(2) is not applicable), s54(1) applies.

6.16 These examples however disguise the fact that s54 has thrown up some challenging issues for the courts. Merkin describes s54 as 'perhaps the most difficult section in the entire Insurance Contracts Act 1984,'[27] but nevertheless argues that with the s54 approach, most serious criticisms of the law on warranties disappear.[28] One of the principal problems with s54, which has seen so many judges 'struggling with issues of construction and application of the words adopted by parliament,'[29] is that if the section is given a large ambit, 'it might effectively permit courts to repair all kinds of "omissions" on the part of insured persons and third parties and effectively to rewrite insurance policies accordingly.'[30] It is accepted that s54 offers many benefits over the historic approach to breaches of warranties, as well as some advantages over the Insurance Act 2015, however it will be argued that it represents an unnecessarily complex solution and one which, even after 35 years of litigation, is still subject to evolving judicial interpretation. The following sections will focus on the component elements underpinning the operation of s54, the issues and uncertainties relating thereto and the courts' evolving interpretation of the section.

26 Emphasis added.

27 R Merkin, Reforming Insurance Law: Is There a Case for Reverse Transportation?; A Report for the English and Scottish Law Commissioners on the Australian Experience of Insurance Law Reform; available at http://www.lawcom.gov.uk/app/uploads/2015/03/ICL_Merkin_report.pdf or at https://eprints.soton.ac.uk/27860/.

28 R Merkin, 'Australia: Still a Nation of Chalmers?' (2011) 30(2) University of Queensland Law Journal, University of Queensland 189–224.

29 *Greentree v FAI General Insurance Co Ltd* [1998] NSWSC 544; (1998) 44 NSWLR 706 at 714 per Mason P.

30 *FAI Insurance Limited v Aust Hospital Care Pty Ltd* [2001] HCA 38; 204 CLR 641; 75 ALJR 1236 (27 June 2001) Kirby J at 63.

Substance over form

6.17 On one aspect at least the courts' position has been consistently clear: in interpreting s54 the courts will adopt a 'substance over form' approach. In *Antico v Heath Fielding Australia Pty Ltd* the court determined that s54 is 'remedial in character and its language should be construed so as to give the most complete remedy that is consistent with the actual language employed and to which its words are fairly open.'[31] In *East End Real Estate Pty Ltd v CE Heath Casualty & General Insurance Ltd*,[32] Gleeson CJ indicated

> In my view, by choosing words of generality and avoiding reference to the particular type of contractual provision that might produce the result that the insurer may refuse to pay a claim, the legislature has evinced an intention to avoid the result that the operation of s54 depends upon matters of form.[33]

The approach was endorsed by the majority in *FAI General Insurance Co Ltd v Australian Hospital Care Pty Ltd* where Kirby J stressed that

> no distinction can be made, for the purposes of s54, between provisions of a contract which define the scope of cover, and those provisions which are conditions affecting an entitlement to claim. The substantive effect of the contract can be determined only by examination of the contract as a whole.[34]

This in turn was reinforced by Meagher JA in *Prepaid Services Pty Ltd v Atradius Credit Insurance NV* where he emphasised that the effect of a contract of insurance must be determined as a matter of construction, unconstrained by distinctions between provisions which define the scope of cover and conditions or exclusions which impact the entitlement of the insured to claim.[35] Meagher's approach was followed in *Pantaenius Australia Pty Ltd v Watkins Syndicate 0457 at Lloyd's*,[36] while the High Court in *Maxwell v Highway Hauliers*[37] again emphasised the importance of substance over form in interpreting s54.

The key elements of s54

6.18 This section will outline the key elements required in order to trigger the application of s54 and discuss the courts' interpretation of each element in a number of key cases. Inevitably several of these cases have individually discussed some or all of the key features of s54; however it is important to deal separately with each element in order fully to appreciate the complexity of the section and the courts' evolving interpretation of s54. We will then examine in detail four cases that have come before the courts in recent years. These cases have not only sought to clarify judicial interpretation in a number

31 (1997) 188 CLR 652, at 675.

32 (1991) 25 NSWLR 400; 7 ANZ Ins Cas 61–092.

33 (1991) 25 NSWLR 400; 7 ANZ Ins Cas 61–092 at 403 c-d to 404B.

34 [2001] HCA 38; (2001) 204 CLR 641 (McHugh, Gummow and Hayne JJ), at 655–656 [32] – [33].

35 P Mann, Mann's Annotated Insurance Contracts Act, 7th Edition, Thompson Reuters, Sydney, 2016, at page 422, citing *Prepaid Services Pty Ltd v Atradius Credit Insurance NV* (2013) 302 ALR 732; 17 ANZ Ins Cas 61–981; [2013] NSWCA 252.

36 [2016] FCA 1.

37 [2014] HCA 33, 10 September 2014.

of key areas, but also, importantly, demonstrate that the evolving interpretation of s54 remains at the cutting edge of Australian insurance law, notwithstanding over 35 years' experience of the section.

(A) Questions of scope: when does s54 apply?

6.19 By definition an event that is beyond the scope of an insurance policy is not a breach of that policy: it is simply not covered by it.[38] Again, in circumstances where there is a failure to meet a condition precedent to the attachment of risk, the policy merely fails to come on risk. In the latter case it is clear s54 has no role: the section applies only to contracts of insurance that have become effective. But does s54 have a role in addressing issues of scope?

6.20 At the WA Court of Appeal hearing of *Maxwell v Highway Hauliers*[39] McLure P set out the following steps in determining the application of s54:

(1) Identify the relevant s54 act or omission;
(2) Determine whether the act or omission is one to which s54(2) applies. If yes, determine whether s54(3) or s54(4) applies. If s54(2) does not apply, determine whether s54(1) applies;
(3) In assessing whether s54(1) applies:
    (a) Determine whether there are any restrictions or limitations inherent in the actual claim by reference to the type or kind of insurance in issue. If the facts of the claim are outside any inherent restrictions or limitations, it will not be a claim under the insurance contract, and s54(1) will not apply;
    (b) Determine whether the effect of the insurance contract is that the insurer may refuse to pay the claim in question (in whole or in part) by reason of the act or omission; and
    (c) Determine whether the insurer is refusing to pay the claim by reason only of that act or omission. If yes, the insurer may not refuse to pay the claim (but the insurer's liability may be reduced to the extent its interests were prejudiced as a result of the act or omission).

6.21 S54 applies only to insurance contracts that have come into effect.[40] Accordingly it is clear that s54 does not apply to pre-contractual non-disclosure or misrepresentation. Hawke has argued that one of the key challenges in relation to s54 is to ensure that the remedial purpose of the section (preventing insureds losing the benefit of cover because of conduct that is irrelevant to the risk insured) is not frustrated by drafting devices, while at the same time ensuring that section cannot be used to enlarge the scope of cover.[41] However in the 1990s a series of cases appeared to establish a line of thinking that suggested that s54 *could* be utilised to vary the risk definition of a policy and alter the scope of cover.

38 *Sutton on Insurance Law*, eds Merkin, Kirby and Enright, 4th Edition, Lawbook Co., 2015.

39 (2013) 45 WAR 297, at para 75. Although the case went to the High Court on appeal this nevertheless remains a good summary of the approach courts take to s54.

40 This poses potential problems with claims made policies where events from which the claim arises occur before policy commenced.

41 F Hawke, S54: 'Where to Draw the Line?' (2012) 23 *Insurance Law Journal* 223–244.

It is argued that such a development would represent a very worrying trend and one fraught with commercial uncertainty for all parties. It would surely throw into question the right of parties to determine the terms under which they contract. It is hard to see why piercing the sanctity of scope should be a one-way ticket (in favour of the insured). At its extreme, such a development would leave both parties with no commercial certainty as to the bargain they had struck. Accordingly it is surely essential that s54 is not permitted to encroach into issues of scope.

6.22 However in *East End Real Estate Pty Ltd v CE Heath Casualty & General Insurance Ltd*[42] (subsequently approved by the High Court in *Antico v Heath Fielding Australia Pty Ltd:* see later in this chapter) under a claims made policy, a claim was made against the insured during the policy period, but the insured failed to notify the insurer until after the end of the period. The insurer argued that s54 did not deal with matters concerning scope: it could not be used to widen scope. In rejecting the insurer's argument, the court observed: 'It would hardly be consistent ... to construe the language of s54 in such a way as to make its operation depend upon the choice that is made between various available drafting techniques.'[43] Mahoney CJ held that the immediate reason that the insurer could refuse to meet the claim was because it was not in cover, however 'it was not within cover by reason of an omission of the insured. Therefore the entitlement to refuse arose by reason of that omission' and as a result s54(1) applied. Does the decision in this case suggest that s54 could be used to vary the definition of risk that was accepted and underwritten and thus the scope of the cover? Does an insurer's potential ability to claim prejudice under s54(1) offer adequate protection to what otherwise could be a dangerous blurring of risk definition? Sutton suggests that the court appears to have construed the application of s54 widely, such that it applied to both the scope of the cover and the conditions of the policy.[44] Certainly the comments of Gleeson CJ appear to support this:

> it is perfectly appropriate to say in the present case that the effect of the contract of insurance is such that, but for s54, the respondent may refuse to pay the appellant's claim. The circumstance that this comes about, because of the language of that part of the contract of insurance which defines the risk, rather than by reason of a breach of a condition of the policy, does not seem to me to be material.[45]

As a result Sutton suggests that after *East End* it is possible to argue that where there is 'an act of the insured or some other person' which is the subject of a term of the policy, s54 will apply, even if the act in question is one which goes to the heart of the risk which is being underwritten.[46] Indeed Clarke JA even argued in *East End* that 'on one view, the effect of the application of the statute is to enlarge the cover.'[47] Sutton argues that the court gave a liberal interpretation to s54 and emphasised that the section looked to the effect of the

---

42 (1991) 25 NSWLR 400; 7 ANZ Ins Cas 61–092.

43 (1991) 25 NSWLR 400; 7 ANZ Ins Cas 61–092.

44 *Sutton on Insurance Law,* eds Merkin, Kirby and Enright, 4th Edition, Lawbook Co., 2015, page 206.

45 *East End Real Estate Pty Ltd v CE Heath Casualty & General Insurance Ltd* (1991) 25 NSWLR 400; 7ANZ Ins Cas 61–092 at 403 (NSWLR).

46 *Sutton on Insurance Law,* eds Merkin, Kirby and Enright, 4th Edition, Lawbook Co., 2015, page 207.

47 *East End Real Estate Pty Ltd v CE Heath Casualty & General Insurance Ltd* (1991) 25 NSWLR 400; 7 ANZ Ins Cas 61–092 400 (NSWLR) at 410.

contract and not merely to the precise terms of the risk covered.[48] The decision in *East End* appears to have transformed a 'claims made and notified' policy into a 'claims made' policy with the failure to notify the insurer of submission of the claim being seemingly viewed as essentially a procedural matter (as opposed to something that lay outside the scope of cover).[49] Despite concerns about the impact this decision might have on claims made and notified policies, the decision has endured.

6.23 In *FAI General Insurance Co Ltd v Perry*[50] in connection with a claims made and notified policy, the insured became aware of circumstances (that might give rise to a claim) during the policy period, but did not notify the insurer during the policy period. On appeal the New South Wales Court of Appeal held that the failure to notify the circumstance was an 'inaction' and not an 'act or omission' and that s54 therefore did not apply. Gleeson CJ commented:

> When one is dealing with claims that are mere future possibilities, a decision not to elect to expand the scope of the cover to include such claims does not seem to me to constitute an omission of the kind with which s54 is concerned.[51]

He stressed that the key issue was the element of choice on the part of the insured in deciding whether or not to notify the insurer of the relevant circumstances and thus increase the coverage of the policy.

6.24 The decision in *Perry* was criticised in *Antico v Heath Fielding Australia Pty Ltd.*[52] The case concerned a Directors' and Officers' legal expenses policy under which Antico was indemnified for legal expenses incurred in actions taken against him as a director during the period of cover. However, the indemnity was conditional upon the insurer consenting to defend the claim – consent that it was required to furnish if 'reasonable grounds' for a defence existed. Antico failed to obtain consent and argued, inter alia, that this failure could be excused under s54(1). Finding in favour of the insured, the court emphasised that it was essential that the remedial effect of s54 was not undermined by matters of form, e.g. including operational terms in the definition of the risks to which policy responds. *Antico* established that s54 takes as its starting point the existence of a claim and of a contract, where the effect of the contract is that the insurer may refuse to pay that claim as a result of some act which the insured (or someone else) has done or omitted to do after the contract was entered into; it does not imply that a liability of the insurer to pay the claim has been established.[53] In the words of Brennan CJ s54(1)

> focuses not on the legal character of a reason which entitles an insurer to refuse to pay a claim – falling outside a covered risk, coming within an exclusion or non-compliance with a condition – but on the actual conduct of the insured, that is, on some act which the insured does or omits to do. ... It is engaged when the doing of an act or the making of

48 *Sutton on Insurance Law,* eds Merkin, Kirby and Enright, 4th Edition, Lawbook Co., 2015, page 207, *citing East End Real Estate Pty Ltd v CE Heath Casualty & General Insurance Ltd* (1991) 25.

49 *Greentree v FAI General Insurance Co Ltd* (1998) 44 NSWLR 706; 10 ANZ Ins Cas 61–423; 158 ALR 592 at 595, 601.

50 *FAI General Insurance Co Ltd v Perry* (1993) 30 NSWLR 89; 7 ANZ Ins Cas 61–194.

51 *FAI General Insurance Co Ltd v Perry* (1993) 30 NSWLR 89; 7 ANZ Ins Cas 61–194 at 93 (NSWLR).

52 [1997] 188 CLR 652; 146 ALR 385; 71 ALJR 1210; BC9703412.

53 *Maxwell v Highway Hauliers Pty Ltd* [2014], HCA 33, 10 September 2014 citing *Antico* [1997] 188 CLR 652, 669.

> an omission would excuse the insurer from an obligation to pay a claim for a loss actually suffered by the insured.'[54]

On face value this would seem to suggest that the bargain struck by the parties in relation to scope can be challenged where there has been an act or omission by the insured (or on occasion some other party). This seems hard to justify.

6.25 The court stressed however the distinction between terms of a policy which should be seen as conditions to be met by the insured and terms which might expand the scope of the policy. The court recognised that the distinction was difficult to express definitively. However, Brennan's position in *Antico* was supported by the decision in *FAI General Insurance Co Ltd v Australian Hospital Care Pty Ltd (AHC)*.[55] In *Hospital Care* the insured (AHC) was covered by a policy of professional indemnity insurance with FAI from 20 June 1992 to 20 June 1993. In circumstances similar to those in *FAI v Perry*, the contract 'deemed' claims to have been made within the policy period if the insured notified the insurer within that period of circumstances that gave rise to a subsequent claim. Despite being aware of an injury occurring prior to the FAI cover ending, AHC failed to notify the insurer and take advantage of the deeming condition as it was 'not expected ... that a claim would be made.' The actual claim by the third party was not made until after the policy year. The insured argued that this was an omission that could be cured by s54(1). Determining that the situation was one that attracted the application of s54, the court held that s54(1) directed attention to the effect of the contract of insurance on the claim of the insured which the insured had in fact made and that no distinction could be made, for the purposes of the section, 'between provisions of a contract which define the scope of cover, and those provisions which are conditions affecting an entitlement to claim.'[56]

6.26 In *Greentree v FAI General Insurance Co Ltd* the NSW Court of Appeal held that a failure by a third party to make a claim on the insured within the period of insurance cover under a claims made and notified policy was not an omission by some other party under s54.[57] Spigelman CJ described the failure on the part of a third party to make a demand as 'an event wholly external to the policy.'[58] The reasoning in *Greentree* was subsequently rejected in *Hospital Care*,[59]although the court agreed with the decision. In *Hospital Care* the court held that s54(1) 'does not operate to relieve the insured of restrictions or limitations that are inherent in the claim.'[60] The court illustrated this as follows:

> The restrictions that are inherent within a claim vary according to the type of insurance in issue. Under an "occurrence" based contract, no claim can be made under the contract unless the event insured against takes place during the period of cover. Under a "claims made and notified" policy, if no "demand" (the court distinguished between a third party "demand" and a "claim" made by the insured) is made by a third party upon the insured during the period of insurance, any claim that may subsequently be made by the insured on the insurer (that is, the claim to which s54 refers) would necessarily acknowledge that

54 [1997] HCA 35; (1997) 188 CLR 652 at 660–661.
55 [2001] HCA 38; (2001) 204 CLR 641.
56 [2001] HCA 38; (2001) 204 CLR 641 at 656 [33].
57 (1998) 44 NSWLR 706; 147 FLR 422; 158 ALR 592; 10 ANZ Ins Cas 61–423.
58 (1998) 158 ALR 592 at 595.
59 [2001] HCA 38; (2001) 204 CLR 641 at 658–660 [39] – [46].
60 [2001] HCA 38 (27 June 2001) at para 41.

indemnity is sought in relation to a demand not of a type covered by the policy (because it not within the temporal limits that identify those demands in relation to which indemnity must be given).[61]

6.27 The position adopted in *Hospital Care* can be contrasted with *Kelly v New Zealand Insurance Co Ltd*[62] where it was held that a failure to declare items of unique value under a property policy which would have extended the sum insured to cover those items was not something to which s54 responded. The reason s54 did not apply was because the insured had chosen not to extend the scope of the policy under the provision allowing for this.[63] Hawke argues that it is not easy to reconcile *Kelly* with *Hospital Care*,[64] however in *Kelly* there was a clear (proactive) decision by the insured not to extend the policy and had he done so he would have been obliged to pay an additional premium. In contrast in *Hospital Care*, it is argued that the case arose from a simple oversight/omission by the assured and there was of course no question of an additional premium. Nevertheless, *Hospital Care* does blur the sanctity of scope.

6.28 In *Prepaid Services Pty Ltd v Atradius Credit Insurance NV*, the NSW Court of Appeal held that s54 did not apply because the reason the insurer was able to refuse payment was because the insured's claim was in respect of a payment default which was not covered by the policy.[65] Stressing that in interpreting the effect of the contract the court should adopt a substance over form approach, Meagher JA commented that it remained necessary 'to have regard to the nature of the risk and subject matter insured, as well as the commercial or other context in which the insurance is written.'[66]

6.29 In this case, Prepaid Services, Optus Mobile Pty Limited and Virgin Mobile (Australia) Pty Limited all supplied prepaid mobile recharge vouchers to Bill Express Limited, which in turn sold the vouchers to customers. Atradius Credit Insurance NV issued a trade credit policy to Prepaid, Optus and Virgin that indemnified them for Bill Express's failure to meet payment obligations during the policy period. A proposal submitted by the companies prior to the policy being issued was expressly incorporated into the policy terms. The proposal provided that credit terms for supply to Bill Express were '21 days with weekly settlement.'

6.30 However no written agreement between Optus Mobile and Bill Express was provided to Atradius prior to the policy being issued. Bill Express defaulted on its payments, and PrePaid, Optus and Virgin made a claim on the policy. Atradius denied the claim made by Optus in respect of unpaid invoices it issued to Bill Express on the grounds that the policy only insured defaults under a contract requiring Bill Express to pay up to 30 days from the date of the invoice. However, the unpaid amounts claimed by Optus arose under a contract requiring payment by Bill Express 30 days from the date Optus issued a statement to Bill Express (which amounted in effect to payment terms of 30 to

61 [2001] HCA 38; (2001) 204 CLR 641 at 658–660 [42].

62 (1993) 7 ANZ Ins Cas 61–197.

63 *Kelly v New Zealand Insurance* (1996) 9 ANZ Ins Cas 61–317 at 67,518. Merkin takes a similar view: R Merkin, Reforming Insurance Law: Is There a Case for Reverse Transportation?; A Report for the English and Scottish Law Commissioners on the Australian Experience of Insurance Law Reform; available at http://www.lawcom.gov.uk/app/uploads/2015/03/ICL_Merkin_report.pdf or at https://eprints.soton.ac.uk/27860/.

64 F Hawke, S54: 'Where to Draw the Line?' (2012) 23 *Insurance Law Journal* 223–244.

65 (2013) 302 ALR 732; 17 ANZ Ins Cas 61–981; [2013] NSWCA 252.

66 (2013) 302 ALR 732; 17 ANZ Ins Cas 61–981; [2013] NSWCA 252, at 776 [135–136].

60 days). Atradius maintained that the claim did not therefore arise under a contract between Optus and Bill Express that was insured by the policy, and accordingly, that it fell outside the scope of the policy's cover. Optus argued that its supply of recharge vouchers to Bill Express under a contract requiring payment more than 30 days from invoice was an act or omission by Optus to which s54 applied, preventing Atradius from denying the claim. The Court of Appeal held that the policy provided indemnity against Bill Express's failure 'to meet a payment obligation under, and by the time required by, a specified contract' and in the absence of that contract the parties adopted terms based on the substance of the proposal. On the facts, the court concluded that Atradius refused Optus Mobile's claim because the 'effect' of the policy (to use the language of s54(1)) was that the insurer could refuse to pay the claim because it was for a payment default not covered by the policy, not because Optus Mobile had contracted with Bill Express on different terms. Accordingly s54 had no application; the specified contractual terms formed part of the risk insured, the 'effect' of the policy.

6.31 In seeking to digest the implications of the various decisions regarding the interaction of s54 with issues of scope up to the decision in *PrePaid*, Hawke argues that, if the insurer's right to avoid payment arises by virtue of an intrinsic limitation on the application of the contract to the circumstances of the claim, then s54 cannot be invoked.[67] He stresses that s54 is concerned with the policy as it is, not the policy as it might have been had the insured procured different terms.[68] He suggests that the courts' approach is to determine whether the policy is one which normally covers a loss of the relevant type, but that the insurer can refuse to pay because of insured's post-contract conduct, as opposed to a situation where the policy simply does not cover the loss, even though this may have come about because of an omission by the insured.[69] Hawke argues that, as highlighted in *Hospital Care*, a key question is whether the claim is covered by the insurer's 'core promise.'[70] In *Hospital Care* McHugh J indicated that [s54] 'does not operate to relieve the insured of restrictions or limitations that are inherent in the claim.'[71] Pynt suggests that in a 'losses occurring' policy an insurer's 'core promise' will generally coincide with the scope of the insuring clause, such that situations that fall outside the scope of the clause will be regarded as having fallen outside the insurer's 'core promise' and thus will not attract the operation of s54.[72] The courts will look at the relevant 'substance' or 'essence' of the contract, rather than detailed drafting. S54 will have no application where the insurer's right to refuse payment arises from 'an inherent limitation or restriction' (in the words of the judgement in *Hospital Care*) in the claim.[73] This approach was subsequently endorsed in *Maxwell v Highway Hauliers*[74] the details of which are discussed later in this chapter. The High Court in *Maxwell* indicated the insurers were wrong to equate the statement (from the plurality in *Australian Hospital Care*) that s54 does not operate to relieve the insured of restrictions or limitations that are inherent

67 F Hawke, S54: 'Where to Draw the Line?' (2012) 23 *Insurance Law Journal* 223–244.

68 F Hawke, S54: 'Where to Draw the Line?' (2012) 23 *Insurance Law Journal* 223–244.

69 F Hawke, S54: 'Where to Draw the Line?' (2012) 23 *Insurance Law Journal* 223–244.

70 F Hawke, S54: 'Where to Draw the Line?' (2012) 23 *Insurance Law Journal* 223–244.

71 McHugh J in *FAI General Insurance Co Ltd v Australian Hospital Care Pty Ltd.* (2001) 204 CLR 641.

72 G Pynt, *Australian Insurance Law: A First Reference,* Butterworths, Chatswood, Australia, 3rd Edition, 2015, page 365.

73 G Pynt, *Australian Insurance Law: A First Reference,* Butterworths, Chatswood, Australia, 3rd Edition, 2015, page 365.

74 [2014] HCA 33.

in the claim with any restriction or limitation on the scope of the cover that is provided under the contract.

> A restriction or limitation that is inherent in the claim which an insured has in fact made, in the sense in which the plurality in [*Australian Hospital Care*] used that terminology, is a restriction or limitation which must necessarily be acknowledged in the making of a claim, having regard to the type of insurance contract under which that claim is made.[75]

Applying this logic to *Hospital Care*, it was part of the insurer's core promise to cover claims of the type that were the subject of the appeal and the only reason the insurer could refuse to indemnify was that the circumstances had not been notified in a timely fashion.[76] Accordingly the situation attracted the application of s54.[77] In defining criteria for the application of s54, McClure P observed in *Allianz Australia Insurance Ltd v Inglis*

> what must be acknowledged in the claims is that the third party respondents were insured under the Policy for legal liability, that bodily injury the subject of the claims, occurred during the period of insurance and was caused by an accident within the geographic area covered by the Policy.[78]

6.32 Reflecting these judgements, Mann suggests that it is not possible to equate restrictions and limitations in claims which do not engage s54 with the scope of cover under a contract of insurance: the two are not coextensive.[79] Certainly it seems clear that the structure of s54 means that the boundary between legitimate resort to s54 and the sanctity of scope will always be somewhat blurred and will often require judicial interpretation. It is submitted that the decision in *Hospital Care* is a step too far (see the detailed discussion in Omissions later in this chapter), but even if it is accepted as being reasonable on the facts, it leaves the insurer open to an ill-defined time period during which he may be exposed to claims. In any event, it has taken significant litigation and judicial deliberation to reach the current position and it is submitted that it is certainly possible to improve upon the absence of precision inherent in this context in s54.[80]

---

75 *Maxwell v Highway Hauliers Pty Ltd* (2014) 88 ALJR 841; 18 ANZ Ins Cas 62–035; [2014] HCA 33 at 23.

76 [2001] HCA 38; (2001) 204 CLR 641 at 658–660 [at 46]. See also the discussion of what constitutes an omission for the purposes of s54 later in this chapter.

77 The majority in *Hospital Care* indicated that s54 will apply to events which fall within the description of 'the event insured against' and as 'an event of the type contemplated by the contract' and noted that this will vary according to 'the type of insurance in issue': *FAI General Insurance Co Ltd v Australian Hospital Care Pty Ltd* (2001) 204 CLR 641; 75 ALJR 1236; 11 ANZ Ins Cas 61–497; [2001] HCA 38 at 41 and 42.

78 [2016] WASCA 25 at 60. This case is considered in detail later in the chapter.

79 P Mann, *Mann's Annotated Insurance Contracts Act,* 7th Edition, Thompson Reuters, Sydney, 2016, at page 426.

80 In *Harrison v Retail Employees Superannuation Pty Ltd* (2016) 19 ANZ Ins Cas 62–091; [2015] NSWSC 1665 (10 November 2015) a life insurer contended that the employee's disablement (TPD: total and permanent disability event) occurred outside the 12-month period of deemed cover and, in the absence of an application to it to become a full insured member (for cover beyond the 12-month period), that the TPD claim was not payable because cover had ceased. Lindsay J found that the disablement occurred during the period of deemed cover. However, he suggested that, if (contrary to his finding) the employee's disablement occurred after the period of deemed cover (in circumstances in which, for want of an 'application,' cover had ceased), s54 would operate to preclude the life insurer from refusing to pay the claim by reason only of the want of an 'application.' Lindsay J cited *Antico* and noted that an act or omission which engaged s54 may be a failure to exercise a right, choice or liberty, which an insured enjoys under the contract of insurance. The judge suggested that to the extent that the employee's claim might be said to have been based on a TPD event that occurred outside 'the period of cover,' any

6.33 These shortcomings were again illustrated in *Johnson v Triple C Furniture*.[81] In a somewhat surprising conclusion, the Queensland Court of Appeal interpreted the ruling in *Hospital Care* (that section 54(1) did not operate to relieve the insured of any restrictions or limitations that are inherent in its claim) as meaning that an insurer could avoid s54 by demonstrating that a claim that had been made was not for an insured risk. *Johnson* was however overturned by the High Court in *Maxwell v Highway Hauliers*[82] as addressed in detail later in this chapter.

(B) The requisite effect

6.34 For s54 to be activated, the 'effect of a contract of insurance' must be that the insurer may refuse to pay a claim by reason of a relevant act or omission. This 'effect' must come from the contract of insurance. If the contract of insurance itself does not give the requisite 'effect,' then the requirement within s54(1) is not satisfied and s54 is not triggered. In *East End Real Estate Pty Ltd v CE Heath Casualty & General Insurance Ltd*.[83] in a claims made and notified policy, a demand was made on the insured by a third party, but the insured failed to notify the insurer until some six weeks after the period of cover had expired. Under the terms of the policy, the insurer would have been entitled to deny liability based on the failure to notify. The NSW Court of Appeal (Gleeson CJ, Mahoney and Clarke JJA) held that it did not matter from where in a contract of insurance the 'effect' came. In this instance the effect arose

> by reason merely of the fact that, the making of the claim upon the insurer not having been "notified" to the insurer, the claim was not within the cover. But it was not within the cover by reason of an omission of the insured. Therefore the entitlement to refuse arose by reason of that omission.[84]

6.35 This decision was approved in *Antico v Heath Fielding Australia Pty Ltd*: 's 54(1) refers not to precise concepts of form but to the effect of the contract and asks whether that effect is that the insurer may refuse payment "by reason of" the relevant act or omission.'[85] Specifically, as we have seen, in the comments of Dawson, Toohey, Gaudron and Gummow JJ

> Section 54 takes as its starting point the existence of a claim and a contract to the effect that the insurer may refuse to pay the claim. The section directs attention to the reason founding the refusal, namely a particular act or omission on the part of the insured or of some other person.[86]

---

restriction or limitation on the entitlement to claim a TPD benefit was not inherent in the claim (as per *Australian Hospital Care* and *Highway Hauliers*), but arose by reason of an omission by the employee to make, and an omission on the part of the trustee to obtain from the employee, an application to become a full 'insured member.' These omissions occurred after the policy had been entered into and while it remained operative and were thus within the ambit of s54. While this may be a sound interpretation of the effect of s54, this example again in this author's view strays too close to effectively re-drafting the scope of cover and as a result again raises concerns as to the robustness of the s54 solution.

81 *Johnson v Triple C Furniture* [2010] QCA 282. The case is addressed in detail later in this chapter.

82 [2014] HCA 33.

83 (1991) 25 NSWLR 400; 7 ANZ Ins Cas 61–092.

84 *East End Real Estate Pty Ltd v CE Heath Casualty & General Insurance Ltd* (1991) 25 NSWLR 400; 7 ANZ Ins Cas 61–092 Mahoney JA (at 407 (NSWLR); 77,363 (ANZ Ins Cas)).

85 (1997) 188 CLR 652; 71 ALJR 1210; 146 ALR 385; 9 ANZ Ins Cas 61–371; [1997] HCA 35.

86 (1997) 188 CLR 652, 669.

Antico confirmed that the act or omission to which the section applies may be that of a person who is not a party to the insurance contract, but the failure by a third party to make a claim on the insured during the period of cover in a claims made and notified policy was not an omission to act of some other person within the meaning of s54(1): this was conduct wholly external to the policy itself. In *Gibbs Holdings Pty Ltd v Mercantile Mutual Insurance (Australia)* Thomas JA argued that the 'act' referred to in s54(1) is 'the act by reason of which the insurer is entitled to refuse to pay the claim.'[87]

6.36 In *FAI General Insurance Co Ltd v Australian Hospital Care Pty Ltd*[88] the High Court held that

> s54 directs attention to the effect of the contract of insurance on the claim of the insured which the insured has in fact made. It is not concerned with some other claim that the insured might have made at some other time, or in respect of some other event or circumstance. It requires the precise identification of the event or circumstance in respect of which the insured claims payment or indemnity from the insurer.[89]

The court held that a failure to give notice of facts that might give rise to a claim in accordance with a policy requirement was an omission within the meaning of s54 because *the effect was that the insurer could refuse to pay the claim.*[90] The High Court overruled the decision of the NSW Court of Appeal in *FAI General Insurance Co Ltd v Perry*[91] (see later in this chapter). The majority in *Australian Hospital Care* drew attention to the differences between 'occurrence-based' contracts of insurance and 'claims made and notified' policies. They distinguished the insured's 'claim' within the meaning of that term in s54(1) from that of the third party claim on the insured (such as those made in a claims made policy), which they referred to as a demand.' The court held that there was a relevant effect of the contract of insurance because the deeming clause allowed for the notification of facts (circumstances) such that any subsequent claim would be deemed to have been made within the period of insurance in which the circumstances were notified. The existence of the deeming clause meant that the effect of the contract of insurance, but for s54, would be that the insurer could refuse to pay the insured's claim by reason only of the omission of the insured to notify the facts (circumstances) that might subsequently give rise to a claim.[92]

6.37 If the policy did not contain a 'deeming clause' allowing for the notification of circumstances (that might give rise to a claim) by the insured it has been held that there was no requisite effect under the contract of insurance: *Gosford City Council v GIO General Ltd.*[93] In *Gosford City Council*[94] a claims made and notified policy did not contain a deeming clause

---

87 *Gibbs Holdings Pty Ltd v Mercantile Mutual Insurance (Australia)* (2002) 1 Qld R 17 Thomas JA at para 30.

88 (2001) 204 CLR 641; 75 ALJR 1236; 11 ANZ Ins Cas 61–497; [2001] HCA 38.

89 *FAI General Insurance Co Ltd v Australian Hospital Care Pty Ltd* (2001)(at 659 (CLR); 75,761–75 (ANZ Ins Cas)).

90 (2001) 204 CLR 641; 75 ALJR 1236; 11 ANZ Ins Cas 61–497; [2001] HCA 38 (emphasis added).

91 (1993) 30 NSWLR 89; 7 ANZ Ins Cas 61–164.

92 As cited in Mann's Annotated Insurance Contract Act, Peter Mann, 7th Edition, 2016, Thomson Reuters, Sydney, page 472.

93 (2003) 56 NSWLR 542; 12 ANZ Ins Cas 61–566; [2003] NSWCA 34.

94 (2003) 56 NSWLR 542; 12 ANZ Ins Cas 61–566; [2003] NSWCA 34 See also *CA & MEC McInally Nominees Pty Ltd v HTW Valuers (Brisbane) Pty Ltd.* [2009] 2 Qd R1; (2001) 166 FLR 271; 11 ANZ Ins Cas 61–507; [2001] QSC 388.

or any other provision requiring the notification of facts (circumstances); the court held that there was no relevant effect of the contract of insurance, and therefore no 'omission,' where there had been a late notification of facts (circumstances) that could give rise to a claim. The court also found that s40(3) did not imply a term to the same effect as s54(1) so as to create the requisite 'effect' and therefore an 'omission' within the meaning of s54 in the event that there was a failure to notify facts. S40(3) states

> Where the insured gave notice in writing to the insurer of facts that might give rise to a claim against the insured as soon as was reasonably practicable after the insured became aware of those facts but before the insurance cover provided by the contract expired, the insurer is not relieved of liability under the contract in respect of the claim, when made, by reason only that it was made after the expiration of the period of insurance cover provided by the contract.[95]

Accordingly if the contract of insurance itself does not give the requisite 'effect,' none will be implied and in such circumstances the s54(1) will not apply. Mann argues that as a result of these decisions most Australian professional indemnity policies do not contain deeming clauses and have a narrow definition as to what constitutes a claim in order to avoid the requisite 'effect.'[96]

6.38 As we have seen in *PrePaidServices Pty Ltd v Atradius Credit Insurance NV*,[97] Meagher J held that the effect of a contract of insurance must be determined as a matter of construction, unconstrained by distinctions between provisions which define the scope of cover and conditions or exclusions which affect the entitlement of an insured to claim.[98] However Meager J concluded that s54 did not prevent the insurer from refusing to pay the claim because, in the language of s54(1), the 'effect' of the policy was that the insurer may refuse to pay the insured's claim because it was in respect of a payment default which was not covered by the policy.

(C) The treatment of omissions

6.39 As a result of s54(6) an 'act' under s54(1) includes an omission.[99] A central issue under s54 is whether a failure by an assured to exercise an option that would entitle him to cover (had he exercised the option) is an 'omission' for the purposes of s54.[100] In *FAI General Insurance Co Ltd v Perry*,[101] the Court of Appeal held by a majority that a failure by an insured to notify facts (circumstances) that might give rise to a claim in accordance with an optional provision of a policy (in terms similar to s40) would not constitute an omission within s54.

95 S40(3) Insurance Contracts Act 1984.

96 P Mann, *Mann's Annotated Insurance Contracts Act,* 7th Edition, Thompson Reuters, Sydney, 2016, at page 421.

97 (2013) 302 ALR 732; 17 ANZ Ins Cas 61–981; [2013] NSWCA 252.

98 P Mann, Mann's Annotated Insurance Contracts Act, 7th Edition, Thompson Reuters, Sydney, 2016, at page 422, citing *Prepaid Services Pty Ltd v Atradius Credit Insurance NV* (2013) 302 ALR 732; 17 ANZ Ins Cas 61–981; [2013] NSWCA 252

99 S54(6) reads: 'A reference in this section to an act includes a reference to:
(a) an omission.'

100 R Merkin, Reforming Insurance Law: Is There a Case for Reverse Transportation?; A Report for the English and Scottish Law Commissioners on the Australian Experience of Insurance Law Reform; available at http://www.lawcom.gov.uk/app/uploads/2015/03/ICL_Merkin_report.pdf or at https://eprints.soton.ac.uk/27860/.

101 (1993) 30 NSWLR 89; 7 ANZ Ins Cas 61–164.

In *Kelly v New Zealand Insurance Co Ltd*[102] an election by an insured not to expand the scope of cover by providing the insurer with a list of valuable contents was held to be inaction and not an omission within s54: The court observed: 'Liability was denied not because the [insured] failed to do something, but because he deliberately elected not to extend the scope of cover beyond that specifically provided for.'[103]

6.40 In *Antico v Heath Fielding Australia Pty Ltd*[104] the High Court felt there was no reason why an omission may not be a failure to exercise a right, choice or liberty that the insured enjoyed under the contract of insurance.[105] Accordingly the High Court rejected part of the reasoning in *Perry*.[106] Mann argues that this led to what he describes as the 'omission/non-event dichotomy.'[107] In *Permanent Trustee Australia Ltd v FAI General Insurance Co Ltd.*[108] the issue concerned the failure by the insured to notify facts (circumstances) that might give rise to a claim where no claim had been made within the period of insurance cover. Hodgson CJ in Eq argued in obiter comments that a refusal by the insurer to pay the insured's claim on the ground that no claim was actually made within the period of insurance, and that no claim was deemed to have been made, *focused on the non-occurrence of an event, rather than an omission of the insured or anyone else to do something*, so that s54 did not apply.[109] In this way he sought to argue that *Perry* was not inconsistent with *Antico* on the grounds that in *Perry* the issue was the non-occurrence of a claim, or anything else deemed to be a claim; and not that the insured omitted to notify circumstances. In *Greentree v FAI General Insurance Co Ltd*[110] the NSW Court of Appeal held that a failure by a third party to make a claim on the insured within the period of insurance cover under a 'claims made and notified' policy was not an 'omission ... of some other person' within s54(1). Spigelman CJ argued that in the context of liability insurance, the failure of a third party to make a claim should be regarded as an event wholly external to the policy and should precede any consideration of the policy's 'effect.'[111]

6.41 As we have seen, in *FAI General Insurance Co Ltd v Australian Hospital Care Pty Ltd*[112] the insured owned a hospital and failed to notify the insurer of an inquiry by patient's solicitor during the period of insurance in a claims made and notified policy. The insured was aware that the solicitor appeared satisfied that there was no indication of malpractice. However, the patient subsequently made a claim after the policy had expired. The court indicated that s54(1) was unable to remedy an inherent restriction or limitation in the

102 (1993) 7 ANZ Ins Cas 61–197.

103 *Kelly v New Zealand Insurance Co Ltd,* Owen J at 67,518 (ANZ Ins Cas).

104 (1997) 188 CLR 652; 71 ALJR 1210; 9 ANZ Ins Cas 61–371; [1997] HCA 35.

105 An insured's agreement to a retrospective endorsement to cover is not an 'act' within s54: *Sienkiewicz (As Trustee for the Sienkiewicz Superannuation Fund) v Salisbury Group Pty Ltd (in Liquidation) (No 2)* [2015] FCA 147 (6 March 2015) where it was argued that the act of the insured in agreeing to an endorsement to cover fell within s54, such that the insurers should not be able to rely on the endorsement to refuse to pay the claim.

106 (1997) 188 CLR 652; 71 ALJR 1210; 9 ANZ Ins Cas 61–371; [1997] HCA 35 at 669–670 (CLR); 77,082 (ANZ Ins Cas).

107 P Mann, *Mann's Annotated Insurance Contract Act,* 7th Edition 2016, Thomson Reuters, Sydney, page 434.

108 (1998) 153 ALR 529; 10 ANZ Ins Cas 61–408.

109 Emphasis added.

110 (1998) 44 NSWLR 706; 147 FLR 422; 158 ALR 592; 10 ANZ Ins Cas 61–423.

111 *Greentree v FAI General Insurance Co Ltd* (1998) 44 NSWLR 706; 147 FLR 422; 158 ALR 592; 10 ANZ Ins Cas 61–423 at 74,741 (ANZ Ins Cas).

112 (2001) CLR 641. This decision overruled *FIA General Insurance v Perry* [1993] 30 NSWLR 89 and the rationale in *Greentree v FAI General Insurance Co Ltd.* [1998] 158 ALR 592.

insured's claim, but held that the insured's failure to notify the circumstances constituted an omission within terms of s54 because the effect of the contract was that the insurer could refuse to meet the claim by reason only of the fact that the insured did not give notice of the occurrence to the insurer. Accordingly the court held that s54 required that the insurer could not refuse to pay the insured's claim. The court rejected the reasoning in *Greentree* and *Permanent Trustee* (although finding the decision to be correct in each case).[113] The decision appears to represent a significant extension of the law as it previously stood and as a result has been the subject of considerable criticism on the basis that it represents a step too far in the insured's favour.

6.42 Certainly it appears to be the case that

(i) If a policy (for example in a typical Directors' and Officers' liability policy) expressly permits notification of circumstances as a trigger for liability, then the assured's failure to notify within the policy period itself, is capable of being excused under s54 to the extent that there is no prejudice to the insurers and
(ii) If a claim is made against the assured, but he fails to notify it within the time permitted by the policy, i.e., as soon as reasonably practicable, but in any event within the policy (or permitted extended) period, there is an omission which falls within s54 and it may be excused to the extent that it has not caused prejudice.[114]

6.43 Without further clarification it has been argued that this could potentially result in a claim being notified years after it was first presented to the assured.[115] This has the potential to cause insurers a raft of challenges and uncertainties and would surely tilt the playing field too far in favour of the insured. At an extreme, it seems possible to argue that in *Hospital Care* the claim was held not within scope as a result of an omission of the insured, hence the insurer's entitlement to refuse indemnity arose by reason of that omission and thus triggered the application of s54. In seeking to rationalise *Hospital Care* (and picking up the distinction alluded to in the judgement) it has been argued that the decision sought to draw a distinction between an inherently essential element of a claim as a matter of law (which, if omitted, s54(1) cannot cure) and other merely ancillary or procedural matters (breach of which can be cured by s54).[116] It is submitted however that this is an unconvincing argument.

6.44 As it stands, Merkin argues convincingly[117] that as a result of *Hospital Care* it is now clear that if the policy permits the assured to notify circumstances that may give rise to a loss during the currency of the policy, and the assured fails to do so, this is an omission falling within s54(1). Approaching it from a different angle, Mann argues that *Hospital Care* may

113 (2001) CLR 641. This decision overruled *FIA General Insurance v Perry* [1993] 30 NSWLR 89 and the rationale in *Greentree v FAI General Insurance Co Ltd.* [1998] 158 ALR 592.

114 Australian Insurance Law Association, Geoff Masel Memorial Lecture 2009, Directors' and Officers' Insurance and the Global Financial Crisis, Robert Merkin.

115 Australian Insurance Law Association, Geoff Masel Memorial Lecture 2009, Directors' and Officers' Insurance and the Global Financial Crisis, Robert Merkin.

116 M Muscillo, The Lesser of Two Evils: *FAI General Insurance Co Ltd v Australian Hospital Care Pty Ltd* (2001) 1(2) QUTLJJ 304–311.

117 R Merkin, Reforming Insurance Law: Is There a Case for Reverse Transportation?; A Report for the English and Scottish Law Commissioners on the Australian Experience of Insurance Law Reform; available at http://www.lawcom.gov.uk/app/uploads/2015/03/ICL_Merkin_report.pdf or at https://eprints.soton.ac.uk/27860/.

represent the end of a judicial search for one definition of what constitutes an omission and that instead, cases that involve a failure to notify facts (or circumstances) in a 'claims made and notified' policy will turn on the question of whether the *effect of the contract of insurance* is that the insurer may refuse to pay a claim (see discussion earlier).[118] As we have seen,[119] Mann argues that after *Hospital Care*, if a claims made and notified policy of insurance contains a clause that provides for the notification of facts (circumstances) that might give rise to a claim (a deeming clause), then there could be a relevant 'effect of the contract of insurance' and an 'omission' for the purposes of s54 in the event of a failure to notify. If however the policy did not include a 'deeming clause' he argues that, in the event of a failure by the insured to notify, there would then likely be no relevant 'effect of the contract of insurance' and no 'omission.' If the contract of insurance itself does not give the requisite 'effect' then the requirement within s54(1) is not satisfied and s54 does not come into play and there is thus no question of an 'omission': *Gosford City Council v GIO General Ltd.*[120] As a consequence, as we have seen, insurers are increasingly omitting a 'deeming' clause in order to avoid a requisite 'effect' and therefore the possibility of an 'omission' under s54.[121] In *Gosford City Council* a claims made policy, which attached only if a claim was made against the assured during the currency of the policy, could not operate to allow the assured to seek indemnity for a claim made against him after the policy had expired as there was no relevant act or omission on the part of the assured.

6.45 Following *Hospital Care* the Australian Treasury Department commissioned a review of the operation of s54.[122] The Report (which is examined in more detail later in this chapter) recommended that s54 should not be used to condone, after the expiry of the policy period, notification of circumstances potentially leading to a claim. Specifically the Review recommended that notification by an assured to the insurers outside the period of cover, of facts or circumstances which might give rise to a claim, should be excluded from the relief provided under s54. The Review did not however take the further step of recommending any restriction on the use of s54 to justify notification of actual claims outside the year of the policy, on the basis that the industry had accepted the position. Although the proposals formed part of the draft Insurance Contracts Amendment Bill 2007, the Bill was not passed into law.[123] While the Insurance Contracts Amendment Act 2013 was passed it did not contain amendments to s54.[124]

6.46 In *Johnson v Triple C Furniture and Electrical Pty Ltd.*[125] the court held that there can be a failure to do something in breach of a clause in a contract of insurance that is not an omission under s54 where the thing omitted is not within that person's control

118 P Mann, *Mann's Annotated Insurance Contracts Act,* 7th Edition, Thompson Reuters, Sydney, 2016, at page 430.

119 See The Requisite Effect, earlier in this chapter.

120 (2003) 56 NSWLR 542; 12 ANZ Ins Cas 61–566; [2003] NSWCA 34. See also the discussion of the requisite effect of the contract of insurance earlier in this chapter.

121 P Mann, *Mann's Annotated Insurance Contracts Act,* 7th Edition, Thompson Reuters, Sydney, 2016, page 421.

122 Review of the Insurance Contracts Act 1984 (Cth), Report into the Operation of Section 54, Alan Cameron and Nancy Milne, October 2003, Commonwealth of Australia Department of Treasury.

123 Australian Insurance Law Association, Geoff Masel Memorial Lecture 2009, Directors' and Officers' Insurance and the Global Financial Crisis, Robert Merkin.

124 The Insurance Contracts Amendment Act 2013 received Royal Assent on 28 June 2013.

125 (2010) 243 FLR 336; 16 ANZ Ins Cas 61–866; [2010] QCA 282.

or capacity to do. In *Triple C* an exclusion clause was triggered by the failure of a pilot of a plane that crashed to complete a required periodic flight review test. The court ruled that s54 did not apply because, as the pilot was unable to control the outcome of the test (it depended on third party assessment), his failure satisfactorily to complete an aeroplane flight review was not an omission under s54. This strange, and somewhat contorted, finding seemed to suggest that post-contractual conduct could now be relied on by insurers to deny claims, whereas previously s54 had prevented this occurring. To the relief of many, *Johnson v Triple C* was overturned by the High Court in *Maxwell v Highway Hauliers.*[126]

6.47 In *Allianz Australia Insurance Ltd v Inglis*,[127] the Supreme Court of Western Australia held that a 'state of affairs' was not an act or omission for the purposes of s54. This is addressed in detail later in this chapter.

6.48 Mann points out that it may have been that the intent of the ALRC was that the s54 remedy would be available for breaches of the contractual duty of utmost good faith. The Notes to the Draft Insurance Contracts Bill 1982 state that the remedies for breach of contract, for example s54, will be available for a breach of the duty of utmost good faith. However, as Mann observes, s54 requires the existence of a contract of insurance and it thus seems clear that it cannot apply to a pre-contractual breach of the duty of utmost good faith.[128]

(D) Does s54(1) or s54(2) apply and what amounts to prejudice?

6.49 Once it is clear that the situation is one to which s54 applies, the court must then consider if the act or omission is one which, by its nature, could reasonably be regarded as capable of causing or contributing to the sort of loss which the policy covers. If it is, then s54(2) applies and the onus is on the insured to show some or all of the loss was not caused by the act or omission (under s54(3) or (4)). S54(2) applies a loose form of causal connection test, such that a determination is required as to whether an act or omission *could reasonably have been regarded as capable of causing, or contributing to*, a loss which falls within the scope of the policy.[129] If there is no such possibility, then the matter is dealt with under s54(1) and the burden is on the insurer to demonstrate he has suffered prejudice and to establish the value of that prejudice. In ALRC 20 the Commission had recommended a proportionality test framed in terms of prejudice to the insurer, with damages being the measure of prejudice suffered as a consequence of the insured's conduct. If the assured's breach is not one that would have produced any different result, then there is likely no prejudice (see more detail later in this chapter).

6.50 If the possibility of causation exists, s54(3) comes into play. Under s54(3), if the assured can prove that no part of the loss was caused by the act or omission and that the loss arose from a completely separate source, the insurers will be liable for the full amount of the claim, notwithstanding the assured's breach. If the assured is unable to utilise s54(3), s54(4) provides that the insurer will not be able to refuse a claim (by reason only of the assured's breach) where the assured proves that some part of the loss was not caused by his breach. In

126 [2014] HCA 33.
127 [2016] WASCA 25.
128 P Mann, *Mann's Annotated Insurance Contracts Act* 7th Edition, Thompson Reuters, Sydney, 2016 at page 483.
129 Emphasis added.

these circumstances the insurer must pay out that part of the loss that was caused by factors other than the assured's breach.

6.51 In ALRC 20 the Commission gave an example of how it envisaged the interaction between the sections might work.[130] In the Commission's example a motor vehicle was modified in breach of a warranty in the policy. The modification increased the risk of the brakes malfunctioning. An accident occurred, but the brakes functioned normally. In this instance it seems that s54(2) would apply (and s54(1) would therefore not) as the modification *could* have contributed to the accident and the onus would thus be on the insured to establish under s54(3) or 54(4) that the modification did *not* contribute to the loss, or if it did, it was only partially responsible.

6.52 In *Ferrcom Pty Ltd v Commercial Union Assurance Co of Australia Ltd*[131] the High Court suggested

> The dichotomy between the two classes of acts or omissions [those under s54(1) and those under s54(2)] is not entirely clear. It seems that the effect of an act that has not caused a loss or part of a loss depends on whether the act "could reasonably be regarded as being capable of causing or contributing to [the] loss".[132]

6.53 The case involved a mobile crane and the policy contained a condition precedent to the insurer's liability requiring notification 'as soon as possible ... of any change materially varying any of the facts and circumstances existing at the commencement of [the] policy.' The crane was subsequently registered as a motor vehicle, but Ferrcom's agent failed to pass this information to the insurer. It was common ground that the failure to notify the registration of a mobile crane for road use could not 'reasonably be regarded as being capable of causing or contributing to *the* loss' and thus fell to be considered under s54(1).[133] Note that s54(2) refers to 'capable of causing or contributing to *a* loss in respect of which insurance cover is provided.' The distinction has however not been picked up and the *Ferrcom* approach (referring to *the* loss) now seems to be accepted. The court defined prejudice as

> the existence of a liability which, in whole or in part, would not have been borne by the insurer if the act had not been done or the omission had not been made or in the non-receipt of an additional premium to which the insurer would have been entitled by reason of the doing of the act or the making of the omission.[134]

6.54 The insurer had lost its opportunity to go off risk because of the insured's failure to notify a material alteration of the risk and this lost opportunity was equal to the prima facie liability imposed by s54(1), which was thereby reduced to nil. In *Moltoni Corporation Pty Ltd v QBE Insurance Ltd* prejudice was held to be the actual financial damage that has been or will be sustained as a result of the relevant act or omission: 'the relevant prejudice suffered is

130 ALRC 20, para 228.

131 (1993) 176 CLR 332.

132 *Ferrcom Pty Ltd v Commercial Union Assurance Co of Australia Ltd* (1993) 176 CLR 332 at 339–340 (CLR); 7 ANZ Ins Cas 61–156.

133 Emphasis added.

134 *Ferrcom Pty Ltd v Commercial Union Assurance Co of Australia Ltd* (1993) 176 CLR 332 at 339–340 (CLR); 7 ANZ Ins Cas 61–156 (at 77,831 (ANZ Ins Cas)).

to be measured by reference to what would have happened (as distinct from what could or might have happened) if the act or omission had not occurred.'[135]

6.55 Thomas JA argued in *Gibbs Holdings Pty Ltd v Mercantile Mutual Insurance (Australia)*[136] that 'logically the first task of a court in applying s54 is to ascertain whether the case is one to which s54(2) applies.'[137] In this case a failure to notify a material alteration of risk (as required under the policy) arising from a plastics manufacturer taking occupancy of the insured premises was held to be an act that failed to satisfy s54(2) and was therefore covered by s54(1). The court held that the relevant act (for the purposes of triggering the application of s54) could not be confined to the acceptance of the plastics manufacturer as a tenant or to the insured permitting the use of its premises by a plastics manufacturer (either of which could potentially have fallen within s54(2)). In the view of Thomas JA, 'An "act" for the purposes of s54 must be one by reason of which the insurer is entitled to refuse to pay the claim.' There could be more than one such act, but each must possess that requisite quality. The insured, as the party who pleads the application of s54, was 'entitled to seek judgment on the basis of the act that will give the insured the most favourable result.'[138] The case illustrates the knots that a court can tie itself in applying s54(1) or (2).

6.56 In *Mercantile Mutual Insurance (Aust) Ltd v Schigulski* Olsson J noted that it was difficult to see why an un-occupancy clause in a policy for premises could not be reasonably regarded as capable of causing or contributing to a loss caused by vandals.[139] In *McNeill v O'Kane* Holmes J held that a failure to set an alarm in accord with a policy requirement could reasonably be regarded as being capable of causing or contributing to a loss by arson: 'The question to be asked for the purpose of [s54(2)] is not whether the failure to set the alarm did cause or contribute to the loss by arson, but whether it could be reasonably regarded as being capable of doing so.'[140] In *Bunting v Australian Associated Motor Insurers Ltd* the failure by the insured to apply the brakes of his vehicle while driving under the influence of alcohol was held to be capable of causing or contributing to the loss sustained.[141] In *Matton Developments Pty Ltd v CGU Insurance Ltd (No 2)* a boom of a crane collapsed having been used in a manner other than that for which it was designed; it was not used in compliance with relevant Australian Standards and was being operated contrary to manufacturer's guidelines. Flanagan J (Qld Sup Ct) held that the act could reasonably be regarded as being capable of causing or contributing to the collapse of the boom.[142]

6.57 Under s54(1) the onus is on the insurer to establish prejudice. Merkin argues that there is a two-step test to determining prejudice: the insurers have to prove that they would have relied upon the assured's act or omission in order to defeat the claim and they have to

135 (2001) 205 CLR 149; 76 ALJR 337; [2001] HCA 73.

136 *Gibbs Holdings Pty Ltd v Mercantile Mutual Insurance (Australia)* (2002) 1 Qld R 17.

137 *Gibbs Holdings Pty Ltd v Mercantile Mutual Insurance (Australia* (2002) 1 Qld R 17, Thomas JA at para 21.

138 *Gibbs Holdings Pty Ltd v Mercantile Mutual Insurance (Australia)* (2002) 1 Qld R 17, Thomas JA at para 34. Pincus JA dissenting found that the basis for the insurer refusing to pay was a composite of causes comprising letting the plastics manufacturer in and failing to advise the insurer of and secure the insurer's agreement. He was of the view that it was wrong to consider only that part of the composite which was of such a kind that it could not possibly cause any loss to the insured and to ignore that part which could do so.

139 (1993) 172 LSJS 173.

140 (2003) 12 ANZ Ins Cas 61–554; [2002] QSC 144 at 56.

141 [1994] TASSC 9.

142 (2015) 18 ANZ Ins Cas 62–061; [2015] QSC 72 (15 April 2015).

prove that their inability to do so means that they have suffered monetary prejudice.[143] In *Moltoni Corporation Pty Ltd v QBE Insurance Ltd*[144] the High Court held that quantification of the insured's prejudice required the identification of the financial consequences that had, in fact, or would be, caused by the relevant act or omission under s54. The court provided guidance on the tests necessary for establishing prejudice:

> Yet it is only if, first, the right would have been exercised, but was not, and secondly the insurer has suffered resulting prejudice that can be represented in monetary terms that the provision of s54(1) allowing reduction in the insurer's liability is engaged[145]; ... If the right would not have been exercised, the insurer has not suffered prejudice ... if the insurer does not prove, on the balance of probabilities, that it would have exercised the right in question, it fails to demonstrate that its liability for the claim should be reduced.[146]

6.58 Generally the courts take the view that if the assured's breach is not one that would have produced any different result, then there is no prejudice.[147] On the other hand if the insurer can show that he would have come off risk had he been aware of the insured's breach, the likelihood is that prejudice will be assessed at 100% (as in *Ferrcom*, earlier). As a result failure by the assured to give the insurers due notice of a claim against him which prevents the insurer from defending the claim properly will only give rise to prejudice if the insurers can show that their defence would have made a difference to the outcome.[148]

6.59 A number of other cases further illustrate the courts' approach to issues of prejudice under s54(1). In *Australian Associated Motor Insurers Ltd v Ellis*[149] the insured failed to notify the insurer of his intention to modify a motor vehicle. Had it been notified, the insurer would have continued the insurance, but would have imposed a condition excluding its liability whilst the car was being driven by a person under the age of 25. The insured's daughter, who was 23 years of age, was driving the motor vehicle when the accident which gave rise to the claim occurred. The court held that the extent to which insurer's rights were prejudiced was full amount of insured's claim. In *East End Real Estate Pty Ltd v CE Heath Casualty & General Insurance Ltd*[150] the insurer refused to indemnify the insured for late notification of a claim on the grounds that its interests had been prejudiced to the extent that it was required to pay the costs of the proceedings. The court held that the insurer's interests were not prejudiced by the insured's action, but by its own decision to litigate and by the failure of that litigation. In *Zollo v National Australia Bank (No 2)*[151] the court held there was no prejudice where there was no evidence that the late notification of a disability

143 R Merkin, Reforming Insurance Law: Is There a Case for Reverse Transportation?; A Report for the English and Scottish Law Commissioners on the Australian Experience of Insurance Law Reform; available at http://lawcommission.justice.gov.uk/docs/ICL_Merkin_report.pdf.

144 (2001) 205 CLR 149; 76 ALJR 337; 11 ANZ Ins Cas 61–512; [2001] HCA 73 at 17.

145 (2001) 205 CLR 149; 76 ALJR 337; 11 ANZ Ins Cas 61–512; [2001] HCA 73, at 162 (CLR).

146 *Moltoni Corporation Pty Ltd v QBE Insurance Ltd* (2001) 205 CLR 149; 76 ALJR 337; 11 ANZ Ins Cas 61–512; [2001] HCA 73, at 162 (CLR).

147 *Antico v Heath Fielding Australia Pty Ltd* (1997) 188 CLR 652 (no prejudice); *FAI General Insurance Ltd v Jarvis* (1999) 19 ANZ Ins Cas 61–426 (prejudice).

148 *Antico v Heath Fielding Australia Pty Ltd* (1997) 188 CLR 652 (no prejudice); *FAI General Insurance Ltd v Jarvis* (1999) 19 ANZ Ins Cas 61–426 (prejudice).

149 (1990) 54 SASR 61; 10 MVR 143; 6 ANZ Ins Cas 60–957.

150 (1991) 25 NSWLR 400; 7 ANZ Ins Cas 61–092.

151 [1997] SASC 6060.

claim (and the attendant right of the insurer to commission an earlier medical examination) would have made any difference.

The cutting edge: recent cases that illustrate that s54 continues to generate controversy

6.60 Four more recent high profile cases have demonstrated that s54 continues to be a source of complex litigation. This section will review three cases, *Maxwell v Highway Hauliers*[152]; *Pantaenius Australia Pty Ltd v Watkins Syndicate 0457 at Lloyd's*[153] and *Allianz Australia Insurance Ltd. v Inglis*[154] in detail and will seek to identify the key issues and conclusions arising. These cases highlight some of the problems with s54 and demonstrate that, after over 35 years, judicial interpretation is still evolving. The 2019 case of *DIF III – Global Co-Investment Fund LP v Babcock & Brown International Pty Limited*[155] which was less controversial, is also examined. The cases provide further evidence that, while it may have many benefits, the Australian model for addressing breaches of insurance warranties is far from perfect and is unnecessarily complex.

(i) *Maxwell v Highway Hauliers*

6.61 The issue of scope and the application of s54 were considered by the High Court in *Maxwell v Highway Hauliers*. Highway Hauliers (HH) operated a fleet of freight trucks running across Australia. In the light of the assured's claim record, the insurance policy covering the fleet required all drivers to undertake a 'PAQS' test. The policy provided that there was no cover for drivers on the east-west run who did not have a PAQS score of at least 36 and excluded claims involving drivers in respect of whom the underwriters had not received a driver's declaration at the time of an occurrence (unless the underwriters subsequently chose to accept one). Two trucks were damaged in two separate incidents. In neither case had the driver undertaken a PAQS test or been declared. The underwriters refused indemnity on those grounds. The insurers sought to deny the claim by relying on *Johnson v Triple C Furniture and Electrical Pty Ltd.*[156] and characterising the post-contractual failures of the insured's truck drivers (to achieve minimum scores on a driving test and to be pre-approved as drivers) as an inherent limitation in the claim which s54 could not remedy. They argued that because the relevant endorsement was expressed in terms of there being 'no indemnity' if the driver was not accredited, coverage never arose and s54 could not be permitted to allow the insured to circumvent deficiencies in a claim that resulted from it being outside the scope of cover. As the court put it, the insurer's case came down 'to the proposition that the "claim" to which s54(1) refers, is limited to a claim for an insured risk.'[157] However the Court of Appeal of the Supreme Court of New South Wales in *Prepaid Services Pty Ltd v Atradius Credit Insurance NV*[158] had declined to follow *Johnson*. Certainly if the insurer's approach were adopted it would result in a significant narrowing of s54's effectiveness as it would open the door to exclusions and

152 [2014] HCA 33, 10 September 2014.
153 [2016] FCA 1.
154 [2016] WASCA 25.
155 [2019] NSWSC 527.
156 (2010) 243 FLR 336; 16 ANZ Ins Cas 61–866; [2010] QCA 282.
157 *Maxwell v Highway Hauliers Pty Ltd* [2014] HCA 33, 10 September 2014, at 596 [17].
158 [2014] NSWSC 21.

endorsements being drafted as carve-outs from the scope of cover which would then be beyond the reach of s54.

6.62 At first instance, the Supreme Court of Western Australia distinguished *Triple C* on its facts and held that s54 did apply to excuse the insured's omissions. This result was confirmed unanimously by the Western Australian Court of Appeal. The insurers conceded that the fact that each vehicle had been operated by an untested driver could not reasonably be regarded as being capable of causing or contributing to any loss incurred by the insured as a result of each accident. Consequently, s54(2) had no application. The insurers also conceded that there was no prejudice arising from the breaches.

6.63 Stressing the importance of substance over form in interpreting s54, the High Court noted that the objectives of s54 as described by the ALRC included striking a fair balance between the interests of an insurer and an insured with regard to contractual terms designed to protect the insurer from an increase in risk.[159] That balance was to be struck irrespective of the form of that contractual term. The court highlighted the ALRC's proposition[160] that no difference be drawn between a policy term framed as:

- An obligation of the insured (e.g. 'the insured is under an obligation to keep the motor vehicle in a roadworthy condition');
- A continuing warranty of the insured (e.g. 'the insured warrants he will keep the motor vehicle in a roadworthy condition');
- A limitation on the defined risk (e.g. 'this contract provides cover for the motor vehicle while it is roadworthy'); or
- A temporal exclusion from cover (e.g. 'this cover will not apply while the motor vehicle is unroadworthy').

6.64 The High Court held that

> it is sufficient to engage s54(1) that the effect of the Policy is that the Insurers may refuse to pay those claims by reason only of acts which occurred after the contract was entered into. Precisely how the Policy produced that effect was not to the point.[161]

The court ruled that the reference in *FAI v Hospital Care* to section 54(1) being unable to remedy an inherent restriction or limitation in the insured's claim was intended to refer to how a claim was made having regard to the type of insurance contract involved. The relevant restriction or limitation would arise where:[162]

(i) Under a 'claims made and notified' policy, a claim was made outside of the period of cover. The court re-iterated that a claim under a 'claims made and notified' contract necessarily acknowledged that the indemnity sought could only be in relation to a demand made on the insured by a third party during the period of cover. The section did not operate to permit indemnity to be sought in relation to a demand

159 Australian Law Reform Commission, *Insurance Contracts*, Report No 20, (1982) at xxxi-xxxii, 132–140.

160 Australian Law Reform Commission, Insurance Contracts, Report No 20, (1982). See also Australia, House of Representatives, Insurance Contracts Bill 1984, Explanatory Memorandum at 78–80.

161 *Maxwell v Highway Hauliers Pty Ltd* [2014] HCA 33, 10 September 2014, P12/2014, at para 27.

162 *Maxwell v Highway Hauliers Pty Ltd* [2014] HCA 33, 10 September 2014, P12/2014, at paras 24 and 25.

that the third party omitted to make on the insured during the period of cover, but made after that period expired;

(ii) Under a 'discovery' or a 'claims-made and circumstances notified' policy, where a claim was made in respect of a circumstance that the insured was not aware of during the period of cover. The claim necessarily acknowledged that the indemnity sought could only be in relation to an occurrence of which the insured became aware during the period of cover; and

(iii) Under an 'occurrence-based' policy, where indemnity was sought for an event that occurred outside of the period of cover. In relation to a claim under an occurrence-based policy, the claim necessarily acknowledged that the indemnity sought could only be in relation to an event that occurred during the period of cover.[163]

6.65 The High Court found that:

- The fact that each vehicle was being operated at the time of the accident by an untested driver was an act that occurred after the contract of insurance was entered into;
- There was an omission of the Insured in failing to ensure that each vehicle was operated by a driver who had undertaken a PAQS test or an equivalent program approved by the Insurers. That omission occurred during the Period of Insurance; and
- HH having claimed under the policy for accidents that occurred during the period of insurance, it was sufficient in order to engage section 54(1) that the effect of the policy was that the underwriters might refuse to pay the claims, by reason only of acts which occurred after the policy was entered into. Precisely how the Policy produced that effect was not to the point.[164]

As a result the court held that the insurers were liable to indemnify the assured and pay damages for breach of the policy.

6.66 The High Court stated that the finding in *Johnson v Triple C Furniture & Electrical Pty Ltd*[165] was erroneous (although it should be noted that if s54(2) had been applied the outcome would likely have remained a finding for the insurer). The operation of the aircraft in breach of air safety regulations was an 'act' which occurred after the contract was entered into and the temporal exclusion did not qualify the claim that was made.[166] The court indicated that any act or omission that took place after the insurance contract was entered into, and which would otherwise give the insurer a contractual right to deny indemnity, will be subject to s54. The type of contractual term that an insurer relies on to deny indemnity was not relevant in determining whether s54 applied; the issue was one of substance over form. Consequently, it now seems settled that it will be very difficult for insurers to draft policy wording that seeks to avoid s54 where it would otherwise be applicable.

6.67 The analysis of Corboy J in the Court of Appeal is helpful in viewing *Maxwell v Highway Hauliers*. Corboy J concluded that it was the act of HH that triggered the exclusions, thereby removing claims from coverage, rather than a 'state of affairs' to which the policy

163 *Maxwell v Highway Hauliers Pty Ltd* [2014] HCA 33, 10 September 2014, P12/2014, at para 25.

164 *Maxwell v Highway Hauliers Pty Ltd* [2014] HCA 33, 10 September 2014, P12/2014, at para 27.

165 [2012] 2 Qd R 337.

166 *Maxwell v Highway Hauliers Pty Ltd* [2014] HCA 33, 10 September 2014, P12/2014, at para 28.

did not respond.[167] He argued that the policy was not concerned with drivers as such; rather it was concerned with the vehicles and their use. The policy was an insurance against loss of, or damage to, vehicles and third party liabilities arising from use of them. It was not confined to the risk of accidental damage caused by a driver. 'The PAQS endorsement conditioned the insurer's obligation to meet a particular claim that otherwise fell within the scope of the cover: it did not form part of the way in which the scope of the policy was defined.'[168]

6.68 S54 was designed, inter alia, to safeguard against insurance cover being frustrated by drafting devices, particularly in circumstances where a breach of a warranty or other policy term had no causal link with the loss incurred and did not prejudice the insurer's interests.[169] The difficulty facing the courts had been striking a balance between that aim and ensuring that the sanctity of the scope of cover agreed by the parties was not eroded by s54. *Highway Hauliers* provides another example of the challenges that the courts face in finding that balance. It is submitted that the decision in *Highway Hauliers* pushes at the boundary of what is sensible and equitable in terms of an encroachment into matters of scope. The court indicated that any clause – seemingly even one which was clearly intended to operate as a restriction of the cover – can potentially attract the operation of s54. While the decision on the facts is supportable, it is of concern that in the future courts may be tempted to use the decision in *Highway Hauliers* to push still further at that boundary. The worry is that the decision in *Highway Hauliers*, like that in *Hospital Care*, has left the law teetering on the edge of a slippery and dangerous slope to a world where insurers can no longer be certain that the risk they have bargained for and for which they have calculated the premium, is the risk they will end up being held liable for, unless they can establish either causation under s54(2) or prejudice under s54(1).

(ii) *Pantaenius Australia Pty Ltd v Watkins Syndicate 0457 at Lloyd's*[170]

6.69 The case, considered by the Federal Court, involved the loss of a luxury yacht. The appellant was an insurance company who had admitted liability, but sought a contribution from the respondent, another insurance company. The latter denied liability on the grounds that a clause in their policy provided that, in the event that the vessel intended to enter foreign waters, all cover under the policy would be suspended between the time when the vessel cleared Australian Customs for the purpose of leaving Australian waters and the time when it cleared Australian Customs on its return. The relevant clause stated: 'All cover provided by the policy will be automatically suspended when your boat clears Australian Customs and Immigration for the purpose of leaving Australian waters and will recommence when it clears Australian Customs and Immigration on return.' The respondent argued that, at the time when the vessel ran aground, because it had not yet cleared Australian Customs (on its return from a race in Bali), cover under its policy was suspended.

6.70 The appellant's position was that s54(1) applied and that accordingly the respondent was obliged to contribute. The respondent argued that the policy was an occurrence based

167 In connection with a ruling on what constitutes a 'state of affairs' see *Allianz Australia Insurance Ltd v Inglis* [2016] WASCA 25 and later in this chapter.

168 [2012] WASC 53 at 99–101.

169 R Giblett and N Wiesener, The Long Haul: High Court Endorses Broad Application of S54 of the Insurance Contracts Act, Norton Rose Fulbright, September 2014.

170 [2016] FCA 1.

policy, subject to prescribed geographic limits and that the description of those limits included specific terms governing the scope of cover in circumstances where the insured vessel intended to leave Australian waters. The appellant maintained that the relevant clause was an exclusion clause, rather than a limitation of scope. The policy covered loss and damage occasioned to the vessel while it was in Australian waters i.e. the loss occurred within the geographic limits of the policy and that the claim was within the risk covered by the policy, subject to the operation of any relevant exclusions. Accordingly the exclusion clause should be subject to s54 because the suspension did not go to the nature of the risk covered by the policy, but was simply an exclusion.

6.71 The court (Foster J) ruled that the clear intent of the policy was that cover was not provided in respect of journeys where the intention of the person in charge of the insured vessel was to leave Australian waters.[171] The court held that the geographical limits on the policy constrained the scope of the policy.[172] The suspension provision was an exclusion and did not operate as one of the contractually prescribed elements of the geographic limits on the scope of cover itself. It was accordingly subject to the operation of s54.

6.72 The applicant argued that the relevant act or omission for the purposes of s54 was the sailing or presence (re-entry into) of the vessel in Australian waters without having cleared Australian Customs on its return from Indonesia. The respondent's position was that the failure to clear customs was not an act or omission, but a non-event. Adopting neither position, the court held that the relevant act was the clearing of customs on departure with the intention of leaving Australian waters:

> By causing the vessel to clear Australian Customs for the purpose of leaving Australian waters in order to compete in the Fremantle to Bali sailboat race, Mr Phillips committed an act or acts within the meaning of that term in s54(1) which led the respondent to refuse to pay his claim, being an act which occurred after the Nautilus policy was entered into.[173]

6.73 The respondent further argued that by re-entering Australian waters the insured committed an act capable of causing or contributing to the loss under s54(2), on the grounds that there was a direct causative link between entering those waters and the loss of the vessel: had it not embarked on the relevant voyage it would not have run aground. The court held that the correct approach was a 'with and without' test of causation and that the nature of the risk would have been precisely the same whether the vessel had cleared Australian Customs or not.[174] No causation had thus been established under s54(2) and no prejudice established under s54(1) as the act of clearing customs on departure and sailing from Fremantle had not increased the risk that the vessel would run aground.

6.74 As the court was of the view that scope was in this instance geographically defined, this raises the question of what the court's view would have been if the loss had occurred just outside Australian territorial waters. On the basis of the court's geographical approach to scope, the logic of the court's position would presumably be that it would have assessed such a loss to be outside the scope of the policy. But what if, without any intent to participate in an overseas race, the insured vessel had inadvertently sailed half a mile beyond Australian

171 [2016] FCA 1 at 70.
172 [2016] FCA 1 at 77.
173 [2016] FCA 1 at 84 and 89.
174 [2016] FCA 1 at 96.

waters and was lost to fire? Would s54 come to the insured's aid? On some interpretations of s54 it may well do: would this amount to a 'limitation of the defined risk,' something that the ALRC (and the Explanatory Notes to the Bill) specifically indicated should be caught by s54?[175] This again illustrates the lack of clarity in relation to s54 and matters of scope. Again, we have seen that under s54(2) the test is whether the act (or omission) *could* reasonably be regarded as being capable of causing or contributing to the loss.[176] Surely it is at least arguable that on the facts, the act of clearing customs with the intention of racing in offshore waters *could* have contributed to the loss? Surely the fact that the nature of the risk was not changed does not of itself mean that the act was not *capable* of contributing to the loss? If this analysis is correct, the onus should have been on the insured to show under s54(3) (or as appropriate s54(4)) that, on the facts, the act did not contribute to the loss. This is not to suggest the finding of the court regarding causation was necessarily incorrect, merely that the logic steps it took to reach its conclusions may have been flawed.

6.75 While on its face the judgement seems reasonable, albeit somewhat tortuous, it is submitted that the potential difficulty it poses is that it comes close to asserting that an 'intention' (in this case an intention to leave Australian waters) is sufficient to trigger the operation of s54. Surely by definition, an 'intention' can never be an act or omission? Nevertheless, on the basis of the policy wording, the outcome of the case can be supported. The case does however represent another example of the courts straining at the limits of s54 and highlights again the inherent uncertainty, lack of precision and unnecessarily complex nature of s54.

(iii) *Allianz Australia Insurance Ltd v Inglis*[177]

6.76 The case concerned a home and contents policy that also provided legal liability cover. The latter was subject to an exclusion for 'injury to any person who normally lives with you, or damage to their property.' The insured's daughter was seriously injured when run over by the insured's ride-on lawnmower at a neighbour's property; the lawnmower was driven by the neighbour's son. The insured issued proceedings against the neighbour claiming damages for negligently caused personal injuries. The neighbours issued third party proceedings against the insured claiming an indemnity, or alternatively a contribution, under s7 of the Law Reform (Contributory Negligence and Tortfeasors Contribution) Act (WA) for the injuries suffered by the insured's daughter. The insurer (Allianz) declined to indemnify the insured on the grounds of the exclusion clause. In the case before the Federal Court, Allianz claimed the trial judge had erred in holding (i) that the fact that the insured's daughter was living with the insured was an 'act' for the purposes of s54, rather than a state of affairs; (ii) the 'act' occurred after the contract was entered into; (iii) that the relevant act could not reasonably be regarded as capable of causing or contributing to a loss in respect of which insurance cover was provided (and that s54(2) thus had no application); and (iv) that the class of persons who normally live with the insured was not a restriction or limitation inherent in the type of policy. Allianz contended that the expression 'a person

175 Australian Law Reform Commission, Insurance Contracts, Report No 20, (1982). See also Australia, House of Representatives, Insurance Contracts Bill 1984, Explanatory Memorandum at 78–80.

176 In ALRC 20 the Commission specifically envisaged s54(2) applying to circumstances where the act or omission *could* have contributed to the accident/loss. In such circumstances the onus would be on the insured to show under s54(3) or (4) that the act did not in fact so contribute, or if it did, it did so only partially.

177 [2016] WASCA 25.

who normally lives with you' did not contain or constitute an 'act' under s54(1) but rather was a state of affairs, or the status or description of a person. The insured argued that the exclusion did not apply to the insured's daughter, but that if s54 applied, then so too did s54(5)(b), on the grounds that it was not reasonably possible for the insured or other person not to do the act.

6.77 The Federal Court (McLure P) held the exclusion clause applied to the insured's daughter and further that the fact that the insured's daughter normally lived with the insured did not constitute an 'act' within the meaning of s54(1).[178] In reaching her conclusion, McLure P was guided by the finding in *Antico v Heath Fielding Australia Pty Ltd*[179]: s54 of the ICA was remedial in character and its language should be construed so as to give the most complete remedy which was consistent with the actual language employed and to which its words were fairly open. The judge indicated that the assessment of whether a person normally lives with another depended on the 'drawing of an inference from the conduct of all relevant persons over an extended period.' In the final analysis the issue did not turn on the 'act of the insured or of some other person'; it was properly characterised as a 'state of affairs or description of a relationship.' It was analogous to the analysis necessary to 'inform and determine whether the relationship of employer and employee exists.'[180]

6.78 While the decision was sufficient to settle the case, the judge went on to consider the other grounds of appeal as if the daughter living with the insured *did* constitute an act for the purposes of s54(1). Allianz had argued that if the fact that Georgia Inglis was normally living with the insured was an act for the purposes of s54, the act occurred before the policy was entered into and according to s54 would not be applicable. McLure P indicated that the fact that the insured's daughter was normally living with the insured before (and after) entry into the policy did not take the act outside the scope of s54(1) which applied to 'an act that occurred after the contract was entered into.' Section 54 was intended to apply to temporal exclusions such as the one in the policy and the section was responsive to factual changes during the period of the insurance. If during the period of cover a claimant ceased to normally live with the insured before any relevant legal liability was incurred, the exclusion would not apply.[181] If the facts supported the inference that on the date of the accident the insured's daughter was normally living with the insured (and they did), that was an act that occurred after the policy was entered into for the purpose of s54(1) of the ICA.[182] In terms of the question whether s54(2) applied to the circumstances of the case (the third ground of appeal), the judge held that in order for s54(2) to be applicable, the act in question must be one that was reasonably regarded as legally capable of satisfying the requirement that the act could potentially cause or contribute to an accident and any consequential harm. The judge held that the 'act,' had there been one, would have increased the risk of a financial loss in respect of which cover was provided, but it was incapable of satisfying the causation requirements for legal liability and accordingly s54(2) had no application.[183] If there was an 'act,' the increase in risk of financial loss might

178 [2016] WASCA 25 at 43.
179 [1997] HCA 35; (1997) 188 CLR 652, at 675.
180 [2016] WASCA 25 at 42.
181 [2016] WASCA 25 at 46.
182 [2016] WASCA 25 at 47.
183 [2016] WASCA 25 at 54.

arguably have constituted prejudice for the purposes of s54(1), but it did not bring the act within s54(2). S54(5) was part of a connected subset of the legislative scheme together with s54(2), s54(3) and s54(4) it was highly artificial to seek to apply s54(5) to an act which failed to meet the criteria for s54(2).[184]

6.79 Allianz's final ground for appeal was that insureds' claims were in respect of liability of a kind not dealt with by the policy because the claim was not for injury to a person within the classes of cover; accordingly, the reason for refusal of the claim was not some act or omission on the part of the insured or some other person, but because the policy did not extend to the claim. The judge held that the temporal exclusion in this case was not a restriction or limitation which must necessarily be acknowledged in the making of a claim, having regard to the type of insurance contract under which that claim is made (as per *Maxwell v Highway Hauliers*[185]). Applying *Maxwell* to the facts of this case, the judge indicated that what must be acknowledged in the claims was that the third party respondents were insured under the policy for legal liability, that the bodily injury which was the subject of the claims occurred during the period of insurance and was caused by an accident within the geographic area covered by the policy. The final ground of appeal would accordingly have been dismissed.

6.80 It is submitted that the decision represents a sensible victory for common sense and restores the focus to the need for an 'event' (comprising either an act or an omission) in order for s54 to be applicable. Nevertheless, it is contended that the structure of s54 inherently makes determinations at the margin fraught with difficulty. The result is that the section will continue to attract litigation and controversial decisions that push (in both directions) at the boundaries of what represents a fair balance between the interests of insureds on the one hand and insurers on the other.

6.81 It was unfortunate that McLure P felt it appropriate (unlike her colleagues) to give hypothetical rulings on the remaining grounds of appeal. It is submitted that this additional deliberation is only likely to cause further confusion. It is hard to see how (in the context of the second ground of appeal) a circumstance that does not change from before the time of entry into the contract could be regarded as an 'act' that occurred after the contract was entered into for the purposes of s54. The judge's analysis serves only to confuse the emphasis inherent in her primary decision of the importance of focusing on an 'event.' There are also grounds for taking issue with the judge's position in relation to s54(2). The wording of the subsection makes it clear that the threshold is that the 'act' 'could reasonably be regarded as being capable of causing or contributing to a loss.'[186] Although the relevant cover was for legal liability, it is surely at least arguable that the judge erred in defining the test in this instance as being an act that was reasonably regarded 'as legally capable of satisfying the causation elements or requirements of legal liability for a loss.'[187] If the act was one (as the judge indicated it was[188]) that would have increased the risk of a financial loss in respect of which cover was provided, is that not a sufficient trigger for s54(2), because in those circumstances surely it is an act which is *capable* of

184 [2016] WASCA 25 at 54.
185 [2014] HCA 33, 10 September 2014, P12/2014 at 23–25.
186 S54(2) Insurance Contracts Act 1984.
187 [2016] WASCA 25 at 54.
188 [2016] WASCA 25 at 54.

contributing to a loss (in respect of which cover is provided)? For example, who is to say that a settlement might not be agreed, despite the circumstances falling short of the standards necessary for legal liability?

(iv) *DIF III – Global Co-Investment Fund LP v Babcock & Brown International Pty Limited*[189]

6.82 A case arising from the collapse in 2009 of Babcock and Brown Ltd, a specialist advisory and investment firm, involved claims regarding the application of s54 against both D&O and PI Insurers. The court held that s54 did not cure a lack of notification of circumstances if those circumstances were not known (to the insured) during the policy period.

6.83 The PI Insurers conceded that any failure to give notice of known circumstances that could reasonably be anticipated to give rise to a claim could be cured under s54, but argued that s54 could not cure a failure to give notice of circumstances that were not known. The insured sought to rely on a number of documents which, they argued, were sufficient to constitute notice of a claim against the Manager or provide evidence that (in accordance with the policy) the insured's management first became aware during the policy period of a 'fact, circumstance or event which could reasonably be anticipated to give rise to' the claim which subsequently came to pass. On the facts it was held that the evidence did not establish that the insured's management had any basis, during the policy period, for thinking that a claim would be brought. In these circumstances, s54 could not apply.

6.84 The D&O Policy contained a deeming provision which gave the insured an option to notify, within the policy period, circumstances out of which a claim might arise. The insurers accepted that, in light of the deeming provision, s54 could operate to cure late notification of circumstances, but submitted that the claims in respect of which indemnity was sought did not arise out of the notification of circumstances relied on. Although evidence of notification of a potential claim was submitted, the court held that there was insufficient connection between this and the claim which was eventually brought. The insured was also unable, on the facts, to prove the existence, during the relevant period, of circumstances that might reasonably be expected to give rise to a claim in respect of which, failure to notify might have been forgiven by s54. The insured subsequently referred to a separate notice given to the insurers and in an obiter observation the judge commented that it might have been arguable that s54 would have applied to this notice (subject (under s54(1)) to any prejudice suffered by the insurers as a result of the late notification). However, as the notice was not pleaded, it could not be relied upon.

6.85 In the light of this decision, it seems clear that if the policy wording requires relevant knowledge on the part of an insured in the policy period, s54 will not cure any failure to give notice of circumstances which were not known in the period. This seems sensible.

189 [2019] NSWSC 527.

Review of s54 of the ICA by Cameron and Milne, commissioned by and submitted to the Australian Government, October 2003

6.86 In 2003 the Australian Government announced it would commission a wide-ranging review of the Insurance Contracts Act. The objective of the Review was, inter alia, to 'assess whether the rights and obligations of insurers and insureds under the Act continue to be appropriate'; to determine if any amendments to the Act were required; and to make recommendations aimed at improving the overall operation of the Act by correcting deficiencies and clarifying ambiguities in its operation. The Review was conducted by Alan Cameron AM and Nancy Milne. The first stage of the Review looked specifically at the operation of s54.

6.87 One of the key drivers for the Review was the concern expressed after the judicial interpretations in some of the cases referenced earlier about the application of s54 to claims made and claims made and notified policies. As we have seen, where such policies contained a 'deeming provision,' this provided that where an insured notified facts or circumstances which might give rise to a claim during the policy period, any claim which ultimately eventuated from those facts and circumstances was treated as a claim under that policy.

6.88 The Review recognised that in respect of many professions, claims made policies offered some specific advantages for all parties as compared with 'occurrence based' policies. These included:

Greater stability and certainty for the insurance industry:

- 'Claims made' insurance eased the burden of the insurer provisioning for long-tail insurance. In that regard, 'claims made' insurance reduced insurer risk. This in turn led to lower premiums both directly and indirectly by encouraging greater insurer competition.

Consumer confidence in the adequacy of coverage:

- 'Claims made' insurance was more likely to provide adequate coverage for a claim as the policy period was more closely aligned with the time of the claim. In long-tail insurance, the event that leads to the claim may occur long before the claim itself. This time lapse may result in coverage (that was perceived adequate at the time of the occurrence) being inadequate when the claim is made several years later.

6.89 As a result of the decisions in some of the cases discussed previously, there was concern that s54 allowed an insured who entered into a 'claims made' or 'claims made and notified' insurance contract, to alter the nature of the contract from that of 'claims made' to one of 'occurrence.' Specifically, concern had arisen over judicial interpretation of subsection 54(1) which had excused the insured from the consequences of a failure to notify claims or circumstances which might give rise to a claim during the period of cover (even where the decision not to notify was deliberate), such that coverage was still available for those losses for an indeterminate period after the policy had expired. The concern was that this resulted in the policy being converted into an 'occurrence trigger contract,' with the consequence that insurers must provide for 'incurred but not reported claims' as in traditional accident-based liability insurance.

The problem defined

6.90 Kirby J defined claims made policies as follows in *FAI General Insurance Company Ltd v Australian Hospital Care Pty*:

> Claims made type policies ... differ from "occurrence" policies in that, instead of attaching the insurer's liability to indemnify the insured to the happening of an occurrence during the period of cover, they attach the liability in various ways (according to the description in the policy) to the making of a claim against the insured, its notification by the insured to the insurer or the "discovery" of a claim within the period of cover.'[190]

The judge further observed:[191]

> The essence of the problem, that has seen so many judges struggling with issues of construction and application of the words adopted by parliament in s54 of the Act, is that if the section is given the large ambit argued for it by the insured, it might effectively permit courts to repair all kinds of "omissions" on the part of insured persons and third parties and effectively to rewrite insurance policies accordingly. Courts could do so in a way that would essentially destroy the basic foundation upon which claims made type policies are based, [and] it would be surprising if the Act were to permit "omissions" to make or notify claims, or to notify occurrences, within the period of cover that had the effect of altering the essential character of the cover provided in the contract of insurance. It would be surprising if it permitted an insured, at its option, *to convert a claims made policy, effectively, to a kind of occurrence policy for which a substantially higher premium would ordinarily have been levied by the insurer.*[192]

However, although conscious of the detrimental impact such a finding would have on the availability of claims made and notified policies, his honour nevertheless concluded

> Unless the meaning of the section, derived from its language, permits or requires a Court to confine relief in such [claims made and notified] cases, any dissatisfaction with the operation of the section in respect of this class of insurance is a matter for legislative amendment. The judicial "struggle" with the requirements of the provision, as such requirements are found to be inherent in its language and apparent purpose, can only go so far.

6.91 Commenting on the *Australian Hospital* decision, Professor Sutton had observed that the ruling might 'lead to the imposition of much greater risks on insurers, with the consequence that premiums will increase and the Australian insurance industry will be out of step with international practice.'[193] As a result he feared that the long-tailed nature of occurrence based policies was back with a vengeance, albeit that the trigger for the cover to respond was awareness of a potential claim against the assured. Sutton further observed that relying on an assessment of the prejudice suffered by the insurer could be a flawed attempt at ameliorating the adverse impact of the section because (as Gleeson CJ observed in *Australian Hospital Care*), it could be very difficult to measure that prejudice. As a minimum, Sutton felt that such an approach would require a greatly expanded definition of prejudice to incorporate, for

190 [2001] HCA 38 at para 64.
191 (2001) 204 CLR 641 at para 73; (2001) 11 ANZ Ins Cas at para 63.
192 Emphasis added.
193 Report 250 of Australian and New Zealand Insurance Law.

example, the loss that an insurer would suffer from having to maintain adequate contingency funds to meet possible future claims of which it knows nothing.

6.92 Chesterman J in *FAI v Australian Hospital Care Pty Ltd* summarised the operation of section 54 as follows:

> The result (that s54(1) responds to an insured's failure to notify circumstances during the policy period) does not give rise to any particular sense of satisfaction, but seems compelled by the explanation of s54 found in *Antico*. So understood, the section appears to produce a policy of insurance rather different from the one agreed upon by the parties. ... *The effect of the section is to distort the contractual arrangement made by the parties.*[194]

6.93 Cole J in *Breville Appliances Pty Ltd v Harold Duvernay Ducrou & Ors* put the issues that could arise as follows:

> To construe s54 to convert a Claims Made and Notified Policy into a Claims Made Policy seems to me, to go far beyond that which the legislature intended. There is, I would have thought, a clear distinction between denying an insurer a right to refuse indemnity because of an act or omission of the insured on the one hand, *and effectively broadening the scope of cover by denying an insurer the right to define cover*, and thus assessment of risk and consequential assessment of premium, on the other.[195]

Impact of s54 on the market

6.94 Consultations undertaken by Cameron and Milne suggested that generally the industry was happy with the operation of s54 and that there was no demand for an amendment to s54 in relation to occurrence policies. A large number of submissions to the Review however suggested that s54 was not drafted with 'claims made' and 'claims made and notified' insurance in mind. Nevertheless, the Review concluded that it was virtually impossible to articulate the exact role the interpretation of s54 had played in the reduction in availability of professional indemnity insurance in Australia. The Review's soundings did however make it clear that some insurers (particularly London insurers) had withdrawn from the professional indemnity insurance market in Australia, or had altered their policies in an effort to reduce the impact of the recent decisions relating to the application of s54 to claims made and notified policies. Others would likely leave the market if the withdrawal of deeming clauses proved to be an ineffective way of preserving the 'claims made' nature of such policies.

6.95 Cameron and Milne concluded that improving the availability of professional indemnity insurance in the Australian market required that insurers had certainty. However, the Review determined that insurers faced a high degree of uncertainty in provisioning for 'incurred but not reported' insurance claims, primarily as a result of the operation of s54. The Review suggested that s54 was a material component in the group of causes that were discouraging insurance providers from offering, increasing the cost of and reducing the breadth of coverage of 'claims made' insurance in Australia.[196]

---

194 *FAI General Insurance Co Ltd v Australian Hospital Care Pty Ltd* (1999) 10 ANZ Ins Cas 61–445. Emphasis added.

195 (1992) 7 ANZ Ins Cas 61–125 at 77 628–77 629. Emphasis added.

196 Review of the Operation of s54 of the ICA by Alan Cameron and Nancy Milne, October 2003.

6.96 A survey by the Association of Consulting Engineers Australia supported the Review's findings, concluding that

(i) The percentage of income spent on PI insurance by engineering firms had doubled in each of the last three preceding years.
(ii) One third of firms had their profits affected. As a result, nearly 1 in 5 had reduced services to the community.
(iii) About 20% of firms were recovering only half their PI costs from clients.
(iv) Nearly 30% (mostly small firms) were unable to pass the increases on at all.[197]

6.97 As we have seen, as a result of the decision in *Hospital Care*, in an attempt to address the perceived shortcomings with s54 and its impact on late notification of circumstances, insurers issuing claims made policies adopted an approach of omitting the deeming clause. Cameron and Milne concluded that this was an undesirable development. Further in *Gosford Council v GIO General Limited*, as we have seen, the court held that s54 would not apply in relation to the statutory right provided by s40(3) (which provides the insured rights similar to that which would apply if a deeming provision were included in the policy)[198] because s54 provided relief from the 'effect of the contract,' not from a requirement imposed by law.[199]

6.98 The Review concluded that the position regarding s54 and the impact of deleting deeming clauses remained unsatisfactory because:

(i) The outcome of any High Court appeal on this issue was uncertain;
(ii) There was still a degree of uncertainty about the application of s54 to 'claims made' policies that did not include a deeming provision; and
(iii) The practice of omitting deeming provisions from 'claims made' policies for this kind of reason was undesirable: insureds should be able to understand the effect of the policy without having to consult lawyers.[200]

6.99 The Review was concerned that many insureds and their advisers might not understand that without deeming provisions, 'claims made' policies might no longer enable s54 to excuse the late notification of circumstances. The Review felt that if s54 were amended so as not to excuse the late notification of circumstances under a 'claims made' policy, the benefit would be the provision of certainty to insurers and insureds and increased contract clarity through encouraging the re-introduction of deeming provisions into 'claims made' policies. The Review felt that the plain English impact of deeming provisions would allow an insured to understand his rights and obligations under an insurance policy by simply reading the terms of the contract, whereas the current trend of claims made policies without deeming provisions required insureds to be aware of, and understand the effect of,

---

197 Association of Consulting Engineers Australia, The Impact of Changes in Professional Indemnity (PI) Insurance on Costs and Fees for Consulting Engineering Firms, May 2003.

198 S40(3) reads as follows: 'Where the insured gave notice in writing to the insurer of facts that might give rise to a claim against the insured as soon as was reasonably practicable after the insured became aware of those facts but before the insurance cover provided by the contract expired, the insurer is not relieved of liability under the contract in respect of the claim, when made, by reason only that it was made after the expiration of the period of the insurance cover provided by the contract.'

199 [2002] NSWSC 511 and [2003] NSW CA 34.

200 Review of the Operation of s54 of the ICA by Alan Cameron and Nancy Milne, October 2003.

the Insurance Contracts Act in conjunction with their insurance contract, in order properly to understand their rights regarding the notification of circumstances to an insurer.[201] The Review felt that an amendment to s54 that clarified the position would leave third parties no worse off than they were prior to such an amendment.

Review recommendations

6.100 The Review recommended that s54 be amended so that notifications of facts or circumstances which might give rise to a claim would be excluded from the relief provided under s54. S54 would still provide relief to an insured in respect to a claim made against the insured during the period of cover, but notified to the insurer outside that period.[202] The amendment would be limited to 'claims made' and 'claims made and notified' policies, or, simply those policies which were subject to s40(3) of the Insurance Contracts Act. In addition, the Review recommended that insurers should be required to notify insureds not earlier than one month and no later than seven business days prior to the expiration of the relevant policy, of the importance of notifying facts or circumstances, unless the insured was, to the insurer's knowledge, advised by an insurance broker.[203] The Review saw the application of s54 to late notification of circumstances as anomalous. The Review suggested that any class of contract prescribed by regulation or declared by the Australian Securities and Investments Commission (ASIC) could, if need be, be excluded from the operation of the amendment. Alternatively the amendment could be crafted to apply solely to identified types of insurance as follows:

- Contracts of professional indemnity insurance;
- Contracts of insurance that provided cover for liability of a person in their capacity as a director or officer of a corporation, including any related contract of insurance which provided cover for a corporation in respect of its liability to indemnify a person in their capacity as a director or officer of that corporation;
- Contracts of insurance that provided cover for liability arising from employment practices;
- Contracts of insurance that indemnified a trustee or trust fund in relation to a loss or liability incurred by the trustee in the course of carrying out the trustee's functions in relation to the trust;
- Contracts known as errors or omissions contracts of insurance;
- Contracts of insurance commonly known as a product recall or product guarantee insurance contracts; and
- Contracts of medical malpractice insurance.

6.101 The Review recognised that if s54 were amended as recommended it would be necessary to provide for an extended reporting period of facts or circumstances that might give rise to a claim for policies which were subject to s40 of the Act,[204] not least because

201 Review of the Operation of s54 of the ICA by Alan Cameron and Nancy Milne, October 2003.

202 Review of the Operation of s54 of the ICA by Alan Cameron and Nancy Milne, October 2003.

203 Review of the Operation of s54 of the ICA by Alan Cameron and Nancy Milne, October 2003.

204 S40 applies to contracts of liability insurance the effect of which is that the insurer's liability is excluded or limited by reason that notice of a claim is not given before the expiry of the cover.

awareness of circumstances may arise late on the last day of cover, making notification impossible before expiration.[205] Accordingly, the Review recommended that there should be an extended reporting period of 45 days for facts or circumstances that might give rise to a claim for policies that were subject to s40 of the Act. Circumstances notified during that period, but of which the insured became aware during the previous period, would be taken as covered by the policy for the previous period. The Review observed that a failure to exercise a right, choice or liberty should not be an omission for purposes of s54.[206] An alternate approach (with the same outcome) was to hold that s54 did not apply to a deliberate failure of an insured to extend cover under a general insurance policy.

6.102 The amended s54, as recommended by the Review, would read as follows:

s54A Subsection 54(1) not to apply to certain omissions in relation to liability insurance contracts

(1) This section applies if, apart from this section, s54(1) would have the effect that an insurer may not refuse to pay a claim, either in whole or in part, by reason only that the insured, having become aware before the insurance cover provided by the contract expired of facts that might give rise to a claim against the insured, did not give notice in writing to the insurer of those facts during a period provided for in the contract, or in this Act, for giving such notice.

(2) S54(1) does not have that effect if the contract is a contract of liability insurance the effect of which is that:
  (a) the insurer's liability is excluded or limited by reason that a claim against the insured in respect of a loss suffered by some other person is not made before the insurance cover provided by the contract expires; or
  (b) the insurer's liability is excluded or limited by reason that:
    (i) a claim against the insured in respect of a loss suffered by some other person is not made before the insurance cover provided by the contract expires; and
    (ii) notice of such a claim is not given to the insurer before the insurance cover provided by the contract expires.[207]

6.103 Notwithstanding the apparently broad consensus reflected in submissions to the Review, its recommendations have not been implemented. It seems the feeling was that although the decision in *Hospital Care* had caused a considerable stir when delivered, the market had adjusted its practices accordingly and so the need for reform was felt to have diminished. This is regrettable; however, implementation of the Review's recommendations would not, of itself, be sufficient to overcome the reservations discussed previously about s54 as a template for addressing breaches of insurance warranties and other terms.

Marine insurance and ALRC

6.104 In 2001 the ALRC undertook a review of the Marine Insurance Act 1909.[208] One of the main questions it examined was whether there remained a justification for

205 Review of the Operation of s54 of the ICA by Alan Cameron and Nancy Milne, October 2003.
206 Review of the Operation of s54 of the ICA by Alan Cameron and Nancy Milne, October 2003.
207 Review of the Operation of s54 of the ICA by Alan Cameron and Nancy Milne, October 2003.
208 Its conclusions were published in ALRC 91, Review of the Marine Insurance Act 1909, May 2001.

maintaining two separate statutory regimes for insurance, the Insurance Contracts Act 1984 (governing the vast majority of commercial insurance contracts) and the Marine Insurance Act 1909. Following its review, the ALRC recommended in ALRC 91[209] the maintenance of two separate regimes.

6.105 In ALRC 91, the Commission recommended that warranties should disappear and be replaced (if required by the insurers) by express contract terms under which insurers would be relieved from liability in the event of a breach which was the proximate cause of the loss, even if there were other proximate causes (recommendations 7–9). A breach that was remedied before any loss would cease to be of significance. In the absence of any relevant express term, insurers would be entitled only to damages on breach. The burden of proving a breach would rest on the insurers, although the burden of showing that the breach was not the proximate cause of the loss would be borne by the assured (recommendation 19).

6.106 However, the ALRC decided against introducing an element of proportionality as found in s54 of the ICA. Under the ALRC's recommendations, the insurer would not be able to refuse to pay a claim where the breach was something less than the proximate cause, but nevertheless did somehow worsen the situation.[210] Other recommendations were: (i) the removal of personal/domestic risks from the MIA to the ICA, and (ii) the inclusion in the MIA of coverage of commercial vessels on the seas or inland waters. While consistency may have been a sound rationale for following the ICA, the ALRC, somewhat surprisingly, indicated it felt that s54 was inappropriate for marine insurance.

6.107 ALRC 91 proposed the abolition of the implied seaworthiness warranty, to be replaced, where appropriate, with express terms.[211] An insurer would be discharged from liability only where the assured knew or ought to have known of the relevant circumstances that rendered the vessel unseaworthy and failed to take such remedial steps as were reasonably available to him.[212] Such an approach has merit given that the implied warranty of seaworthiness is of limited relevance in the modern world. As an alternative, the ALRC proposed that MIA1909, s46(2) should be repealed and the implied warranty of seaworthiness in both time and voyage policies should follow the time model in MIA 1909, s45(5).[213]

6.108 As far as the implied warranty of legality is concerned, ALRC 91 proposed that the implied warranty should be repealed and replaced with an express term if required,[214] and that either any breach of an express term should discharge the insurers from liability[215] or that any breach of an express term should discharge the insurers from liability insofar as loss was attributable to the breach.

209 ALRC 91, Review of the Marine Insurance Act 1909, May 2001.

210 As we have seen, s54(2) of the ICA permits the insurer to refuse to pay a claim where the act or omission could reasonably be regarded as being capable of causing or contributing to a loss in respect of which insurance cover is provided by the contract. However, this is subject, inter alia, to the following: (i) if the assured proves that no part of the loss was caused by the breach the insurer may not refuse to pay the claim by reason only of that act (ICA, s54(3)): i.e. in such circumstances s54(1) applies; (ii) if the assured proves that some part of the loss was not caused by the breach, the insurers must pay that part (ICA, s54(4)).

211 ALRC 91, recommendation 10.

212 ALRC 91, recommendation 11.

213 Where, with the privity of the assured, the ship is sent to sea in an unseaworthy state, the insurer is not liable for any loss attributable to unseaworthiness.

214 ALRC 91, recommendation 11.

215 ALRC 91, recommendation 14.

6.109 Lewins was of the view that under the proposed reforms, the pendulum had perhaps swung too far to the insurer's disadvantage, though insurers may nevertheless prefer the proposed approach to that of s54.[216]

Insurance Contracts Act or Marine Insurance Act?

6.110 As Lewins put it, given the significant difference between the regimes, 'The problem of determining the applicable legal regime for a particular contract of insurance is unique to Australia.'[217] Merkin sees no convincing reason for the maintenance of a parallel system of statutory regimes and describes ALRC 91 as 'a document with modest objectives.'[218] In Merkin's view the vast bulk of the Marine Insurance Act is inconsistent with modern practice, obsolete or unnecessary and bringing marine insurance within the Insurance Contracts Act 1984 would be relatively straightforward.[219] Calls for reform have increased with the introduction of the Insurance Act 2015 in the UK, as reflected in the comment of the Chief Justice of Australia's Federal Court, James Allsop, that, '[w]hilst the [Aus MIA] has served the community for a century, one wonders whether the marine insurance markets would not be better served by a more up to date and comprehensively adopted contemporary model.' While there is some merit in Merkin's views, the ALRC's recommendation to abolish warranties is nevertheless a significant proposal, one which, if it were implemented, would likely have far reaching consequences. Merkin acknowledges that it might also be necessary to add a small number of sections to deal with marine insurance matters, although in his view far fewer than ALRC 91 suggested.

6.111 Merkin defines warranties as either a statement by the assured that a state of affairs exists at the date the statement was made (a present warranty) or a promise that the assured will act or refrain from acting in a given way during the currency of the policy (a future warranty).[220] Merkin argues that the ICA approach to warranties has much to commend it, not least as s24 disposes of present warranties by the simple device of treating every statement as a representation, rather than as a warranty, so that the breach does not have any automatic effect, but rather attracts the ordinary rules which govern misrepresentation as set out in ICA 1984, ss23 and 28. He argues that warranties are gradually falling into disuse and that recent English cases have recognised the draconian nature of warranties and have attempted to construe them as narrowly as the language will bear.[221]

216 ALRC 91 Lewins, Kate 'Marine Insurance Reform – Rocking the Boat?' (2001) 79 *Australian Law Reform Commission Reform Journal* 48.

217 ALRC 91 Lewins, Kate 'Marine Insurance Reform – Rocking the Boat?' (2001) 79 *Australian Law Reform Commission Reform Journal* 48.

218 R Merkin, 'Australia: Still a Nation of Chalmers?' (2011) 30(2) *University of Queensland Law Journal,* University of Queensland 189.

219 R Merkin, 'Australia: Still a Nation of Chalmers?' (2011) 30(2) *University of Queensland Law Journal,* University of Queensland 189.

220 R Merkin, 'Australia: Still a Nation of Chalmers?' (2011) 30(2) *University of Queensland Law Journal,* University of Queensland 189.

221 *Pratt v Aigaion Insurance* [2009] Lloyd's Rep IR 149 (crewing warranty applicable only where vessel preparing for or actually sailing). Cf *Switzerland Insurance Australia Limited v Mowie Fisheries Pty Ltd* [1997] FCA 231 (a warranty that vessel would remain in survey was not broken simply because the assured was in breach of a condition attached to the survey certificate).

6.112 For Merkin the differences between the ALRC 91 recommendations and ICA 1984, s54 were 'too subtle for the present writer's grasp.'[222] He viewed the main difference being, as we have seen, that if any part of the loss was proximately caused by the assured's breach of an express term, ALRC 91 would remove all recovery, whereas ICA 1984 s54 would involve apportionment. In Merkin's view MIA, 1909 ss39–41 should be repealed and ICA 1984, s54 should govern express warranties. This approach would merit support if the s54 approach was less flawed. This however is not the case: on the contrary, as demonstrated previously, the s54 approach has a number of shortcomings; for this reason, although supporting the move to one comprehensive legislative framework, Merkin's proposal cannot be supported in the Australian context, unless there were simultaneous reforms to address the issues with s54.

6.113 As far as implied warranties were concerned, Merkin's view was that the ALRC failed to show any convincing reason why s54 should not govern the position. As far as voyage policies were concerned, in Merkin's view the implied warranty of seaworthiness would be swept away by s54, and replaced with a causation test under s54(3), whereby insurers would have a proportionate defence to the extent that the unseaworthiness contributed to the loss. As far as time policies are concerned, Merkin argued that English law had now moved ahead of the ICA after the Supreme Court ruled in *Global Process Systems Inc v Berhad, The Cendor Mopu*[223] that if there had been a peril of the seas affecting an unseaworthy vessel then the assured was entitled to recover. While many of Merkin's concerns about the implied warranty of seaworthiness are valid, it is argued that, for the reasons explained, the solution is not simply for them to be replaced by s54. The preferred approach to the reform of the implied warranty of seaworthiness is set out in Chapter 12.

6.114 Merkin rejects the ALRC's approach to the implied warranty of legality on the grounds that the common law already provides an adequate remedy.[224] He argues that if the contract itself contemplates an illegal venture, it will be void on public policy grounds. Alternatively, if there is no illegality in formation, but only in performance, the guilty party cannot recover if, to do so, he must pray in aid his own illegality. Merkin argues that MIA 1909, ss43–47 should be repealed and ICA s54 should govern any express provision made by the parties. There is much to commend this approach: in relation to the implied warranty of legality, concerns about illegality are largely addressed by existing principles of public policy and incidental illegality, which has no relevance to the claim, would not provide grounds for an insurer to avoid liability. As will be argued later, however,[225] this author's proposed approach is for the implied warranty of legality to be abolished.

6.115 The majority of the ALRC's recommendations in ALRC 91 have yet to be acted upon.[226] On balance, it is submitted that ALRC 91 was a missed opportunity. To have two separate regimes for commercial insurance is unnecessary and can only be an additional source of uncertainty. It is much better that all commercial insurance falls under

222 R Merkin, 'Australia: Still a Nation of Chalmers?' (2011) 30(2) *University of Queensland Law Journal,* University of Queensland 189–224.

223 [2011] UKSC 5.

224 R Merkin, 'Australia: Still a Nation of Chalmers?' (2011) 30(2) *University of Queensland Law Journal,* University of Queensland 189.

225 See Chapter 12, Proposed Solution.

226 S9(a) of the ICA now provides that the Act now extends to 'pleasure craft,' defined as vessels which are owned by individuals and used or intended to be used wholly for recreational activities, sporting activities, or both and otherwise for reward.

one regime. This view is supported by the stress testing undertaken in Chapter 10. There is merit in many of Merkin's arguments, however, in an ideal world, the answer would not lie in a binary choice between the Marine Insurance Act and s54 of the Insurance Contracts Act, but rather in a more nuanced approach which also took the opportunity to amend some of the shortcomings of s54 that have been highlighted earlier. Nevertheless, it needs to be recognised that, after some initial difficulties, the s54 regime is now, by and large, well regarded by the industry in Australia. If the political (and professional) will to re-visit s54 does not exist, and all the evidence suggests that it does not, then maintenance of the two separate regimes would represent a marginally better option than seeking to apply the unreformed s54 approach to marine insurance. However, the primary objective of this volume is not to opine on the best pragmatic solution in a given territory, but rather to seek out, in the light of experience and precedent in a number of jurisdictions, the optimum solution for the treatment of breaches of insurance warranties and similar provisions.

NSW Insurance Act 1902

6.116 Given the reservations expressed previously with s54, it is worth considering whether the approach in the NSW Insurance Act 1902 offers any useful precedents and pointers in seeking a methodology for dealing with insurance warranties and similar provisions.

6.117 Section 18 of the Insurance Act 1902 (NSW) permits a court to excuse a breach, by the insured, of a term or condition of the contract of insurance where the breach does not prejudice the insurer. It is important to note that, as inconsistent state law, under s109 of the Constitution, the relevant sections of the Insurance Act do not apply to contracts that are otherwise subject to the Insurance Contracts Act or the Marine Insurance Act and, therefore, have limited practical impact as the NSW government no longer operates a state insurer. Nevertheless, the NSW Act is relevant as it provides an illustration of an alternate approach to the treatment of breaches of warranties and similar terms that may be of benefit in considering what constitutes an optimal solution.

6.118 Section 18 states:

> 18 (1) In any proceedings taken in a court in respect of a difference or dispute arising out of a contract of insurance, if it appears to the court that a failure by the insured to observe or perform a term or condition of the contract of insurance may reasonably be excused on the ground that the insurer was not prejudiced by the failure, the court may order that the failure be excused.
>
> (2) Where an order of the nature referred to in subsection (1) has been made, the rights and liabilities of all persons in respect of the contract of insurance concerned shall be determined as if the failure the subject of the order had not occurred.

6.119 The key difference from s54 is that s18(1) only applies where the insurer is *not* prejudiced by the insured's failure. Thus, if an insurer *is* prejudiced by the breach of contract, then the insured is *not* entitled to relief from the consequences of that breach, no matter how slight that prejudice. In *Allianz Australia Insurance Ltd v BlueScope Steel Ltd*[227] the decision of

227 [2014] NSWCA 276.

the court confirmed that the insurer must establish that any asserted prejudice is 'real' and not merely theoretical.

6.120 The section applies to policy terms that impose a positive obligation on the insured, such as a requirement to give notice of a loss,[228] and to policy terms that exclude the insurer's liability.[229] The effect is to provide relief where insurers seek to rely on non-compliance with a term of the contract, even though the insurer was not prejudiced by that non-compliance.[230] Some observers have expressed a preference for the structure of the New South Wales provision over that of s54 of the ICA on grounds of simplicity and apparent flexibility, features possibly more in keeping with the style of the MIA. The NSW provision is narrower than s54 of the ICA in that it is limited to providing relief in the event of a failure by the insured to 'observe or perform a term or condition' of the contract, whereas s54 operates whenever some act or omission of the insured or some other person could lead the insurer to refuse to pay a claim.[231]

6.121 The Insurance Act (NSW) applies to all contracts of insurance except those set out in section 21 of the Act and the regulations made under that section. The effect of the Insurance Regulations 1998 (NSW) is that the parts of the Insurance Act (NSW) dealing with general insurance law principles do not apply to:

(a) Contracts of insurance that are subject to The Insurance Contracts Act;
(b) Contracts of marine insurance;
(c) Contracts of life insurance; and
(d) Sections 18A and 18B do not apply to provisions of contracts of insurance in respect of which the following acts apply:
  (i) Motor Vehicles (Third Party Insurance Act) 1942 (NSW);
  (ii) The Workers Compensation Act 1997 (NSW); and
  (iii) Section 41 of The Legal Profession Act 1987 (NSW).

Put another way, the Act applies to those contracts of insurance (apart from marine insurance and life insurance) that are excluded from the operation of the Insurance Contracts Act 1984 by section 9 of that Act.

6.122 As a result of The Insurance Regulation 2009, it is now clear that the relevant provisions of the Insurance Act (NSW) will not apply to any reinsurance contract entered into from 1 September 2009 and which is subject to New South Wales law. Where it applies, the Insurance Act affects the following areas:

- The right of an insurer to rely on a failure by an insured to comply with a term of the insurance contract;
- The right of an insurer to rely on a misrepresentation or non-disclosure by an insured;
- The right of an insurer to rely on an exclusion clause; and
- The right of an insured to commence Court proceedings notwithstanding an arbitration clause.

---

228 F Marks and A Balla, *Guidebook to Insurance Law in Australia,* CCH, North Ryde, NSW, 3rd Edition, 1998, 1503.

229 *Accident Insurance Mutual Ltd v Sullivan* (1986) 4 ANZ Ins Cas 60–748.

230 *Accident Insurance Mutual Ltd v Sullivan* (1986) 4 ANZ Ins Cas 60–748.

231 *East End Real Estate Pty Ltd v CE Heath Casualty & General Insurance Ltd* (1991) 25 NSWLR 400, 403.

6.123 Section 18A Insurance Act 1902 (NSW) provides, in essence, that a contract of insurance may not be avoided because of a misrepresentation or non-disclosure by an insured, unless it was fraudulent or the insured knew or a reasonable person in the insured's circumstances ought to have known, that the statement was material to the insurer in relation to the contract of insurance. The relevance of this provision to this volume is that it negates the effect of 'basis of contract clauses' and any scope for the doctrine of 'constructive materiality.' S18A prevents an insurer from relying on such a basis of contract clause to avoid a contract where the relevant misrepresentation or non-disclosure was not material. S18A clearly requires the court to consider the circumstances of the particular insured. This offers greater protection to insureds who are naive in insurance matters, but arguably offers less protection to, for example, insurance lawyers.

6.124 S18B excludes the operation of certain limitations or exclusions in contracts of insurance applying to the happening of an event or the existence of a circumstance, where the relevant loss was not caused or contributed to by the happening of those events or the existence of those circumstances. Section 18B was intended to allow a court to permit an insured person to remain indemnified in the face of a clause in an insurance contract that specifically excludes or limits the liability of the insurer, where there is no connection between the loss and the event or circumstances triggering an exclusion or limitation.[232]

The definition of scope

6.125 As with s54 of the ICA, issues of scope have exercised the courts in interpreting the NSW Insurance Act. In *HIH Casualty and General Insurance Limited (In Liquidation) v R J Wallace and Ors*,[233] the court held that s18B was concerned with policy limitations or exclusions triggered by particular events or circumstances and not with the underlying scope of cover. The scope of cover does not depend on the happening of events, the occurrence of circumstances or the triggering of anything. In *Westport Insurance Corporation v Gordian Runoff Ltd*[234] the NSW Supreme Court held that the decision of the arbitrators had conflated the scope of cover with the exclusions or limitations, whereas an exclusion or limitation is something that only becomes an issue once the class of business has been determined. An exclusion or limitation explained

> the circumstances where, although a policy issued by the insurer is within the class of business of the reinsurance treaty, the happening of a particular event or the existence of a particular circumstance has the effect of excluding or limiting the reinsurer's obligation to indemnify the insurer for any claims arising under that policy.[235]

Einstein J:

> The grammatical, as well the natural, sense of section 18B(1), read as a whole, is that it is concerned with policy exclusions or limitations, which are triggered by a particular

232 Clayton Utz, 'Include Me Out: Exclusion Clauses, Reinsurance, and Section 18B of the Insurance Act,' 10 October 2011; available at https://www.claytonutz.com/knowledge/2011/october/include-me-out-exclusion-clauses-reinsurance-and-section-18b-of-the-insurance-act.

233 [2006] NSWSC 1150.

234 [2011] HCA 37.

235 [2011] HCA 37.

> event or circumstance, where the loss claimed is causally unrelated to that event or circumstance. The section could not be concerned with the underlying scope of cover. That is because the scope of cover does not depend on the happening of an event or the occurrence of a circumstance. . . . It is qualitatively different from a policy exclusion or limitation.[236]

This is a useful distinction. Einstein found that s18B was concerned with exclusions and limitations as opposed to terms defining agreed scope of cover. On appeal Einstein's judgement was overturned, but restored on appeal to High Court.

The NSW Insurance Act: an assessment of relevance

6.126 The NSW Insurance Act is relevant to this volume not because of the significance of its role in Australian insurance law, but because it provides an example of an alternate approach to the treatment of breaches of insurance warranties and similar terms. Unlike the ICA, which requires an act or omission (s54(6)), the trigger for application of the Insurance Act is a failure to observe or perform a condition of the contract. As we have seen, the approach in the ICA raises unhelpful uncertainties regarding what constitutes an act or omission for the purposes of the ICA.

6.127 Whereas the premise for s54 is whether the act or omission of the insured was capable of causing or contributing to the loss (a 'could have' test in effect), the NSW Insurance Act is based, in the context of s18B, on a requirement that the loss was 'caused or contributed to' by the insured's failure to observe the contract: a more direct causal test, without incorporation of the *possibility* of causation. In most situations, it is argued that this is a preferable approach. However, the ICA in part addresses this potential shortcoming by allowing the insured to recover (and for the insurer to remain liable) in circumstances where the insured shows that no part of the loss was in practice caused or contributed to by the relevant act or omission. Unlike the ICA, the NSW legislation provides no relief for an insured where the insurer has suffered prejudice; neither is there any allowance for proportionality in the NSW legislation in order to allow the court to take account of the degree and extent of causation. These omissions are flaws in the NSW approach and the provisions for prejudice and proportionality incorporated in s54 are to be preferred. Falling short of the abolition of basis clauses, s18A of the NSW legislation provides an effective foil to undue reliance by insurers on basis clauses by preventing an insurer from relying on a basis of contract clause to avoid a contract where the relevant misrepresentation or non-disclosure was not material. The approach requires the court to take account of the individual insured's own knowledge and experience. This approach has much to commend it, although as we shall see, there should be no difficulty with an outright abolition of basis clauses. As with the ICA, we have seen that issues of scope have again been a focus of attention in relation to the NSW legislation. This however is not directly as a result of the provisions of the NSW statute. While we have seen that case law relating to the NSW Act has been useful in articulating what constitutes the scope of a policy, the principle should be clear: any provision dealing with a breach of warranty or other term is only of relevance in circumstances where the matter is within the scope of the policy. If it is

236 [2011] HCA 37.

outside the scope, the insurer should have no liability and there should be no issue for a court to address.

The verdict: an analysis of the effectiveness of s54 as a mechanism for dealing effectively with breaches of warranties and other conditions

6.128 Like Merkin, this author sees the approaches in New Zealand and Australia as a great improvement on the formalistic approach adopted by the common law.[237] In both Australia and New Zealand[238] if the clause is not a risk clause, its enforcement rests upon prejudice. If it is a risk clause, its enforcement rests upon causation.[239] Merkin has described the foundations of s54 as 'the need for a causal link between the assured's breach of contract and the loss and, if there is such a link, reduction of the claim on a proportionate, rather than absolute, basis.'[240] One of the advantages of s54 is that it has the merit of being wide-ranging in its application, applying to any contractual obligation that has 'the effect' of entitling insurers to refuse to pay a claim. However, the Law Commission has observed that s54 'is a complex provision, which has proved difficult to interpret.'[241] Certainly the Australian approach has not been without its critics.[242] In 2001 the Australian Law Reform Commission noted that the 'question concerning categories of act or omission covered by Section 54 has been a matter of some legal controversy.'[243] Nevertheless, consultations undertaken by Cameron and Milne suggested that generally the industry was happy with the operation of s54 and that there was no demand for an amendment to s54 in relation to occurrence policies. Merkin acknowledges there is a possible need to modify the section so that it no longer condones notification of circumstances under a claims made policy where the policy has expired;[244] in the main however Merkin is supportive of s54. By contrast the New Zealand Law Reform Commission regarded s54 as being, in general, 'sweeping and unfocused,' out of sympathy with the habits of insurers and insurance law practitioners, likely to provoke litigation and, ultimately, unlikely to prove judge-proof.[245] Similarly, this author does not believe s54 represents an optimum template for addressing breaches of warranties and similar provisions.

237 R Merkin and O Gurses, 'Insurance Contracts after the Insurance Act 2015' (2016) 132(3) LQR 445.

238 See Chapter 7 for an assessment of the New Zealand approach.

239 R Merkin and O Gurses, 'Insurance Contracts after the Insurance Act 2015' (2016) 132(3) LQR 445.

240 R Merkin, Reforming Insurance Law: Is There a Case for Reverse Transportation? Report for the English and Scottish Law Commissions on the Australian Experience of Insurance Law Reform, para 7.4.

241 The Law Commission Consultation Paper No. 204, Insurance Contract Law: The Business Insured's Duty of Disclosure and the Law of Warranties, June 2012, para 13.14.

242 See for example, Schoombee, 'Antico's Case and Other Recent Decisions on Notification of Claims and Circumstances: Sections 54 and 40 of the Insurance Contracts Act' (1997) 8 Ins LJ 167; Mead, The Effect of Section 54 of the Insurance Contracts Act 1984 and Proposals for Reform, (1997) 9 Ins LJ 1; J Clarke, 'After the Dust Settles on Antico: *FIA v Perry Lives*' (1997) 9 Ins LJ 29; Sutton, 'The High Court Widens the 'Reach' of the Insurance Contracts Act' (1998) 26 *Australian Business Law Review* 57; G Masel, 'Taking Liberties with Claims Made Policies' (2000) 11(2) Ins LJ 104.

243 ALRC Report 91 (2001).

244 R Merkin, Reforming Insurance Law: Is There a Case for Reverse Transportation? Report for the English and Scottish Law Commissions on the Australian Experience of Insurance Law Reform, para 7.20.

245 NZLRC Report Some Insurance Law Problems cited in Irish Law Reform Commission Consultation Paper Insurance Contracts, (LRC CP 65–2011), December 2011, para 5.74.

6.129 A major shortcoming with s54 is that it risks blurring the boundary between the historic flaws that s54 was designed to safeguard against, such as insurance cover being frustrated by drafting devices, particularly in circumstances where a breach of a warranty or other policy term had no causal link with the loss incurred and did not prejudice the insurer's interests, and the limits of cover set by the scope of the policy. As Merkin has observed, the goal is to find a mechanism that distinguishes between terms that define the very risk that is covered by the policy and terms that remove liability in particular circumstances.[246] Merkin argues that the prime merit in the Australian approach is that it 'removes all distinctions between classes of terms and is concerned only with the relationship between the operation of the provision and the loss suffered by the assured.'[247] Certainly this is a significant feather in s54's cap. Additionally, the ability to take account of prejudice suffered by the insurer and to accommodate proportionality when determining causation are excellent features: the omission of such flexibility from the Insurance Act 2015 is regrettable. The difficulty facing the courts however has been striking a balance between achieving the benefits offered on the one hand and ensuring that the sanctity of the scope of cover agreed by the parties is not eroded by s54 on the other. We have seen how the courts have struggled with achieving that balance. It has been argued that the decision in *Highway Hauliers*[248] pushes at the boundary of what is sensible and equitable in terms of an encroachment into matters of scope and opens the door to potential further erosion of the sanctity of the scope of contract. In contrast this text has argued that scope should be sacrosanct and not open to interference in this way from the courts. The structure of s54 means that the boundary between legitimate resort to s54 and the sanctity of scope will always be somewhat blurred and will often require judicial interpretation. Masel has argued that if the courts cannot accommodate a workable distinction, exempting acts and omissions which define or extend the scope of cover from the operation of s54, legislative intervention may provide the only solution.[249] Significantly, the reservations expressed previously in relation to the impact of s54 on matters of scope, were shared by the ALRC itself. In 2001, the ALRC, in its Review of the Marine Insurance Act, rejected s54 as a model for reform of the Marine Insurance Act in these terms: 'In important respects, the practical effect of the operation of s54 is to allow the insured to unilaterally alter the bargain made by the parties, arguably to the extent of fundamentally changing the scope of the insurance.'[250] This is surely evidence enough that s54 should not be used as a template for reform.

6.130 This volume is concerned with the regime in commercial insurance contracts. Interestingly, submissions to the ALRC when reviewing the marine insurance regime in Australia, suggested that the consumer protection provisions in the ICA were generally considered inappropriate for marine insurance, where the interests of the parties in

246 R Merkin, Reforming Insurance Law: Is There a Case for Reverse Transportation? Report for the English and Scottish Law Commissions on the Australian Experience of Insurance Law Reform, para 7.19.

247 R Merkin, Reforming Insurance Law: Is There a Case for Reverse Transportation?; A Report for the English and Scottish Law Commissioners on the Australian Experience of Insurance Law Reform, para 7.20.

248 [2014] HCA 33, 10 September 2014, P12/2014.

249 G Masel, 'Taking Liberties with Claims Made Policies' (2000) 11(2) *Insurance Law Journal* 104, at 111.

250 ALRC 91 Review of the Marine Insurance Act 1909, para 9.120.

retaining flexibility and full freedom of contract should be the paramount consideration.[251] This author supports the implicit criticism of the Insurance Contracts Act as being too rigid and lacking the degree of flexibility and freedom to contract, ideal for commercial insurance.[252]

6.131 Despite the fact it does offer several positive features, in the round, for the reasons discussed previously, s54 is not seen as an optimised template for reform.

251 Submissions to the ALRC referenced in ALRC 91 including P Grieve Submission 6; Law Society of WA Submission 7; K Carruthers Submission 9; Law Council of Australia Submission 10; Insurance Council of Australia Submission 11; MLAANZ Submission 12.

252 P Grieve Submission 6 to the ALRC Review of the Marine Insurance Act 1909.

CHAPTER 7

The law on insurance warranties in New Zealand

Legislative reform of warranties and other provisions

7.1 The Contractual Remedies Act 1979 abolished the right of a contracting party to avoid a contract for misrepresentation, or to terminate a contract for breach, and replaced those remedies with a single remedy of cancellation. This has now been replaced by ss36–40 of the Contract and Commercial Law Act 2017. Subject to express contractual provisions to the contrary (s34), s36(1) of the Act provides that 'a party to a contract may cancel the contract if, by words or conduct, another party (B) repudiates the contract by making it clear that B does not intend to –

(a) perform B's obligations under the contract; or
(b) complete the performance of B's obligations under the contract.'

S37(1) provides a party to a contract may cancel it if –

(a) the party has been induced to enter into it by a misrepresentation, whether innocent or fraudulent, made by or on behalf of another party to the contract; or
(b) a term in the contract is breached by another party to the contract; or
(c) it is clear that a term in the contract will be breached by another party to the contract.

7.2 The right to cancel is constrained to circumstances where the parties have expressly or impliedly agreed that the truth of the representation or, the performance of the term is essential to the cancelling party (s37(2)(a)); or where, inter alia, the effect of the breach would be to, in relation to the cancelling party, make the benefit or burden of the contract substantially different from that represented or contracted for (s37(2)(b)(iii)).

7.3 The question arises whether these provisions are applicable to warranties. Merkin argued in relation to s7 of the previous Contractual Remedies Act that, as the statute referred to situations where a contractual party had an *option* to rescind/treat the contract as discharged, (s7(1) referred to circumstances where a party to a contract '*may* rescind it, or treat it as discharged, for misrepresentation or repudiation or breach'), it could not apply to warranties where a breach *automatically* discharges the insurer from liability.[1] This analysis seems logical and as s40 of the Contract and Commercial Law Act states

1 Merkin and Nicoll, *Colinvaux's Law of Insurance in New Zealand,* Thompson and Reuters NZ, Wellington, 2nd Edition, 2017, para 5.5.8, page 357.

DOI: 10.4324/9781003031734-7

> Sections 36 to 39 have effect in place of the rules of the common law and of equity governing the circumstances in which a party to a contract *may*[2] rescind it, or treat it as discharged, for misrepresentation, repudiation, or breach

it would appear that the same logic would apply. As an alternate it could perhaps be argued that inclusion of a warranty in the insurance contract amounts to the express provision to the contrary for the purposes of s34, with the consequence that it will therefore prevail over ss36–40 of the Act.[3] However this argument, in situations where warranties are included in the contract, but the remedy of automatic discharge from liability is not expressly stated on the face of the contract, seems more questionable. To date the application of the Contract and Commercial Law Act to insurance warranties has not been tested in court.

7.4 Of direct relevance to insurance warranties is the Insurance Law Reform Act 1977. Sections 5 and 6 of the Act remove the right of avoidance for a mis-statement which is not material and not substantially incorrect. (S4 relates to mis-statements in contracts of life insurance.) Specifically ss5 and 6 read as follows:

Section 5 Mis-statements in other contracts of insurance

(1) A contract of insurance shall not be avoided by reason only of any statement made in any proposal or other document on the faith of which the contract was entered into, reinstated, or renewed by the insurer unless the statement –
   (a) was substantially incorrect; and
   (b) was material.
(2) Nothing in this section shall –
   (a) apply in respect of any contract of insurance embodied in a life policy; or
   (b) limit the provisions of sections 4 and 7.

Section 6 Incorrectness and materiality defined

(1) For the purposes of sections 4 and 5, and notwithstanding any admission, term, condition, stipulation, warranty, or proviso in the application or proposal for insurance or in the life policy or contract of insurance, a statement is substantially incorrect only if the difference between what is stated and what is actually correct would have been considered material by a prudent insurer.
(2) For the purposes of sections 4 and 5, and notwithstanding any admission, term, condition, stipulation, warranty, or proviso in the application or proposal for insurance or in the life policy or contract of insurance, a statement is material only if that statement would have influenced the judgment of a prudent insurer in fixing the premium or in determining whether he would have taken or continued the risk upon substantially the same terms.

7.5 Merkin suggests that the clear intention behind ss5 and 6 is to prevent reliance upon present warranties and to treat them as representations that, as such, have to be judged

---

2 Emphasis added.

3 Merkin and Nicoll, *Colinvaux's Law of Insurance in New Zealand,* Thompson and Reuters NZ, Wellington, 2nd Edition, 2017, page 362.

for their effectiveness against the usual tests for misrepresentation at common law. Merkin however argues that, contrary to that intention, a present warranty is not affected by the Act on the grounds that breach of a present warranty has never at common law given a right of avoidance, only a right to treat the risk as never having attached (this is because compliance with a present warranty acts as a condition precedent to the attachment of risk under the policy).[4] This author agrees that this analysis seems sound.

7.6 The courts however have disagreed with Merkin's hypothesis and have applied ss5 and 6 to present warranties. In *Gold Star Insurance Co Ltd v Tegas* the assured made a number of false statements regarding disqualification from driving and convictions. The court held that the insurer was not liable under the policy: the statements made were material and not substantially correct. Importantly the judge held that the basis clause in the policy had been dis-applied by ss5 and 6 of the 1977 Act and that accordingly it was necessary to assess the misrepresentation by reference to ordinary common law principles as codified in the 1977 Act.[5] This decision was followed in *McLeod v SIMU Mutual Assoc*: the assured provided a false answer to a question concerning the criminal convictions of the driver of the vehicle. The court again disregarded the basis clause and assessed the rights of the insurer by reference only to the tests in the 1977 Act.[6] In *Hing v Security & General Insurance Co (NZ) Ltd* the assured proposed to relocate his house and stated in the proposal that haulage would be performed by a particular firm of haulage contractors. The proposal form contained a basis clause. In practice the relocation was undertaken by a combination of a different firm and an inexperienced bulldozer operator. During the removal, part of the house was damaged beyond repair. The court held that the statement in the proposal was both substantially incorrect and material within the meaning of s5 of the 1977 Act.[7] Merkin argues that this was an inappropriate application of s5 as the assured's commitment was at least arguably a continuing warranty.[8] Merkin argues that ss5 and 6 have no application to continuing warranties.[9] He suggests that by its nature a breach of a continuing warranty cannot amount to an incorrect 'misstatement' in a proposal or document on the basis of which the policy is issued, reinstated or renewed within the meaning of ss4 and 5. He further argues that the Contracts and Commercial Law Reform Committee did not refer to continuing or promissory warranties in its report Aspects of Insurance Law (1 July 1975), which led to the enactment of the Insurance Law Reform Act 1977. Borrowdale supports this analysis, arguing that the Act can be 'twisted to cover promissory [continuing] warranties only by uncomfortable linguistic contortions.'[10]

4 Merkin and Nicoll, *Colinvaux's Law of Insurance in New Zealand,* Thompson and Reuters NZ, Wellington, 2nd Edition, 2017, para 5.5.8 page 359.

5 Unreported, 30 September 1986, NZHC.

6 (1987) 4 ANZ Ins Cas 60–784 (HC).

7 (1988) 5 ANZ Ins Cas.

8 Merkin and Nicoll, *Colinvaux's Law of Insurance in New Zealand,* Thompson and Reuters NZ, Wellington, 2nd Edition, 2017, para 5.5.8 page 360.

9 Merkin and Nicoll, *Colinvaux's Law of Insurance in New Zealand,* Thompson and Reuters NZ, Wellington, 2nd Edition, 2017, para 5.5.8 page 360.

10 A Borrowdale, 'Insurance Law Reform Acts in Practice (I)' (1987) NZLJ 30 at 31.

Section 9 of the Insurance Law Reform Act

7.7 S9 of the Insurance Law Reform Act relates to the imposition of time limits on claims made by the assured under contracts of insurance and prevents reliance by an insurer on any contractual claims time limit other than to the extent that prejudice has been suffered.[11] As the section deals exclusively with the claims process, it is not directly relevant to the main subject matter of this book, however it is nevertheless noteworthy for the provision it makes in s9(1)(b) and s9(2) for prejudice suffered by the insurer to be taken into account in terms of evaluating the consequences of a breach by the insured of a term of the contract. As we will see, this is something that is lacking in the Insurance Act 2015, despite being present in both the Australian Insurance Contracts Act and the Insurance Law Reform Act in New Zealand.

The common law before s11 of the Insurance Law Reform Act

7.8 The position relating to continuing warranties may have been altered by s11 of the Insurance Law Reform Act. When recommending the introduction of s11, the Contracts and Commercial Law Reform Committee suggested that as the law stood, an insurer could escape liability in situations where the assured was, for example, run into from behind while his vehicle was un-roadworthy, but the assured had no knowledge of that fact, and there was no causal connection between the breach and the loss incurred. The Committee suggested that 'it is unreasonable for insurers to avoid liability on the grounds that the risk is increased where the loss results from some cause other than circumstances relied on as increasing the risk.'[12]

7.9 In *Trickett v Queensland Insurance Co Ltd*[13] a motor insurance policy was held to be 'suspended' while the vehicle was driven contrary to an exclusion relating to the vehicle being in a damaged or unfit condition. In *Public Trustee v NIMU Insurance Co*[14] in relation to an exclusion specifying driving under the influence of intoxicating liquor, the court held that it was the driving or being in charge of the vehicle while in the defined state or condition in relation to intoxicating liquor which was the exception. It was not necessary to establish a causal linkage between the damage incurred and that condition. The use of the word 'while,' used in conjunction with an 'unsafe condition' exception was purely temporal in meaning. In *Parsons v Farmers Mutual Insurance Assoc*[15] the Court of Appeal approved *Public Trustee v NIMU* where an exception was framed as triggering 'whilst' the relevant condition applies. In *Parsons* the policy included an exclusion from cover whilst the driver was intoxicated. The provision became relevant after the insured was killed when the vehicle he was driving struck a bridge. Although the fact that he was intoxicated was not disputed, there was little evidence to suggest this had contributed to the accident. Nevertheless, the New Zealand Court of Appeal held that the exclusion

11 The full text of s9 of the Insurance Law Reform Act is set out in Appendix 2.

12 NZLRC Contracts and Commercial Law Reform Committee Aspects of Insurance Law (1 July 1975) at [29].

13 [1932] NZLR 1727 (CA).

14 [1967] NZLR 530 (SC).

15 [1972] NZLR 966 (CA).

gave an (*sic*) insurance company a broad means of relieving the company from liability, the underlying consideration being that he who is intoxicated is far more likely to suffer bodily injury by accident than he who is sober. It is clear that the word "whilst" does not import a causative relationship between the state of intoxication and the happening of the event amounting to accident.'[16]

7.10 In *State Insurance General Manager v Harray*[17] the insurer refused to indemnify the insured for damage to the insured motor vehicle, relying upon the exclusion 'whilst [the vehicle was] being driven in an unsafe condition' because on the facts the tyres were badly worn. However, the actual road conditions at time of accident meant that the worn tyres would not have resulted in the car being unsafe. The court held that the exception did not apply as the test of safety was restricted to the specific circumstances applying at the time when the damage was incurred. The court further approved the finding in *Parsons* that the exclusion did not require a causal connection to be established linking the damage to the breach of the condition.

Section 11 of the Insurance Law Reform Act

7.11 In its report, Some Insurance Law Problems,[18] the New Zealand Law Commission indicated that the purpose of s11 was to prevent exclusions being used to exclude liability where the circumstances, and so the increase in risk, existed, but the loss was not attributable to that increase. The Contracts and Commercial Law Reform Committee indicated s11 was introduced as a temporary measure,[19] that the Committee's intention was for s11 to 'tackle the problem of non-causative exemptions.'[20] In its Report Aspects of Insurance Law, the Committee indicated that the long-term answer would be considered in a future report and might involve (1) extending power to the courts to strike out unjust or inequitable provisions or (2) legislating standard forms of contract for the more common classes of insurance.

7.12 Section 11 reads as follows:

Where –

(a) by the provisions of a contract of insurance the circumstances in which the insurer is bound to indemnify the insured against loss are so defined as to exclude or limit the liability of the insurer to indemnify the insured on the happening of certain events or on the existence of certain circumstances; and

(b) in the view of the court or arbitrator determining the claim of the insured the liability of the insurer has been so defined because the happening of such events or the existence of such circumstances was in the view of the insurer likely to increase the risk of such loss occurring,

16 [1972] NZLR 966 at 976, (MacArthur J), citing *Public Trustee v NIMU Insurance Co* [1967] NZLR 530 and *Abraham v Norwich Union Fire Insurance Society Ltd* [1970] NZLR 968.

17 [1974] 1 NZLR 199 (CA).

18 New Zealand Law Commission: Some Insurance Law Problems May 1998 Report 46.

19 Contracts and Commercial Law Reform Committee Aspects of Insurance Law (1 July 1975).

20 Contracts and Commercial Law Reform Committee Aspects of Insurance Law (1 July 1975) at 29 and 30.

> the insured shall not be disentitled to be indemnified by the insurer by reason only of such provisions of the contract of insurance if the insured proves on the balance of probability that the loss in respect of which the insured seeks to be indemnified was not caused or contributed to by the happening of such events or the existence of such circumstances.

7.13 The burden is on the insurer to show that the restriction on cover applies in the circumstances of the case; the burden then shifts to the insured to establish the absence of a causal linkage. If there is no evidence as to what actually happened, s11 cannot be utilised.[21] In summary, s11 applies when: (a) the policy excludes or limits the liability of the insurers to provide an indemnity; (b) the exclusion or limitation applies on the happening of certain events or on the existence of certain circumstances; (c) the clause was present because, in the view of the insurer, the events or circumstances were likely to increase the risk of loss; and (d) the assured proves on the balance of probabilities that the loss was not caused or contributed to by the happening of those events or the existence of such circumstances. Unlike sections 10 and 11 of the Insurance Act 2015, it is not possible to contract out of section 11 of the NZ Insurance Law Reform Act.[22]

7.14 Several cases have considered the application of s11. In *Norwich Winterthur Insurance (New Zealand) Ltd v Hammond*,[23] Heron J held that the insurer had the burden of establishing that the facts fell within the exception and, if successful, the insured must then show that the breach has not caused or contributed to the accident. Another worn tyres and a roadworthy exclusion case, on the facts the insured was successful as the court accepted evidence from an expert witness that the condition of the tyres was not the reason for the accident, but rather that speed and wet conditions alone were the probable cause. In *AA Mutual Insurance Co v Stevens*[24] the insurer refused to indemnify the insured because he had driven contrary to his doctor's instruction. In refusing to provide indemnity, the insurer sought to rely on a condition which provided: 'The insured shall take all reasonable steps to safeguard the insured vehicle and its accessories and spare parts from loss or damage and maintain it in efficient condition.' The Court of Appeal held that the clause referred to the physical condition of the vehicle, not to the health of the driver. To fall within the ambit of s11, the clause or clauses in question must relate to circumstances or events likely to increase the risk of loss:[25] *Hall v FP North Ltd*. In this case the court held that neither the relevant exclusion, nor the endorsement in question, defined events or circumstances that were likely to increase the risk of liability arising in the first place, and as a result they failed to satisfy s11(b).

7.15 S11 has been interpreted as applying in a situation where the insured paid a lesser premium in return for motor vehicle cover, on the basis that it was confined to a named driver, but the insurer was nevertheless required to indemnify for loss caused when the vehicle was in the control of a different driver: *State Insurance Ltd v Lam*.[26] It is suggested

21 *Culham v Lumley General Insurance (New Zealand) Ltd* Unreported, 6 November 2000, NZHC. *Lotus Manufacturing Co Ltd v Sun Alliance Insurance Ltd* (1987) 4 ANZ Ins Cas 60–782; *Teal Electrical Ltd v New Zealand Insurance Ltd* Unreported, 31 July 1990; *Slebos v Antrone Holdings Ltd* [1999] BCL 184.

22 S15 NZ Insurance Law Reform Act.

23 (1985) 3 ANZ Ins Cas 60–637 (HC).

24 [1982] 1 NZLR 349 (CA).

25 (2009) 16 ANZ Ins Cas 61–831 (HC).

26 Unreported, 10 October 1996, CA 159/96.

that this is a questionable decision on the grounds that it is at least arguable that the court should have found the loss to be outside the scope of the policy. In *New Zealand Insurance Co Ltd v Harris*[27] the court held that once it has been established that the facts fell within the relevant exclusion in the policy, determining whether s11 applied was dependent upon a two stage process: (i) establishing whether the insurer's liability had been so defined because the happening of the events or the existence of the circumstances was in the view of the insurer likely to increase the risk of occurrence of the loss; and then (ii) determining, using an objective test, whether the loss in respect of which the insured sought to be indemnified, was caused or contributed to by the happening of the events or the existence of the circumstances. In this case the court held that s11 prevented the insurer from declining liability to indemnify for losses to a tractor from fire that arose during commercial use, notwithstanding that the cover was by its terms confined to private use. The court rejected an argument that 'but for' the breach, the tractor would not have been where it was when the fire occurred: 'In construing a statutory provision of this kind designed for practical application on a day to day basis, refined analysis in terms of metaphysical inquiries into causation should be eschewed.'[28] This author however agrees with Merkin who cautions that a 'but for' test will often be relevant in such cases. For example where the relevant exclusion would prevent the use of the insured item in a situation where the resulting risk of loss, following use, could be shown to be greater.[29] If there is no evidence as to what actually happened, and thus no ability to establish the *absence* of a causal linkage, s11 will be of no assistance to an assured, notwithstanding that the breach of an exclusion clause has been established. For example in *Tweddle v State Insurance Ltd* the insured was unable to show that high winds alone caused the collapse of a building after he had demolished a wall in breach of the policy. As a result he was unable to satisfy the second limb of the s11 test and the insurer was able to escape liability.[30]

7.16 S11 does not seek to excuse pre-contractual statements or failures to disclose.[31] Equally, it has been held not to apply to a statement made by the assured prior to the inception of the contract that has been warranted, because in such a case there is no risk at all.[32] The decision in *Womersley v Peacock*[33] suggests that s11 does not override statutory implied terms, specifically the warranties implied in the Marine Insurance Act 1908. This view was supported in the earlier decision in *Harbour Inn Seafood Ltd v Switzerland General Insurance Ltd*.[34] As a result of s11(b), it is clear that s11 would not affect a clause that requires an insured to give notice of a loss within a given period of time. This is because a failure to give notice could not increase the risk of a loss occurring, as the clause would only apply once a loss had happened. (As we have seen s9 of the ILRA prevents reliance by an insurer on any contractual claims time limit other than to the extent that prejudice has been

27 [1990] 1 NZLR 10 (CA) at 15.

28 *New Zealand Insurance Co Ltd v Harris* [1990] 1 NZLR 10 (CA) at 16.

29 Merkin and Nicoll, *Colinvaux's Law of Insurance in New Zealand,* Thompson and Reuters NZ, Wellington, 2nd Edition, 2017, citing DF Dugdale, 'Insurance Law: Sorting out Section 11' (1992) NZLJ 99 at 101.

30 (1991) 6 ANZ Ins Cas 61–052 (HC).

31 *Sampson v Gold Star Insurance* [1980] 2 NZLR 742; *Kinred v State Insurance General Manager* (1989) 5 ANZ Ins Cas 75–924.

32 *Gold Star Insurance Co Ltd v Tegas* Unreported, 30 September 1986, NZHC.

33 (Unreported) High Court of NZ, Christchurch Registry CP 24/98, 8 September 1999.

34 (1991) 6 ANZ Ins Cas 61–048; although in that case a breach of the warranty of legality by sailing in breach of collision regulations was causative of the loss.

suffered.) As a result, s11 of the Insurance Law Reform Act has a significantly narrower coverage than s54 of the ICA in Australia.

Issues of scope

7.17 S11 applies to exclusions for perils that are otherwise covered by the policy, not to risks that are outside the scope of the policy. In *Barnaby v South British Insurance Co Ltd*[35] a policy on a building excluded liability for 'fault, defect, error or omission in design.' A wall collapsed in bad weather and was found to have been constructed with a defect. The question arose did the policy cover a wall, but excluding the risk of its collapse due to a defect, or did it cover only a wall free of defects?[36] Hardie Boys J observed:

> The key to this section is to be found in the last words of paragraph (b): the section is designed to deal with those kinds of exclusion clauses which provide for circumstances likely to increase the risk of a loss which the policy actually covers ... the section is not designed to deal with exclusion clauses which specify the kind of loss or the quantum of loss to which cover does not apply at all.[37]

In this instance it is submitted that the court's ruling that the facts were outside the scope of the policy is questionable on the grounds that it opens the section up to attempts to circumvent it through drafting semantics. As it happened, on the facts of the case, this distinction would have made no difference to the outcome as there was a causal linkage between the defect and the loss, so the insured would anyway have been unable to avail himself of the dispensation offered by s11.

7.18 In *Hall v FP North Ltd*[38] the case involved the provision of financial advice and a professional indemnity policy covering breach of contract for the provision of professional services. The policy was endorsed against depreciation in value of the recommended investments or for loss 'relating directly or indirectly' to the insolvency of any financial institution or fund manager. Firms in which the adviser suggested the insured invest subsequently went bankrupt. The High Court found that the s11 did not apply because the relevant endorsements were part of the definition of cover, rather than descriptions of events or circumstances that excluded liabilities that would otherwise exist under the policy. This seems a clearer example of a matter that was outside the scope of the policy.

7.19 In *Nelson Forests Ltd v Three Tuis Ltd.*[39] cover was provided for legal liability for accidents 'in connection with' the operation of a lifestyle farm business. There was a fire that arose in connection with tourism activities undertaken on the property by the assured. The insurance company argued that s11 did not apply at all, because the relevant policy limitation (occurrences in connection with farming operations) did not merely limit existing cover, but was more fundamental because it defined the risk that the insurer had agreed to cover in the first place. The court rejected utilisation of s11 on the grounds that the section only applied to exclusions for loss otherwise covered by the policy, while the relevant clause defined the

35 (1980) 1 ANZ Ins Cas 60–401 (HC).

36 R Merkin and O Gurses, 'The Insurance Act 2015: Rebalancing the Interests of Insurer and Assured' (2015) 78(6) *Modern Law Review* 1004–1027.

37 *Barnaby v South British Insurance Co Ltd* (1980) 1 ANZ Ins Cas 60–401 (HC) at 77,008.

38 (2009) 16 ANZ Ins Cas 61–831 (HC).

39 HC Nelson CIV-2010–442–84, 9 December 2010.

risk from the outset in terms restricted to the farming operation (not tourism). It was held that s11 could not operate to give the assured cover for a kind of liability that the insurer had never agreed to cover in the first place, i.e. in relation to non-farming operations. It is submitted that this appears to be a clear case of the matter in question being outside the agreed scope of the policy. In both *Nelson Forests Ltd v Three Tuis Ltd.* and *Hall v FP North Ltd*, the court distinguished between policy terms that defined the kind of risk which the insurer agreed to cover (issues of scope), and policy terms that defined circumstances in which an otherwise covered risk was excluded. As we have seen in dealing with s54 of the Australian Insurance Contracts Act, this distinction is, as also illustrated by *Barnaby*, not always easy to define and can present challenges in distinguishing between clauses that define the kind of risks to be covered in the first place (scope and thus outside/not covered by s11), and those which merely define circumstances in which those covered risks are excluded (i.e. legitimate exclusion clauses which are prima facie caught by s11). However, it is submitted that it is reasonably clear that exclusions that apply temporally (e.g. excluding cover whilst the driver is under the influence) generally (if not always) fall into the category of provisions which define circumstances in which an otherwise covered risk is excluded. The challenge for the courts can be seen by considering that, in *Barnaby*, if the policy had been construed as covering the construction of a wall, then as Merkin suggests, the construction of the wall with a defect would arguably amount to 'the existence of certain circumstances' within the scope of the policy and thus within the section.[40] In reality, the interpretation the court put on the policy was that it defined the risk (and therefore provided cover for) only in relation to buildings that did not contain design defects. Again as already discussed, in *State Insurance Ltd v Lam*,[41] this author believes there is at least an argument that the court should have ruled that s11 did not apply on grounds that the unauthorised usage was outside the scope of the policy. While obviously particular to the circumstances of the NZ legislation, the cases nevertheless illustrate more generally the onus placed on the courts and the legislature to seek to ensure that the intent of legislative reform is not open to being undermined by drafting manipulation.

7.20 In *Price v New Zealand Insurance Ltd*[42] the court ducked the question of whether the limitation of a motor policy to vehicles which had not been modified was a restriction on the class of risk covered, or whether it was an exclusion for a risk which was otherwise covered and which therefore fell within s11. In *Culham v Lumley General Insurance (New Zealand) Ltd*[43] the court held that the unauthorised modification of premises by the assured was not an excluded risk under the definition of the risk, but rather a condition whose breach could be excused under s11. In *Hing v Security & General Insurance Co (NZ) Ltd*, s11 was held to apply to a term in a contractors' all-risks policy that excluded liability in the event of any change in the method of removal work being undertaken.

7.21 Referencing *Barnaby*, Merkin queries if there is any material difference between a defective means of construction and a changed means of construction.[44] Merkin argues

40 Merkin and Nicoll, *Colinvaux's Law of Insurance in New Zealand,* Thompson and Reuters NZ, Wellington, 2nd Edition, 2017, para 5.6.7.

41 (Unreported, 10 October 1996, CA 159/96).

42 Unreported, 25 July 2003, DCNZ.

43 (1985) 4 ANZ Ins Cas 60–696 (HC).

44 Merkin and Nicoll, *Colinvaux's Law of Insurance in New Zealand,* Thompson and Reuters NZ, Wellington, 2nd Edition, 2017, para 5.6.7.

the *Barnaby* approach could be applied to policy terms denying cover to unlicensed or young drivers on the grounds that these would seem to be descriptive of the risk run and not exclusions from cover. This author supports Merkin's assertion, but surprisingly, the point has not been argued.[45] In *Sun Alliance Insurance Ltd v Travel the Earth Ltd*[46] the policy covered the assured while travelling and not while employed overseas. She was injured while recreational skiing after work, when employed as a lift attendant at a Japanese ski resort. S11 was held to be applicable, but the other requirements of s11 were not met because regular access to a hazardous ski field increased the risk of injury. It could be argued that if the policy covered the assured while travelling and not while working, then there was no insurance in place in any period during which the assured was travelling for work. In Merkin's view the relevant provision appeared to have been descriptive of the risk, but the point was not taken. However, it is respectfully submitted that it would be something of a stretch to suggest that the *recreational*[47] skiing which the assured undertook amounted to travel to work. These narrow distinctions might be seen as a fatal flaw in the s11 approach, but issues of scope are always going to be something that will arise in cases involving insurance warranties, exclusion clauses and similar conditions.[48] This volume argues that what is important is that the court retains sufficient discretion to enable it to interpret questions of scope on a case by case basis. Any effective approach to the issue of breaches of insurance warranties/other contractual provisions which enable the insurer to escape liability must contain sufficient flexibility to enable interpretation by the courts: such flexibility should be welcomed as an essential ingredient in an effective solution.[49]

Conditions precedent

7.22 Does s11 apply to conditions precedent? It is important to distinguish between a condition precedent to the validity of the contract, a condition precedent to the attachment of risk and a condition precedent to the insurer's liability. The first must be satisfied in order for there to be a contract. The latter category of condition presupposes a valid contract, but one under which the insurer is not liable until the assured has met the requisite conditions. In the view of this volume, s11 has no application in relation to conditions precedent to the contract. This is because s11 requires there to be a valid contract of insurance.[50] This author submits however that there is no reason why s11 should not apply to conditions precedent to the attachment of a specific risk. Take for example a property policy which contained a condition precedent that the insurer would have no liability for any losses relating to fire under the contract unless a specific specification of sprinkler system were fitted and was operational. Let us suppose that the relevant sprinkler system was not fitted at the date the policy came into effect. It is submitted that such a provision could be held to be a valid condition precedent, but still be subject to s11 should there be a loss which the insured was able to demonstrate was not caused or contributed to by the failure to fit the specified system. It is submitted that the

45 Merkin and Nicoll, *Colinvaux's Law of Insurance in New Zealand,* Thompson and Reuters NZ, Wellington, 2nd Edition, 2017, para 5.6.7, citing *Sun Alliance Insurance Ltd v Travel the Earth Ltd* [1997] DCR 331 (DC).

46 [1997] DCR 331 (DC).

47 Emphasis added.

48 See Chapter 11, Issues: Problems with the Law on Warranties and Potential Solutions for Resolving Them.

49 For details of this volume's recommendations regarding an optimal approach see Chapter 12.

50 Non risk CPs such as those that involve the service of notice of loss on the insurer will fail to meet the requirements of s11(b).

requirement for the sprinkler system meets the needs of s11(a) as the condition is defined to exclude liability in the event the building does not have the specified fire protection system. It is submitted that the requirements of s11(b) would also clearly be met as the requirement for the sprinkler system had been so defined because the absence of the system was, in the view of the insurer, likely to increase the risk of such loss occurring. Assuming this analysis was accepted by the court, the insurer would be liable, notwithstanding the assured's failure to meet the specified requirements. The contrary argument would presumably be that s11 is intended only to apply to exclusion clauses, but it is submitted such a distinction is rather semantic and would simply encourage provisions to be drafted as conditions precedent, rather than an exclusion clause, in order to avoid the reach of s11.

7.23 Again, let us suppose that a property policy for a storage warehouse contains a condition that provides the insurer will have no liability for theft losses unless a particular deadbolt is fitted to the main doors to the warehouse and that this provision is drafted in the form of a condition precedent. The insured fails to fit such a lock and suffers losses through pilfering by a member of staff, the theft occurring during normal working hours when the main door would have been unlocked. It is submitted that in these circumstances the conditions of s11 of the Insurance Law Reform Act have again been met. First it is clear there is a valid contract and it is evident that, regardless of the condition precedent to the insurer's liability for theft losses, the insurer is on risk for non-theft risks. Again the requirements of s11(a) and 11(b) have both been met. It should be relatively easy for the insured to establish the absence of a causal link between the failure to fit the deadbolt and pilfering which occurred during hours when the main door would in any event have not been locked. As a result, there seems no reason, therefore, why the section would not apply. Accordingly the insurer would be liable to meet the losses arising from the pilfering. This position is supported by *T&G Processed Foods v Hawk*[51] where the argument was made that s11 did not apply to conditions precedent. Although the presiding judge did not rule on the point, she indicated she was unimpressed with the argument.

7.24 It is submitted that s11 would normally not apply to a condition precedent to the liability of the insurer where this is a non-risk clause and imposes for example a requirement for the provision of notice to the insurer: this would fail to meet the requirements of s11(b) that the provision had been 'so defined because the happening of such events or the existence of such circumstances was in the view of the insurer likely to increase the risk of such loss occurring.'

Does s11 apply to warranties?

7.25 When introducing the legislation, the New Zealand Minister of Justice stated,

> Clause 11 deals with what are called non-causative exemptions. Insurance policies commonly exclude liability in certain instances. For example, a motor vehicle policy may exclude liability while the vehicle is being driven in an unsafe condition. If the vehicle were hit while stopped at traffic lights, the insurer would be able to avoid liability, even though the unsafe condition had nothing to do with the accident. The clause confines the right to avoid the policy to those instances where the circumstances specified in the exemption contributed to the accident.[52]

51 [2019] NZHC 643.

52 Parliamentary debates House of Representatives 6 July 1977, 1207.

The Contracts and Commercial Law Reform Committee observed 'it is unreasonable for insurers to avoid liability on the grounds that the risk is increased where the loss results from some cause other than circumstances relied on as increasing the risk.'[53]

7.26 Merkin suggests that the Contracts and Commercial Law Reform Committee in proposing the reform that subsequently became s11 of the Insurance Law Reform Act were focused on temporal exclusion clauses. The Committee was of the view that cases such as *State Insurance General Manager v Harray*[54] confirmed the principle that 'whilst' had a temporal and not a causative meaning. Merkin argues that this, coupled with the examples used by the Committee to illustrate its points (mainly relating to consumer motor insurance, (for example a vehicle being driven whilst in an unsafe condition) which have been interpreted as being suspensive in nature), suggests the Committee assumed that the policy would survive a breach. This, he argues, means the section was not intended to apply to warranties, where the insurer's liability ceases automatically on breach without any prospect of reinstatement.[55] However in *Sampson v Goldstar Insurance Company Ltd*[56] Mr Justice Baker held that the section applied to provisions other than temporal exclusions, including conditions subsequent.[57] Merkin suggests that s11 cannot apply to present warranties, because s11 regulates indemnity where there is valid cover in place and breach of a present warranty means a policy never comes on risk as the present warranty acts as a condition precedent to the attachment of risk. In circumstances where the risk does not attach at all this may be logical and is supported by the decision in *Gold Star Insurance Co Ltd v Tegas*. However, such approach sits less comfortably with the courts' application of ss5 and 6 to present warranties such that they be treated as representations, subject to the usual tests for misrepresentation at common law.

7.27 Merkin further argues that s11 will apply to continuous warranties where loss and breach are coterminous. He suggests that where there has been a breach of warranty, but the loss resulted from some other cause, the assured has the ability to argue that the loss would have happened irrespective of the breach of warranty, and thus the circumstances relating to the warranty did not cause or contribute to the loss.[58] He asserts that if the breach and loss are not coterminous, then logically the section should have no application at all. Respectfully, this author rejects this argument.

7.28 It is submitted that there is nothing in s11 which indicates that it was not intended to apply to continuous warranties and that it would be perverse for them to be excluded without such indication, when, in all other respects, they meet the requirements of s11. It surely should not matter that upon a breach of a continuous warranty cover ceases automatically and is not restored. Whether the assured is able to obtain comfort from s11 will depend on his ability to prove, on a balance of probabilities, that the loss was 'not caused or contributed to by the happening of such events or the existence of such circumstances.'

53 NZLRC Contracts and Commercial Law Reform Committee Aspects of Insurance Law (1 July 1975) at [29].

54 [1974] 1 NZLR 199 (CA).

55 Merkin and Nicoll, *Colinvaux's Law of Insurance in New Zealand,* Thompson and Reuters NZ, Wellington, 2nd Edition, 2017.

56 [1980] 2 NZLR 742, 745.

57 1980 1 ANZ Ins Cas 60–043.

58 Merkin and Nicoll, *Colinvaux's Law of Insurance in New Zealand,* Thompson and Reuters NZ, Wellington, 2nd Edition, 2017, para 5.5.8 page 360.

The decision in *Tweddle v State Insurance Ltd*[59] would seem to support this position. In this case s11 was applied to two 'conditions' in a houseowner's policy. The first provision specified that the insurance would 'cease to attach' should the property be changed to increase the risk of loss. The second provided that 'all insurance under this policy shall cease immediately' upon any 'fall or displacement' of the insured property. The assured removed a wall from the property and on the facts, it was clear that this contributed to the property being blown over a cliff in a strong gale. Accordingly the insured was unable to obtain any relief under s11. Although described as conditions, it is likely that both provisions would have been held to be continuous warranties had the issue been argued in court.[60] Although it is unclear from the judgement whether it was argued that the cover came to an end as soon as the wall was removed (and that s11 was accordingly not applicable), it is clear that the court was of the view that s11 *did* apply.

7.29 Merkin seems to assert that it flows from the decision in *Barnaby* that, because a warranty is a method of defining risk, it follows that s11 should have no application to warranties.[61] This author cannot agree with this argument. The decision in *Barnaby*[62] was that the loss was outside the *scope* of the policy, it is argued that it was for this reason that s11 had no application: it is the assertion of this author that this is different from saying that s11 should have no application to warranties because the latter are a mechanism for defining risk. In *New Zealand Insurance Co Ltd v Harris*[63] s11 was applied to a provision that 'warranted' that the insured vehicle would not be let out on hire. Merkin argues that had the point been put to the court, the clause might have been found to be a suspensory provision on the grounds that such 'conditions of use' provisions in motor insurances were normally regarded as suspensory conditions.[64] Merkin asserts that the insurance company clearly regarded the provision as suspensory on the grounds that it was not argued on its behalf that cover ceased immediately when the tractor was let out on hire. Surely it is also possible that this was not argued because it was assumed that s11 *did* apply to continuous warranties? This author asserts that a more compelling argument than that proposed by Merkin might have been to argue that commercial hire of the tractor was outside the *scope* of the policy, as in *Barnaby*. Had the latter argument been successful, the court would have held that s11 had no application, but it would not have established that s11 did not apply to continuous warranties.

7.30 However in *Lobb v Phoenix Assurance Co Ltd*[65] a marine policy on a yacht contained a 'warranty' prohibiting use of the vessel outside New Zealand waters. On the facts the court found that the provision had not been broken, but it seems clear that the court proceeded on the assumption that, had the provision been a warranty and had it been broken, the insurer could have 'avoid[ed] liability on the policy.'[66] In

59 (1991) 6 ANZ Ins Cas 61–052 (HC).

60 Merkin and Nicoll, *Colinvaux's Law of Insurance in New Zealand,* Thompson and Reuters NZ, Wellington, 2nd Edition, 2017, para 5.6.9 (3).

61 Merkin and Nicoll, *Colinvaux's Law of Insurance in New Zealand,* Thompson and Reuters NZ, Wellington, 2nd Edition, 2017, para 5.6.9 (2).

62 *Barnaby v South British Insurance Co Ltd* (1980) 1 ANZ Ins Cas 60–401 (HC).

63 (1990) 1 NZLR 10 (CA).

64 Merkin and Nicoll, *Colinvaux's Law of Insurance in New Zealand,* Thompson and Reuters NZ, Wellington, 2nd Edition, 2017, para 5.6.9 (3).

65 [1988] 1 NZLR 285 CA.

66 [1988] 1 NZLR 285 CA at 288.

Hing v Security & General Insurance Co (NZ) Ltd[67] a contractors' all-risks policy required the insured to use professional contractors to undertake a house removal operation. In practice after commencement, the assured, who had no relevant experience, undertook part of the work. The house was damaged beyond repair. At first instance it was held that the breach was material and, as such, this was sufficient under ss5 and 6 of the Insurance Law Reform Act 1977 to prevent the assured from recovering. In obiter comments, s11 was assumed to apply, but was of no assistance to the assured, given the causal linkage between breach and loss. On appeal s11 received very little attention and this volume suggests that as a result the case is of little direct assistance. The application of s11 to basis clauses was questioned in *Harbour Inn Seafoods Ltd v Switzerland General Insurance Ltd.*[68] Fisher J stated,

> S11 of the Insurance Law Reform Act in its use of the words "in the view of the insurer" is, in my view, inconsistent with promises which become part of the contract, not because of any view of the insurer, but because of the intentions of the legislature.

Similar doubt has been cast on the application of the section to implied warranties: in *Womersley v Peacock*[69] Pankhurst J observed

> exemptions, or warranties, implied by statute were not seemingly considered when s11 was drafted with reference to the circumstances in "a contract of insurance" (s11(a)) and "the view of the insurer" as to increased risk (s11(b)). As a result ... I think it is doubtful whether s 11 can override a statutory warranty.

This author asserts that the implication in both these cases however is that, subject to the carve outs of each particular case, s11 was assumed to apply to continuous warranties.

7.31 Accordingly it is submitted that, while it may be the case that it has not been categorically determined by the courts that s11 applies to continuous warranties, should the position be directly challenged in courts, the likelihood is that s11 would be held to apply to continuous warranties. As such this author disagrees with Merkin when he asserts that s11 only applies to suspensory conditions and not to 'true' warranties.[70] Certainly the view held by this author seems to be supported by several international commentators. In its report ALRC 91, the Australian Law Reform Commission, commenting on the approach adopted to insurance warranties in other jurisdictions, observed that while it was clear that s11 applied to express warranties, there had been obiter suggestions that it does not apply to implied warranties.[71] Again, in its Joint Consultation Report 204 Insurance Contract Law: The Business Insured's Duty of Disclosure and the Law of Warranties, the Law Commission of England and Wales asserted that s11 of the Insurance Law Reform Act 'covers not just warranties but also

67 (1985) 4 ANZ Ins Cas 60–696 (HC).

68 (1991) 6 ANZ Ins Cas 61–048.

69 (Unreported) High Court of NZ, Christchurch Registry CP 24/98, 8 September 1999.

70 Merkin and Nicoll, *Colinvaux's Law of Insurance in New Zealand,* Thompson and Reuters NZ, Wellington, 2nd Edition, 2017, para 5.6.9 (3).

71 ALRC 91 para 9.55; See also 'The Marine Insurance Act Out of Warranty?' Quintin Rares (2013) 27 A&NZ Mar LJ where again the author takes it as a given that s11 applies to warranties.

other terms which have a similar function.'[72] The Law Commission was of the view that the decision in *Norwich Winterthur Insurance (New Zealand) Ltd v Hammond*[73] confirmed that s11 applied to warranties, notwithstanding that some academics had asserted that originally the provision was only attended to apply to definitions of the risk.[74] Note however that the ALRC observed that

> a reading of the Report that led to the passing of the Act suggests that the section was intended to deal with exclusions from cover, not warranties. The prime aim of the section was avowedly to introduce a causal element into exclusions of a temporal nature.[75]

Nevertheless, the Australian Department of Justice opined that in its view s11 applied to warranties: 'the section provides that the insured remains entitled to be indemnified if he or she proves on the balance of probabilities that the loss was not caused or contributed to by the breach of warranty.'[76]

Overseas assessment of s11

7.32 The Australian Law Reform Commission rejected s11 as a model because of its failure to take into account the statistical likelihood factor.[77] For its part, the Irish Law Commission preferred the New Zealand approach to s54 in Australia, believing it to have 'considerable attractiveness ... that it is relatively easier to understand than the Australian provision.'[78] The Irish Commission also preferred the New Zealand approach over that proposed by the Law Commission in England and Wales in 1980, and the latter's proposed causal connection test set out in its 2007 Joint Consultation Paper.[79] The Irish Law Commission believed the New Zealand approach 'struck a reasonable balance insofar as the insured is required to prove that the event did not cause or contribute to the event.'[80] In its report LCCP 204, the Law Commission of England and Wales was rather less enthusiastic, opining that the New Zealand experience 'illustrates the difficulties of distinguishing between terms which define the risk, and those which limit liability in defined circumstances.' The Commission felt that a causal connection test that was suitable for specific warranties about locks, alarms

72 Law Commission of England and Wales Joint Consultation Report 204 Insurance Contract Law: The Business Insured's Duty of Disclosure and the Law of Warranties, para 13.3; available at www.http.scotlaw.gov.uk.

73 (1985) 3 ANZ Ins Cas 60–637 (HC).

74 See discussion in ALRC 20, Insurance Contracts (1982) at para 223. The ALRC suggested that a reading of the Report from the Contracts and Commercial Law Reform Committee (page 15) suggests that the section was intended to deal with exclusions from cover, rather than warranties.

75 ALRC 20 para 223.

76 Australian Justice Dept Terms of Reference for a Review of the Marine Insurance Act 1909 by the ALRC, para 5.38.

77 Insurance Contracts, ALRC 20, December 1982, para 228. The NZ Law Reform Commission had a similar view and observed that the way the section had been interpreted took no account of the extent to which an exclusion might be framed with the statistical likelihood of a particular loss occurring in mind: see further discussion later in this chapter.

78 Law Reform Commission of Ireland, Consultation Paper LRC CP 65–2011, Insurance Contracts, December 201, para 5.77.

79 Law Reform Commission of Ireland, Consultation Paper LRC CP 65–2011, Insurance Contracts, December 201, para 5.77.

80 Law Reform Commission of Ireland, Consultation Paper LRC CP 65–2011, Insurance Contracts, December 201, para 5.77.

or sprinklers 'may not be suitable for terms which defined the nature of the business or the geographical limits of the policy.'[81]

An analysis of the New Zealand approach

7.33 As we have seen, the clear intention behind ss5 and 6 of the Insurance Law Reform Act was to prevent reliance upon present warranties and to treat them as representations, which, as such, have to be judged for their effectiveness against the usual tests for misrepresentation at common law. Putting aside the issue of whether the statute is successful in achieving this goal, this author welcomes and supports this intent. Section 11 of the Act is applicable to any condition in the policy in the nature of an exclusion or limitation on the liability of the insurer to indemnify; in the event of a breach of a warranty that is a condition precedent to the attachment of a specific risk it is submitted that s11 could apply, subject, inter alia, to the assured being able to demonstrate that the loss was not caused or contributed to by the failure to meet the conditions specified for the inception of that risk under the contract. S11 has no application in relation to a condition precedent to the contract coming into effect. Failure to meet the condition precedent would result in there being no contract and as a result s11 would have no application. If (as the courts have interpreted the situation) present warranties were caught by ss5 and 6, this would not, in this author's view, represent a problem.

7.34 This volume shares the observations of the Law Commission of England and Wales that matters of scope sometimes pose difficult challenges, but rejects the implicit suggestion that the New Zealand approach is particularly vulnerable to such challenges. Rather, this author is of the view that questions of scope are issues that (i) should always be borne in mind in assessing breaches of warranties/other conditions where, in the event of breach, the policy purports to provide the insurer with the right to avoid liability; and that (ii) the courts are the right place for such issues to be assessed. Nevertheless, this volume accepts that the interpretation of s11 by the courts has at times seemed harsh on insurers. How can it be right that an assured can drive his vehicle intoxicated, in flagrant breach of both the policy terms and the law, and yet potentially obtain the benefit of insurance cover if the cause of the damage to his vehicle was not linked to the assured's breach? Further we have seen that the section has been interpreted in a way that prevented insurers from declining liability to indemnify for losses to equipment during commercial use when the cover, by its terms, was confined to private use.[82] This author would argue that this must surely be an unjustifiable tilting of the playing field in favour of the insured, as in normal circumstances an insurer would, reflecting the relevant risks inherent in each category of usage, charge a lesser premium for use confined to personal use, compared to a policy that also provides cover for commercial usage. The NZ Law Reform Commission was sympathetic to this view. In its report Some Insurance Law Problems, the NZLRC suggested that the problem with s11 was that the way it had been interpreted took no account of the extent to which an exclusion might be framed with the statistical likelihood of a particular loss occurring

81 The Law Commission Consultation Paper No. 204, Insurance Contract Law; The Business Insured's Duty of Disclosure and the Law of Warranties, June 2012.

82 *New Zealand Insurance Co Ltd v Harris* [1990] 1 NZLR 10.

in mind.[83] The Commission proposed a solution that sought to retain the substance of s11 (which the Commission believed in the main to be operating well), but with additional wording to address the particular issue identified. The revised section would read as follows:

Increased risk exclusions

(1) An insured is not bound by an increased risk exclusion if the insured proves on the balance of probability that the loss in respect of which the insured seeks to be indemnified was not caused or contributed to by the happening of an event or the existence of a circumstance referred to in the increased risk exclusion.
(2) For the purposes of this section, an increased risk exclusion is a provision in a contract of insurance that
    (a) defines the circumstances in which the insurer is bound to indemnify the insured against loss so as to exclude or limit the liability of the insurer to indemnify the insured on the happening of certain events or on the existence of certain circumstances; and
    (b) so defined the liability of the insurer, in the view of the court or arbitrator determining the claim of the insured, because the happening of such events or the existence of such circumstances was in the view of the insurer likely to increase the risk of loss occurring.
(3) a provision is not an increased risk exclusion for the purposes of this section that
    (a) defines the age, identity, qualifications or experience of a driver of a vehicle, a pilot of an aircraft, or an operator of a chattel; or
    (b) defines the geographical area in which a loss must occur if the insurer is to be liable to indemnify the insured; or
    (c) excludes loss that occurs while a vehicle, aircraft, or other chattel is being used for commercial purposes other than those permitted by the contract of insurance.

7.35 The NZLRC indicated that the intention of s11 was to prevent insurers relying on provisions excluding cover in situations of increased risk where the increased risk did not in fact cause the loss. It was argued that it was unfair to insurers, however, to prevent their relying on such provisions where the excluded situation was one where the loss becomes statistically more likely. Subsection (3) was intended to exclude from the operation of the section situations within that category.[84]

7.36 While expressing some sympathy for the concerns expressed by the NZLRC,[85] nevertheless the Law Commission in England and Wales was critical of the proposed reform to s11, on the basis that the proposed list of exceptions in the draft section 11(3) was arbitrary, applying, for example, to a ship where the policy excludes cover whilst in the English

83 New Zealand Law Commission: Some Insurance Law Problems May 1998 Report 4, para 43.

84 New Zealand Law Commission: Some Insurance Law Problems May 1998 Report 4, para C10.

85 'There comes a point where the activity generating the loss is so far removed from the activity covered by the policy that the policy should not apply at all.' The Law Commission Consultation Paper No. 182, Insurance Contract Law: Misrepresentation, Non-Disclosure and Breach of Warranty by the Insured, A Joint Consultation Paper, para 8.35.

Channel, but not where an insurer specified that the ship should retain its classification.[86] This author agrees with this criticism, but nevertheless feels the proposed reform was a step in the right direction. The New Zealand Government's preliminary analysis of the issues identified by the NZ Law Reform Commission concluded that further work was needed. The Government indicated that this work would be considered for inclusion on the Government's work programme, subject to other priorities.

7.37 In 2019 the New Zealand Government established a Review of Insurance Contract Law. The purpose of the Review was to: 'ensure New Zealand's insurance contract law was facilitating insurance markets that work well and enable individuals and businesses to effectively protect themselves against risk.'[87]

7.38 In relation to s11 of the Insurance Law Reform Act, in submissions to the Review, the Government summarised that s11 provided that if a policy exclusion applied in relation to a claim, but the exclusion did not cause or contribute to the loss, the insurer was obliged to accept the claim, for example where a policy excluded cover if the insured vehicle was driven for commercial purpose, where this provision was breached, but the commercial driving of the vehicle did not contribute to the loss as the vehicle was hit by another vehicle while stationary at a stop light. The Government suggested that some circumstances raised a greater statistical likelihood of loss even if they do not cause the loss. For example there was a greater likelihood of loss for commercial vehicles because they tend to be driven more than private vehicles. It was argued that s11 limited insurers' ability to exclude such risks or charge higher prices.[88] Accordingly the Review recommended that it be provided that certain policy exclusions should not be subject to section 11. Specifically it was proposed that the Minister make decisions on the details having regard to the recommendations of the Law Commission – the Government anticipated that was likely to include situations where a vehicle was used for a commercial purpose when this was not permitted by the policy, as well as conditions relating to the qualifications of the driver of a vehicle. It was proposed to introduce a regulation-making power so that regulations could be added such that further types of exclusions not subject to section 11 could be added in due course. At the time of writing it remains to be seen if these initiatives will be pursued by the New Zealand Government. It should be remembered that similar reforms have previously been proposed without legislation subsequently being introduced.[89]

7.39 Notwithstanding the issues identified by the NZLRC in Some Insurance Law Problems, and in the 2019 Review of Insurance Contract Law, it is submitted that the New Zealand approach has much to commend it. The simple causal linkage approach adopted in s11, with the burden on the insured, is welcomed by this author. S11 has no provision for suspension of the insurer's liability, and it can be argued that such provisions are not required

86 The Law Commission Consultation Paper No. 182, Insurance Contract Law: Misrepresentation, Non-Disclosure and Breach of Warranty by the Insured, A Joint Consultation Paper, para 8.37.

87 www.mbie.govt.nz/business-and-employment/business/financial-markets-regulation/insurance-contract-law-review/ Note that in relation to s9 of the Insurance Law Reform Act the Review proposed that s9 be amended such that an insurer under certain types of liability policies could decline a claim if the policyholder notified the claim or the circumstances giving rise to a claim after a defined period after the end of a policy term; but that if the policyholder was not aware of the relevant circumstances until after the end of the policy term, the policyholder should be able to claim under their next policy (if any).

88 www.mbie.govt.nz/business-and-employment/business/financial-markets-regulation/insurance-contract-law-review/ Annex 2.

89 New Zealand Law Commission: Some Insurance Law Problems May 1998 Report 4, para 43.

because, even if the contract provided for suspension, this would seemingly not apply when the conditions of s11 have been met. Nevertheless, this author is of the view that there is merit in an explicit provision, like that in the Insurance Act 2015, which makes it plain that a breach of warranty is henceforth only suspensive in consequence.

7.40 Unlike s9 of the Insurance Law Reform Act, s11 makes no provision for any prejudice suffered by the insurer. In the view of this author, this is a shortcoming. Further, the test for causal linkage in s11 is a modest one: it requires it be shown that the event (breach) did not, on a balance of probabilities, cause or contribute to the loss. On face value if would appear that any contribution toward the loss, however small, would be sufficient to ensure that the insurer escapes liability. It is submitted that an approach that accommodates proportionality, and which thus enables the actual estimated contribution to be measured, would be preferable. Finally this volume questions the rationale for the second element of the s11 conditions:

> in the view of the court or arbitrator determining the claim of the insured the liability of the insurer has been so defined because the happening of such events or the existence of such circumstances was in the view of the insurer likely to increase the risk of such loss occurring.'

7.41 It is not clear to this author why the genesis of a particular provision should be relevant to ensuring an equitable balance between the interests of the insured and insurer. Indeed, it can be argued that it is where conditions have been introduced *without* regard to the likelihood of increased risk, that the insured is in most need of protection. As we shall see, s11 would have failed to provide protection to the insured in *Yorkshire Insurance Co v Campbell*.[90]

7.42 In summary, this volume believes that the New Zealand approach is preferable to that in s54 of the Australian Insurance Contracts Act. Further, the simple causal linkage approach is preferred over the mechanisms in the Insurance Act 2015.[91] Nevertheless, there remains room for improvement. This author believes that the New Zealand solution goes too far in favour of the insured, is scarred by the absence of any account of prejudice or proportionality and, like its Australian counterpart, leaves too much room for uncertainty in relation to matters of scope.

90 [1917] 2 KB 433. Stress testing of the New Zealand approach is undertaken in Chapter 10.

91 See Chapter 9 for a detailed analysis of the Insurance Act.

CHAPTER 8

2014 Law Commission proposals

The Commission's recommendations

8.1 The Commission's Report in 2014 included draft legislation. The key provisions in the draft legislation that are relevant to this volume were clauses 9, 10 and 11. These are set out in full next.

Clause 9

Warranties and representations

(1) This section applies to representations made by the insured in connection with
  (a) a proposed non-consumer insurance contract, or
  (b) a proposed variation to a non-consumer insurance contract.

(2) Such a representation is not capable of being converted into a warranty by means of any provision of the non-consumer insurance contract (or of the terms of the variation), or of any other contract (and whether by declaring the representation to form the basis of the contract or otherwise).

Clause 10

Breach of warranty

(1) Any rule of law that breach of a warranty (express or implied) in a contract of insurance results in the discharge of the insurer's liability under the contract is abolished.

(2) Subject to section 11, an insurer has no liability under a contract of insurance in respect of any loss occurring, or attributable to something happening, after a warranty (express or implied) in the contract has been breached but before the breach has been remedied.

(3) But subsection (2) does not apply if
  (a) because of a change of circumstances, the warranty ceases to be applicable to the circumstances of the contract,
  (b) compliance with the warranty is rendered unlawful by any subsequent law, or
  (c) the insurer waives the breach of warranty.

(4) Subsection (2) does not affect the liability of the insurer in respect of losses occurring, or attributable to something happening
  (a) before the breach of warranty, or
  (b) if the breach can be remedied, after it has been remedied.

DOI: 10.4324/9781003031734-8

(5) For the purposes of this section, a breach of warranty is to be taken as remedied
   (a) in a case falling within subsection (6), if the risk to which the warranty relates later becomes essentially the same as that originally contemplated by the parties,
   (b) in any other case, if the insured ceases to be in breach of the warranty.
(6) A case falls within this subsection if
   (a) the warranty in question requires that by an ascertainable time something is to be done (or not done), or a condition is to be fulfilled, or something is (or is not) to be the case, and
   (b) that requirement is not complied with.
(7) In the Marine Insurance Act 1906
   (a) in section 33 (nature of warranty), in subsection (3), the second sentence is omitted,
   (b) section 34 (when breach of warranty excused) is omitted.

Clause 11

Terms relevant to particular descriptions of loss

(1) This section applies to any term (express or implied) of a contract of insurance compliance with which would tend to reduce the risk of one or more of the following:
   (a) loss of a particular kind,
   (b) loss at a particular location,
   (c) loss at a particular time.
(2) Breach of such a term may not be relied upon by the insurer to exclude, limit or discharge its liability for, respectively:
   (a) loss of a different kind,
   (b) loss at a different location,
   (c) loss at a different time.
(3) This section may apply in addition to section 10.

8.2 The key recommendations of the Commission were as follows:

(i) Clause 9: basis clauses: the Commission proposed that basis of the contract clauses in non-consumer insurance contracts should be of no effect. Representations should not be capable of being converted into warranties by means of a policy term or statement on the proposal form.[1] The Commission recommended that this change should be mandatory: not capable of change by agreement between the parties.[2] This proposal is to be welcomed and is viewed as uncontroversial.
(ii) Clause 10: warranties should become 'suspensive conditions': the Commission recommended that the existing remedy for breach of warranty (automatic discharge

1 Recommendation 22, Law Commission and Scottish Law Commission, Insurance Contract Law: Business Disclosure; Warranties; Insurers' Remedies for Fraudulent Claims; and Late Payment Law Com No 353 / Scot Law Com No 238 Cm 8898 SG/2014/131 July 2014 para 16.3. Available at: http://lawcommission.justice.gov.uk/docs.

2 Recommendation 23, Law Commission and Scottish Law Commission, Insurance Contract Law: Business Disclosure; Warranties; Insurers' Remedies for Fraudulent Claims; and Late Payment Law Com No 353 / Scot Law Com No 238 Cm 8898 SG/2014/131 July 2014 para 16.3. Available at: http://lawcommission.justice.gov.uk/docs.

of the insurer's liability) should be removed. Instead, the insurer's liability should be suspended from the point of the breach of warranty.[3] Accordingly an insurer would not be liable for losses under the policy while the insured was in breach of a warranty, but the insurer's liability would be restored if the breach of warranty were remedied.[4] A breach of warranty would generally be regarded as remedied where the insured ceased to be in breach of it.[5] For time-specific warranties which applied at, or by, an ascertainable time, the Commission proposed that a breach should be regarded as remedied if the risk to which the warranty related later became essentially the same as that originally contemplated by the parties.[6] The Commission proposed that these recommendations apply to both express and implied marine insurance warranties.[7] Crucially, the Commission proposed that an insurer would not be liable for any loss that was 'attributable to something happening' while the breach remained un-remedied.[8] The Commission illustrated the intended operation of this provision with the example of a policy covering the storage of fine wine.[9] In this example the policy included a warranty requiring the wine to be stored 'horizontally in a cool cellar.' In fact, the wine was stored for a period upright in a warm room. The error was discovered, and the policyholder remedied the breach of warranty by placing the bottles into horizontal cool storage. However, as a result of the breach, the corks had been damaged, permanently increasing the risk that the wine would oxidise or otherwise deteriorate. The Commission indicated that although the breach had been 'remedied,' the insurer would not be liable for the loss. This was because the loss was 'attributable to something happening' during the period of breach. In the view of this author this is akin to saying the loss was 'caused by' the breach: causal linkage.

(iii) Clause 11: where a term was designed to reduce the risk of a particular type of loss, or the risk of loss at a particular time or place then, if the insured was in

3 Recommendation 24, Law Commission and Scottish Law Commission, Insurance Contract Law: Business Disclosure; Warranties; Insurers' Remedies for Fraudulent Claims; and Late Payment Law Com No 353 / Scot Law Com No 238 Cm 8898 SG/2014/131 July 2014 para 17.84. Available at: http://lawcommission.justice.gov.uk/docs.

4 Recommendation 25, Law Commission and Scottish Law Commission, Insurance Contract Law: Business Disclosure; Warranties; Insurers' Remedies for Fraudulent Claims; and Late Payment Law Com No 353 / Scot Law Com No 238 Cm 8898 SG/2014/131 July 2014. Available at: http://lawcommission.justice.gov.uk/docs.

5 Paragraph 17.34, Law Commission and Scottish Law Commission, Insurance Contract Law: Business Disclosure; Warranties; Insurers' Remedies for Fraudulent Claims; and Late Payment Law Com No 353 / Scot Law Com No 238 Cm 8898 SG/2014/131 July 2014. Available at: http://lawcommission.justice.gov.uk/docs.

6 Recommendation 26, Law Commission and Scottish Law Commission, Insurance Contract Law: Business Disclosure; Warranties; Insurers' Remedies for Fraudulent Claims; and Late Payment Law Com No 353 / Scot Law Com No 238 Cm 8898 SG/2014/131 July 2014 para 17.84. Available at: http://lawcommission.justice.gov.uk/docs.

7 Recommendation 27, Law Commission and Scottish Law Commission, Insurance Contract Law: Business Disclosure; Warranties; Insurers' Remedies for Fraudulent Claims; and Late Payment Law Com No 353 / Scot Law Com No 238 Cm 8898 SG/2014/131 July 2014 para 17.84. Available at: http://lawcommission.justice.gov.uk/docs.

8 Recommendation 28, Law Commission and Scottish Law Commission, Insurance Contract Law: Business Disclosure; Warranties; Insurers' Remedies for Fraudulent Claims; and Late Payment Law Com No 353 / Scot Law Com No 238 Cm 8898 SG/2014/131 July 2014. Available at: http://lawcommission.justice.gov.uk/docs see also para 15.9 of the same report.

9 Paragraph 17.29 Law Commission and Scottish Law Commission, Insurance Contract Law: Business Disclosure; Warranties; Insurers' Remedies for Fraudulent Claims; and Late Payment Law Com No 353 / Scot Law Com No 238 Cm 8898 SG/2014/131 July 2014. Available at: http://lawcommission.justice.gov.uk/docs.

breach of that term, the insurer would only be able to refuse claims for losses falling within that specific category of risk.[10] For example, where there was a breach of a warranty designed to reduce the risk of damage caused by fire, the insurer's liability under the contract would be suspended only in respect of fire losses. The insurance contract would continue to operate normally in all other ways.[11] The determination of whether a term fell within this definition should *be objectively based on whether compliance with that term would tend to reduce the risk of the occurrence of that category or those categories of loss.*[12] However would all provisions in a policy for a building be caught on the grounds that, by definition, they relate to a particular location? The Commission's Report makes it clear that this additional provision was not confined to warranties and was not intended to apply where a clause went to the entirety of the nature of the risk (such as a requirement that a ship remains in class, or that a vehicle is not used commercially).[13] Crucially the Commission specifically asserted that a causal linkage was not required for the suspension to be effective;[14] rather the Commission indicated the test was intended to simply be a question of whether compliance might usually be thought to reduce the chances of the particular type of loss being suffered.[15] The Commission's intention was that clauses 10 and 11 apply together. This would only be relevant where a given term was found to be a warranty; in this case the insurer's liability under *the contract as a whole*[16] would be suspended until the breach was remedied, *unless*[17] the term was held to fall within the ambit of clause 11, in which case the breach would only suspend the insurer's liability in relation to losses of the relevant type.[18]

---

10 Recommendation 28, Law Commission and Scottish Law Commission, Insurance Contract Law: Business Disclosure; Warranties; Insurers' Remedies for Fraudulent Claims; and Late Payment Law Com No 353 / Scot Law Com No 238 Cm 8898 SG/2014/131 July 2014. Available at: http://lawcommission.justice.gov.uk/docs.

11 Paragraph 17.55 Law Commission and Scottish Law Commission, Insurance Contract Law: Business Disclosure; Warranties; Insurers' Remedies for Fraudulent Claims; and Late Payment Law Com No 353 / Scot Law Com No 238 Cm 8898 SG/2014/131 July 2014. Available at: http://lawcommission.justice.gov.uk/docs.

12 Emphasis added. Recommendation 29, Law Commission and Scottish Law Commission, Insurance Contract Law: Business Disclosure; Warranties; Insurers' Remedies for Fraudulent Claims; and Late Payment Law Com No 353 / Scot Law Com No 238 Cm 8898 SG/2014/131 July 2014. Available at: http://lawcommission.justice.gov.uk/docs.

13 Paragraph 18.4 Law Commission and Scottish Law Commission, Insurance Contract Law: Business Disclosure; Warranties; Insurers' Remedies for Fraudulent Claims; and Late Payment Law Com No 353 / Scot Law Com No 238 Cm 8898 SG/2014/131 July 2014. Available at: http://lawcommission.justice.gov.uk/docs.

14 Para 18.5, Law Commission and Scottish Law Commission, Insurance Contract Law: Business Disclosure; Warranties; Insurers' Remedies for Fraudulent Claims; and Late Payment Law Com No 353 / Scot Law Com No 238 Cm 8898 SG/2014/131 July 2014. Available at: http://lawcommission.justice.gov.uk/docs see also para 15.9 of the same report.

15 Para 18.16, Law Commission and Scottish Law Commission, Insurance Contract Law: Business Disclosure; Warranties; Insurers' Remedies for Fraudulent Claims; and Late Payment Law Com No 353 / Scot Law Com No 238 Cm 8898 SG/2014/131 July 2014. Available at: http://lawcommission.justice.gov.uk/docs see also para 15.9 of the same report.

16 Emphasis added.

17 Emphasis added.

18 Paragraph 18.48 Law Commission and Scottish Law Commission, Insurance Contract Law: Business Disclosure; Warranties; Insurers' Remedies for Fraudulent Claims; and Late Payment Law Com No 353 / Scot Law Com No 238 Cm 8898 SG/2014/131 July 2014. Available at: http://lawcommission.justice.gov.uk/docs.

8.3 The Commission proposed that its recommendations regarding clauses 10 and 11 should be a default scheme: parties should be able to contract out if they wished.[19]

8.4 Contrary to the position it took in 2007, following comments from the insurance industry, the Commission recommended that there should be no statutory right of cancellation: this should be left to the terms of the contract.[20] This author regards this as a mistake: the position would, it is submitted, be improved if the insurer was granted a right to terminate the policy on, say, 14 days' notice. Crucially the Commission was of the view that a causal link between the breach and the ultimate loss should not be required for the suspension of the insurer's liability to be effective.[21]

8.5 The proposal to make a breach of warranty suspensory is to be applauded and guarded welcome is given to the proposal to limit suspension to the category of risk covered where a provision is tailored to a specific class of risk.[22] However it is submitted that the absence of a requirement for a causal linkage between breach and the ultimate loss[23] is a key failing in the proposals. The Commission suggested that the consequences of breach should *not*[24] be considered in light of what had actually happened. Under the Commission's proposals it was not relevant whether or not the breach of the term actually contributed to the loss which had occurred:[25] it was sufficient that the term was relevant to the particular kind, time or place of loss.[26] If that were the case (and the assured was in breach), the insurer would not be liable for the actual loss.

8.6 The Commission's original draft of clause 11 of the Insurance Bill was dropped prior to the Bill being submitted to Parliament on the grounds that its provisions were not without controversy. During the Special Purpose Committee Stage of the Bill a revised clause 11 was submitted and subsequently approved as s11 of the Insurance Act. That provision requires that non-compliance with the relevant term could not have increased the risk of the loss which actually occurred in the circumstances in which it occurred. This revised provision received very little attention during the passage of the Bill through

19 Law Commission and Scottish Law Commission, Insurance Contract Law: Business Disclosure; Warranties; Insurers' Remedies for Fraudulent Claims; and Late Payment Law Com No 353 / Scot Law Com No 238 Cm 8898 SG/2014/131 July 2014 para 18.68, page 204. Available at: http://lawcommission.justice.gov.uk/docs.

20 Paragraph 17.61 Law Commission and Scottish Law Commission, Insurance Contract Law: Business Disclosure; Warranties; Insurers' Remedies for Fraudulent Claims; and Late Payment Law Com No 353 / Scot Law Com No 238 Cm 8898 SG/2014/131 July 2014.

21 Paragraph 18.5 Law Commission and Scottish Law Commission, Insurance Contract Law: Business Disclosure; Warranties; Insurers' Remedies for Fraudulent Claims; and Late Payment Law Com No 353 / Scot Law Com No 238 Cm 8898 SG/2014/131 July 2014. Available at: http://lawcommission.justice.gov.uk/docs.

22 Recommendations 24 through 28, Law Commission and Scottish Law Commission, Insurance Contract Law: Business Disclosure; Warranties; Insurers' Remedies for Fraudulent Claims; and Late Payment Law Com No 353 / Scot Law Com No 238 Cm 8898 SG/2014/131 July 2014. Available at: http://lawcommission.justice.gov.uk/docs.

23 Paragraphs 18.38 to 18.40 Law Commission and Scottish Law Commission, Insurance Contract Law: Business Disclosure; Warranties; Insurers' Remedies for Fraudulent Claims; and Late Payment Law Com No 353 / Scot Law Com No 238 Cm 8898 SG/2014/131 July 2014. Available at: http://lawcommission.justice.gov.uk/docs.

24 Emphasis added.

25 Law Commission and Scottish Law Commission, Insurance Contract Law: Business Disclosure; Warranties; Insurers' Remedies for Fraudulent Claims; and Late Payment Law Com No 353 / Scot Law Com No 238 Cm 8898 SG/2014/131 July 2014 para 18.5. Available at: http://lawcommission.justice.gov.uk/docs.

26 Clause 11 of The Draft Insurance Contracts Bill 2014 submitted by the Commission at the same time as their report and available at http://lawcommission.justice.gov.uk.

Parliament. It is argued that this was unfortunate. The relevant provisions of the Insurance Act as passed are considered further in Chapter 9.

Time specific warranties

8.7 In its report, the Law Commission observed that warranties could be viewed as risk control measures.[27] As a result the Commission argued that when the risk remained the same following the remedying of a breach, it was logical that the insurer should be on risk. Using this logic the Commission proposed that time specific warranties should be treated as 'remedied' if, once the specified requirement had been met (albeit later than specified), the risk was restored to the position it would have been had the breach not taken place.[28] The Commission argued that the correct approach to take when considering whether a time-specific warranty had been remedied was to look at the purpose for which the warranty was inserted in the contract and to ask whether that purpose has been frustrated or whether, due to the actions taken to remedy the breach of warranty, the purpose was, in substance, fulfilled and the risk profile restored to that which the insurer had accepted.[29] Clauses 10(5) and 10(6) contain these provisions.

Relationship between clauses 10 and 11

8.8 The original clause 10(2) was expressly stated to be subject to clause 11 because, in the Commission's words, 'not all warranties are aimed at reducing particular risks.'[30] The Commission's clause 11 had the potential to apply to warranties, but also to other terms that sought to exclude or limit an insurer's liability. Clearly some contract terms, other than warranties, could be caught by clause 11, but not by clause 10. While clause 10 would apply to all warranties, clause 11 would only apply to those provisions (including warranties) aimed at particular risks. The Commission sought to provide examples of warranties that would fall outside of clause 11, highlighting those relating to a policyholder's criminal record, that a ship remains in a given class, those defining the scope of the contract as a whole, (such as a term restricting cover to personal (and not commercial) use) and those with no bearing on risk of loss at all, such as premium payment warranties.[31] As already

27 Paragraph 17.37 Law Commission and Scottish Law Commission, Insurance Contract Law: Business Disclosure; Warranties; Insurers' Remedies for Fraudulent Claims; and Late Payment Law Com No 353 / Scot Law Com No 238 Cm 8898 SG/2014/131 July 2014. Available at: http://lawcommission.justice.gov.uk/docs.

28 Paragraph 17.43 Law Commission and Scottish Law Commission, Insurance Contract Law: Business Disclosure; Warranties; Insurers' Remedies for Fraudulent Claims; and Late Payment Law Com No 353 / Scot Law Com No 238 Cm 8898 SG/2014/131 July 2014. Available at: http://lawcommission.justice.gov.uk/docs. This approach was subsequently replicated in s10(5) of the Insurance Act 2015.

29 Paragraph 17.48 Law Commission and Scottish Law Commission, Insurance Contract Law: Business Disclosure; Warranties; Insurers' Remedies for Fraudulent Claims; and Late Payment Law Com No 353 / Scot Law Com No 238 Cm 8898 SG/2014/131 July 2014. Available at: http://lawcommission.justice.gov.uk/docs.

30 Paragraph 18.44 Law Commission and Scottish Law Commission, Insurance Contract Law: Business Disclosure; Warranties; Insurers' Remedies for Fraudulent Claims; and Late Payment Law Com No 353 / Scot Law Com No 238 Cm 8898 SG/2014/131 July 2014. Available at: http://lawcommission.justice.gov.uk/docs.

31 Paragraph 18.44 Law Commission and Scottish Law Commission, Insurance Contract Law: Business Disclosure; Warranties; Insurers' Remedies for Fraudulent Claims; and Late Payment Law Com No 353 / Scot Law Com No 238 Cm 8898 SG/2014/131 July 2014. Available at: http://lawcommission.justice.gov.uk/docs. This approach was subsequently replicated in s10(5) of the Insurance Act 2015.

indicated, it seems clear (not least because of the words 'subject to clause 11' in clause 10(2), words which, interestingly, were omitted in the version passed into law in the Insurance Act), that a suspension under clause 10 would apply to the whole of the policy unless the provision was caught by clause 11, in which case the suspension would be limited to the particular risk.

8.9 The Commission indicated that it had been influenced by experience in New Zealand and in particular the recommendations (which as we have seen have not yet been implemented) of the New Zealand Law Reform Commission in its report Some Insurance Law Problems (1998) NZLC R46.[32] The Law Commission indicated that it felt the target of the proposed NZ reforms was provisions which 'go to the heart of the risk profile which the insurer is willing to accept, so that any breach of such a provision should allow the insurer to avoid liability.'[33] The Commission felt such provisions[34] would fall outside clause 11. The Commission's objective was to prevent insurers being able to rely on breaches where the type of loss which occurred was not one which compliance with the warranty or condition could have had any chance of preventing: 'The real mischief this recommendation is designed to address is reliance on breach of blatantly irrelevant warranties in order to escape liability for an unconnected loss.'[35]

Causal linkage or particular risk

8.10 Crucially the Commission was of the view (both in relation to its original clause 11 and the Insurance Act as enacted), that a causal link between the breach and the ultimate loss should not be required. As will be seen, it is submitted that this is a significant flaw in the proposals.[36] The Commission accepted that the approach set out in the proposed clause 11 (and indeed that subsequently adopted in the amended version that became s11 of the Insurance Act) posed a new challenge for parties and the courts, but it argued that it was not a challenge that was completely foreign to the courts. The Commission suggested that when assessing the result that compliance would tend to have, whether or not breach of the term actually contributed to the loss which had occurred, was not relevant. It would be sufficient, it argued, that the term was relevant to the particular kind, time or place of loss. If that was the case, the insurer would not be liable for the actual loss. It was argued that the insurer

32 New Zealand Law Commission: Some Insurance Law Problems May 1998 Report 46, pages 28 and 29.

33 Paragraph 18.34 Law Commission and Scottish Law Commission, Insurance Contract Law: Business Disclosure; Warranties; Insurers' Remedies for Fraudulent Claims; and Late Payment Law Com No 353 / Scot Law Com No 238 Cm 8898 SG/2014/131 July 2014. Available at: http://lawcommission.justice.gov.uk/docs.

34 As we have seen, the target of the proposed NZ reforms were provisions which:

(1) Define the age, identity, qualifications or experience of a driver of a vehicle, a pilot of an aircraft, or an operator of a chattel; or

(2) Define the geographical area in which a loss must occur if the insurer is to be liable to indemnify the insured; or

(3) Exclude loss that occurs while a vehicle, aircraft or other chattel is being used for commercial purposes other than those permitted by the contract of insurance.

35 Paragraph 18.20 Law Commission and Scottish Law Commission, Insurance Contract Law: Business Disclosure; Warranties; Insurers' Remedies for Fraudulent Claims; and Late Payment Law Com No 353 / Scot Law Com No 238 Cm 8898 SG/2014/131 July 2014. Available at: http://lawcommission.justice.gov.uk/docs.

36 See Chapter 9.

therefore retained a broader remedy than it would have under a causation test.[37] In an example offered by the Commission, it suggested that a requirement to fit a particular type of lock, if breached, would excuse the insurer for liability, not only for losses arising from theft, but also related events such as arson and vandalism.[38] This volume argues that this illustrates one of the problems with a formulation of the type proposed by the Commission: defining what category of losses *are* covered by a given provision. Is arson or vandalism really in the same category of loss as theft? Admittedly, one of the problems with the alternate causal linkage approach is defining the limits of causation: did the absence of a specified lock on the door to the insured property *cause* the loss occasioned by the burglar accessing the property through a window? It is clear that under the Commission's example it would not matter if the insured's loss arose as a result of the intruder accessing the premises through a window, rather than the door that had not been fitted with the required lock, because the suspension was linked to the *category* of risk and thus the actual *cause* was not relevant.[39] In some circumstances it might be possible successfully to argue a causative linkage on the grounds that the absence of the appropriate security measures on the door may have attracted the attention of the burglar to the property. Alternatively it may also be possible to argue that there was no causal link in such circumstances on the grounds that entry by a window has no causal linkage with an inadequately secured door. Nevertheless, as argued later,[40] the need to appraise the degree of causation arising in any individual situation should not be a bar to utilising a causation approach.

More warranties?

8.11 The Commission acknowledged that, once implemented, the Insurance Act would mean that warranties would have less draconian consequences than a policy provision not drafted as a warranty, but which stated that the insurer's liability would cease in the event of a breach of the term. The Commission argued that, in the light of this, it expected the courts, in circumstances of ambiguity, would seek to classify terms as warranties, even if they were not expressly categorised as such in the policy.[41]

37 Paragraph 18.39 Law Commission and Scottish Law Commission, Insurance Contract Law: Business Disclosure; Warranties; Insurers' Remedies for Fraudulent Claims; and Late Payment Law Com No 353 / Scot Law Com No 238 Cm 8898 SG/2014/131 July 2014. Available at: http://lawcommission.justice.gov.uk/docs.

38 Paragraph 18.40 Law Commission and Scottish Law Commission, Insurance Contract Law: Business Disclosure; Warranties; Insurers' Remedies for Fraudulent Claims; and Late Payment Law Com No 353 / Scot Law Com No 238 Cm 8898 SG/2014/131 July 2014. Available at: http://lawcommission.justice.gov.uk/docs.

39 Emphasis added.

40 See Chapter 12, A Proposed Solution.

41 Paragraph 17.74, Law Commission and Scottish Law Commission, Insurance Contract Law: Business Disclosure; Warranties; Insurers' Remedies for Fraudulent Claims; and Late Payment Law Com No 353 / Scot Law Com No 238 Cm 8898 SG/2014/131 July 2014 para 18.68. Available at: http://lawcommission.justice.gov.uk/docs see also para 15.9 of the same report.

CHAPTER 9

The Insurance Act 2015

An effective reform of the law on warranties and other provisions?

Insurance Act 2015: key provisions

9.1 For the purposes of this volume, the relevant clauses of the Insurance Act 2015 are the following:

Section 9 Warranties and representations

Section 10 Breach of warranty

Section 11 Terms not relevant to the actual loss

Section 16 Contracting out: non-consumer insurance contracts

Section 17 The transparency requirements

Section 9 Warranties and representations

9.2 Section 9 reads as follows:

(1) This section applies to representations made by the insured in connection with –
  (a) a proposed non-consumer insurance contract, or
  (b) a proposed variation to a non-consumer insurance contract.

(2) Such a representation is not capable of being converted into a warranty by means of any provision of the non-consumer insurance contract (or of the terms of the variation), or of any other contract (and whether by declaring the representation to form the basis of the contract or otherwise).[1]

9.3 Section 9 abolishes basis clauses. As discussed elsewhere, this author, like most other commentators, welcomes the abolition of basis clauses, regarding it as a reform that is long overdue. It may be thought that s9 will likely reduce the number of present fact warranties as the section outlaws the automatic 'conversion' of representations into warranties. However, this text doubts this will be the outcome: instead it is suggested additional, separate, warranties will simply be added to the policy by insurers, mirroring provisions that would

1 S9 Insurance Act 2015.

DOI: 10.4324/9781003031734-9

otherwise have been 'converted' into warranties by basis of contract provisions. The Law Commission's Report supports this assertion.[2]

Section 10 Breach of warranty

9.4 S10 of the Insurance Act 2015 reads as follows:

S10(1): Any rule of law that a breach of a warranty (express or implied) in a contract of insurance results in the discharge of the insurer's liability under the contract is abolished.

S10(2): An insurer has no liability under a contract of insurance in respect of any loss occurring, or attributable to something happening, after a warranty (express or implied) in the contract has been breached but before the breach has been remedied.

S10(3) But subsection (2) does not apply if –

- (a) because of a change of circumstances, the warranty ceases to be applicable to the circumstances of the contract,
- (b) compliance with the warranty is rendered unlawful by any subsequent law, or
- (c) the insurer waives the breach of warranty.

S10(4) Subsection (2) does not affect the liability of the insurer in respect of losses occurring, or attributable to something happening –

- (a) before the breach of warranty, or
- (b) if the breach can be remedied, after it has been remedied.

S10(5) For the purposes of this section, a breach of warranty is to be taken as remedied –

- (a) in a case falling within subsection (6), if the risk to which the warranty relates later becomes essentially the same as that originally contemplated by the parties,
- (b) in any other case, if the insured ceases to be in breach of the warranty.

S10(6) A case falls within this subsection if –

- (a) the warranty in question requires that by an ascertainable time something is to be done (or not done), or a condition is to be fulfilled, or something is (or is not) to be the case, and
- (b) that requirement is not complied with.

S10(7) In the Marine Insurance Act 1906 –

- (a) in section 33 (nature of warranty), in subsection (3), the second sentence is omitted,
- (b) section 34 (when breach of warranty excused) is omitted.

9.5 In essence, the impact of s10 is that a breach of warranty cannot be relied upon by the insurer to escape liability, unless the assured was in breach at the time of the loss, or at least at the time of the happening of the event that gave rise to some future loss. The risk is simply suspended during any period of breach. It is submitted that it seems clear as a result of s10(2) ('An insurer has no liability under a contract of insurance') that the suspension applies

2 See in particular para 16.11 Law Commission and Scottish Law Commission, Insurance Contract Law: Business Disclosure; Warranties; Insurers' Remedies for Fraudulent Claims; and Late Payment Law Com No 353 / Scot Law Com No 238 Cm 8898 SG/2014/131 July 2014. Available at: http://lawcommission.justice.gov.uk/docs.

to the whole contract of insurance. As we have seen in the Commission's draft legislation clause 10(2) was stated to be subject to s11. This wording was however dropped from the legislation adopted by Parliament as s10(2). Although s11 can apply *in addition* to s10 (s11(4) refers), s10(2) is no longer *subject* to s11. Under the Commission's original proposals, where a warranty was shown to relate to a particular risk it was clear that the policy would only be suspended in relation to that risk. The reasons for the change in the final version of the Act are not clear and are considered further later in this chapter.

9.6 The Act makes no change to the existing law in relation to the standard of compliance required: it is still the case that a warranty 'must be exactly complied with, whether material to the risk or not.'[3] The effect of s10(2) is that a breach of a warranty by an insured suspends the insurer's liability under the insurance contract from the time of the breach, until such time as the breach is remedied.[4] The insurer will have no liability for anything which occurs, or which is 'attributable to something occurring,' during the period of suspension.[5] The 'attributable ... occurring' wording in s10(2) is intended to cater for the situation in which the loss arises as a result of an event which occurred during the period of suspension, but is not actually suffered until after the breach has been 'remedied.' For example where a vessel enters a prohibited zone and incurs damage there, but the damage does not become apparent until after the vessel has left the prohibited zone (and the breach has therefore prima facie been 'remedied'). While the concept may appear clear, it is argued that the implementation of this section may not be straightforward. As Soyer has indicated, it is likely that to avail himself of the benefit of this provision, an insurer will need to establish a causal linkage between an event occurring during the period of suspension and a loss that arises after cover has been re-instated.[6] Despite the Commission's stated opposition to the concept, causal linkage again appears relevant in the context of s10(4) where the Act confirms that the insurer remains liable in respect of losses occurring, 'or attributable to something happening' before the breach of warranty or after it has been remedied. Soyer asserts that causal linkage is again relevant: if the insurer is to avoid liability after a breach has been remedied he must demonstrate that the risk has acquired new characteristics as a result of the breach and that the loss that results after the breach is remedied is attributable to these new characteristics.[7] Soyer offers the example of a motor insurance policy which contains a warranty indicating that the insured vehicle will not be used in racing competitions. If the insured breaches this condition and, in the following week, an engine breakdown arises then, in order to deny liability, the insurer would be required to prove that 'something happened' during the race which led to the mechanical breakdown after the cover was reinstated. The fact that the insured vehicle took part in a race on its own will not be enough to afford a defence to the insurer under s10(2);[8] a causal link between the events will need to be established. This analysis seems sound. It seems odd that a causal linkage approach should be

3 S33(3) Marine Insurance Act 1906. See also paragraph 85, Explanatory Notes to the Insurance Bill 2014–2015 available at http://http://services.parliament.uk/bills/.

4 S10(2) Insurance Act 2015 available at http://services.parliament.uk/bills/ and Paragraph 86, Explanatory Notes to the Insurance Bill 2014–2015 available at http://services.parliament.uk/bills/.

5 S10(2) Insurance Act 2015.

6 B Soyer, *Warranties in Marine Insurance,* 3rd Edition, Routledge, London, 2017, page 180, para 5.54.

7 B Soyer, *Warranties in Marine Insurance,* 3rd Edition, Routledge, London, 2017, page 180, para 5.54.

8 B Soyer, 'Risk Control Clauses in Insurance Law: Law Reform and the Future' (2016) 75 *Cambridge Law Journal* 109–127.

judged acceptable to establish liability or otherwise of the insurer in s10(2) and 10(4), but is seemingly rejected as an appropriate mechanism elsewhere in the Act.[9] The result is an inconsistent application of causal linkage in the Insurance Act.

9.7 Section 10(4)(b) provides that the insurer will be liable for losses occurring after a breach has been remedied, but acknowledges that some breaches of warranty cannot be remedied.[10] Section 10(5)(b) provides that a warranty will normally be remedied when the assured is no longer in breach.[11] As we have seen, in its report the Law Commission indicated that where the risk, post 'remedy,' is essentially the same as that prior to the breach, the insurer will be liable, even if the loss may not have occurred, save for the breach.[12] For example the insurer will remain liable where a vessel takes a short cut through a prohibited zone but, having exited the latter, is hit by a storm (which it would otherwise not have met) and is lost. This seems reasonable: the risk of this occurring is normally the same post remedy as it was pre-breach. It is also consistent with the common law, which suggests there is no causation as a matter of law in such arbitrary instances.[13]

9.8 Where a warranty requires something to be done by a specific time or date, but that deadline is missed, sections 10(5)(a) and 10(6)(a) and (b) provide that the breach of warranty will be treated as being remedied if the requirement of the warranty is met, albeit late,[14] and provided the risk is essentially the same as that originally contemplated by the parties.[15] This approach, which addresses remedies for breaches that are usually in practice trivial but, as they are time based, in theory could not be remedied, is welcomed. Soyer argues that s10(5) and (6) will require the courts to consider the purpose for which the warranty was inserted into the policy and analyse whether that purpose has been frustrated as a result of the breach which was later remedied.[16] If so, he argues that the insurer's liability for any loss which arises will be avoided. Soyer uses the example of a fishing policy that contains a warranty that the vessel should not be left unoccupied for more than 60 days a year. Suppose the vessel is in fact unoccupied for 75 days, but the assured then 'remedies' the breach by ensuring the vessel is occupied for the remainder of the policy period. As the extended period of non-occupancy has potential risk consequences (it could for example increase the risk of vandalism or theft), and because the commercial purpose of the warranty has arguably been frustrated, Soyer suggests that the breach is not capable of remedy. This seems reasonable; but what if the vessel was unoccupied for 61 days? This volume argues that the courts will need to assess each instance on its facts and reach a conclusion regarding the risk consequences of any breach.

9 Although as will be demonstrated, it appears to have inadvertently crept into s11(3).

10 Section 10(4)(b) Insurance Act 2015 and Paragraph 87, Explanatory Notes to the Insurance Bill 2014–2015 available at http://http://services.parliament.uk/bills/.

11 S10(5)(b) Insurance Act 2015.

12 Paragraph 17.36 Law Commission and Scottish Law Commission, Insurance Contract Law: Business Disclosure; Warranties; Insurers' Remedies for Fraudulent Claims; and Late Payment Law Com No 353 / Scot Law Com No 238 Cm 8898 SG/2014/131 July 2014. Available at: http://lawcommission.justice.gov.uk/docs.

13 See for example *The Estrella* [1977] I LLoyd's Rep 525 and *NV Koninklijke Rotterdamsche Lloyd v Western Steamship Co Ltd (The Empire Jamaica)* [1957] AC 386.

14 Ss10(5)(a) and 10(6)(a) and (b) Insurance Act 2015 available at http://http://services.parliament.uk/bills/ and Paragraph 89, Explanatory Notes to the Insurance Bill 2014–2015 available at http://http://services.parliament.uk/bills/.

15 S10(5)(a) Insurance Act 2015.

16 Soyer, *Warranties in Marine Insurance,* 3rd Edition, Routledge, London, 2017, page 181, para 5.55.

Treatment of conditions precedent

9.9 How are warranties that are also conditions precedent affected by section 10 of the Insurance Act 2015? S10 applies to breaches of warranties and does not differentiate between different types of warranty (for example between 'affirmative' or 'present' warranties and 'future' warranties); as such, it is submitted that it must surely be taken to apply to *all* warranties. A condition precedent by definition requires something to be done (or not done) by an ascertainable time ... often the date at which it is intended the contract will come into effect. Conditions precedent are often expressed as warranties. Merkin and Gurses assert that ss10 and 11 of the Insurance Act 2015 do not apply to conditions precedent.[17] This author respectfully disagrees in relation to s10[18] and submits that there are circumstances in which s10 can apply to conditions precedent. The combination of subsections 10(5)(a) and 10(6) have typically been regarded as applying to situations where, at the time the contract comes into effect, or after the contract has come into effect, there is a time dependent warranty that has not been met. As we have seen in accordance with these two subsections, any breach (e.g. failure to have the inspection carried out by the given date) will be treated as remedied once the condition has been met and provided the risk is essentially the same as that originally contemplated by the parties. As conditions precedent are by definition time dependent, this volume argues that a remedy of a breach of a condition precedent can fall to be considered under ss10(5)(a) and 10(6) and that accordingly for the remedy to take effect (and thus for example, for the contract to come on risk in relation to a given exposure), the risk must be as originally contemplated by the parties. Accordingly it is submitted that somewhat perversely, where a warranty that is a condition precedent is initially not met, a contract may nevertheless subsequently come into effect if the condition precedent is subsequently met *and*[19] the risk to which the warranty/condition precedent relates becomes essentially the same as that originally contemplated by the parties.[20] Were this interpretation not correct, it might be argued that any breach of a warranty that is also a condition precedent could prima facie be caught by s10(5)(b) which has no requirement for the risk to be essentially the same as originally contemplated, only that the insured ceases to be in breach of the warranty; such an outcome could be potentially commercially catastrophic for insurers. This author would however argue that given that any condition precedent by definition has a time dependent element, the insured would still be in breach and that accordingly s10(5)(b) could not apply: the insurer would remain not liable. Soyer does not directly address the question of whether s10(5) can have application to conditions precedent. By implication however he suggests it does not, arguing, for example, that in the case of a policy requiring that a specific type of security alarm be fitted, that, in circumstances where the specified alarm is not installed by the policy commencement date, the policy would be suspended from the outset, without the insured having any possibility of remedying the breach.[21] But this surely cannot be right if, for example, the specified alarm is operational within just a few hours of the deadline. In such circumstances the facts surely fit directly within ss10(5)(a) and 10(6) and the risk to which the warranty relates is essentially 'the same as originally contemplated by the

17 R Merkin and O Gurses, 'The Insurance Act 2015: Rebalancing the Interests of Insurer and Assured' (2015) 78(6) *Modern Law Review* 1004–1027.

18 The application of s11 of the Insurance Act to conditions precedent is considered later in this chapter.

19 Emphasis added.

20 S10(5)(a).

21 Soyer, *Warranties in Marine Insurance,* 3rd Edition, Routledge, London, 2017, page 232–3, para 8.2.

parties.'[22] If there was a substantial delay in fitting the alarm, this could well impact the risk, such that it is no longer the same as that originally contemplated by the parties. In such circumstances the breach would not be capable of remedy.

9.10 In a separate example, Soyer references the situation where a policy contains a warranty that the insured yacht is registered in Australia.[23] Soyer argues that if at the commencement date, the yacht is not registered in Australia, cover will be suspended from the outset, again without the insured having any possibility of remedying the breach. To support this proposition Soyer argues that the breach would result in the insurer never coming on risk as compliance with a warranty of this kind would be viewed as a condition contingent to the attachment of risk; he references the comments of Lord Mansfield in *De Hahn v Hartley*. Lord Mansfield declared:

> A warranty in a policy of insurance is a condition or contingency, and unless that can be performed there is no contract. It is perfectly immaterial for what purpose a warranty is introduced, but, being inserted, the contract does not exist unless it be literally complied with.[24]

9.11 Soyer argues that the contractual analysis would remain the same after the Insurance Act. He suggests that an 'affirmative warranty' assists an underwriter in rating the scope of the proposed insured risk, suggesting the underwriter agrees to take on the risk relying on the contractual undertaking that is the basis of the warranty. Accordingly, Soyer argues, in the event of a breach, the insurer is misled with regard to the nature and extent of the risk and this is the rationale for him not coming on risk at all. But if the yacht were registered in Australia shortly after the contract commencement date, this surely again fits the situation envisaged in s10(5)(a) and (6), which relate to the situation where, following rectification, the risk 'becomes essentially the same as that originally contemplated by the parties.'[25] This author respectfully suggests that Soyer's analysis is not consistent with the wording of the Act and, in particular, s10(5)(a) and (6). Accordingly this volume submits that, in the circumstances described previously, there is no reason to believe section 10(5)(a) and (6) cannot cover warranties that are also conditions precedent. The Law Commissioners seem to agree with this analysis. They use the example of the *De Hahn*[26] case and argue that, when the additional seamen required in order to meet the warranty that the vessel sail with not less than 50 hands came aboard, 'the risk was restored to the state in which the insurer was prepared to accept it'[27] and that accordingly the insurer should at that point come on risk: the Commissioners implicitly acknowledged that the insurer had, prior to that point, not come on risk because of the breach.[28]

22 In accordance with s10(5)(a) of the Insurance Act 2015.

23 Soyer, *Warranties in Marine Insurance,* 3rd Edition, Routledge, London, 2017, page 179, para 5.53.

24 (1786) 1 TR 343 at 345–46.

25 S10(5)(a) Insurance Act 2015.

26 (1786) 1 TR 343.

27 Para 17.45 Law Commission and Scottish Law Commission, Insurance Contract Law: Business Disclosure; Warranties; Insurers' Remedies for Fraudulent Claims; and Late Payment Law Com No 353 / Scot Law Com No 238 Cm 8898 SG/2014/131 July 2014. Available at: http://lawcommission.justice.gov.uk/docs.

28 Para 17.45 Law Commission and Scottish Law Commission, Insurance Contract Law: Business Disclosure; Warranties; Insurers' Remedies for Fraudulent Claims; and Late Payment Law Com No 353 / Scot Law Com No 238 Cm 8898 SG/2014/131 July 2014. Available at: http://lawcommission.justice.gov.uk/docs.

Section 11 Terms not relevant to the actual loss

9.12 S11 of the Insurance Act provides as follows:

S11 Terms not relevant to the actual loss

S11(1): This section applies to a term (express or implied)[29] of a contract of insurance, other than a term defining the risk as a whole, if compliance with it would tend to reduce the risk of one or more of the following –

(a) loss of a particular kind,
(b) loss at a particular location,
(c) loss at a particular time.

S11(2): If a loss occurs, and the term has not been complied with, the insurer may not rely on the non-compliance to exclude, limit or discharge its liability under the contract for the loss if the insured satisfies subsection (3).

S11(3): The insured satisfies this subsection if it shows that the non-compliance with the term could not have increased the risk of the loss which actually occurred in the circumstances in which it occurred.

S11(4): This section may apply in addition to section 10.

Changes to draft provisions

9.13 We have seen that the original clause 11 incorporated in the draft Bill recommended by the Law Commission was dropped prior to the Bill being placed before Parliament on the grounds that it did not have universal support and was therefore too controversial to go through the Special Procedure for Uncontroversial Law Commission Bills under which the Insurance Bill was considered. The format that finally appeared in the Act was proposed during the Special Public Bill Committee consideration of the Bill and in reality received very little debate prior to being passed into law.[30] In the view of this author, this was unfortunate because it has resulted in the revised provision being passed into law without a full analysis of its implications.

9.14 The wording of s11 as enacted contains two main changes from the original Bill that formed part of the Law Commission's report. First, the words 'other than a term defining the risk as a whole' have been added to subsection (1). The intent may have been to ensure that clauses that relate to the scope of cover are not caught; if so, it is submitted that it fails in its objective. Merkin and Gurses argue that the final form of s11 results in three classes of clause: one which defines the risk; one which does not define the risk and relates to loss of a particular kind, at a particular location or at a particular time; and one which does not define the risk and which does not relate to kind, location or time.[31] In the second change, under the original wording the insurer could not rely upon a kind, location or time exclusion where the loss was of a different kind, at a different location or at a different time. This has been replaced by a more general provision referring to the risk of the loss which actually occurred. Merkin and Gurses suggest that the intent here was to create an approach not based on causation. However, this volume would argue that s11(3) sets what amounts,

29 The Insurance Act 2015 leaves the definition of an implied warranty unchanged.

30 See transcript of the Special Public Bill Committee on the Insurance Bill [HL], Committee Stage, 15 December 2014, pages 12–14, available at http://www.parliament.uk.

31 R Merkin and O Gurses, Insurance Contracts after the Insurance Act 2015, (2016) 132(3) LQR 445–469.

in essence, to a causation test: 'if it shows that the non-compliance with the term could not have increased the risk of the loss which actually occurred in the circumstances in which it occurred.'[32]

Does s11 apply to warranties?

9.15 The wording of s10(2), by stating that the insurer has no liability for any loss after the breach of a warranty and before its remedy, implies that there is no recovery whatever the cause of the loss.[33] But s11(4) indicates that s11 (which provides for breaches of certain provisions to be ignored in assessing whether an insured is able to recover) may apply in addition to s10. Further, it is clear from the Law Commission's documents and illustrations that the original intention was to subject s10(2) to s11[34] This apparent dilemma is considered in more detail later in this chapter. Merkin and Gurses argue that it would have been preferable for the Act to do away with warranties as a separate category.[35] In addition they suggest that as the Act leaves the common law definition of warranties in place, it is at least arguable that s11 does not apply to 'true' warranties.[36] They argue that the absence of a definition means the Act leaves in play the description of warranties in *HIH Casualty and General Insurance Co v New Hampshire Insurance Co*[37] where Rix LJ suggested that the characteristics of a warranty were that it went to the root of the transaction, was not only so described (as a warranty), but that the provision bore materially on the risk and that damages would not be an adequate remedy to the insurers for breach. Accordingly Merkin and Gurses argue that 'true' warranties are thus risk-defining and outside s11.[38] This author would argue however that this approach ignores the fact that s11 distinguishes between provisions which define the risk as a whole (which are outside s11) and those (which are within s11) which tend to reduce (and thus by definition, 'define') the risks of loss of a particular kind, at a particular location or at a particular time. Further, the Explanatory Notes to the Act make it clear that s11 is intended to apply to warranties as well as other terms of insurance contracts.[39] The Explanatory Notes also specifically refer to conditions precedent and exclusion clauses as being within the ambit of s11(1), provided those terms relate to a particular type of loss or loss at a particular location or time.[40] These are considered in more detail later in this chapter.

S11 as a constraint on s10

9.16 It is submitted that it seems clear that under s10(2) when a warranty has been breached the insurer's liability is suspended across the whole of the contract of insurance

---

32 S11(3) Insurance Act 2015.

33 S10(2) Insurance Act 2015.

34 See especially Law Com No 353 Insurance Contract Law: Business Disclosure; Warranties; Insurers' Remedies for Fraudulent Claims; and Late Payment at [18.44]. However, as already indicated the wording specifically making cl10(3) subject to cl11 is missing from the Insurance Act as passed into law.

35 R Merkin and O Gurses, 'Insurance Contracts after the Insurance Act 2015' (2016) 132(3) LQR 445–469.

36 R Merkin and O Gurses, 'Insurance Contracts after the Insurance Act 2015' (2016) 132(3) LQR 445–469.

37 [2001] EWCA Civ 735, [2001] 2 Lloyd's Rep 161, [2001] LLR IR 224.

38 R Merkin and O Gurses, 'Insurance Contracts after the Insurance Act 2015' (2016) 132(3) LQR 445–469.

39 Insurance Act 2015 Explanatory Notes, Commentary on Sections, para 92, available at http://www.legislation.gov.uk.

40 Insurance Act 2015 Explanatory Notes, Commentary on Sections, para 94, available at http://www.legislation.gov.uk.

until (and if) the breach is remedied. This is because s10(2) refers to the insurer having '*no liability under a contract of insurance in respect of any loss occurring*, or attributable to something happening, after a warranty (express or implied) in the contract has been breached but before the breach has been remedied.'[41] It has already been argued that s11 is intended to apply to any term of an insurance contract (including warranties), save for those defining the risk as a whole, if compliance with those terms would tend to reduce the risk of loss of a particular kind, at a particular location, or at a particular time (s11(1)). S11(3) however provides that where a breach of such a term remains un-remedied, the insurer is unable to escape liability because of the breach if the insured shows that the breach could not have increased the risk of loss that actually occurred in the circumstances in which it occurred. As s11(4) indicates that s11 can apply in addition to s10, this volume submits that it seems clear that where a breach falls within s11(1), then s11(2) and (3) will act to constrain the ability of the insurer to escape liability, notwithstanding the provisions of s10(2) and as such, when in play, these provisions act as a constraint on s10(2). This view is supported by comments from the Law Commission in its Report: in paragraph 18.45 it stated 'where a warranty does fall within 11(1), then the insurer's liability will be suspended under 10(2) only in respect of losses of the particular kind, or loss at the particular time or location.'[42] While these comments of course referred to the original clause 11, the observations about the manner in which the section will influence s10(2) can, it is submitted, be taken to apply to the revised version of s11.

9.17 The problem with this analysis however is that (i) as we have seen, the original clause 10(2) was prefaced by the words 'subject to s11' but these words were specifically omitted from the version that formed s10 of the Insurance Act and nowhere does the Act say that s10 is subject to s11; and (ii) s11(4) only states that s11 may apply *in addition* to s10; nowhere does it say it takes precedence over s10. Merkin and Gurses observe it is curious that s10(3) does not refer to s11 as an express modification.[43] It is of course perfectly possible to have a warranty that is not complied with (and is thus covered by s10) and which also falls within the ambit of s11. We have seen that under s10 liability is suspended across the contract as a whole until, and if, the breach is remedied (s10(2)). Under s11 where a provision which has been breached relates to a particular risk, the insurer cannot rely on the breach to avoid liability where the insured shows the 'non-compliance could not have increased the risk of loss that actually occurred in the circumstances in which it occurred.'[44] Assuming the insured is able to satisfy the latter requirement, the provisions in s11 are in conflict with s10, yet all the Act says is that s11 may apply *in addition to* s10.[45] Notwithstanding these clear difficulties, this author is, on balance, of the view that a court would hold that in such circumstances s11 does act as a constraint on s10.

9.18 Merkin has sought to argue that while it was the clear intention of the Commission that s11 should apply to warranties, if the Act were to carry through this intent, it is strange that s10(3), which identifies circumstances in which an insurer cannot rely upon

41 Emphasis added.

42 Paragraph 18.45, Law Commission and Scottish Law Commission, Insurance Contract Law: Business Disclosure; Warranties; Insurers' Remedies for Fraudulent Claims; and Late Payment Law Com No 353 / Scot Law Com No 238 Cm 8898 SG/2014/131 July 2014. Available at: http://lawcommission.justice.gov.uk/docs.

43 R Merkin and O Gurses, 'Insurance Contracts after the Insurance Act 2015' (2016) 132(3) LQR 445.

44 S11(3) Insurance Act 2015.

45 S11(4) Insurance Act 2015, emphasis added.

a (un-remedied) breach of warranty to avoid liability, makes no reference to s11.[46] As we have seen, nowhere does the Act specify that s10, and specifically s10(2), is subject to any provisions of s11 and s11(4) simply states that s11 *may*[47] apply in addition to s10. Given this, it is possible, Merkin suggests, to argue that the only way that sections 10 and 11 work together (as envisaged by s11(4)), is for s10 to apply to 'warranties' (presumably 'true' warranties in Merkin's parlance) and for s11 to apply to other contractual terms. If this were the case, s11 would then only apply in addition to s10 in circumstances where s10 has been triggered in relation to a warranty and s11 came into play in relation to some other contractual provision. It is clear however that this was not the intended interaction between these provisions: the Explanatory Notes to s11 of the Act indicate 'Section 11 applies to any warranty or other term which can be seen to relate to a particular type of loss, or the risk of loss at a particular time or in a particular place.'[48] Accordingly this author respectfully rejects Merkin's suggested approach; nevertheless, the possibility of this interpretation provides evidence of the uncertainty surrounding the application of the new provisions.

Non-risk clauses

9.19 It seems clear from the wording of s11 that it was not intended to cover non-risk clauses, such as those relating to the claims procedure. s11 appears only to deal with risk clauses (and indeed only those risk clauses compliance with which would tend to reduce the risk of a particular kind, at a particular location or at a particular time). It makes no provision for, and thus presumably has no application to non-risk clauses such as premium clauses and notice obligations, even where these can provide the insurer with the opportunity to avoid liability under the policy. The only way such clauses are potentially caught by the Insurance Act is if they are expressed as warranties in which case s10 may apply. This volume views this as a further problem with s11.

9.20 However, while this author views this a regrettable omission, he would however stop short of agreeing with Merkin and Gurses who view the failure of the Act to deal with non-risk clauses as one of its greatest weaknesses.[49]

The risk as a whole

9.21 One of the key uncertainties in the interpretation of the Insurance Act is the meaning of the 'risk as a whole' as referenced in s11. For clauses other than those that define the risk as a whole, the Explanatory Notes indicate that the intention of s11 is to prevent an insurer relying on non-compliance with a relevant contractual term except in circumstances where the non-compliance could potentially have had some bearing on the risk of the loss which actually occurred.[50] The Explanatory Notes rather unhelpfully confirm that s11 is not intended to relate to provisions that define the risk as a whole, and in this context the Notes provide as an example clauses that impose a requirement that a

46 R Merkin and O Gurses, 'Insurance Contracts after the Insurance Act 2015' (2016) 132(3) LQR 445–469.

47 Emphasis added.

48 Insurance Act 2015 Explanatory Notes, Commentary on Sections, para 92, available at http://www.legislation.gov.uk.

49 R Merkin and O Gurses, 'Insurance Contracts after the Insurance Act 2015' (2016) 132(3) LQR 445–469.

50 Insurance Act 2015 Explanatory Notes, Commentary on Sections, para 92, available at http://www.legislation.gov.uk.

property or vehicle is not to be used commercially.[51] On this basis, it could surely be argued that a requirement that the vehicle be maintained in a roadworthy condition would also be treated as one defining the risk as a whole (and thus similarly outside the ambit of s11). Does this suggest that the intention was that the risk as a whole was intended to equate to terms which directly or indirectly defined the scope of cover? Soyer appears to hint at such a suggestion.[52] Gurses seems to support this proposition, arguing that if the facts of *De Hahn v Hartley*[53] were to be subjected to the application of the Insurance Act, the question of whether s11 would apply would turn on whether the requirement for 50 members of crew was 'an essential part of the definition of the subject-matter insured.'[54] While that may have been the intent, the wording of the section does not make this clear. Gurses argues that the process identified in Australia in interpreting s54 of the Insurance Contracts Act of 'understanding what the restrictions or limitations are that are inherent in the claim' and which is 'one that involves the construction of the policy'[55] is similar to the process required under s11: one of understanding the essential character of the contract. Gurses suggests that the process would involve the identification of the nature and limits of the risks that are intended to be accepted, paid for and covered. Certainly this author agrees that a scope defining clause is one that defines the risk as a whole; however, it is respectfully suggested that this is not the same as confining the application of the s11 carve out to provisions that define the scope of contract. Gurses asserts that a term that limits the risk to be run describes the risk for the purposes of s11. In this context she references *Farr v Motor Traders' Mutual Insurance Society*,[56] where it was held that the assured's statement described and therefore limited the risk to be run. (In *Farr* as we have seen, the assured warranted that the insured taxi would be driven for only one shift each day. However, for a short time it was driven for two shifts. An accident happened after this practice ceased. It was held that the term was merely descriptive of the risk, so that the insured was entitled to recover for an accident happening at a time when the vehicle was being operated in accordance with the policy.) According to this assessment the insured in *Farr* would be unable to utilise s11, but would benefit under s10 as the breach of warranty had been remedied prior to the loss.[57] Gurses asserts that if the clause relates to some evident aspect of the risk, without which the risk could potentially increase, that is a risk-mitigation clause. The latter she argues would be subject to s11(3).[58]

9.22 Soyer suggests that it would be difficult to persuade a court that a provision which required an insured vessel not to deviate from its specified course (consistent with s46 of the Marine Insurance Act 1906) was a term that defined the risk as a whole. This seems sensible. If a requirement that a vehicle be maintained in a roadworthy condition defines the

51 Insurance Act 2015 Explanatory Notes, Commentary on Sections, para 94, available at http://www.legislation.gov.uk.

52 B Soyer, *Warranties in Marine Insurance,* Routledge, London, 3rd Edition, 2017, page 230–231.

53 (1786) 1 TR 343. See also Stress Testing of the Insurance Act provisions in Chapter 10.

54 O Gurses, 'Section 11 of the Insurance Act 2015: When Does a Term Define the Risk as a Whole in an Insurance Contract? Balancing the Interest of the Assured and Insurer' (2020) 3 J.B.L. 184–201.

55 *Watkins Syndicate 0457 at Lloyd's v Pantaenius Australia Pty Ltd* [2016] FCAFC 150 at [40].

56 [1920] 3 KB 669.

57 O Gurses, 'Section 11 of the Insurance Act 2015: When Does a Term Define the Risk as a Whole in an Insurance Contract? Balancing the Interest of the Assured and Insurer' (2020) 3 J.B.L. 184–201.

58 O Gurses, 'Section 11 of the Insurance Act 2015: When Does a Term Define the Risk as a Whole in an Insurance Contract? Balancing the Interest of the Assured and Insurer' (2020) 3 J.B.L. 184–201.

risk as a whole, how would a requirement that the driver of that vehicle hold a particular driving qualification be treated? Is there an argument for saying this should also be regarded as defining the risk as a whole? In the view of this author, that would be a step too far. What of a requirement in a marine policy that a vessel should always utilise the services of a pilot to navigate into and out of port? For this author, it would be easier to make the case that this is a term that defined the risk as a whole, but there can be no certainty about this. Such examples illustrate the difficulties that are likely to come before the courts as a result of the wording of the section.

9.23 Merkin and Gurses express concern that the Act may result in problems arising in relation to issues of risk definition versus exclusion. They argue that the courts will have to develop some sense as to when a clause defines the risk and when it excludes liability or imposes a condition upon which liability depends.[59] For example they argue that in a motor vehicle policy the outcome may vary depending upon whether the policy defines the risk as driving for private purposes or defines the risk as driving, but with an exclusion for loss incurred while the vehicle is being used for business purposes: they suggest s11 is excluded in the former case, but potentially applicable to the exclusion clause in the latter. If this is right, the danger is that the formulation used in the statute could open the door to attempts to draft around the provisions of Act. Surely it was not the intention that the interpretation of s11 would be down to drafting semantics?

9.24 This author would respectfully argue that the exclusion clause (of the type referenced in Merkin and Gurses' second example) surely also has an impact on defining the risk as a whole, and if so, the logic is surely that such a provision will also be outside the reach of s11, notwithstanding any intention for exclusion clauses to fall within the ambit of the section. As will be seen,[60] it is the position of this author that it is essential for exclusion clauses to be covered by any reform of the law in this area: a failure to do so would, it is submitted, represent a major gap in the effectiveness of the reform.

9.25 It is relatively easy to offer examples that clearly fall within the ambit of s11: for example a requirement in a property policy that a particular form of lock be fitted. The challenge arises in situations that fall on the margin. The Law Commission's own examples again illustrate some of the problems with the s11 approach: a marine seaworthiness warranty or a motor roadworthiness warranty at first sight appear to be provisions defining the risk as a whole. However, the Law Commission argues that s11 would apply and that if there were a breach of the provision, a loss unconnected to seaworthiness or roadworthiness would nevertheless be recoverable.[61]

9.26 The reality is that in many instances an insurer could argue that a particular clause is one that defines the risk as a whole, whereas the insured would argue that the same provision relates to a particular location, time or kind of loss. There is a clear contradiction here as a given clause can, at least arguably, relate to both. For example if the policy relates to a particular property, is it the case that the correct interpretation is that every clause in the policy falls within clause 11(1)(b), because the policy relates to loss at a particular location? This author submits that this is clearly not what was intended. If the policy contains a

59 R Merkin and O Gurses, 'Insurance Contracts after the Insurance Act 2015' (2016) 132(3) LQR 445–469.

60 See Chapter 12.

61 LC Report No 353 Law Com No 353 Insurance Contract Law: Business Disclosure; Warranties; Insurers' Remedies for Fraudulent Claims; and Late Payment.

requirement that a security guard is present 24 hours a day, is this a provision that defines the risk as a whole? Surely it does at least add an element of definition to the *whole* risk and not just part of it. If there was a requirement to post a nightwatchman, the insurer might argue that this defines the risk as a whole, at least for a period of time, but the assured would likely argue that it relates to a particular time: 'night.' The Law Commission, in discussion of the original clause 11, observed that 'breach of a condition that a vessel in port must retain a night watchman would mean suspension of the insurer's liability for losses occurring while the watchman should have been present.'[62] It is clear from the Commission's comments that it envisaged *all* liability under the policy being suspended while the breach continued. It could be argued that, if the consequence of breach is that the insurer's liability is suspended across the policy as a whole, then surely the term must be defining the risk as a whole, albeit only for a period. Does a clause that relates to the risk as a whole, but only for a particular time, fall outside the reach of s11? What constitutes a *particular* time in this context will be a matter of interpretation and inevitably, it is submitted, contention.

9.27 While this text would expect a court to show an inclination to favour the insured, this author submits that the concept of 'defining the risk as a whole' is a flawed one and the lack of clarity surrounding it will inevitably result in considerable uncertainty and litigation. Furthermore, given the potential for different subjective interpretations, there is no guarantee that extensive litigation will provide any greater degree of clarity on the issue.

Exclusion clauses

9.28 As described by MacDonald Eggers QC in *Crowden v QBE Insurance (Europe) Ltd*,[63] an exclusion clause 'is not designed to exclude, restrict or limit a primary liability on the part of the insurer; instead, it is intended to define the risk which the insurer is prepared to accept by way of the insurance contract.' If this definition is to be taken at face value, it would seem that exclusion clauses are outside the reach of s11 of the Insurance Act. Certainly as we have seen, an argument can be made that exclusion clauses assist the definition of the risk as a whole and, as such, should fall outside s11. We have seen that the Law Commission suggested in its Report No 353 that exclusion clauses should fall within the ambit of the original draft clause 11[64] and the Explanatory Notes to the Bill which became the Insurance Act, also suggested that exclusion clauses would fall within the ambit of s11.[65] Gurses asserts that whether an exclusion clause falls within or outside

62 Paragraph 18.4 (2), Law Commission and Scottish Law Commission, Insurance Contract Law: Business Disclosure; Warranties; Insurers' Remedies for Fraudulent Claims; and Late Payment Law Com No 353 / Scot Law Com No 238 Cm 8898 SG/2014/131 July 2014. Available at: http://lawcommission.justice.gov.uk/docs.

63 *Crowden v QBE Insurance (Europe) Ltd* [2018] Lloyd's Rep IR 83 at [60].

64 The Law Commission suggested that exclusion clauses would come under the original draft cl 11 of its draft statute: 'Our recommendation could apply to terms including warranties (including the implied marine warranties), conditions precedent, definitions of risk and exclusion clauses.' Law Commission and Scottish Law Commission, Insurance Contract Law: Business Disclosure; Warranties; Insurers' Remedies for Fraudulent Claims; and Late Payment Law Com No 353 / Scot Law Com No 238 Cm 8898 SG/2014/131 July 2014, para 18.41. Available at: http://lawcommission.justice.gov.uk/docs.

65 Insurance Act 2015 Explanatory Notes, Commentary on Sections, para 95, available at http://www.legislation.gov.uk. The Law Commission suggested that exclusion clauses would come under s11 of the Insurance Act: Law Commission and Scottish Law Commission, Insurance Contract Law: Business Disclosure; Warranties; Insurers' Remedies for Fraudulent Claims; and Late Payment Law Com No 353 / Scot Law Com No 238 Cm 8898 SG/2014/131 July 2014, at A 82. Available at: http://lawcommission.justice.gov.uk/docs.

s11 will depend on its scope and the way that it is expressed in the contract.[66] If it is directly relevant to the scope of the cover, it will be outside the reach of s11. She argues that exclusions on the basis of the geographical areas in which the insurer provides cover fall under this category. In her view a failure to comply with requirements regarding a nightwatchman or a burglar alarm or a sprinkler system would fall within s11. This author would respectfully disagree; it is submitted that, depending on the specific, context the latter could still have the effect of defining the risk as a whole: see the section on Stress Testing the Insurance Act[67] where it is argued that the facts of *Forsakringsaktielselskapet Vesta v Butcher*[68] would fall outside s11.

9.29 What about circumstances where the triggering of an exclusion clause does not require 'non-compliance'? Even if exclusion clauses that suspend liability across the policy are not judged to be provisions which define the risk as a whole (as we have seen, if they do define the risk as a whole then, by virtue of s11(1), they receive no benefit from s11), s11 specifically requires there to have been *non-compliance* with a term of the contract (s11(2)) and many exclusion clauses do not require any form of 'non-compliance' to trigger their operation. Take for example the exclusion clause in *Pantaenius Australia Pty Ltd v Watkins Syndicate 0457 at Lloyd's*.[69] In this instance a marine policy on a yacht contained the following clause: 'All cover provided by the policy will be automatically suspended when your boat clears Australian Customs and Immigration for the purpose of leaving Australian waters and will recommence when it clears Australian Customs and Immigration on return.' It is surely the case that clearance of Australian Customs by the boat would not constitute 'non-compliance' with a term of the policy, but would nevertheless trigger the exclusion clause. In such circumstances the exclusion clause would surely clearly lie outside s11. Merkin and Gurses assert that although in the Insurance Act the question is framed in terms of the assured's conduct, the UK legislation is in effect the same as in s54 of the Insurance Contracts Act in Australia, given that it refers to 'compliance,' i.e. an act or omission.[70] For the reasons given, this author respectfully disagrees with this analysis. As argued previously, this volume believes that on balance exclusion clauses that suspend liability across the whole policy define the risk as a whole and thus should also be excluded from s11. Accordingly, this author submits that, while some exclusion clauses may be caught by s11 of the Act, any exclusion clauses that suspend the liability of the insurer across the contract as a whole, and additionally any which do not require non-compliance with a term of the policy to trigger their operation, will fall outside s11.

Does s11 apply to conditions precedent?

9.30 We have seen how condition precedents that are also warranties are addressed under s10. How are conditions precedent to be treated under s11? Once again, the Explanatory Notes to the Insurance Bill indicated that the intention was that s11 would apply to conditions precedent, provided the other requirements of the section were

66 R Merkin and O Gurses, 'Insurance Contracts after the Insurance Act 2015' (2016) 132(3) LQR 445–469.

67 See Chapter 10.

68 [1989] 1 Lloyd's Rep 331.

69 [2016] FCA 1 The potential treatment of this case under the Insurance Act is discussed in detail in Chapter 10.

70 R Merkin and O Gurses, 'Insurance Contracts after the Insurance Act 2015' (2016) 132(3) LQR 445.

met.[71] Confusingly, the Law Commission in its consultation document Insurance Law: The Business Insured's Duty of Disclosure and the Law of Warranties suggested that its proposals did not cover condition precedents to the attachment of risk.[72] These two positions may, in practice, not be inconsistent. We have seen that in determining whether or not s11 of the Insurance Act is applicable, it does not matter whether a provision is a warranty or not. The first key test (set by s11(1)) is whether the relevant provision is a term that defines the risk as a whole. If it does, s11 has no application.[73] This author submits that if the provision in question is a condition precedent to the attachment of risk across the contract as a whole then, by definition, it is a term which defines the risk as a whole and as such will be outside the reach of s11. As we have seen, if the term is a warranty it may be caught by s10(5) and (6), providing that when the breach (in this instance a failure to comply with the terms of the condition precedent) is remedied/the conditions have been met, the risk is essentially the same as that originally contemplated by the parties.[74] If on the other hand the condition precedent relates only to the attachment of a specific risk (or it is otherwise clear that the term does not define the risk as a whole), then it is submitted that a breach of the term could be caught by s11. If the term that has not been complied with is a condition precedent to the liability of the insurer and has no bearing on risk (such as for example the provision to the insurer of notice of loss[75]), whether across the contract as a whole, or in relation to a specific risk, this is not a provision which, as required by s11(1), would 'tend to reduce the risk' of loss at a particular kind, at a particular location or at a particular time.[76] Such a provision is in essence a non-risk provision and as such would be outside the reach of s11. It is possible however for provisions which are conditions precedent to liability to be risk provisions and therefore potentially to be caught by s11 (providing the provision does not relate to the risk as a whole). Clause 34 of the IHC 2003 is, this author would argue, essentially a condition precedent to the liability of the insurer and yet is not a non-risk clause. In summary the clause requires that if a vessel has been laid up for 180 consecutive days or more, the assured must arrange for an examination by the classification society and for any recommended repairs to be undertaken. Soyer argues that clause 34 is potentially caught by s11[77]; this author would respectfully disagree on the grounds that a provision of this kind is likely one that defines the risk as a whole.

9.31 This author would further respectfully submit that if the provision that has not been complied with is a condition precedent to the attachment of risk across the contract,

71 Insurance Act 2015 Explanatory Notes, Commentary on Sections, para 94, available at http://www.legislation.gov.uk. The Law Commission suggested that some (but not all) condition precedents and exclusion clauses would come under s11 of the Insurance Act: Law Commission and Scottish Law Commission, Insurance Contract Law: Business Disclosure; Warranties; Insurers' Remedies for Fraudulent Claims; and Late Payment Law Com No 353 / Scot Law Com No 238 Cm 8898 SG/2014/131 July 2014, at A 82. Available at: http://lawcommission.justice.gov.uk/docs.

72 This comment also applied to s10 of the Bill (as it was at that stage). The Law Commission Consultation Paper No. 204 and The Scottish Law Commission Discussion Paper No. 155 Insurance Contract Law: The Business Insured's Duty of Disclosure and the Law of Warranties, A Joint Consultation Paper, para 16.24.

73 S11(1) Insurance Act 2015.

74 S10(5) and (6) Insurance Act 2015.

75 For example clause 43.1 of IHC 2003 is a condition of this kind: it requires the assured to give notice to the lead underwriter(s) as soon as possible in the event of an accident or loss which may result in a claim under the policy.

76 S11(1) Insurance Act 2015 refers.

77 B Soyer, *Warranties in Marine Insurance*, Routledge, London, 3rd Edition, 2017, page 46.

it is anyway at least arguable that there is no contract of insurance as required by s11(1). While, as Gurses points out,[78] a failure to meet the terms of a condition precedent to the attachment of risk does not, of itself, affect the validity of the contract, is what remains a contract *of insurance* as required by s11(1)? The fact that in such circumstances any premium that has been paid may be liable to be refunded might seem to support the proposition that there is not.[79] Of course the same argument might be deployed to suggest that s10 does not therefore apply to breaches of warranties that are also conditions precedent; however, in this instance it is submitted that s10(5) and (6) make it clear that the section will have application where, when the specified conditions of the warranty are met, the risk remains essentially the same as that originally contemplated.

9.32 Even if a condition precedent to the attachment of risk (across the contract) did *not* define the risk as a whole, it is submitted that there is anyway a further argument for s11 having no application. This author would argue that it would be bizarre if s11 enabled the non-compliance with such conditions precedent to be ignored if (but only if) the conditions of s11(3) are met: this would surely challenge the whole rationale for conditions precedent as well as the basis on which they operate. Putting it another way, if s11 were to apply to such a condition precedent, it would be impossible for the parties to know whether a given policy was on foot or not until (and if) a loss had been incurred. Even then, the determination of whether the policy was on foot would depend on the nature of the loss incurred: it would be deemed to be on foot only if the insured was able to demonstrate that the non-compliance could not have 'increased the risk of the loss which actually occurred in the circumstances in which it occurred.'[80] How can it be that the determination of whether or not a contract is on foot be based on a post hoc analysis of whether or not a given non-compliance could have increased the risk of a given (but currently unknown) loss? Surely such an approach would represent a completely untenable and intolerable commercial position for all parties? It is surely a fundamental commercial necessity that the parties are able to determine from the outset whether insurance is in place or not. Determination of whether a contract is on risk cannot turn on completely unpredictable post-contract events. While a similar argument could in theory be made in relation to a condition precedent that related to the attachment of a specific risk, this author is satisfied that it is easier to make the case that the statute was intended to apply to such circumstances.

9.33 As we have seen, as s11 only applies to risk clauses, it would have no application to conditions precedent relating to the claims process. This, it is submitted, is another significant omission, unlike in New Zealand where s9 of the Insurance Law Reform Act permits forgiveness of non-compliance by the assured with time limits in the claim process, provided such non-compliance does not prejudice the insurer.[81] As Merkin and Gurses point out, under English Law a perfectly reasonable claim can be defeated by the failure

78 O Gurses, 'Section 11 of the Insurance Act 2015: When Does a Term Define the Risk as a Whole in an Insurance Contract? Balancing the Interest of the Assured and Insurer' (2020) 3 J.B.L. 184–201.

79 See s84(1) and (2) of the Marine Insurance Act 1906.

80 S11(3) Insurance Act 2015.

81 See Chapter 7. S54(1) of the Australian Insurance Contracts Act makes a similar provision for prejudice to be taken into account.

to observe the terms of a condition precedent (to liability), notwithstanding that the non-compliance was trivial and inconsequential so far as the insurer was concerned.[82]

Causal linkage?

9.34 In circumstances where a relevant term has not been complied with and is otherwise within s11, the Explanatory Notes confirm that an insurer will be unable to rely on the breach as a reason for avoiding or limiting liability if the insured shows that the non-compliance could not have increased the risk of the loss which actually occurred in the circumstances in which it occurred. This of course adds little to the language used in the statute.[83] In order to seek to illustrate the point, the Explanatory Notes use the example of a property that has been damaged by flooding. The Notes indicate that it would be expected that an insured could show that a failure to comply with a warranty (or other condition) to use a specified type of lock on a window could not have increased the risk of loss from flooding. Accordingly the insurer would be obliged, under s11, to pay out on the flood claim, notwithstanding the insured's breach of the lock provision.[84] This looks like a causation test. Merkin and Gurses provide an example of where the wording of 11(3) may part from a standard causation test: a motor vehicle policy excludes liability whilst the vehicle is being driven by a learner driver. The vehicle is driven by a learner who crashes, having passed out while driving. They argue that the fact that the vehicle was being driven by a non-qualified driver may have increased the chances of the loss that actually occurred (crash), but not the chances of a loss in the circumstances in which it occurred.[85] We have seen that in its final report the Law Commission deliberately sought to move away from the concept of causation or causal linkage in determining liability for breaches of insurance conditions. In line with the Law Commission's final position, the Explanatory Notes indicate that a direct causal link between the breach and the ultimate loss is not required. The Notes stress that the relevant test is *not*[86] whether the non-compliance actually caused or contributed to the loss that has been suffered.[87] This volume argues that in practice this is at best a pedantic distinction and that in the vast majority of cases[88] s11(3) in practice represents a causal linkage formulae inadvertently (as a result of it being incorporated into the draft Bill at a very late stage) admitted through the back door. Merkin and Gurses would appear to hold a similar view.[89] They argue that it was probable that the Commissioners intended that the test would be not straight causal, but whether non-compliance with the term could have increased the risk in the circumstances that the loss occurred. To achieve this they argue that it would have

82 R Merkin and O Gurses, 'The Insurance Act 2015: Rebalancing the Interests of Insurer and Assured' (2015) 78(6) *Modern Law Review* 1004–1027.

83 S11(3) Insurance Act 2015.

84 Explanatory Notes to the Insurance Bill para 95.

85 R Merkin and O Gurses, Insurance Contracts after the Insurance Act 2015, (2016) 132(3) LQR 445.

86 Emphasis added.

87 Explanatory Notes to the Insurance Bill para 96.

88 An exception is discussed at para 8.10.

89 R Merkin and O Gurses, 'The Insurance Act 2015: Rebalancing the Interests of Insurer and Assured' (2015) 78(6) *Modern Law Review* 1004–1027.

been sensible to delete the words 'in the circumstances' from s11(3).[90] Soyer agrees with this author that it is very likely that s11 will re-introduce causation via the back door.[91]

Potential problems with s11

9.35 Some of the problems likely to arise as a result of s11 can be illustrated by considering the facts of *Hibbert v Pigou*,[92] where the policy included a warranty that the vessel should sail in convoy. The vessel failed to do so and was lost in a storm. As the warranty remained un-remedied at the time of loss, the insured would be unable to rely on s10.[93] Under s11, this author suggests that the most likely interpretation would be that the warranty applied to the risk as a whole and not to a particular kind, location or time. If this was upheld, s11 would not apply and the outcome would be that the insurer would be able to avoid the contract, notwithstanding that there was clearly no causal linkage between the breach and loss. However, this volume also submits that it would be perfectly possible to argue that the provision could be taken as referring to a particular risk, loss by enemy action, in which case the insured *would* be able to claim, providing he was able to establish that non-compliance did not increase the risk of loss that actually occurred (loss of the ship) in the circumstances in which it occurred (as a result of a storm). The insured would surely be able to satisfy this test. If there had been a warranty that the vessel be equipped with particular defensive measures (e.g. some particular weaponry), rather than the more general requirement that the vessel travel in convoy and the assured failed to ensure the equipment was installed and the vessel lost in a storm, then the likelihood is again that the insured would be able to claim, but in this instance the case (that the requirement related to a particular risk) would be easier for the insured to argue. This volume fails to see the logic for the outcome turning on such imprecise and ultimately subjective definitional distinctions.

9.36 Again suppose the policy were for a fleet of trucks and required that they be fitted with particular satellite navigation systems, providing that failure to do so released the insurer from liability under the policy. It is hard to see that this requirement applies to either a loss of a particular kind (this text would argue that it is difficult to see how a navigational system goes to reducing a risk for which the insurer may be liable under the policy), or at a particular location or at a particular time; accordingly this author submits that this presumably means that it applies to the risk as a whole. If this is correct, a breach by the insured of this provision will mean that, assuming the breach is un-remedied at the time of loss, the insured is unable to claim under s11 for a loss arising from an unrelated loss such as theft or fire. If on the other hand the provision is held to be a non-risk defining term, s11 will anyway have no application and will again offer no assistance to the assured. It is arguable that the same situation could apply to a range of minor, but general, provisions of this kind where it may be difficult to single out the individual/particular risks (but assuming the relevant provision *is* a risk provision) to which they apply. Thus, perversely s11 would not apply and the insurer would be able to escape liability as the insured would be unable to

90 R Merkin and O Gurses, 'Insurance Contracts after the Insurance Act 2015' (2016) 132(3) LQR 445.

91 Soyer, 'Risk Control Clauses in Insurance Law: Law Reform and the Future' (2016) 75 *Cambridge Law Journal* 109–127.

92 (1783) 3 Doug KB 213.

93 S10(2) Insurance Act 2015.

avail himself of the exception in s11(3), notwithstanding that the failure to comply related to a relatively minor provision. This volume submits that such an outcome surely flies in the face of the general intent of the provisions of the Insurance Act 2015 in this area and demonstrates a further fragility in the statute's provisions.

9.37 Merkin[94] gives the example of a driver who is over the drink drive limit and is hit from behind while waiting at traffic lights; Merkin argues that under the Insurance Act 2015 as the test is 'the non-compliance with the term could not have increased the risk of the loss which actually occurred in the circumstances in which it occurred'[95] and that this appears to have been satisfied, the assured's claim would likely be allowed to proceed. This author not only believes this would be regrettable were it the case, but also respectfully suggests that an alternate interpretation is more likely. If there were no specific warranty in relation to a prohibition on drink driving under the policy (or other similar provision), s10 would have no application. (If s10 were applicable then, subject to s11 not also being applicable, the insured would be unable to claim as the policy as a whole would be suspended while the breach remained un-remedied.[96]) The next question is whether s11 applies. If there is a provision that forbids drink driving (either specifically or indirectly through a general provision requiring the policy holder to adhere to motoring laws etc.), it is clear the assured is in breach. (In the unlikely event that there was no such provision, s11 would have no application as there would have been no breach.) This volume suggests that such a prohibition, given the potential implications of breach are wide-ranging, would be viewed as a term which defined the risk as a whole and which thus fell outside the reach of s11. Accordingly the assured would be unable to claim under s11. Even if this is not correct, this text suggests that the assured would anyway not be able to satisfy the test in s11(3) that breach of the term 'could not have increased the risk of the loss that actually occurred in the circumstances in which it occurred.'[97] This is because it is perfectly possible for the driver's intoxicated state to have contributed to the loss. This turns on the words *could not*[98] (have increased the risk): it is possible to conceive of several ways in which the driver's intoxicated state *could* have contributed to the loss. Of course any such contribution to the risk must be in the context of the loss 'that actually occurred in the circumstances in which it occurred,' but this volume submits that this formula still allows for a number of possible scenarios. For Merkin's interpretation to hold good, it is respectfully suggested that the words 'could not' must, in effect, be read as 'did not.' This author believes that the interpretation set out previously would represent a positive outcome and that in these circumstances the Insurance Act operates effectively. It surely cannot be right that an insured could flagrantly breach a key provision (one which clearly has an impact on the insurer's risk/premium calculation) of the policy and the law, and yet still benefit under the policy.

9.38 In its report the Commission argued that the decision in *Forsikringsaktielselskapet Vesta v Butcher*[99] (where it was held that under the Marine Insurance Act, the failure of the assured owner of a fish farm to comply with a warranty requiring a 24-hour watch to be

94 Merkin and Hemsworth, *The Law of Motor Insurance,* 2nd Edition, 2016, Chapter 2.
95 S11(3) Insurance Act 2015.
96 S10(2) Insurance Act 2015.
97 S11(3) Insurance Act 2015.
98 S11(3) Insurance Act 2015, emphasis added.
99 [1989] AC 852.

maintained, was fatal to the assured's claim for loss from storm damage) would be different applying their proposals (i.e. the original clause 11, as discussed earlier), on the grounds that the insurer's liability would only have been suspended in relation to losses that a watchman might have been able to do something to prevent or mitigate.[100] This volume considers this to be a possible, although improbable, interpretation of the way the Commission's original proposals would have actually worked in this instance and assumes that losses that the watchman could have prevented were a *particular* kind of loss for these purposes. Applying s10 and (the final version of) s11 of the Insurance Act to the facts of *Forsikringsaktielselskapet Vesta v Butcher*, this text believes that a court would more likely find that the warranty in question did *not* fall within the s11 exemption because it would be hard to argue in this volume's view that it was anything other than a term that defined the risk as a whole. As such, s11 would have no application. Applying this logic therefore, the decision would fall to be decided under s10(2) and, as the insurers liability would have been suspended at the time of loss in accord with that section, the original decision would be unchanged under the Insurance Act: the insurer would avoid liability.

9.39 Again, the Commission argued that on the facts of *Bamcell II* [101] (where a warranty which required the posting of a nightwatchman was breached; the vessel was, however, lost during daytime as a result of the negligence of a crew member), the application of the Commission's original clause 11 would mean that the insurer's liability was suspended only in relation to losses occurring at night: the insurer would be liable for other losses. Applying s11 of the Insurance Act to these facts, it is at least arguable that the requirement to post a nightwatchman is a provision that defines the risk as a whole. Were this correct, in the event of a breach, this would mean that the insurer would escape liability. However, this volume acknowledges that an alternate interpretation, that the provision defines the risk of loss at a particular time, is perhaps more likely. In these circumstances the likelihood is that the insured would be able to satisfy the court that the non-compliance could not have increased the risk of loss that actually occurred in the circumstances in which it occurred. Accordingly the insurer would be liable. As we have seen, what is not clear is what s11 means for a term that defines the risk as a whole, but only for a particular time. This volume would argue that losses of a particular kind or at a particular location cannot, by definition, be the same as the risk as a whole. It is submitted that this is not necessarily true of a temporal measure. While the intent may have been that the temporal element ('for a particular time') in s11(1)(c) should take precedence, the first paragraph of s11(1) specifically excludes provisions that apply to the risk as a whole. This is a further example of the Insurance Act lacking precision.

9.40 Interestingly the Law Commission felt that in marine insurance where the subject matter of the policy was a ship, the qualifications of the captain would affect either the policy as a whole, or a significant part of the risk. Following this logic, if one considers a policy for a fleet of trucks where there is a requirement that drivers must have a particular level of experience and/or qualification (as per *Maxwell v Highway Hauliers*[102]), surely such a requirement could be taken as defining the risk as a whole? It could perhaps be argued

100 Paragraph 18.57 Law Commission and Scottish Law Commission, Insurance Contract Law: Business Disclosure; Warranties; Insurers' Remedies for Fraudulent Claims; and Late Payment Law Com No 353 / Scot Law Com No 238 Cm 8898 SG/2014/131 July 2014. Available at: http://lawcommission.justice.gov.uk/docs.

101 [2002] 1 AC 252.

102 [2014] HCA 33, 10 September 2014.

that the requirement would tend to reduce the risk of loss of a particular kind (presumably loss caused by a road traffic accident?), but this author submits that this possibility merely flags the inherent flaw with the s11 formulation: how is 'defining the risk as whole' to be interpreted? If in the example of the fleet of trucks, the provision is held to apply to the risk as a whole (which to this author seems to be the sensible approach), s11 will not apply. Accordingly if the breach is un-remedied at the time of loss the insurer would, it appears, be able to avoid liability, regardless of the nature of the loss. This seems irrational in circumstances where the loss is unconnected with the requirement for particular experience or qualifications.

No account of prejudice

9.41 Whereas, as we have seen, legislation in other jurisdictions provides for allowance to be taken of prejudice suffered by the insurer,[103] the Insurance Act contains no such provision. This author regards this as an unfortunate and significant omission. In *Ferrcom Pty Ltd v Commercial Union Assurance Co of Australia Ltd*[104] the court defined prejudice as

> the existence of a liability which, in whole or in part, would not have been borne by the insurer if the act had not been done or the omission had not been made or in the non-receipt of an additional premium to which the insurer would have been entitled by reason of the doing of the act or the making of the omission.[105]

While the reference to act or omission is clearly tailored to the provisions of the Insurance Contracts Act, the generic description of prejudice nevertheless, it is submitted, holds good. Using this definition it is perfectly possible to envisage circumstances where an insurer may, as a result of, say, s11 of the Insurance Act, be required to meet a liability, notwithstanding a breach by the insured in circumstances where the insurer would otherwise have been entitled to an additional premium. Take for example the situation where a policy provides that a factory must be fitted with a specified burglary alarm, but the insured fails to fit the alarm. Assume that a loss is suffered as a result of a fire in the factory, unconnected with the absence of the burglary alarm. In these circumstances, it is reasonable to assume that the insurer would be liable under s11 of the Insurance Act on the grounds that compliance would have tended to reduce the risk of a particular kind, but that the non-compliance could not have increased the risk of loss which actually occurred in the circumstances in which it occurred (s11(3)). Let us further suppose that, by referencing other policies it has issued, the insurer is able to demonstrate that, had it known that no alarm would be fitted, it would have charged an additional £1500 premium per annum. Notwithstanding the

103 For example s54(1) of the Insurance Contracts Act in Australia provides for the insurer's liability in respect of the claim to be reduced by the amount that fairly represents the extent to which the insurer's interests were prejudiced as a result of the breach. Again s9 of the New Zealand Insurance Law Reform Act provides that 'a provision of a contract of insurance prescribing any manner in which or any limit of time within which notice of any claim by the insured under such contract must be given or prescribing any limit of time within which any suit or action by the insured must be brought shall ... bind the insured only if in the opinion of the arbitrator or court determining the claim the insurer has in the particular circumstances been so prejudiced by the failure of the insured to comply with such provision that it would be inequitable if such provision were not to bind the insured.'

104 (1993) 176 CLR 332.

105 *Ferrcom Pty Ltd v Commercial Union Assurance Co of Australia Ltd* (at 77,831 (ANZ Ins Cas)).

obligation to meet the liability, it seems that under the Insurance Act no account would be taken of the fact that the insurer has, in effect, forgone a premium (i.e., it is argued, suffered prejudice to the extent) of £1500. This seems irrational and inequitable; after all, if such prejudice had been reflected by an additional provision in the policy, indicating that in the event the alarm was not fitted, the premium would increase by £1500, it would not have been open to the insured to seek to avoid the additional payment.

Right of termination

9.42 The Insurance Act contains no right of termination in the event of a breach of warranty or other term: seemingly this is to be left to the terms of the contract.[106] This author considers this to be a mistake: for the reasons explored elsewhere in this volume,[107] the position would, it is submitted, be improved if, on breach of warranty or other provision giving the insurer the right to avoid liability, the insurer was granted a right to terminate on, say, 14 days' notice.

Treatment of implied warranties under the Insurance Act 2015

9.43 We have seen[108] that the Marine Insurance Act 1906 provides for implied warranties in relation to seaworthiness and legality. How are these affected by the Insurance Act 2015?

Section 10

9.44 Section 10 of the Insurance Act applies to warranties and is specifically stated to apply to implied warranties in addition to express ones.[109] Accordingly it appears clear that, as with express warranties, under s10(2) a breach of the implied warranty of seaworthiness suspends, rather than terminates, the insurer's liability under the policy. As we have seen (subject to any application of s11 as discussed later in this chapter), the insurer's liability is suspended across the whole of the policy while the breach remains un-remedied. Under s10(4) the insurer's liability under the policy is prima facie restored once the breach has been remedied. However, as we have seen, under s39(1) of the Marine Insurance Act 1906[110] the implied warranty of seaworthiness applies, in the case of a voyage policy, at the commencement of the voyage: it is not a continuing warranty. In circumstance where this warranty has been breached and the vessel has commenced its journey in an unseaworthy state, is it in fact possible for the breach to be remedied? This question has not arisen in the past, given that a breach of warranty was not capable of remedy and automatically discharged the insurer from liability. It could be argued that a breach of the implied warranty

106 Para 17.61 Law Commission and Scottish Law Commission, Insurance Contract Law: Business Disclosure; Warranties; Insurers' Remedies for Fraudulent Claims; and Late Payment Law Com No 353 / Scot Law Com No 238 Cm 8898 SG/2014/131 July 2014 para 18.68. Available at: http://lawcommission.justice.gov.uk/docs.

107 See Chapters 3, 11 and 12.

108 Chapter 4 refers.

109 S10(1) of the Insurance Act reads 'Any rule of law that a breach of a warranty (express or implied) in a contract of insurance results in the discharge of the insurer's liability under the contract of insurance is abolished.' Again s10(2) is expressly stated to apply to both express and implied warranties.

110 S39(1) of the Marine Insurance Act 1906 is not affected by the Insurance Act 2015.

of seaworthiness, because it applies 'at the commencement of the voyage,' is not capable of remedy, in which case, notwithstanding the wording of s10(1) of the Insurance Act, s10 will be of no assistance to the insured. This author submits however that a more likely interpretation will be that a breach of the implied warranty of seaworthiness would fall to be considered under ss10(5) and 10(6) of the Insurance Act. The implied warranty requires the vessel to be seaworthy at the time the voyage is commenced and thus can be said to fall within s10(6); if the rectification undertaken was sufficient to restore the risk to the same as originally contemplated by the parties, this author would argue that s10(5) kicks in and the insurer's liability is restored. While this outcome may seem equitable, it cannot be taken for granted until, and if, the issue is tested in court. For the reasons discussed previously, it would be quite feasible for a court to hold that s10 has no application in the context of a breach of the implied warranty. What is the situation in relation to a time policy where a vessel is sent to sea in an unseaworthy state with the privity of the assured (s39(5) of the Marine Insurance Act 1906 refers)? S39(5) provides that there is no implied warranty of seaworthiness in relation to time policies but that where, with the privity of the insured a vessel is sent to sea in an unseaworthy state the insurer is not liable for any loss attributable to unseaworthiness. As a result s10 will have no application.

9.45 As s10 applies only to (express or implied) warranties, it is submitted that it is clear therefore that it has no impact on the implied voyage conditions set out in ss42–49 of the Marine Insurance Act.

Section 11

9.46 S11 of the Insurance Act is stated to apply to terms, whether express or implied of a contract of insurance. It thus seems clear that the intent was that s11 apply to implied warranties. This author struggles to see how this works in practice. As we have seen, the Marine Insurance Act 1906 provides for implied warranties in relation to seaworthiness (s39(1), and (3), and in more limited circumstances s39(5)) and legality (s41). S39(2) provides an implied warranty that the vessel will be able to manage the ordinary perils of port. This author submits that surely in the context of marine insurance, the implied warranty of seaworthiness can often, if not ordinarily, be considered as applying to the risk as a whole, in which case s11 of the Insurance Act 2015 will not apply to any breach. If this assessment is not correct then for s11 to apply, seaworthiness would presumably have to be seen as relating to a loss of a particular kind, a stretch in the view of this author, given the breadth of issues that can potentially trigger a breach of the implied warranty of seaworthiness.[111] Nevertheless, applying this latter logic, it could perhaps be argued that if a vessel comes into port to make good defects (for example a defective boiler) which have rendered it unseaworthy and is lost as a result of a fire while in port, the assured would be able to claim, even if the repairs have not been completed at the time of the loss, if he is able to demonstrate under s11(3) that the non-compliance could not have increased the risk of the loss which actually occurred in the circumstances in which it occurred. The same would presumably apply in the context of a breach of s39(5) of the Marine Insurance Act where, in the context of a time policy, the assured knowingly sent a vessel to sea in an

111 See Chapter 4 for illustrations of this.

unseaworthy condition, assuming again the insured could satisfy the requirements of s11(3). Unlike s10, s11 does not require the breach to have been rectified in order for the insured to be able to claim under the terms of the section. Soyer argues that s11 has no application to s43 (Alteration of port of departure) or s44 (Sailing for different destination), as these are explicitly expressed as conditions precedent to attachment of risk and as a result s11 of the Insurance Act has no role to play.[112] This seems sensible. Soyer argues that the position may be different in relation to other voyage conditions such as change of voyage (s45), deviation (s46) and delay in voyage (s48); again this author would concur with this analysis and that accordingly s11 could potentially apply to breaches of these conditions.

What impact do sections 10 and 11 have on the implied warranty of legality?

9.47 We have seen in Chapter 4 that whether or not the implied warranty of legality set out in s41 of the Marine Insurance Act 1906 has been breached will be a question of fact; the answer will not always be obvious. This author submits that it is clear that if the first part of s41, that the adventure insured is a legal one, has been breached, this is not a situation that can be repaired and that accordingly s10 of the Insurance Act will have no bearing as the breach is not capable of remedy as envisaged in s10(2). Does this logic also apply to the second half of s41 of the Marine Insurance Act, that so far as the assured can control the matter, the adventure shall be carried out in a lawful manner? This author would argue that it does. While there will be shades of grey in determining whether the threshold to constitute a breach of s41 has been met, once, on the facts, it has been so met, it is not capable of remedy and accordingly s10 of the Insurance Act will again have no application.

9.48 Does s11 of the Insurance Act 2015 apply to a breach of the implied warranty of legality? As s41 of the Marine Insurance Act refers to the implied warranty of legality in the context of the 'adventure insured,'[113] this volume would submit that it is surely hard to argue that the implied warranty refers to anything other than the risk as a whole. Assuming this is correct, s11 of the Insurance Act will have no application to a breach of the implied warranty of legality.

Contracting out provisions of the Insurance Act 2015

9.49 The Law Commission indicated that for non-consumer insurance, it did not propose to place any restrictions on the extent to which the statutory regime could be altered (or excluded) by contract.[114] The Commission indicated that the contracting out provisions of the Act were intentionally drafted in a broad manner to enable courts to

112 B Soyer, *Warranties in Marine Insurance,* 3rd Edition, Routledge, London, 2017, para 7.18, page 226. While agreeing with Soyer's analysis in relation to the risk attaching (s10(5) and (6) of the Insurance Act 2015 would have no relevance in this instance), this author is of the view that as such a provision clearly relates to the risk as a whole, it is anyway outside the reach of s11.

113 S41 Marine Insurance Act 1906 reads, 'There is an implied warranty that the adventure insured is a lawful one, and that, so far as the insured can control the matter, the adventure shall be carried out in a lawful manner.'

114 Law Commission and Scottish Law Commission, Insurance Contract Law: Business Disclosure; Warranties; Insurers' Remedies for Fraudulent Claims; and Late Payment Law Com No 353 / Scot Law Com No 238 Cm 8898 SG/2014/131 July 2014, para 29.4.

differentiate between different scenarios, from well-advised, commercially aware insurance buyers, to smaller insurers, buying 'off the shelf' and increasingly online.[115] Nevertheless, there is an expectation that these provisions will be amongst the first to be the subject of litigation.[116] Interestingly, in contrast to the expectations of the Law Commission,[117] the UK Government suggested there was 'no pent up demand for widespread contracting out.'[118] Notwithstanding this, the Government committed that a review be undertaken within five years of the enactment of the Insurance Act to assess the situation. It appears the Commission's intention was to avoid the creation of an overly complicated test and the contracting out provisions are accordingly contained in just two sections, ss16 and 17 of the Insurance Act. One of the stated aims of the Act was to 'ensure that the contracting out provisions are not so onerous as to interfere with the smooth running of the insurance market.'[119]

9.50 In summary insurers are at liberty to opt out of the provisions (save in relation to s9: the effective abolition of basis clauses) of the Act, provided they adhere to the transparency provisions of s17. The risk of course is that this flexibility puts at risk the overarching intent of the Act, to achieve a better balance between the interests of the insurer and the insured. One view is that the contracting out provisions were included as a sop to insurers to water down opposition to the Act that might otherwise have existed.[120] An important question in any review of the Act is to ask to what extent the contracting out provisions are likely to erode the impact of the statutory provisions upon commercial insurance practice in England and Wales? To put it another way, what is the impact of the contracting out provisions on the objectives of the Law Commission, to achieve that better balance between the interests of insurers and insureds?

9.51 S16 and s17 read as follows:

Section 16 Contracting out: non-consumer insurance contracts

(1) A term of a non-consumer insurance contract, or of any other contract, which would put the insured in a worse position as respects representations to which section 9 applies than the insured would be in by virtue of that section is to that extent of no effect.

(2) A term of a non-consumer insurance contract, or of any other contract, which would put the insured in a worse position as respects any of the other matters provided for in Part 2, 3 or 4 of this Act than the insured would be in by virtue of

115 Law Commission and Scottish Law Commission, Insurance Contract Law: Business Disclosure; Warranties; Insurers' Remedies for Fraudulent Claims; and Late Payment Law Com No 353 / Scot Law Com No 238 Cm 8898 SG/2014/131 July 2014, para 29.29 (4). Available at: http://lawcommission.justice.gov.uk/docs.

116 B Soyer, 'Risk Control Clauses in Insurance Law, Law Reform and the Future' (2016) 109 CLJ 124.

117 Law Commission and Scottish Law Commission, Insurance Contract Law: Business Disclosure; Warranties; Insurers' Remedies for Fraudulent Claims; and Late Payment Law Com No 353 / Scot Law Com No 238 Cm 8898 SG/2014/131 July 2014, para 29.25. Available at: http://lawcommission.justice.gov.uk/docs.

118 House of Lords debate 29 July 2014, col GC 629.

119 Law Commission and Scottish Law Commission, Insurance Contract Law: Business Disclosure; Warranties; Insurers' Remedies for Fraudulent Claims; and Late Payment Law Com No 353 / Scot Law Com No 238 Cm 8898 SG/2014/131 July 2014, para 29.29 (3). Available at: http://lawcommission.justice.gov.uk/docs.

120 G Leloudas, 'Contracting Out of the Insurance Act 2015' in *Commercial Insurance Contracts, The Insurance Act 2015, A New Regime for Commercial and Marine Insurance Law,* edited by M Clarke and B Soyer, Informa Law for Routledge, London, 2016.

the provisions of those Parts (so far as relating to non-consumer insurance contracts) is to that extent of no effect, unless the requirements of section 17 have been satisfied in relation to the term.

(3) In this section references to a contract include a variation.

(4) This section does not apply in relation to a contract for the settlement of a claim arising under a non-consumer insurance contract.

Section 17 The transparency requirements

(1) In this section, 'the disadvantageous term' means such a term as is mentioned in section 16(2).

(2) The insurer must take sufficient steps to draw the disadvantageous term to the insured's attention before the contract is entered into or the variation agreed.

(3) The disadvantageous term must be clear and unambiguous as to its effect.

(4) In determining whether the requirements of subsections (2) and (3) have been met, the characteristics of insured persons of the kind in question, and the circumstances of the transaction, are to be taken into account.

(5) The insured may not rely on any failure on the part of the insurer to meet the requirements of subsection (2) if the insured (or its agent) had actual knowledge of the disadvantageous term when the contract was entered into or the variation agreed.

9.52 It is important that any disadvantageous term is brought to the attention of the insured prior to the latter signing the slip or accepting the insurance online. When a broker is involved on behalf of the insured, the likely time for any relevant terms to be drawn to his attention would be during placement/renewal discussions. Where a broker is employed, the onus would be on him to inquire as to the specifics. This would often not be the case where there is no broker involved: s17(4) specifies that the characteristics of the insured in each case and the circumstances of the transaction must be taken into account.[121] Examples used by the Commission to illustrate the operation of s17 appear to suggest that a discussion about excluding the provisions of the Act is crucial in order to pass the hurdles in s17.[122] There is however nothing in the Act that specifies the need for such a discussion. S17(2) requires the insurer to bring a disadvantageous term to the attention of the insured (or in practice his broker). What qualifies as crossing the relevant threshold will depend on the facts of each case. The Law Commission has suggested that an asterisk next to the disadvantageous term would constitute the bare minimum necessary to comply with s17(2). It remains to be seen whether the courts will adopt a less onerous threshold for application in sophisticated insurance markets, than that which may be applied in the SME environment. This volume argues that such an approach would be logical.

9.53 S17(5) provides an escape for an insurer who has not drawn the opt out clause to the insured's attention if he is able to demonstrate that the insured had 'actual knowledge' of the disadvantageous clause when the contract or variation was entered into.[123] This

121 S17(4) Insurance Act 2015.

122 Insurance Act 2015 Explanatory Notes, Commentary on Sections, para 125, available at http://www.legislation.gov.uk.

123 S17(5) Insurance Act 2015.

can be an important issue where policy wording is agreed sometime after the slip was entered into. Again what constitutes actual knowledge will depend on the facts of each case. It seems logical that actual knowledge does not include constructive knowledge (that of which he ought to be aware): this text agrees with the assertion by Leloudas that the wording of the statute would surely have indicated this if it were intended to be the case.[124]

9.54 The contracting out clause must be 'clear and unambiguous as to its effect';[125] this presumably means that the clause must be clear in terms of how it will disadvantage the insured.[126] This interpretation is supported by the Law Commission's own observations on this issue. Where a broker is involved it is probably sufficient to state that where the policy 'contracts out,' the effect will be that any breach of warranty will discharge the insurer from any liability from that moment onward, regardless of whether or not the breach is subsequently remedied. Where no broker is involved, then the relevant carve out most likely needs to be explained in relation to each warranty it effects.[127] Leloudas has argued that pragmatism has prevailed over legalism.[128] S17(4) is the crucial provision, and the issue will be to seek to decide how to apply the transparency requirement to different insurance markets. This volume agrees that the section has been drafted with sufficient flexibility to allow the courts to adapt their approach in the light of different insurance markets and differing levels of knowledge and expertise amongst the parties.[129]

9.55 The Law Commission suggested that exclusion clauses would be covered under its original clause 11 of the draft Bill set out in its Report LC 353.[130] If it is correct that exclusion clauses come under s11 of the Insurance Act (and, as we have seen, this volume disputes this,[131] arguing that some, if not all, exclusion clauses would fall outside s11), it has been pointed out[132] that there is nothing to stop an insurer opting out of the provisions

124 G Leloudas, 'Contracting Out of the Insurance Act 2015' in *Commercial Insurance Contracts, The Insurance Act 2015, A New Regime for Commercial and Marine Insurance Law* edited by M Clarke and B Soyer, Informa Law for Routledge, London, 2016.

125 S17(3) Insurance Act 2015.

126 G Leloudas, 'Contracting Out of the Insurance Act 2015' in *Commercial Insurance Contracts, The Insurance Act 2015, A New Regime for Commercial and Marine Insurance Law* edited by M Clarke and B Soyer, Informa Law for Routledge, London, 2016.

127 G Leloudas, 'Contracting Out of the Insurance Act 2015' in *Commercial Insurance Contracts, The Insurance Act 2015, A New Regime for Commercial and Marine Insurance Law* edited by M Clarke and B Soyer, Informa Law for Routledge, London, 2016.

128 G Leloudas, 'Contracting Out of the Insurance Act 2015' in *Commercial Insurance Contracts, The Insurance Act 2015, A New Regime for Commercial and Marine Insurance Law* edited by M Clarke and B Soyer, Informa Law for Routledge, London, 2016.

129 G Leloudas, 'Contracting Out of the Insurance Act 2015' in *Commercial Insurance Contracts, The Insurance Act 2015, A New Regime for Commercial and Marine Insurance Law* edited by M Clarke and B Soyer, Informa Law for Routledge, London, 2016.

130 The Law Commission suggested that exclusion clauses would come under the original draft cl 11 of its draft statute: 'Our recommendation could apply to terms including warranties (including the implied marine warranties), conditions precedent, definitions of risk and exclusion clauses.' Law Commission and Scottish Law Commission, Insurance Contract Law: Business Disclosure; Warranties; Insurers' Remedies for Fraudulent Claims; and Late Payment Law Com No 353 / Scot Law Com No 238 Cm 8898 SG/2014/131 July 2014, para 18.41. Available at: http://lawcommission.justice.gov.uk/docs. This author disputes this analysis: see earlier in Chapter 8.

131 See earlier in Chapter 9.

132 G Leloudas, 'Contracting Out of the Insurance Act 2015' in *Commercial Insurance Contracts, The Insurance Act 2015, A New Regime for Commercial and Marine Insurance Law* edited by M Clarke and B Soyer, Informa Law for Routledge, London, 2016.

of s10 of the Act, while maintaining the position in relation to exclusion clauses (and other relevant provisions) under s11 of the Act. This would have the effect of maintaining the harsh position in relation to warranties under the 1906 Marine Insurance Act, while ensuring that the insured has the burden of proof in relation to any breach of the exclusion clause (or other provision), such that he (the insured) must demonstrate (under s11(3)) that the circumstances that triggered the exclusion clause etc. could not have increased the risk of loss that actually occurred in the circumstances in which it occurred.[133] The argument is thus that in such circumstances the insured is worse off and that the Act is accordingly open to 'manipulation.'[134]

Contracting out: the verdict

9.56 It remains to be seen to what extent insurers will seek to avail themselves of the contracting out provisions. Differing approaches to the level of detail and specificity are likely between differing client industries. While this is to be welcomed, this volume would argue that it is a pity that there is not a little more precision in the contracting out provisions of the Insurance Act. This author welcomes the general approach of seeking to ensure that an insured is made aware of any erosion of the rights and protections he would otherwise have under the Insurance Act. While this volume acknowledges that flexibility is important, it is nevertheless of the view that rather too much has been left to interpretation by the courts. This will lead to uncertainty over how the provisions are to be interpreted, at least for a period. A better approach may have been to follow the lead in Australia and New Zealand where there is no provision for contracting out. Such an approach would however likely have resulted in opposition from the industry and may have as a result delayed or, even derailed, reform.

The Insurance Act 2015: a conclusion

9.57 Regrettably, this author is not as optimistic as Soyer about the changes introduced by the Insurance Act which Soyer sees as providing grounds for there being 'every reason to be hopeful of the future.'[135] Merkin and Gurses argue that the effect of s10 and s11 of the Insurance Act 2015 is to retain warranties, while removing their most offensive features. They argue however that a bolder approach would have been to repeal ss33–41 of the Marine Insurance Act 1906.[136] As we have seen, they suggest that perhaps the greatest weakness of the IA 2015 is its failure to address non-risk clauses.[137] In Australia and New Zealand a finding that the clause is not a risk clause triggers other protective measures relieving the assured in full or in part from the consequences of a breach in the absence of prejudice to the insurers.

133 S11(3) Insurance Act 2015.

134 G Leloudas, 'Contracting Out of the Insurance Act 2015' in *Commercial Insurance Contracts, The Insurance Act 2015, A New Regime for Commercial and Marine Insurance Law* edited by M Clarke and B Soyer, Informa Law for Routledge, London, 2016.

135 B Soyer, 'Risk Control Clauses in Insurance Law: Law Reform and the Future' (2016) 75 *Cambridge Law Journal* 109–127.

136 R Merkin and O Gurses, 'Insurance Contracts after the Insurance Act 2015' (2016) 132(3) LQR 445.

137 R Merkin and O Gurses, 'Insurance Contracts after the Insurance Act 2015' (2016) 132(3) LQR 445.

9.58 This author welcomes the proposal to make a breach of warranty suspensory, together with provisions to abolish basis clauses and gives a guarded welcome to the proposal to limit suspension to a specific category of risk where the clause in question relates to a particular kind of loss, or loss at a particular location or place. Gurses asserts that the reference in s11 to the risk as a whole is a welcome law reform that has rationalised the relationship between the assured and the insurer.[138] Respectfully, this author is of a different view. This volume argues that s11 is loosely drafted and will prove to be a source of considerable uncertainty and litigation.[139] While this author agrees that uncertainty of outcome is inherent in any case where the issue is one of contractual interpretation,[140] in particular it is argued that the concept of the risk as a whole (as referenced in s11) is flawed, as well as being vague and unclear. As this volume has sought to demonstrate, the scope of s11 is far from clear in terms of what provisions are subject to it. It is this author's contention that an effective reform of the law in this area must, in addition to warranties, also address exclusion clauses, and breaches of conditions precedent[141] and other provisions, such as non-risk clauses that seek to release the insurer from liability under the policy. This volume has sought to demonstrate that it is far from clear if, for example, exclusion clauses are subject to s11. It can be argued that exclusion clauses by definition refer to the risk as a whole (and are thus outside s11). Even if this is not correct, it is clear that s11 requires there to be a breach of (or non-compliance with) a provision of the contract. This is unhelpful as it is perfectly possible for an exclusion clause to trigger without a breach; in such circumstances the exclusion clause would seemingly be outside the reach of s11. Again the relationship between s11 and conditions precedent is unclear. This volume has sought to demonstrate that in at least some instances it is unlikely that s11 will apply to conditions precedent. As a minimum, it is surely the case that a condition precedent to the attachment of risk across the contract is by definition a term that defines the risk as whole and would thus be outside the reach of s11.

9.59 We have seen that even the relationship between sections 10 and 11, in terms of whether s10 is subject to s11, is unclear. In addition, while the Law Commission positioned itself firmly against the concept of causal linkage, it is difficult to view the final version of s11(3) as anything other than a form of causal linkage, introduced by the back door. Under s11(3) the insurer is unable to escape liability (assuming the relevant provision falls within s11(1) and (2)), if the insured shows that the non-compliance with the term could not have increased the risk of the loss that actually occurred in the circumstances in which it occurred. Yet the Commission suggested that the consequences of breach should *not*[142] be considered in light of what has actually happened. This volume believes that the outcome is confused and uncertain: far better in the view of this author to adopt a clear causal linkage approach.

138 O Gurses, 'Section 11 of the Insurance Act 2015: When Does a Term Define the Risk as a Whole in an Insurance Contract? Balancing the Interest of the Assured and Insurer' (2020) 3 JBL 184–201.

139 Recommendation 28, Law Commission and Scottish Law Commission, Insurance Contract Law: Business Disclosure; Warranties; Insurers' Remedies for Fraudulent Claims; and Late Payment Law Com No 353 / Scot Law Com No 238 Cm 8898 SG/2014/131 July 2014. Available at: http://lawcommission.justice.gov.uk/docs.

140 O Gurses, 'Section 11 of the Insurance Act 2015: When Does a Term Define the Risk as a Whole in an Insurance Contract? Balancing the Interest of the Assured and Insurer' (2020) 3 JBL 184–201.

141 In certain specific circumstances: see Chapter 12 for details of this author's proposals, including in relation to breaches of conditions precedent.

142 Emphasis added.

9.60 While this author acknowledges that the merits of the arguments made in relation to s11 can be debated, what is surely beyond doubt is that the interpretation of the section is fraught with uncertainty and will likely be the cause of considerable confusion and litigation. This is clearly unhelpful, particularly when one of the aims of reform was to provide greater clarity.

9.61 This author acknowledges and supports the need to strike a better balance between the interest of the insured and insurer. For the most part this translates into the need for greater protection for the insured. Over and above its general reservations about s11, this volume has sought to demonstrate that there are at least two areas where the Insurance Act has missed opportunities to offer reasonable protection to insurers. The absence of any ability to take account of any prejudice suffered by the insurer is unhelpful and difficult to justify. Finally the absence of any right on behalf of the insurer to terminate following a breach of a warranty (or other relevant provision) is, in this author's view, an omission that potentially impacts adversely on both the insured and insurer.

CHAPTER 10

Stress testing the regimes for insurance warranties in Australia, New Zealand and the UK

Stress testing the Australian regime with the facts of historic cases from other jurisdictions

10.1 This volume has already critically examined a number of cases where s54 has been applied. As we have seen,[1] the Australian regime comprises a dual track approach made up of (i) s54 of the Insurance Contracts Act, covering, for the purposes of this text, non-marine commercial insurance and (ii) the Marine Insurance Act 1909. In this chapter it will be assumed that the dual track approach has been retained and that the Marine Insurance Act has been amended in line with the recommendations of ALRC 91.[2] However the likely outcome under the status quo (where the recommendations of ALRC 91 have yet to be implemented) will also be reviewed. ALRC 91 of course has no relevance in non-marine cases.

10.2 *De Hahn v Hartley*[3] In a maritime policy a warranty required the vessel to sail with at least 50 crew members, but it actually left port with only 44. The shortfall was soon made up, but when the vessel was subsequently lost the insurer still escaped liability because of the breach of warranty. As Australia has retained a separate regime for maritime policies, it is assumed these facts would be considered under Australia's Marine Insurance Act 1909. Let us assume that the recommendations of ALRC 91 have been implemented. Accordingly, as ALRC recommended the abolition of warranties, it is assumed that the warranty would be replaced by an express term on similar lines. As the breach was remedied prior to the loss of the vessel, under the recommendations of ALRC 91, the insured would be obliged to indemnify the assured for the loss incurred. This would reverse the original decision and would be an outcome welcomed by this author. Of course in reality, the recommendations of ALRC 91 have yet to be implemented. As a result the governing regime would be essentially the same as when the case was originally heard (i.e. the Marine Insurance Act) and this text submits that it is hard to see why the outcome, on the facts (and ignoring for these purposes the likelihood of held covered clauses being included in a modern day policy), would be any different from the original case. This flags a clear disadvantage, and in the view of this author, a critical failing, with the Australian regime as it currently stands. It is possible that the court would view the provision as a condition precedent to the attachment of risk. Were this to be the case then, whether ALRC 91 had been implemented or not, the policy would never have come on risk and the insurer would escape liability.

1 See Chapter 6.
2 See Chapter 6 for consideration of ALRC 91.
3 (1786) 1 TR 343.

DOI: 10.4324/9781003031734-10

10.3 In *Forsakringsaktielselskapet Vesta v Butcher*[4] it was held that the failure of the assured to comply with a warranty that a 24-hour watch would be maintained on the assured's fish farm was fatal to his claim for loss from storm damage, notwithstanding that it was acknowledged that the presence of a watch would not have had any impact whatsoever on the nature or extent of the loss incurred. If assessed under the Insurance Contracts Act, this author believes that it is clear that the omission to post a watch falls within s54. The question is then, could the omission reasonably be regarded as capable of causing or contributing to the loss under s54(2)? This volume would submit that s54(2) would have no application on these facts. As it is clear that the breach/omission did not cause the loss incurred (or any part thereof), this text would further submit that neither s54(3) nor 54(4) would apply and that accordingly the insurer, having suffered no prejudice as a result of the breach, would be liable to indemnify the loss under s54(1). This volume would welcome this outcome.

10.4 In *Hibbert v Pigou*[5] a ship was warranted to sail with a convoy, but failed to do so and was lost in a storm. The underwriters were held not liable for the loss. Again under the Australian regime it is assumed this case would fall to be considered under the Marine Insurance Act 1909. Assuming the recommendations of ALRC 91 had been implemented, this text submits that as the breach is not capable of remedy, the burden of showing that the breach was not the proximate cause of the loss would be borne by the assured (recommendation 19, ALRC 91). This volume assumes that the assured would be able to meet this burden and that accordingly the insurer would be obliged to indemnify the loss. This would represent a reasonable outcome on the facts. However, as noted previously, ALRC has *not* yet been implemented, so in reality the likely outcome with these facts would be the same as in the original case. This text believes this is hard to support in the modern era.

10.5 *New Zealand Insurance Co Ltd v Harris*[6] In this case the policy 'warranted' that the tractor that was the subject of the policy would not be let out on hire for commercial purposes. This provision was breached and the tractor destroyed in fire. A key question under s54 (or any alternate regime) would be whether the use of the tractor for commercial purposes was outside the scope of cover under the policy. As we have seen, this volume has concerns about the potential for s54 to be interpreted in a way that erodes the clarity that might otherwise exist in relation to issues of scope. The original New Zealand court found the facts to be within the scope of cover and it is assumed a similar finding would be made in Australia. This text believes that an important issue under a s54 evaluation would be whether the act of hiring the tractor for commercial purposes might fall foul of s54(2) and specifically whether doing so might be seen as an act which 'could reasonably be regarded as being capable of causing or contributing' to a loss in respect of which cover is provided. As we have seen, this is subject to the insured being able to prove that no part of the loss was caused by the breach (s54(3)). This volume suggests that an Australian court would likely take a similar view to that of its New Zealand counterparty that 'refined analysis in terms of metaphysical inquiries into causation should be eschewed.'[7] Accordingly, it is

4 [1989] 1 Lloyd's Rep 331.
5 (1783) 3 Doug KB 224.
6 [1990] 1 NZLR 10 (CA).
7 *New Zealand Insurance Co Ltd v Harris* [1990] 1 NZLR 10 (CA) at 16.

argued that an Australian court would likely rule that s54(2) did not apply to these facts. Could it be argued that the insurer has suffered prejudice (s54(1)), possibly in the form of unrealised premium that it would have charged had it known the tractor would be let out for commercial use? This seems possible on the basis of the definition of prejudice used in the *Fercomm* case:

> the existence of a liability which, in whole or in part, would not have been borne by the insurer if the act had not been done or the omission had not been made or *in the non-receipt of an additional premium to which the insurer would have been entitled by reason of the doing of the act or the making of the omission.*[8]

If prejudice was judged to have occurred, the quantum of any premium assessed as reasonable for commercial use of the tractor would be deducted from the claim which the insurer must otherwise meet under s54(1). This volume again sees this as a reasonable outcome.

10.6 In *Nelson Forests Ltd v Three Tuis Ltd.*[9] cover was provided for legal liability for accidents 'in connection with' the operation of a lifestyle farm business. There was a fire that arose in connection with tourism activities undertaken on the property by the assured. The court in New Zealand found that cover was restricted to farming operations and that as a result, tourism was outside the scope of cover provided under the policy. Notwithstanding the tendency[10] for s54 to push at the boundaries of scope, this volume submits that, in this instance, there is no reason to suppose that an Australian court would reach a different conclusion regarding scope and that as a result, the likelihood is that the court would rule that s54 had no application. Under these circumstances the insurer would have no obligation to meet the claim. This volume believes this would represent a sensible and equitable outcome.

10.7 In *Barnaby v South British Insurance Co Ltd*[11] a policy on a building excluded liability for 'fault, defect, error or omission in design.' A wall collapsed in bad weather and was found to have been constructed with a defect. The question arose, did the policy cover a wall, but excluding the risk of its collapse due to a defect, or did it cover only a wall free of defects?[12] The New Zealand court held that the policy only provided cover for buildings that did not contain defects and as result the facts were held to be outside the scope of the policy. The case again illustrates the fine distinctions that can influence decisions on scope and the risk that drafting nuances can get in the way of equitable outcomes. This volume submits that questions of scope are best left for determination by the court, based on the particular facts and wording of the policy, and as such there is an extent to which in this text's view they should be regarded as a separate issue from the question of (albeit with consequences for) the treatment of liability to meet a claim.[13] This volume is of the view that, in the light of approach adopted to s54 by the Australian courts and their (to a degree understandable) determination to ensure its operation does not 'depend upon the choice

8 *Ferrcom Pty Ltd v Commercial Union Assurance Co of Australia Ltd* (at 77,831 (ANZ Ins Cas)) emphasis added.

9 HC Nelson CIV-2010–442–84, 9 December 2010.

10 Demonstrated in Chapter 6.

11 (1980) 1 ANZ Ins Cas 60–401 (HC).

12 R Merkin and O Gurses, 'The Insurance Act 2015: Rebalancing the Interests of Insurer and Assured' (2015) 78(6) *Modern Law Review* 1004–1027.

13 This is explored further in Chapter 12.

that is made between various available drafting techniques,'[14] it is likely that in Australia the facts of *Barnaby* would be held to be within scope and thus subject to the application of s54. In any event, in this instance there was a clear causal linkage between the defect and the loss and as a result this volume argues that the insurer would likely escape liability as a result of s54(2), even if, unlike the NZ court, it was held that a wall with a defect was within scope. (This would be subject to the assured being unable under s54(4) to establish that some part of the loss was not caused by the breach.)

10.8 In *Hing v Security & General Insurance Co (NZ) Ltd*[15] the assured proposed to relocate his house and stated in a basis clause that haulage of the house would be performed by a particular firm of haulage contractors. In fact, the haulage operation was conducted by the insured and others who were also not qualified for the task. The house was damaged beyond repair. On the grounds that the use of unapproved hauliers contributed directly to the loss incurred, it is submitted that s54(2) would apply. It is further submitted that the insured would be unable to gain any relief as a result of either s54(3) or s54(4) as the breach clearly contributed to the loss (and so the insured would fail to show that under s54(3) that no part of the loss had been caused by the breach) and it is unlikely the insured would be able to demonstrate that some part of the loss was not caused by the breach (s54(4)). Accordingly it is suggested the insurer would avoid liability for the loss, the same result as that in the original case in NZ and a sensible outcome.

10.9 In *Sugar Hut v Great Lakes Reinsurance (UK) Plc*[16] the policy required installation of a burglar alarm that rang through to a central monitoring station. Instead, a non-specified alarm was fitted and the premises were subsequently damaged by fire. The court in England held that failure to comply with the burglar alarm provision was sufficient to release the insurers from liability under the policy. This text submits that under s54 it seems likely that the facts would fall within the ambit of s54(1) and that s54(2) would offer no relief to the insurer with the result that the insurer would be obliged to meet the claim. This outcome, which reverses the original decision, would, it is submitted, represent an improvement and a sensible and equitable result.

10.10 In *Printpak v AGF Insurance Ltd*[17] the policy contained a warranty that the insured would maintain a burglar alarm. The Court of Appeal held that the wording of the policy had the effect of limiting the impact of a breach of warranty to circumstances where there was a causal link between the breach and the loss, with the result that the alarm warranty only applied to the risk of theft and not to the risk of fire: the policy consisted of separate schedules, each concerned with a different type of risk. Applying s54 to the facts, it is first important to note that it is irrelevant whether the provision is a warranty or not. Adopting the approach set out by McClure P in *Maxwell v Highway Hauliers*,[18] this volume argues that the first question is do the facts fall within the parameters of s54(2)? It is suggested that it is clear that the breach could not be reasonably regarded as causing or contributing to the loss and so the insurer will gain no benefit under s54(2). The insurer has not suffered any

14 *East End Real Estate Pty Ltd v CE Heath Casualty & General Insurance Ltd* (1991) 25 NSWLR 400; 7 ANZ Ins Cas 61–092.

15 (1986) 4 ANZ Ins Cas 69-696.

16 [2010] EWHC 2636.

17 [1999] Lloyd's Rep IR 542.

18 (2013) 45 WAR 297, at para 75. Although the case went to the High Court on appeal this nevertheless remains a good summary of the approach courts take to s54.

prejudice and the facts otherwise fall within s54(1) with the result that if tried under the Insurance Contracts Act, it is suggested that the insurer would likely be liable to meet the claim. This volume is comfortable with this outcome and believes it is based on a sounder footing than the original decision.

10.11 In *Yorkshire Insurance Co v Campbell*[19] a horse being transported by sea and insured against marine perils and the risks of mortality was warranted, via a basis clause, to be of a certain pedigree. The horse perished during the voyage, but the insurer escaped liability as a result of a breach of the warranty concerning the pedigree of the horse. As Australia maintains its dual track regime, it is assumed these facts would likely not fall to be considered under s54 of the Insurance Contracts Act, but rather would continue to fall under the Marine Insurance Act. If it is assumed that the recommendations in ALRC 91 have been implemented, it is assumed the warranty in this instance is replaced by an express term. Under ALRC 91 the insurers would be relieved from liability in the event of a breach which was the proximate cause of the loss, even if there are other proximate causes. The burden of showing that the breach was not the proximate cause of the loss would be borne by the assured (recommendation 19). This text assumes that the insured would be able to meet this burden, with the result that the insurer would be liable to meet the loss. This outcome is to be welcomed and overturns a clear injustice that was not uncommon under the original warranties regime, where in the event of a breach of warranty, an insurer could escape liability for a loss completely unconnected to the breach. This volume believes that overcoming such injustice represents a minimum threshold for any reform to the law of insurance warranties. However, as the recommendations of ALRC 91 have yet to be implemented in Australia, the reality is that if these facts were litigated again today under the existing regime, based as it is on the original Marine Insurance Act, the outcome would likely be the same as in the original case. This volume submits that this again demonstrates a serious flaw in the Australian regime.

10.12 In *Provincial Insurance Company Ltd v Morgan and Foxton*[20] coal merchants declared that their lorry would be used for coal and this statement was converted to a warranty through a basis clause. The lorry was damaged in an accident and had that same day been used for the transport of timber, although at the time of the accident only coal was on board. In the original case the House of Lords held that on a 'strict but reasonable construction' the clause meant only that transporting coal was to be the normal use and that accordingly transporting other material would not terminate liability under the policy. This text submits that the use of timber would likely qualify as an act or omission for the purposes of s54. Although s54(2) may be held to be prima facie applicable, this volume is of the view that the insured would likely be able to demonstrate under s54(3) that no part of the loss was caused by the breach, with the result that s54(1) would apply. As the insurer has suffered no prejudice he would be obliged to meet the claim. This volume suggests that this represents a sensible outcome. The fact that it accords with the original decision is primarily a function of the gymnastics of the court on that occasion, rather than the merits of the original Marine Insurance Act.

10.13 In *Quebec Marine Insurance Co v Commercial Bank of Canada*, the insured vessel's boiler, which had been defective at the start of the voyage, became unmanageable shortly

19 [1917] 2 KB 433.
20 [1933] AC 240.

after the ship set sail. The boiler was repaired following an unscheduled stop, but the vessel was subsequently lost in severe weather. The Privy Council ruled that the assured had breached the implied warranty of seaworthiness and as a result the insurer was not liable for the loss. Once again these facts would, in Australia, fall to be considered under the Marine Insurance Act, not the Insurance Contracts Act. As we have seen, ALRC 91 recommended the abolition of implied warranties.[21] Accordingly let us assume that a requirement that the vessel be seaworthy on commencement of the voyage is incorporated as an express term. Under ALRC 91 a breach of an express term that was remedied before any loss would cease to be of significance. Accordingly, it seems clear that on these facts, assuming ALRC 91 to have been implemented, the insurer would be obliged to meet the loss. This outcome would once again be welcomed by this volume, but of course the reality is that ALRC 91 has not been implemented. The Australian marine environment remains based on the antiquated Marine Insurance Act. On these facts (and ignoring the likely incorporation into a modern policy of held covered provisions etc.), the insurer would likely continue to escape liability in modern day Australia. Once more this flags a defect in the Australian regime.

10.14 In *Bank of Nova Scotia v Hellenic Mutual War Risks, The Good Luck*[22] the House of Lords held that the effect of a breach of warranty was automatically to discharge the insurer from liability under the policy from the time of the breach. The *Good Luck* was insured by the defendant club and mortgaged to the plaintiff bank. The benefit of the insurance was assigned to the bank and the club undertook to advise the bank promptly if they ceased to insure the vessel. Cover was subject to an express warranty prohibiting the vessel from entering certain areas. In practice the vessel entered the prohibited areas on regular occasions, but the owners did not inform either the insurers or the bank. The club subsequently found out about this practice, but took no action. The vessel was lost after being hit by missiles in a prohibited area. While the club had become aware of the breach of warranty, the bank negligently failed to investigate the possibility. Assuming the loss to be covered, the bank made further advances to the owners. Liability under the policy was rejected and the bank brought a claim against the club for having failed to give prompt notice that they had ceased to insure the vessel. The House of Lords held that the breach of warranty automatically discharged the insurer from the date of the breach of warranty. As a result the club was in breach of its undertaking to inform the bank that it had ceased to insure, given it was discharged from liability as soon as the vessel entered the prohibited area. Again in Australia, the case would fall to be considered under the marine insurance regime. ALRC 91 recommended warranties should disappear and be replaced (if required by the insurers) by express contract terms under which insurers would be relieved from liability in the event of a breach which was the proximate cause of the loss, even if there were other proximate causes (recommendations 7–9). It is submitted that the outcome would likely remain the same under the ALRC 91 regime. In practice as ALRC 91 has not been implemented the facts would fall to be considered under the Marine Insurance Act. As a result the outcome in Australia would, it is suggested, be the same as in the original hearing. On the specific facts of the case, this volume is comfortable with this outcome.

21 ALRC 91, para 172.

22 [1991] 3 All ER 1, 2 Lloyd's Rep 191 (HL).

Stress testing the Australian approach: conclusions

10.15 On the basis of this analysis of past cases, where it applies, the s54 approach would appear to provide reasonably balanced outcomes that address some of the worst failings of the historic law of warranties. This however is not a complete picture. As discussed in Chapter 6, the division of the law between maritime and non-marine commercial insurance is, in this author's view, difficult to justify and results in disparate outcomes without a rational basis for the distinction. The marine regime preserves many of the most extreme aspects of the historic law on warranties. Notwithstanding that commercial practice in marine insurance overcomes many of the shortcomings of the Marine Insurance Act, in the view of this volume it remains difficult to justify the continued preservation of parallel systems. Stress testing has demonstrated how the shortcomings of the marine regime could adversely impact outcomes. The recommendations of ALRC 91, had they been adopted, would be insufficient fully to overcome this text's reservations. In terms of s54, it is clear that the industry has adapted to the mechanisms set out in the statute and in many instances stress testing has demonstrated how the application of those mechanisms would produce equitable outcomes which offer a significant improvement on the original position/that maintained in marine insurance. Nevertheless, it is this author's position that s54 provides a flawed basis for addressing breaches of warranties and other conditions, not least because, as discussed earlier,[23] the mechanism can often result in the blurring of the definition of the scope of contract.

Stress testing section 11 of the NZ Insurance Law Reform Act: applying s11 to the facts of key overseas cases

10.16 Chapter 7 has reviewed and critiqued the operation of the relevant New Zealand provisions and their interpretation by the New Zealand courts. As we have seen, unlike Australia, New Zealand has adopted a unified approach to breaches of warranties and other conditions under the Insurance Law Reform Act. Stress testing on the New Zealand regime will focus on s11 of the Insurance Law Reform Act and for these purposes it will be assumed that s11 does apply to warranties.[24] In common with the approach adopted for evaluating the merits of the provisions in Australia and the UK, the objective is to stress test the New Zealand methodology by hypothetically applying it to the facts of a number of key cases. Stress testing provides a further metric and a basis of evaluation of the New Zealand approach in isolation. In addition however, as already noted, the stress testing of common sets of facts in each of the three jurisdictions enables comparisons to be made about the relative merits of the different approaches, as well as providing useful pointers for the development of the optimised approach set out in Chapter 12.

10.17 *Maxwell v Highway Hauliers.*[25] The facts of *Maxwell* are set out in Chapter 6. If one accepts the proposition adopted by the Australian courts, that the relevant requirement in *Maxwell* (that the drivers should be PAQS qualified and submit a driver's declaration) was a suspensory provision, rather than being a scope defining clause, then it seems clear

23 See Chapter 6.
24 See Chapter 7 for a discussion of this issue.
25 *Maxwell v Highway Hauliers Pty Ltd* [2014] HCA 33, 10 September 2014, P12/2014.

that s11 would be applicable to the *Maxwell* facts. The parties in *Maxwell* accepted that there was no causal linkage between the breach and the accident so, in the same way that the assured was able to access the benefit of s54, it is likely that an equivalent NZ assured would be able to access the relief offered under s11. Certainly the facts seem to fall squarely within the objectives identified for s11 by the Contracts and Commercial Law Reform Committee of tackling 'the problem of non-causative exemptions.'[26] It is further submitted that it is reasonable to assume that a court would find that the requirement for the PAQS endorsement specified in the policy matched the requirements of s11(b) in that the absence of such a qualification would in the insurer's view be 'likely to increase the risk of such loss occurring.'[27] As a result this volume suggests the result under s11 of the NZ Insurance Law Reform Act would mirror the result in Australia.

10.18 *Pantaenius Australia Pty Ltd v Watkins Syndicate 0457 at Lloyd's*.[28] For a summary of the facts see Chapter 6. It is clear from the drafting of the policy that the provision was intended to be suspensory: 'All cover provided by the policy will be automatically suspended when your boat clears Australian Customs and Immigration for the purpose of leaving Australian waters and will recommence when it clears Australian Customs and Immigration on return.'

10.19 On appeal, the Federal Court in Australia made much of whether the clause was properly regarded as an exclusion clause that excluded certain events and circumstances on the happening of specific events, or whether the clause was one that was targeted at defining the scope of the insurance offered. This was crucial because, as we have seen, had the court decided that it was a clause defining scope, s54 would have had no application. Similarly under s11 of the Insurance Law Reform Act, it seems clear that s11 has no application to perils that are outside the scope of the policy in the first place.[29] This was confirmed by Hardie Boys J in *Barnaby v South British Insurance Co Ltd*:

> The key to this section is to be found in the last words of paragraph (b): the section is designed to deal with those kinds of exclusion clauses which provide for circumstances likely to increase the risk of a loss which the policy actually covers ... the section is not designed to deal with exclusion clauses which specify the kind of loss or the quantum of loss to which cover does not apply at all.'[30]

The analysis of whether the provision is an exclusion clause or a provision defining scope is likely, it is submitted, to be the same whether it is conducted in connection with s54 (of the ICA) or s11 of the Insurance Law Reform Act. While such analysis is, as we have seen, fraught with difficulty, there is no reason to suppose that a New Zealand court would reach a different conclusion from its Australian counterpart. As a result it is suggested that s11 would, in principle, be held as potentially applicable to the facts in this case.

10.20 According to the ruling in *New Zealand Insurance Co Ltd v Harris*,[31] establishing whether s11 applies depends on a two-stage process: (i) determine whether the insurer's

26 Contracts and Commercial Law Reform Committee Aspects of Insurance Law (1 July 1975) at 29 and 30.

27 S11(b) Insurance Law Reform Act 1977.

28 [2016] FCA 1.

29 Merkin and Nicoll, Colinvaux's Law of Insurance in New Zealand, Thompson and Reuters NZ, Wellington, 2nd Edition, 2017, page 372.

30 *Barnaby v South British Insurance Co Ltd* (1980) 1 ANZ Ins Cas 60–401 (HC) at 77,008.

31 *New Zealand Insurance Co Ltd v Harris* [1990] 1 NZLR 10 (CA).

liability has been so defined because the happening of the events or the existence of the circumstances was in the view of the insurer likely to increase the risk of occurrence of the loss; and (ii) determine whether the loss in respect of which the insured seeks to be indemnified was caused or contributed to by the happening of the events or the existence of the circumstances. If this latter test is satisfied there is a presumption of causal linkage.

10.21 With regard to the first element identified in *Harris*, this is an objective test. It is argued by this volume that the likelihood is that a New Zealand court would find that the exclusion clause in *Pantaenius* had been drafted with increased risk in mind, being the increased risk attendant with sailing outside Australian territorial waters. With regard to the second element, this text argues that, as with the finding in the Australian courts, a New Zealand court would likely find that in *Pantaenius* there was no causal linkage. Support for this argument can be found in *New Zealand Insurance Co Ltd v Harris* where the court rejected a 'but for' approach in determining the second leg (such that 'but for' the breach, the tractor in *Harris* would not have been in the lessee's possession where it was when the fire occurred). 'In construing a statutory provision of this kind designed for practical application on a day to day basis, refined analysis in terms of metaphysical inquiries into causation should be eschewed.'[32] It would, it is submitted, be bizarre to find otherwise given, absent the intention to participate in a race outside territorial waters, the vessel could have run aground at the same location as that at which the loss occurred and been covered by the policy. It was the intention to participate in a race outside territorial waters that triggered the potential increased risk that concerned the insurer, not the course navigated in territorial waters by the vessel. This is consistent with the finding in the Australian court. In the hearing in Australia the court held that the correct approach was a 'with and without' test of causation and that the nature of the risk would have been precisely the same whether the vessel had cleared Australian Customs or not (see Chapter 6). Accordingly under this analysis, the insured could establish the absence of a causal linkage and thus be able to avail himself of the benefit of s11, with the result that the insurer would be unable to avoid liability. However, in this text's submission, from a causal connection perspective, the fact that the loss occurred inside Australia's territorial waters would likely be pivotal, given that, absent this particular exclusion clause, Australian territorial waters were covered by the policy. If the loss had occurred outside Australian territorial waters there is, it is suggested, a stronger argument for the existence of a causal connection between the action that led to the exclusion clause being triggered and the loss incurred, as the only reason in such circumstances that the vessel was outside territorial waters, and the only reason it ran aground where it (hypothetically) did, would presumably be because it had participated (or was intending to participate) in an overseas race.

10.22 *Allianz Australia Insurance Ltd v Inglis*.[33] The case concerned a home and contents policy with legal liability cover. The facts are set out in Chapter 6, but in brief involved an injury to the assured's daughter caused by a lawnmower being used at a neighbour's property. The neighbour counter claimed asserting, inter alia, contributory negligence. The assured's insurer declined to indemnify on grounds of an exclusion clause covering 'injury to any person who normally lives with you, or damage to their property.' This volume

32 *New Zealand Insurance Co Ltd v Harris* [1990] 1 NZLR 10 (CA) at 16.

33 [2016] WASCA 25.

submits that it seems reasonable to assume that the exclusion clause in this instance would satisfy the requirements of s11(a) and (b) of the Insurance Law Reform Act 1977 and that a court would hold that the clause was drafted to limit the liability of the insurer and had been so drafted with the objective of reducing risk under the policy because the presence of someone living with the assured was likely in the insurer's view to increase the risk of [such] loss under the policy occurring.

10.23 Accordingly, it is submitted that analysis would turn on whether the insured was able, on a balance of probability, to establish that the loss in respect of which he sought to be indemnified was 'not caused or contributed to by the happening of such events or the existence of such circumstances.'[34] We have seen (see Chapter 6) that when considered under s54 of the Australian Insurance Contracts Act, McClure P observed in obiter comments that (had the situation constituted an 'act' for the purposes of s54) it would have increased the risk of a financial loss in respect of which cover was provided, but it was incapable of satisfying the causation requirements for legal liability and accordingly s54(2) had no application. As argued in Chapter 6, this volume believes that, under the specific requirements of s54, this analysis was flawed. While the test under s11 of the NZ Insurance Law Reform Act is more specific than that under s54(2) of the ICA, this text submits that for the purposes of s11 of the NZ Act, the insured would likely be able to establish that 'the existence of such circumstances' (being the daughter living with the assured) had not caused the loss. This would mean that the assured was able to take advantage of s11 and that accordingly he would be able to recover, despite the exclusion clause in the policy. This conclusion would produce a different outcome to that resulting from the decision of the Federal Court in Australia under s54 of the ICA. Of course, if the court were instead to conclude that the fact that the daughter was living with the assured *was* capable of constituting a causal linkage with the loss, the assured would be unable to take advantage of s11.

10.24 This volume submits that this analysis demonstrates that, as with any approach based on causal linkage, s11 of the Insurance Law Reform Act is open to differing interpretations of a given set of facts. It is submitted that no solution can be flawless in this regard.

10.25 In *Greentree v FAI General Insurance Co Ltd*[35] the NSW Court of Appeal held that a failure by a third party to make a claim on the insured within the period of insurance cover under a 'claims made and notified' policy was not an 'omission ... of some other person' within s54(1). The court held that the failure of a third party to make a claim should be regarded as an event wholly external to the policy and should precede any consideration of the policy's 'effect'[36] under s54 of the Australian Insurance Contracts Act. This author would argue that on similar facts, a court in New Zealand would also likely find that the facts meant that the insured's claim was outside the scope of contract and, as a result, s11 of the NZ Insurance Law Reform Act would be of no assistance. This is to be welcomed: courts should not be able to re-visit the scope of contract agreed by the parties.

34 S11(b) Insurance Law Reform Act 1977.

35 (1998) 44 NSWLR 706; 147 FLR 422; 158 ALR 592; 10 ANZ Ins Cas 61–423.

36 *Greentree v FAI General Insurance Co Ltd* (1998) 44 NSWLR 706; 147 FLR 422; 158 ALR 592; 10 ANZ Ins Cas 61–423 at 74,741 (ANZ Ins Cas)).

10.26 In *FAI General Insurance Co Ltd v Australian Hospital Care Pty Ltd*[37] the insured, the owner of a hospital, failed to notify the insurer of an inquiry by a patient's solicitor during the tenure of a claims made and notified policy. The insured was aware that the solicitor appeared satisfied that there was no indication of malpractice. Contrary to this expectation, the patient subsequently made a claim after the policy had expired. The court held that s54(1) of the ICA was unable to remedy an inherent restriction or limitation in the insured's claim, but held that the insured's failure to notify the circumstances constituted an omission within terms of s54, because the effect of the contract was that the insurer could refuse to meet the claim by reason only of the fact that the insured did not give notice of the occurrence to the insurer. Accordingly the court held that s54 required that the insurer could not refuse to pay the insured's claim. Applying s11 of the Insurance Law Reform Act to these facts, it is submitted that the facts would fail to meet the requirements of s11(b) of the Act: the requirement on the insured to notify was not one which, of itself, was likely to increase the risk of such loss occurring, because the notification requirement had no direct impact on the likelihood or otherwise of a claim arising. [38] Consequently, it is submitted that a court in New Zealand would likely find in favour of the insurer. On the facts it is argued that this is a preferable outcome to the original decision in the Australian court.

10.27 In *Ferrcom Pty Ltd v Commercial Union Assurance Co of Australia Ltd*[39] a policy on a mobile crane contained a condition precedent to the insurer's liability requiring notification 'as soon as possible ... of any change materially varying any of the facts and circumstances existing at the commencement of [the] policy.' The crane was subsequently registered as a motor vehicle, but Ferrcom's agent failed to pass this information to the insurer. It was accepted by both parties that the failure to notify the registration of a mobile crane for road use could not 'reasonably be regarded as being capable of causing or contributing to the loss.'[40] Applying s54 of the Insurance Contracts Act, the Australian court held that the insurer had lost its opportunity to go off risk/had suffered prejudice because of the insured's failure to notify a material alteration of the risk and this lost opportunity/prejudice was equal to the prima facie liability imposed by s54(1), which was thereby reduced to nil. This volume submits that the facts of *Ferrcom* would not fall within s11 of the NZ Act and would fail to meet the requirements of s11(b) although it is also clear that on the facts the failure to notify the insurer of the change of registration did not contribute to the loss. Accordingly it seems evident that applying the New Zealand legislation to these facts, a court would find in favour of the insurer: effectively the same outcome as in the original case.[41]

---

37 (2001) CLR 641. This decision overruled *FIA General Insurance v Perry* [1993] 30 NSWLR 89 and the rationale in *Greentree v FAI General Insurance Co Ltd.* [1998] 158 ALR 592.

38 s9 of the ILRA 1977 would not apply to permit the court to extend time, because there was no notifiable circumstance during the currency of the policy.

39 (1993) 176 CLR 332.

40 Emphasis added.

41 S9 of the Insurance Law Reform Act relates to the imposition of time limits on claims made by the assured under contracts of insurance and prevents reliance by an insurer on any contractual claims time limit other than to the extent that prejudice has been suffered.

10.28 In *Prepaid Services Pty Ltd v Atradius Credit Insurance NV*,[42] s54 was held not to apply because, on the facts, the court concluded that Atradius refused Optus Mobile's claim because it was for a payment default not covered by the policy, not because Optus Mobile had contracted with Bill Express on different terms. Applying s11 of the New Zealand Act to these facts, this volume submits that there is no reason to believe that a New Zealand court would reach a different conclusion in relation to the question of scope. Accordingly the court would similarly likely find for the insurer. This author has no difficulty with this outcome on the grounds that issues of scope should be assessed on the facts of the individual case.

10.29 In *Antico v Heath Fielding Australia Pty Ltd*[43] a Directors' and Officers' legal expenses policy indemnified the insured for legal expenses incurred in actions taken against him as a director during the period of cover. However, the indemnity was conditional upon the insurer consenting to defend the claim – consent that it was required to furnish if 'reasonable grounds' for a defence existed. The insured failed to obtain consent and argued, inter alia, that this failure could be excused under s54(1). Finding in favour of the insured, the court in Australia emphasised that it was essential that the remedial effect of s54 was not undermined by matters of form, e.g. including operational terms in the definition of the risks to which the policy responds. Applying s11 of the Insurance Law Reform Act to these facts, this volume submits that the circumstances of the case were such that the failure to seek consent was not one which met the requirements of s11(b): the requirement to seek consent had not been 'so defined because the happening of such events or the existence of such circumstances was in the view of the insurer likely to increase the risk of such loss occurring.' Accordingly the court would likely find in favour of the insurer. The original decision has been criticised earlier in this volume[44] and it is submitted that the likely decision under the Insurance Law Reform Act would represent a better outcome than that determined under s54 of the Australian Insurance Contracts Act.

10.30 In *De Hahn v Hartley*[45] we have seen that a vessel was warranted as having sailed with '50 hands or upwards,' but in fact sailed with 44. The manning shortfall was rectified soon afterwards, but the vessel was subsequently lost. Under English law at the time the insurer was able to escape liability. Applying s11 to the facts of *De Hahn v Hartley*, this text submits that it seems clear that the warranty was 'so defined because the happening of such events or the existence of such circumstances was in the view of the insurer likely to increase the risk of such loss occurring,' but that there was no causal linkage between the breach of that warranty and the loss of the vessel. Accordingly the insurer would be unable to rely on the breach of warranty to avoid indemnifying the assured, reversing the decision in the original case. This outcome is to be welcomed. The only caveat to this would be were the court to hold that the requirement for 50 hands was a condition precedent to the attachment of risk across the contract. In such circumstances the policy would not have come on risk and it is possible the insurer would escape liability.

---

42 (2013) 302 ALR 732; 17 ANZ Ins Cas 61–981; [2013] NSWCA 252. See Chapter 6 for an outline of the facts of this case.

43 (1997) 188 CLR 652; 146 ALR 385; 71 ALJR 1210; BC9703412.

44 See Chapter 6.

45 (1786) 1 TR 343.

10.31 As we have seen, in *Yorkshire Insurance Co v Campbell*[46] a horse being transported by sea was insured against marine perils and the risks of mortality. The horse was warranted (through a basis clause) to be of a certain pedigree; the horse died during the voyage, but the insurer escaped liability as a result of a breach of the warranty concerning the pedigree of the horse. Applying s11 to these facts, this volume submits that it is clear that the facts would fail to fall within the wording of s11(b) on the grounds that it would be a stretch to argue that the warranty was 'so defined because the happening of such events or the existence of such circumstances was in the view of the insurer likely to increase the risk of such loss occurring.' If this were correct, s11 would provide no assistance to the insured. However, in the unlikely event that the court were to disagree with this analysis, it is surely certain that applying s11, the insurer would be unable to escape liability on the grounds that it is clear that the breach of warranty did not 'cause or contribute' to the loss. The facts of *Yorkshire Insurance Co v Campbell* are often referred to in order to illustrate the harshness of the traditional approach to the treatment of breaches of insurance warranties. The likely failure of s11 of the Insurance Law Reform Act to assist the insured surely demonstrates that s11 falls short of providing a comprehensive solution to the challenge of providing a more equitable approach to the treatment of breaches of warranties.

10.32 In *Sugar Hut v Great Lakes Reinsurance (UK) plc*[47] the policy required installation of a burglar alarm that rang through to a central monitoring station. Although the alarm was installed, it did not ring through to the central station and the property was subsequently damaged by fire. In the original case the breach was sufficient to enable the insurer to escape liability. Applying s11 to these facts, this text submits that the tests in s11(a) and (b) would likely be satisfied as the warranty was intended to reduce the risk of loss occurring (s11(b)) and the policy provided release from the provision of indemnity in the event of breach (as per s11(a)). Accordingly the decision would likely rest on causation. While it is possible that a court might take the view that the absence of a fully operational burglar alarm may have contributed to the damage caused by fire, this volume is of the view that a more likely outcome is that the court would find that there was no such linkage and that accordingly the insurer would be unable to escape liability to indemnify the assured; a result that would reverse the original decision and one which in the view of this author is to be welcomed.

10.33 In *Provincial Insurance Company Ltd v Morgan and Foxton*[48] coal merchants declared that their lorry would be used for coal and this statement was converted to a warranty through a basis clause. The lorry was damaged in an accident and had that same day been used for the transport of timber, although at the time of the accident only coal was on board. In the original case the House of Lords held that on a 'strict but reasonable construction' the clause meant only that transporting coal was to be the normal use and that accordingly transporting other material would not terminate liability under the policy. This volume submits that it is open to debate whether these facts would pass the hurdle in s11(b): another example of this requirement potentially producing inequitable outcomes for the insured. Putting this potential issue to one side, this text submits that it is otherwise clear that the

46 [1917] 2 KB 433.
47 [2010] EWHC 2636.
48 [1933] AC 240.

court would find for the assured on the basis that the assured would be able to establish the absence of a causal linkage between the breach of warranty and the loss; this would result in the outcome of the case being unchanged from the original decision, an outcome with which this volume is comfortable.

10.34 *Forsakringsaktielselskapet Vesta v Butcher.*[49] In the original case the failure of the assured to comply with a warranty that a 24-hour watch would be maintained on the assured's fish farm was fatal to his claim for loss from storm damage. The absence of any causal linkage was irrelevant. It is assumed that applying s11, a court would be satisfied that the facts meet the requirements of s11(a). Further, assuming that the reference in s11(b) to 'such loss' refers generally to a loss for which the insurer would otherwise be liable to indemnify the insured, then it is submitted that this case would, under s11 in New Zealand, be decided upon causal link issues. Assuming this to be correct, this text submits that the court would thus likely find in the insured's favour on the grounds that the failure to post a watchman had no causal link to damage caused by the storm (this of course assumes that, on the facts, a watchman could have done nothing to mitigate the damage resulting from the storm). This volume submits that such an outcome is preferable to that reached in the original case.

10.35 In *Hibbert v Pigou*[50] the underwriters were held not liable for the loss in circumstances where in breach of a warranty, a vessel failed to sail in convoy and was lost in a storm. Applying s11 of the Insurance Law Reform Act to these facts, this text submits that these circumstances would meet the requirements of s11(a) and s11(b) and as a result would be determined on causation. On the assumption that the court accepts that the failure to sail in convoy had no causal connection with the loss of the vessel in a storm, the insurer would be liable to indemnify the insured, an outcome that overturns the original decision and one that is welcomed by this volume.

10.36 *Printpak v AGF Insurance Ltd*[51]: the facts were outlined previously and applying s11 to those facts, this text submits that it is likely a court would hold that the requirement to fit the specified type of burglary alarm would likely meet the requirements of both s11(a) and (b). As a result the issue would come down to causation. This volume submits that a court would likely find that there was no causal linkage between the failure to fit the requisite alarm and the loss as a result of fire. This would represent the same outcome as in the original case and would be welcomed by this volume.

10.37 In *Allison Pty Ltd v Lumley General Insurance Ltd, The Pilbara Pilot*[52] a vessel was insured under a marine policy that included two warranties requiring that (i) the vessel be moored on cyclone-proof mooring and (ii) the vessel be surveyed, manned, crewed and operated in accordance with the local statutory (i.e. the harbour master's) requirements. The vessel was moved in an effort to protect it from an approaching cyclone, but was lost. The insured did not dispute that the temporary mooring was not an approved mooring, or that the vessel was not moored at a cyclone-proof mooring. The insured did however argue that s84(4) of the Marine Insurance Act (Australia) 1909 meant the express warranties were not applicable. S84(4) puts the assured under a statutory duty to take reasonable measures for the

49 [1989] 1 Lloyd's Rep 331.
50 (1783) 3 Doug KB 224.
51 [1999] Lloyd's Rep IR 542.
52 [2006] WASC 104.

purposes of averting or minimising a loss.[53] The court found in favour of the assured, but the legal rationale for the decision is not entirely clear. Soyer however argues that the obligation under s84(4), as a statutory requirement, takes precedence, with the result that the insured was obliged to take all reasonable steps in order to avert or minimise loss.[54] Accordingly, even though the insured's actions amounted to a breach of warranty, this did not matter as they were reasonable and essential to avert or minimise a potential loss. However, although this volume agrees with Soyer's analysis, s14 of the Insurance Law Reform Act states that 'nothing in the Marine Insurance Act 1908 shall limit any provision of this Act and the provisions of this Act shall prevail in any case where they are in conflict with any provision of that Act.' Does this mean that the arguments made by the insured in the original hearing would not be available in New Zealand and that accordingly the insured would need to seek assistance from s11 of the Insurance Law Reform Act? On the grounds that a s84 provision[55] would potentially constrain the application of s11 on these facts (while not being in direct conflict with s11), the case is at least arguable. It may be however that a court would find that this was not the intent of s14 of the Insurance Law Reform Act, allowing the insured to take advantage of the s84/s78(4)[56] provisions. This volume would support such an approach; however, were the court not to reach this conclusion, the requirements of both s11(a) and (b) would appear satisfied by the warranties that were breached by the insured and so again the issue would likely turn on causation. Although not completely clear from the original case, it may well be that the court would find a causal linkage between the breaches and loss incurred. Were that to be the finding, the insured would ironically receive no assistance from s11 and the result of the original case would be reversed, with the insurer escaping liability. This volume submits that, whether or not on the facts a causal linkage was held to exist, the case nevertheless flags a potential defect in the remedy offered by the Insurance Law Reform Act.

10.38 *Quebec Marine Insurance Co v Commercial Bank of Canada*[57]: the facts of this case, involving the implied warranty of seaworthiness were described previously in the Australian section of this chapter. In the original case the Privy Council ruled that the assured had breached the implied warranty of seaworthiness and as a result the insurer was not liable for the loss, notwithstanding that there was no causal link between breach and loss. Applying the New Zealand legislation to these facts, it seems clear that s14 of the Insurance Law Reform Act would again come into play if these facts arose in a New Zealand context, with the result that s11 of the Act would potentially apply to the breach of implied warranty. However this view was challenged in *Womersley v Peacock*.[58] This text

53 A similar provision is included in The Institute Time Clauses Hulls Port Risks (cl 14.1 and 14.3: the 'sue and labour clause.'

54 Soyer, *Warranties in Marine Insurance*, 3rd Edition, Routledge, London, 2017, para 5.21, page 165, referencing s78(4) of the Marine Insurance Act 1906: 'It is the duty of the assured and his agents, in all cases, to take such measures as may be reasonable for the purpose of averting or minimising a loss.'

55 S78(4) of the Marine Insurance Act (NZ) 1908 is the equivalent NZ provision.

56 S78(4) Marine Insurance Act 1908 (NZ).

57 [1870] LR 3 PC 234.

58 (Unreported) High Court of NZ, Christchurch Registry CP 24/98, 8 September 1999 where Pankhurst J observed:

> exemptions, or warranties, implied by statute were not seemingly considered when s11 was drafted with reference to the circumstances in "a contract of insurance" (s11(a)) and "the view of the insurer" as to increased risk (s11(b)). As a result ... I think it is doubtful whether s 11 can override a statutory warranty.

argues that it is reasonable to assert that the implied warranty of seaworthiness meets the requirements of s11(a) and (b) of the Act and as a result the issue will turn on whether or not there is a causal connection between the breach of implied warranty and the loss. On the facts it is clear that there is no such connection and as a result this text argues that, unlike in Australia, the likely outcome is that the insurer would be obliged to meet the liability arising from the loss, reversing the original decision. This volume believes this outcome is to be welcomed.

10.39 *Bank of Nova Scotia v Hellenic Mutual War Risks, The Good Luck*[59]: the facts have been outlined in the Australian section of this chapter. This text asserts that the terms of the warranty prohibiting the vessel from entering certain areas would be held to meet the requirements of s11(a) and (b) of the Insurance Law Reform Act and as it is clear that there is a causal linkage between the vessel entering the prohibited area and its loss as a result of being hit by missiles, the insurer would likely escape liability. This volume believes that from a strict insurance law perspective this outcome is to be welcomed, however the defendant insurer club would likely still be in breach of its undertaking to inform the bank that it had ceased to insure.

Stress testing the New Zealand approach: conclusions

10.40 The stress testing of s11 of the Insurance Law Reform Act has, it is submitted, demonstrated that the New Zealand approach does hold some advantages over the Australian model. This is in part because in New Zealand there is not a two-tier approach, with marine insurance essentially being subject to the same regime as other commercial insurance in New Zealand. Importantly, the New Zealand model also avoids most of the issues with the blurring of scope encountered under s54 of the Australian Insurance Contracts Act. Additionally the clearer causal linkage approach in the New Zealand model holds, it is argued, advantages over its Australian counterpart. On the other hand, this volume has earlier demonstrated that the New Zealand model strays too far in favour of the insured. Further, it is submitted that the absence of any ability to take account of prejudice suffered by the insurer is an additional drawback, as is the fact that there is no right of termination arising from a relevant breach by the insured. Analysis of *Yorkshire Insurance Co v Campbell*[60] has shown that the wording of s11(b) requiring that the provision be 'so defined because the happening of such events or the existence of such circumstances was in the view of the insurer likely to increase the risk of such loss occurring' can additionally represent an unhelpful impediment.

10.41 Stress testing against the facts of *Allison Pty Ltd v Lumley General Insurance Ltd, The Pilbara Pilot*[61] has demonstrated that s14 of the Insurance Law Reform Act casts into doubt whether there remains a requirement in New Zealand for the insured to take all reasonable steps to avert or minimise a loss. This text believes that such a requirement is to be welcomed and that it is unlikely that it was the intent of s14 of the Insurance Law Reform Act to constrain or abolish it. Were it to do so, it would represent an unnecessary aspect of the New Zealand approach that, in this volume's view, adds no clear benefit.

59 [1991] 3 All ER 1, 2 Lloyd's Rep 191 (HL).
60 [1917] 2 KB 433.
61 [2006] WASC 104.

10.42 In summary, although representing an improvement over its Australian counterpart, the New Zealand model falls short in a number of important respects. Does the UK Insurance Act 2015 offer a more balanced approach?

Stress testing the Insurance Act 2015

10.43 This volume has critically evaluated the Insurance Act 2015 and has sought to argue that it represents a missed opportunity, having failed to address some of the key shortcomings of the law in this area, while at the same time creating additional uncertainties that are likely to lead to increased litigation. This section seeks to examine the application of the Act to the facts of a wide-ranging set of historic cases in an effort to test the Act's agility and its ability satisfactorily to deal with widely varied sets of circumstance. The analysis, it is submitted, again demonstrates some of the key shortcomings of the Act and the uncertainties that it will create. The findings will in turn be utilised to develop and support the optimised approach recommended by this volume.[62]

10.44 *Pantaenius Australia Pty Ltd v Watkins Syndicate 0457 at Lloyd's*[63]: the facts have been outlined previously. No warranty was involved, so it is clear there is no role for s10 of the Insurance Act 2015.[64] The first question in such cases is one of scope: is the risk in question covered by the policy in the first place? In *Pantaenius* the court agreed with the appellant that the relevant clause was an exclusion clause, rather than a limitation of scope. As we have seen, this text submits however that this does not, in and of itself, mean that by entering foreign waters the insured had failed to comply with a term of the policy (as required by s11(2) of the Insurance Act 2015)[65]; rather in this instance it merely meant that he triggered the exclusion clause. The court in Australia held:

> By causing the vessel to clear Australian Customs for the purpose of leaving Australian waters in order to compete in the Fremantle to Bali sailboat race, Mr. Phillips committed an act or acts within the meaning of that term in s 54(1) which led the respondent to refuse to pay his claim, being an act which occurred after the Nautilus policy was entered into.

Accordingly the court held that s54 was applicable to the facts of the case. Could the logic adopted by the Australian court be applied to bring the facts within the purview of s11 of the Insurance Act? This volume submits that it could not. S11 refers explicitly to 'the term has not been complied with.' What term of the *Pantaenius* policy has not been complied with, i.e. *breached*? On the facts of *Pantaenius* it is submitted that there is no failure to comply with a term of the policy. The reason s54 was held to apply was because the section refers to an 'act or omission' of the insured occurring after the policy has come into effect and the court held that clearing customs with the intent to compete in an offshore race was an 'act' for these purposes. It is submitted that this is not always the same as a failure to comply with (i.e. breach of) a [specific] term of the policy, as required by s11 of the Insurance Act. In the view of this volume this is sufficient reason to hold that s11 of the Insurance Act would not apply to the facts of the *Pantaenius* case.

---

62 See Chapter 12.

63 [2016] FCA 1.

64 S10 applies to warranties, not other terms.

65 S11(2) requires that a loss occurs and 'the term has not been complied with.'

10.45 On this logic, for s11 to apply, the *Pantaenius* policy would have had to include a specific term that stated, for example, that the insured would not compete in overseas races during the tenure of the policy and that were the insured to do so, cover would be suspended. Is this drafting semantics? Possibly, but the Act explicitly requires that 'a term has not been complied with' and the mere presence of an exclusion clause is surely NOT the same thing as failure to comply with a term of the policy. S11 would thus not apply and the insured would receive no benefit from it.

10.46 Even if a court were to disagree with this analysis (or if on the facts it was clear that a specific term had been breached), it would nevertheless be necessary to establish that the exclusion clause did not apply to 'the risk as whole' for s11 to be applicable. As we have seen, an argument can surely be made that an exclusion clause that suspends liability across the whole contract must, almost by definition, define the whole risk: once triggered the insurer has *no* exposure so long as the exclusion clause is active. If this analysis were correct, s11 would have no application, even if concerns over the absence of a 'failure to comply' were overcome. Accordingly the insurer would be excused liability. Only if this interpretation were incorrect, would s11 would apply. In these (it is submitted unlikely) circumstances, if the insured were able to establish that the 'non-compliance' 'could not have increased the risk of loss that actually occurred in the circumstances in which it occurred,'[66] then the insurer would be obliged to indemnify the insured, notwithstanding the triggering of the exclusion clause. Given the facts in *Pantaenius*, this text anticipates that it would be possible for the insured to meet this 'causal' requirement and the insurer would in these circumstances be obliged to indemnify; the same outcome as determined by the court in Australia applying s54. But surely this is a long bow and crucially requires significant judicial 'interpretation' of the wording of the Act? Even if the courts were inclined to adopt this approach, can it really be said to offer any benefits over the attempts by the judiciary to ameliorate the harsh effects of the law on warranties contained in the Marine Insurance Act? Indeed, this volume would argue that such an interpretation would open a whole new can of worms. If undertaking an act which is otherwise covered by the provisions of an exclusion clause is a failure to comply with the policy (i.e. a breach of the policy), then by the same token if the insured undertakes an act which is acknowledged to be outside the scope of the policy, should this not also be held to be a 'failure to comply with' (or a breach of) the policy? Where is the logic in that? Surely such an approach could not be supported.

10.47 In *Kelly v New Zealand Insurance Co Ltd* an election by an insured not to expand the scope of cover by providing the insurer with a list of valuable contents was held to be inaction and not an omission within s54 of the Insurance Contracts Act. The court observed: 'Liability was denied, not because the [insured] failed to do something, but because he deliberately elected not to extend the scope of cover beyond that specifically provided for.'[67] Utilising the logic set out previously, this author submits that a court applying the provisions of the Insurance Act 2015 would reach the same conclusion. Even if the case was not decided on the basis of scope, it is submitted that, applying the analysis of the Australian court, as there was no breach, neither s10 nor s11 of the Insurance Act would have any application: both sections require there to have been a breach of a provision of the policy.

66 S11(3) Insurance Act 2015.

67 *Kelly v New Zealand Insurance Co Ltd,* Owen J at 67,518 (ANZ Ins Cas).

Similarly this text submits that under the facts of *Greentree v FAI General Insurance Co Ltd*[68] a court applying the Insurance Act 2015 would reach the same conclusion as that reached in the final Australian court, which ruled that a failure by a third party to make a claim on the insured within the period of insurance cover under a 'claims made and notified' policy was not an 'omission ... of some other person' (as per s54 (1) of the Insurance Contracts Act), but rather an event wholly external to the policy and should preclude any consideration of the policy's 'effect.'[69] It is submitted that a court applying the Insurance Act would likely find the facts to be outside the scope of the policy. Even if the court concluded that the circumstances were not outside the scope of cover, it is hard to see how either s10 or s11 of the Insurance Act would have any impact. S10 would not apply as there has been no breach of a warranty. It is further submitted that s11 would also have no application because the term that has not been complied with (the tenor of the policy) is surely one that applies to the risk as a whole and as such, s11 would have no relevance.

10.48 *Antico v Heath Fielding Australia Pty Ltd* concerned a Directors' and Officers' legal expenses policy under which the insured was indemnified for legal expenses incurred in actions taken against him as a director during the period of cover.[70] However, the indemnity was conditional upon the insurer consenting to defend the claim – consent that it was required to furnish if 'reasonable grounds' for a defence existed. The insured failed to obtain consent and argued, inter alia, that this failure could be excused under s54(1). Finding in favour of the insured, the court stressed that it was essential that the effectiveness of s54 was not undermined by matters of form. Recognising that it remained important to distinguish matters of scope, while at the same time acknowledging it was sometimes difficult to do so, the Australian court stressed the distinction between terms of a policy that should be seen as conditions to be met by the insured, and terms that might expand the scope of the policy. Applying the Insurance Act to these facts, if the requirement to seek consent was a warranty (unlikely as this may be), this text asserts that s10 of the Insurance Act would not assist the assured as the breach was not one which, on the facts, was capable of remedy and so liability would remain suspended under s10(2).[71] In relation to s11, as the provision of the indemnity was conditional upon the insured seeking consent to defend the claim, this volume would submit that it is likely that a court would hold that either the requirement to seek permission was a term which defined the risk as a whole or, much more likely, was a non-risk provision (section 11 of the Insurance Act does not apply to non-risk provisions) and, as such, in either case would fall outside the application of s11 of the Act. If this were correct, the section would also offer no assistance to the insured. We have seen in Chapter 6 that this volume is not uncritical of the original decision in *Antico* and in many ways the likely interpretation under the Insurance Act can thus be considered to offer a better outcome, although as we have seen, this author regards it as a failing that the Insurance Act does not apply to non-risk provisions.

10.49 In *Prepaid Services Pty Ltd v Atradius Credit Insurance NV*,[72] s54 of the ICA was held not to apply because the reason the insurer was able to refuse payment was because the

68 (1998) 44 NSWLR 706; 147 FLR 422; 158 ALR 592; 10 ANZ Ins Cas 61–423.

69 *Greentree v FAI General Insurance Co Ltd* (1998) 44 NSWLR 706; 147 FLR 422; 158 ALR 592; 10 ANZ Ins Cas 61–423 at 74,741 (ANZ Ins Cas).

70 *Antico v Heath Fielding Australia Pty Ltd* (1997) 188 CLR 652.

71 S10 Insurance Act 2015.

72 (2013) 302 ALR 732; 17 ANZ Ins Cas 61–981; [2013] NSWCA 252.

insured's claim was in respect of a payment default which was not covered by the policy: that it was outside the scope of the policy. The Australian court stressed that in interpreting the effect of the contract, the court should adopt a substance over form approach; Meagher JA commented that it remained necessary 'to have regard to the nature of the risk and subject matter insured as well as the commercial or other context in which the insurance is written.' This text submits that a court in England would adopt a similar approach in interpreting issues of scope under the Insurance Act. Accordingly, it is submitted that the decision in England on the same facts would likely be no different from that reached in Australia under the Insurance Contracts Act: the provisions of the Act are substantially irrelevant to determining matters of scope.

10.50 *Ferrcom Pty Ltd v Commercial Union Assurance Co of Australia Ltd*[73] involved a mobile crane, and the policy contained a condition precedent to the insurer's liability requiring notification 'as soon as possible ... of any change materially varying any of the facts and circumstances existing at the commencement of [the] policy.' The crane was subsequently registered as a motor vehicle, but Ferrcom's agent failed to pass this information to the insurer. As the parties in the Australian hearing accepted that the failure to notify the registration of a mobile crane for road use could not 'reasonably be regarded as being capable of causing or contributing to the loss,' the case fell to be considered under s54(1) of the Insurance Contracts Act. The court held that the insurer had suffered prejudice: the insurer had lost its opportunity to go off risk because of the insured's failure to notify a material alteration of the risk and this lost opportunity was held to be equal to the liability imposed by s54(1), which was thereby reduced to nil. If the requirement for notification were held to be a warranty, s10 of the Insurance Act would apply. This volume submits that as the breach remained in place at the time of loss, s10 would offer no assistance to the assured as liability would be suspended (s10(2)). Furthermore this text submits that s10(5) and (6) would also not offer the insured any assistance as the breach had not been remedied/the risk could not be said to be the same as originally contemplated. Would s11 offer any assistance? This volume has argued (see Chapter 9) that s11 can have no application to non-risk provisions. Assuming this to be correct, s11 would also offer no assistance to the insured. This is, in effect, the same outcome as delivered by the Australian court, albeit for different reasons. As we have seen, the Insurance Act also makes no provision for any prejudice suffered by the insurer, something this volume regrets.

10.51 In the unlikely event that the court did not take the view outlined previously, this volume suggests that the term that has not been complied with could be one which relates to (or in the words of s11(1) 'defines') the risk as a whole, in which case s11 would not be applicable and the insured would accordingly again receive no benefit from it. Only in circumstances where the clause in the contract was held not to relate to the risk as a whole (and the court rejected the argument relating to non-risk provisions) would the insured potentially be able to benefit from s11. In this situation the acknowledgment by the parties of the absence of causal linkage would likely mean that the facts would fall within s11(3) of the Insurance Act on the grounds that 'the non-compliance with the term could not have increased the risk of loss which actually occurred in the circumstances in which it occurred.' Were this the case, the insurer would be prevented from relying on the breach by s11(2)

73 (1993) 176 CLR 332.

with the result that, with no ability to take account of prejudice suffered by the insurer in such circumstances, the insurer would likely be held liable. This text submits that this would be both an unlikely and unwelcome outcome. The more likely and supportable outcome under the Insurance Act is that the assured would, for the reasons explained, be offered no assistance by either s10 or s11 of the Act.

10.52 How would a court treat the facts of *FAI General Insurance Co Ltd v Australian Hospital Care Pty Ltd*[74] under the Insurance Act 2015? In this case the insured owned a hospital and failed to notify the insurer of an inquiry by a patient's solicitor during the period of insurance in a claims made and notified policy. The insured was aware that the solicitor appeared satisfied that there was no indication of malpractice. However, the patient subsequently made a claim after the policy had expired. Applying s54 of the Insurance Contracts Act, the court in Australia held that the insured's failure to notify the circumstances constituted an omission within terms of s54 because the effect of the contract was that the insurer could refuse to meet the claim by reason only of the fact that the insured did not give notice of the occurrence to the insurer. Accordingly, the court held that s54 required that the insurer could not refuse to pay the insured's claim. As discussed in Chapter 6, it is submitted that this was a step too far by the Australian courts. In the view of this text, a court applying the provisions of the Insurance Act 2015 would conclude that the provisions relating to the notification of claims were not risk provisions and were accordingly outside the reach of s11 of Insurance Act 2015 and as a result the insured would not receive any assistance from the Act and the insurer would be held not to be liable. For the reasons discussed in Chapter 9, this author views this as a sensible outcome, notwithstanding that he concurs with the views of Merkin and Gurses that the failure of the Insurance Act to address non-risk issues is an omission.[75] On the facts, it is submitted that such an outcome would represent an improvement on the original decision.

10.53 The facts in *Allison Pty Ltd v Lumley General Insurance Ltd, The Pilbara Pilot*[76] have been outlined previously. This text agrees with Soyer's analysis of the likely impact of s78(4) of the Marine Insurance Act[77] and accordingly, were the same facts to be considered now in England (i.e. following the enactment of the Insurance Act), it would seem that prima facie a court would likely reach the same conclusion, finding that s78(4) permitted (as it remains unaltered by the Insurance Act 2015), in effect, certain breaches of warranty, in addition to the forgiving measures set out in s10 and s11 of the Insurance Act. In this instance it seems unlikely that s10 and s11 would offer any assistance to the insured because (a) the breach remained unrectified at the time of loss[78] and (b) there was a likely causal connection between the breach and loss.[79]

10.54 *Allianz Australia Insurance Ltd v Inglis.*[80] The facts have been outlined previously. If the case was to be assessed under the Insurance Act 2015, it is clear that s10 would have no application; the exclusion clause was not in the form of a warranty. Would s11 be applicable? The first question that a court would need to address would be, did the exclusion

74 (2001) CLR 641.

75 R Merkin and O Gurses, 'Insurance Contracts after the Insurance Act 2015' (2016) 132(3) LQR 445.

76 [2006] WASC 104.

77 As discussed in the stress testing of s11 of the NZ Insurance Law Reform Act earlier in this chapter.

78 S10(2) Insurance Act 2015.

79 S11(3) Insurance Act 2015.

80 [2016] WASCA 25.

clause apply to the risk as a whole? This text believes that an argument could certainly be made that the provision does indeed apply to the risk as a whole. As already argued previously, as the clause (and indeed most exclusion provisions), when operative, triggers for the insurer *complete* release from liability, surely it must, by definition, apply to the whole risk? Alternatively, could it be argued that the risk as a whole in this context is the totality of the risk provided by the home and contents policy, of which legal liability was, in effect, a subset, a particular kind of risk for the purposes of s11? On balance, this volume is of the view that the more compelling argument is that in this context, the risk as a whole refers to the legal liability cover, rather than the totality of the cover under the whole home and contents policy. If this is correct s11 of the Insurance Act would have no application and the court would find in favour of the insurer, the same result as in Australia.

10.55 However, even if it were held that the provision does not apply to the whole risk, it is, in the view of this text, doubtful that s11 would offer any assistance to the insured. Following the logic set out earlier in the analysis of the *Pantaenius* case, surely it cannot be argued that the policy, by implication, has a requirement that the insured has no one normally living with him, simply because the exclusion clause triggers in relation to anyone who is living with the insured? In this volume's view there are no grounds for such a proposition. Absent such a requirement (and there was none on the face of the policy either), it is difficult to see how, on the facts, it can be argued that the insured has failed to comply with a term of the policy.[81] Without such a failure to comply, there is no role for s11. Does it make any difference that the trigger in this instance is a 'state of affairs,' rather than an act or omission?[82] It is this volume's position that it does not. There is nothing in s11 to support such a proposition. The fact that the trigger is one that can only be established over a period of time is in no way distinguished in the language in s11. What s11(2) requires is for there to be a term that has not been complied with, i.e. breached. As with the *Pantaenius* case, on these facts there has been no failure to comply and accordingly this text submits s11 would have no application. As a result the insurer would have no liability, the same outcome as under s54 of the Australian Insurance Contracts Act. As we have seen, it is this volume's view that the failure of the Insurance Act to cover exclusion clauses that are triggered without a breach of condition is a significant flaw in the legislation.

10.56 *Maxwell v Highway Hauliers.*[83] The facts have been outlined earlier in this chapter. As we have seen,[84] on appeal the High Court in Australia held that s54 of the Insurance Contract Act applied and that accordingly the insurer was liable for the losses incurred. Even if the requirements relating to the drivers were held to be warranties, s10 of the Insurance Act would offer no assistance to the insured as the breaches remained un-remedied at the time of loss and as a result the policy as a whole would prima facie be suspended.

10.57 Once again in assessing the applicability of s11 of the Insurance Act, the first question is did the relevant term apply to the risk as a whole? If it did, s11 has no application. In the analysis of Corboy J in the Australian Court of Appeal, the policy was

81 S11(2) of the Insurance Act requires that 'the term has not been complied with.'

82 The court in Australia held that the fact that the insured's daughter was living with him at the time of the accident was a 'state of affairs,' rather than an act or omission as required under s54 of the Insurance Contracts Act.

83 [2012] WASC 53.

84 See Chapter 6.

not concerned with drivers as such, rather it was concerned with the vehicles and their use.[85] The policy was an insurance against loss of, or damage to, vehicles and third party liabilities arising from the use of them. If this is a correct analysis, surely it could be argued that the requirement for all drivers to undertake a PAQS test was a requirement that sought to define the risk as a whole (by adding, in effect, a conditionality to the coverage); if that were the case s11 would have no application and the insurer would thus escape liability. At the same time however, Corboy J also acknowledged that the policy was not confined to the risk of accidental damage caused by a driver. Could it not therefore be argued that the requirement for a PAQS test only related to such risks and, as a result, fell *within* the s11 requirement that the relevant clause would tend to reduce the risk of a *particular* kind? This example again highlights the difficulty in interpreting the carve out in s11 of the Insurance Act, that the section will have no application to provisions that define the risk as a whole. Until a number of cases have been tested in the courts it will be very difficult confidently to predict how this provision will be interpreted on a case by case basis. For the purposes of the remainder of this discussion it will be assumed that the facts of *Highway Hauliers do* fall within s11.

10.58 The next question therefore is whether in this instance there is a provision in the policy which has not been complied with (in accordance with s11(2))? While at first sight similar to the cases involving exclusion clauses already examined, this text submits that in this instance s11 of the Insurance Act would likely apply. Although the circumstances were covered by the policy's exclusion clause, in this instance the policy *did* include requirements (the requirement for all drivers to undertake a PAQS test and submit a driver's declaration) that had not been complied with by the insured. Accordingly this text is of the view that, if the requirement for PAQS testing is held to apply to a particular risk, then the circumstances would likely be held to fall within s11. As it was accepted that there was no causal linkage between the breach and loss, it seems likely the insured would be able to satisfy s11(3). In such circumstances, the insurer would be liable – the same outcome as under s54 of the Australian Insurance Contracts Act.

10.59 This volume submits that accordingly it seems clear that s11 will apply to exclusion clauses only where there is a separate provision in the policy that has not been complied with (i.e. has been breached) by the insured and only if it is accepted that the exclusion clause does not define the risk as a whole. It will be observed that this leads to the perverse outcome that, when there are *additional* requirements imposed on the insured and these have been *breached* by the insured, the result, under the Insurance Act, is *less* protection for the insurer. This text suggests that this is at best counter intuitive and at worst undesirable.

10.60 *New Zealand Insurance Co Ltd v Harris*[86]: as we have seen, in this case the policy 'warranted' that the tractor that was the subject of the policy would not be let out on hire for commercial purposes. This provision was breached and the tractor destroyed by fire. In *Harris* the court interpreted s11 of the New Zealand Insurance Law Reform Act in a way that prevented the insurers from declining liability to indemnify for losses to equipment during commercial use when the cover by its terms was confined to private use. The New Zealand court held that cover should not be lost by reason of a hiring which merely set the

85 [2012] WASC 53 at 99–101.
86 [1990] 1 NZLR 10 (CA).

scene for a loss by fire, but could not be regarded as the proximate cause of the loss. S10 of the Insurance Act would again be no assistance to the insured (assuming the provision was held to be a warranty) as the breach subsisted at the time of loss. For the purpose of this stress testing exercise, this text will assume that s11 can apply to warranties in addition to s10.[87]

10.61 In evaluating the relevance of s11 of the Insurance Act 2015, the first question would again be, are the circumstances outside the scope of cover? If they are s11 will offer no assistance to the insured but, for the sake of argument, let us assume a court would hold that the facts were within the scope of the policy. The next issue is does the provision define the risk as a whole? Colinvaux suggests that letting out the tractor on commercial terms could be regarded as a material change in the risk that the insurer had agreed to cover.[88] This text would agree with this analysis and argues that a court would likely find that a condition on these terms does indeed define the risk as whole.[89] In order for s11 to come into play it would be necessary to establish that the provision against commercial use was aimed at reducing a loss of a particular kind, or at a particular location or particular time.[90] While this volume recognises such a conclusion is possible, it argues that it is more likely the court would find s11 did not apply.

10.62 In the perhaps unlikely event that a court reached a different conclusion, it would then be up to the insured to demonstrate that the breach 'could not have increased the risk of loss which occurred in the circumstances in which it occurred' under s11(3). In this context, should special attention be given to the 'could' in s11(3)? This text would argue that surely this widens the test from whether there was *actually* a causal linkage to whether there *could* have been a causal linkage. If this is correct, it will make it a higher bar for the insured to surmount. Might it also bring into play the 'refined analysis in terms of metaphysical inquiries into causation,' rejected by the New Zealand court in *Harris*?[91] We have seen that s54(2) of the Insurance Contracts Act in Australia permits the insurer to refuse to pay a claim where the act or omission *could* reasonably be regarded as being capable of causing or contributing to a loss in respect of which insurance cover is provided by the contract. (As we have seen this is subject to four qualifications, one of which is if the assured proves that no part of the loss was caused by the breach, the insurer may not refuse to pay the claim by reason only of that act (ICA, s54(3)). Certainly the interpretation in Australia has been that if there are circumstances where the act or omission could reasonably have contributed to the loss (regardless in the first instance whether it actually did), the initial test is passed.[92] This text suggests that it seems likely a similar approach would be adopted in the English courts. However, unlike in the Insurance Contracts Act, under s11 of the Insurance Act there is no subsequent opportunity for the insured to demonstrate that, in reality, there was no causal linkage between the breach and loss. Accordingly, this text submits that, on the facts of *Harris*, s11 would likely offer no assistance to the insured. Regrettably, this

87 See Chapter 8 for a discussion of the relationship between s10 and s11(4) of the Insurance Act 2015.

88 Merkin and Nicoll, *Colinvaux's Law of Insurance in New Zealand,* Thompson and Reuters NZ, Wellington, 2nd Edition, 2017.

89 Assuming again that it was in scope, although *Colinvaux's* analysis would suggest otherwise.

90 S11(1) Insurance Act.

91 *New Zealand Insurance Co Ltd v Harris* [1990] 1 NZLR 10 (CA) at 16.

92 The Explanatory Notes to the Draft Insurance Contracts Bill 1982 indicated that the test for s54(2) was whether the relevant conduct could reasonably have been considered capable of contributing to the loss.

volume believes that the formulation in s11(3) of the Insurance Act will only increase the uncertainty regarding the threshold the insured will need to overcome in order to satisfy the requirements of the subsection.

10.63 What if the policy in *Harris* had been drafted as being one that covered private use only of the tractor (without the confirmation that the tractor would not be let out on hire for commercial purposes), could it be said that a term of the policy has not been complied with (breached) if the tractor *was* subsequently let out on commercial terms? In the absence of an explicit term, forbidding the letting out of the tractor on commercial terms, might the court be inclined to take the view that one is implied? Conceivably in the view of this volume, but what really would be the difference between these circumstances and those of *Pantaenius* and *Allianz Australia Insurance Ltd v Inglis* discussed earlier? In neither of these cases was there an explicit term that had been breached; in this instance however it is surely easier to argue that letting the tractor out on commercial terms would represent a breach of the provision for private use only and this author believes a court would find as such. Nevertheless, the other reservations discussed earlier would still need to be overcome for s11 to apply.

10.64 We have seen that in *Sugar Hut v Great Lakes Reinsurance (UK) Plc*[93] the policy required installation of a burglar alarm that rang through to a central monitoring station. Instead, a non-specified alarm was fitted and the premises were subsequently damaged by fire. The court held that failure to comply with the burglar alarm provision was sufficient to release the insurers from liability under the policy. Assuming that the provision was a warranty, s10 of the Insurance Act would apply and under s10(2), as the breach remained un-rectified, liability across the policy as a whole would be suspended with the result that the insurer would prima facie escape liability, as in the original decision. This volume submits however that it is likely that the warranty would likely be held to apply to a loss of a particular kind under s11(1) and that the insured could meet the requirements of s11(3), by demonstrating that non-compliance could not have increased the risk of the loss that actually occurred in the circumstances in which it occurred. Accordingly the insurer would be liable to meet the loss, a much more equitable outcome than originally achieved.

10.65 *Nelson Forests Ltd v Three Tuis Ltd.*[94]: as outlined earlier, in this case the issue that arose was essentially one relating to the scope of the policy. Cover was provided for legal liability for accidents 'in connection with' the operation of a lifestyle farm business. There was a fire that arose from tourism activities undertaken by the assured on the property. The court held that s11 of the New Zealand Insurance Law Reform Act could not operate to give the assured cover for a kind of liability that the insurer had never agreed to cover in the first place, i.e. in relation to non-farming operations. Putting it another way, the NZ court found that the scope of the policy was restricted to lifestyle farming: losses from tourism were outside the scope of the policy. As there is no warranty, s10 of the Insurance Act 2015 would have no application. This text submits that it is clear that for s11 to apply, the risk must be one within the scope of the policy. Accordingly it is argued that an English court would, like its NZ counterpart, likely find that the facts of *Nelson Forests* were outside the scope of the policy and, as a result, that s11 had no application. This seems a sensible approach.

93 [2010] EWHC 2636.

94 HC Nelson CIV-2010–442–84, 9 December 2010.

10.66 *Barnaby v South British Insurance Co Ltd*[95]: in this case, another instance where the determination of the scope of the policy was key to the decision, the assured had built a wall that subsequently collapsed as a result of a defect in its construction. The New Zealand court ruled that, because there was a fault or defect in the construction of the wall, the policy did not provide cover (i.e. the loss was outside the scope of the policy). On the facts, it is arguable that the court could have construed the policy as one that covered the construction of the wall, in which case the building of the wall with a defect would arguably have been 'the existence of certain circumstances' within s11(a) of the New Zealand Act. In these circumstances the assured would prima facie have received protection.[96] Under English law, this text argues that the key issue would also be one of scope. If the court determined that the facts were outside the scope of cover, the Insurance Act would offer no protection to the assured. If the court held that the building of a defective wall was within scope, then, assuming the provision was not held to be a warranty, the court would need to determine if the provision was one that defined the risk as a whole; were if to do so, s11 of the Insurance Act would have no application. Even if the court held that the provision did not define the risk as a whole, this text submits that the insured would likely fail to meet the 'causal linkage' requirements of s11(3) of the Insurance Act[97] and as a result the Act would not come to his aid. Finally there is no exclusion clause and accordingly this would not be an instance where a specific risk, which would otherwise have been covered by the policy, is excluded as a result of the exclusion clause. Had there been such a clause which excluded (for example) damage incurred as a result of defective workmanship, this text would argue that s11 of the Insurance Act would offer no protection as there had been no breach (non-compliance) of a policy term, unless there was also a provision that forbade the building of a wall with a defect (however unlikely such a provision might be), which was then subsequently breached by the assured.

10.67 *Hing v Security & General Insurance Co (NZ) Ltd*[98]: a contractors' all risk house removal policy required a professional firm to undertake the move and excluded liability in the event of any change in the method of removal work being undertaken. In the event the insured did the work himself with others who also had no experience. In the course of the move the house was damaged beyond repair. The New Zealand court found the assured had breached a material warranty and was unable to recover. If the court in England agreed the undertaking was a warranty, s10 of the Insurance Act would apply (as well, potentially, as s11). This text would argue that, on the facts, the insurer would have no liability as a result of s10(2). In this instance the breach would, it is submitted, be incapable of remedy and as a result s10 would offer no assistance to the assured. Does s11 offer any assistance to the assured? Applying s11, this volume submits that a court may well decide that the undertaking was one that went to the definition of the risk as a whole, in which case, as we have seen, s11 would offer no assistance to the assured. If the court

95 (1980) 1 ANZ Ins Cas 60–401 (HC).

96 The interpretation put on the policy by the NZ court was that it defined the risk only in terms of buildings which did not contain design defects. In practice a different interpretation would have made no difference to the outcome as there was a causal link between defect and the claim so there would have been no recovery because of s11(b) of the New Zealand Act.

97 S11(3) requires that the insured demonstrate that non-compliance could not have increased the risk of the loss which actually occurred in the circumstances in which it occurred.

98 (1985) 4 ANZ Ins Cas 60–696 (HC).

did not proceed on these lines, then certainly there had been a non-compliance in line with the requirements of s11(2) and so the issue would then turn on whether the assured was able to satisfy the requirements of s11(3) by demonstrating that his breach could not have increased the risk of loss that actually occurred in the circumstances in which it occurred. It seems inevitable that he would fail to do so and as a result s11 would also offer no assistance to him, an outcome which, given the nature of the breach, is surely to be welcomed.

10.68 It is submitted that the decision in *De Hahn v Hartley*[99] (the facts have been summarised earlier in this chapter) would be reversed were identical facts to come before a court for decision under the Insurance Act 2015, unless the court were to view the undertaking regarding manning levels as a condition precedent to cover. Assuming the warranty requiring the vessel to sail with at least 50 crew was not a condition precedent to cover, then applying the Insurance Act to these facts, under s10(2) the insurer's liability would be suspended from the point the vessel left port undermanned, until such time as the shortfall was rectified. Once the breach had been remedied[100] the insurer's liability would be restored with the result that, unlike in the original case, the insurer would be liable to meet the insured's losses. This outcome is to be welcomed. Although not relevant, as the insured would have received relief under s10, this volume would argue that no relief would be available under s11 as the court would likely find that the requirement for a given level of crew applied to (in effect defined) the risk as a whole. If the court took a different view, relief for the insured would likely be available under s11(2) and (3): the insurer would be unable to avoid liability as the breach could not have increased the risk of the loss which actually occurred in the circumstances in which it occurred.

10.69 What if the provision were viewed as a condition precedent to cover? As we have seen,[101] this volume has argued that, as condition precedents are by definition time dependent (the condition must usually be met by the date the contract is due to come into effect, or on occasion, an earlier date), remedy of a breach of a warranty which is also a condition precedent will potentially fall to be considered under s10(5)(a) and s10(6) as a situation where, in relation to a time dependent warranty the risk, once the conditionality is met, is essentially the same as that originally contemplated by the parties. Accordingly this text would argue that under the facts of *De Hahn v Hartley*, s10(5) and (6) would likely apply, such that the policy would come on risk once the initial failure to meet the terms of the condition precedent was rectified.[102] As a result the insurer would be liable for the loss as the policy would, by the time of the loss, be on risk. This volume has argued that s11 will offer limited assistance in relation to conditions precedent. This volume's case is that the only way a condition precedent could be caught by s11 would be if the provision made clear that it was a condition precedent *only* in relation to the

---

99 (1786) 1 TR 343.

100 It is submitted that bringing the manning level to the warranted quantity would remedy the breach, either on the basis of s10(5)(b) of the Insurance Act; the breach being remedied, or if it was held to fall within the class of remedy covered by s10(6) (time related warranties), because once the manning levels were at the required level, the risk to which the warranty related were essentially the same as originally contemplated (s10(5)(a)).

101 See Chapter 9.

102 As we have seen, a contrary view would argue that if the condition precedent has not been met, there is no contract of insurance as required by s10(2) of the Insurance Act and so s10 has no application and the insurer has no liability.

specific risk, *not* the contract as a whole.[103] Further, this volume has argued[104] that s11 should have no application to CPs to the attachment of risk to the contract because were it to do so, the determination of whether a contract was on foot or not would depend upon whether the insured was able to satisfy s11(3) and as a result this would mean that whether a contract was on foot or not would be dependent on the nature of loss that may, or may not, occur at some point in the future.[105]

10.70 In *Forsakringsaktielselskapet Vesta v Butcher*[106] it was held that the failure of the assured to comply with a warranty that a 24-hour watch would be maintained on the assured's fish farm was fatal to his claim for loss from storm damage. Although the Law Commission claimed the outcome of this case would be reversed under the Insurance Act, we have seen that this volume disputes this.[107] Applying the Insurance Act 2015 to these facts, it is submitted that as the insured was still in breach at the time of loss, s11, rather than s10, would be the relevant provision.[108] Once again in relation to s11, the key question would be, was the relevant term one that defined the risk as a whole? If it was, and this text would argue that it was, s11 would have no application and the insurer will be able to escape liability: the same outcome as in the original case. If the court were not to agree with this assessment, does s11 offer the assured any assistance? If the court were to determine that the provision related to a particular kind of risk (risks that a watch may have been able to ameliorate?), then the insured could be expected to satisfy the requirements of s11(3) and thus the insurer would be held liable for the loss, reversing the original decision. While this would represent an outcome that is to be welcomed, it is unfortunately one that this volume suggests is unlikely on the facts, again flagging the inability of the Insurance Act provisions to provide a comprehensive solution.

10.71 The facts of *Provincial Insurance Company Ltd v Morgan and Foxton*[109] have been summarised previously. Applying the Insurance Act to these facts and assuming the court finds the provision to be a warranty, it is possible that a court would hold that, applying s10 of the Insurance Act, as only coal was on board the lorry at the time of the loss, the insured had ceased to be in breach of the warranty in which case the breach would be taken as remedied and the insurer would be liable to meet the loss. This would seem a sensible and reasonable outcome. This text would argue that it is more difficult to see how s11 could assist the assured. It is submitted that a court would likely find that the provision was one that defined the risk as a whole (mainly because it is hard to see that the term tends to reduce the risk of a particular kind, at a particular location or at a particular time[110]) with the result that the term fell outside s11. Of course if the court were to take the view that the term reduced the loss of a particular kind (the risk from transporting goods other than coal perhaps?), the insured would likely be able to satisfy

103 See Chapter 9.

104 See Chapter 9.

105 See Chapter 9.

106 [1989] 1 Lloyd's Rep 331.

107 See Chapter 9.

108 S10 would offer no assistance to the insured as the policy would be suspended under s10(2) as, on the facts, the breach was not capable of rectification. If the breach had been capable of rectification and had been so rectified the insurer's liability would have been restored under s10(4) of the Insurance Act.

109 [1933] AC 240.

110 Under s11(1) of the Insurance Act a term is taken to apply to the risk as whole unless compliance would tend to reduce the risk of (one or more of) a particular kind, particular location or particular time.

the requirements of s11(3) by demonstrating that the non-compliance with the term had not increased the risk of the loss that actually occurred in the circumstances in which it occurred.[111] This volume would argue that the uncertainty over whether s11 would apply again flags the shortcomings of the section.

10.72 In *Printpak v AGF Insurance Ltd*[112] we have seen that the policy contained a warranty that the insured would maintain a burglar alarm. The Court of Appeal held that the wording of the policy had the effect of limiting the impact of a breach of warranty to circumstances where there was a causal link between the breach and the loss, with the result that the alarm warranty only applied to the risk of theft and not to the risk of fire: the policy consisted of separate schedules, each concerned with a different type of risk. If s10 of the Insurance Act were applied to these facts (i.e. if the provision were held to be a warranty), it would seem likely that, subject to s11 providing any assistance, as there is a clear breach (that had not been remedied at the time of loss) the policy as a whole would be suspended under s10(2) with the result that the original decision would be reversed and the insurer would accordingly escape liability for the loss. Would s11 offer any assistance to the insured? As discussed previously,[113] it is not clear if s10 is subject to s11 (such that if the sections conflict, s11 would take precedence), but for the purposes of stress testing it will be assumed that it is. Consistent with the original decision, it does seem likely that the court would rule that these facts fell within s11(1) and that compliance would tend to reduce the loss of a particular kind. In these circumstances the insured's ability to claim would depend upon his ability to demonstrate under s11(3) that the non-compliance 'could not have increased the risk of loss that actually occurred in the circumstances in which it occurred.'[114]

10.73 Stress testing the Insurance Act against the facts of *Hibbert v Pigou*[115] was considered in Chapter 9, the case again demonstrating the uncertainties likely to arise under the Insurance Act.

10.74 As we have seen, in *Quebec Marine Insurance Co v Commercial Bank of Canada*, the insured vessel's boiler that had been defective at the start of the voyage became unmanageable shortly after the ship set sail. The boiler was repaired following an unscheduled stop, but the vessel was subsequently lost in severe weather. The Privy Council ruled that the assured had breached the implied warranty of seaworthiness and, as a result, the insurer was not liable for the loss. Under the Insurance Act 2015 implied warranties are retained.[116] Accordingly, applying s10 of the Act, once the implied warranty was breached the insurer's liability would be suspended. Following the repair of the defect, under s10(4) and s10(5) and (6) of the Act, the insurer would, this text suggests, again be on risk and as a result would be liable for the losses incurred, reversing the original decision. Again, in this volume's view, this is a preferable outcome compared to that in the original hearing. Access to s11 of the Insurance Act would not be required by the insured; however, it is nevertheless useful to consider how the court might assess its application to the facts. The first question to be addressed

111 S11(3) Insurance Act 2015.
112 [1999] Lloyd's Rep IR 542.
113 See Chapter 8.
114 S11(3) Insurance Act.
115 (1783) 3 Doug KB 224.
116 S10(1) and s11(1) Insurance Act 2015.

is does the implied warranty of seaworthiness apply to the 'risk as a whole'?[117] This author would argue that it surely must be the case that the implied warranty does apply to the risk as a whole and that accordingly s11 has no application. S11 does not explicitly deal with breaches that have been rectified: s11(2) states, 'If a loss occurs and the term has not been complied with'; nevertheless, this author would argue that if it was held that the implied warranty of seaworthiness was *not* a term that applied to the risk as a whole, the insured would likely be able to recover under s11(2) and (3). The fact that the implied warranty had not been complied with at the commencement of the voyage would be sufficient for 11(2), and the insured would likely be able to establish under s11(3) that the breach could not have increased the risk of loss which actually occurred in the circumstances in which it occurred.

10.75 In *Yorkshire Insurance Co v Campbell*[118] the policy provided cover on a horse being transported by sea against marine perils and risks of mortality during the sea voyage. Via a basis clause the horse was warranted to be of a particular pedigree. The horse died during the voyage, but the insurer was able to escape liability as a result of the breach of the warranty regarding pedigree, although it was clear that this had no causal connection with the loss. The case is often quoted as demonstrating one of the main flaws of the 'old' law on warranties: the absence of the need for any connection between breach and loss. Applying the provisions of the Insurance Act 2015 to these facts, the insured was in breach at the time of loss and accordingly s10(2) will apply. As a result it is submitted that s10 will offer no assistance to the insured. Assuming again that s11 can apply in addition to s10, can it offer any assistance to the insured? Under s11 the key initial question will again be does the term define the risk as a whole? As the policy is insuring the horse, this text submits that the court would very likely take the view that the term does indeed define the risk as a whole. Were the court to take this view, any assistance from s11 would be ruled out. If however the court were to determine that the warranty was not one that defined the risk as a whole, does it follow that s11 will be applicable? This text would argue that it does not because in this instance had the pedigree of horse been as warranted, this would prima facie not have *reduced* any of the risks under the policy and accordingly compliance would not have tended to 'reduce the risk of one or more of the following' as required by s11(1). (This volume has earlier demonstrated that s11 has no application to non-risk clauses such as notice provisions and premium clauses.[119]) As a result, it is submitted that the Insurance Act offers no better protection than the original law and indeed reinforces the injustice of the historical position. If the court felt that this failure to comply with s11(1) could somehow be overcome, then s11(3) might be of assistance to the insured on the basis that non-compliance did not increase the loss that actually occurred in the circumstances in which it occurred. This text submits however that it is difficult to see why the failure to meet the risk reduction requirement of s11(1) should be ignored and as a result the Insurance Act would offer no assistance to the insured.

10.76 It is submitted that *Yorkshire Insurance Co v Campbell* demonstrates several of the flaws in the Insurance Act: (i) the uncertainties regarding the concept of what constitutes a term defining the risk as a whole; (ii) the rationale for such a concept in the first place; (iii) the fact that for s11 to offer assistance, the relevant provision must be one that would tend

117 S11(1) Insurance Act 2015.
118 [1917] AC 218.
119 See Chapter 9.

to reduce risk in one or more of the specified categories; (iv) the non-application of s11 to non-risk clauses; and (v) the absence of a simple and practical causal linkage test.

10.77 We have seen that in *Bank of Nova Scotia v Hellenic Mutual War Risks, The Good Luck*[120] the House of Lords held that the effect of a breach of warranty was automatically to discharge the insurer from liability under the policy from the time of the breach. Under s10(1) of the Insurance Act 2015, any rule of law that a breach of an insurance warranty results in the discharge of an insurer's liability is abolished. A breach of warranty now suspends liability under the policy: s10(2). Suspension is now automatic, not termination. However, as the club undertook to advise the bank promptly if they ceased to insure the vessel this text argues that the obligation to notify the bank would likely trigger when the insurance was suspended as at that point the club is no longer insuring the vessel, albeit potentially on a temporary basis. The contrary argument would be that because the vessel was lost prior to the breach being remedied, the insurance ceased at that point and as a result the insured would have been under an obligation to notify the bank only then, at the time of loss (or at least to do so at the point at which the club became aware of the breach and the loss). It could also be argued that while the policy is merely suspended, the insurer would not be obliged to inform the bank: the insurer is still offering insurance and the policy is still on foot, it is just that the insurance is currently suspended. The prudent approach would be for the club to notify the bank when it becomes aware of the breach (assuming this occurs before the loss).

Issues arising as a result of stress testing the Insurance Act 2015

10.78 The stress testing analysis of the Insurance Act undertaken in this chapter has confirmed a number of the weakness in the Insurance Act that were first identified in Chapter 9. These include the following:

(i) The application of s11 only to terms other than those that define the risk as a whole creates an unhelpful and imprecise distinction and one that is fraught with uncertainty, at least until the courts have heard a number of cases on this issue.
(ii) S11 of the Insurance Act (Terms Not Relevant to the Actual Loss) requires that a term of the policy (being a term that does not define the risk as a whole) has not been complied with. While the Insurance Act is silent as to whether it applies to exclusion clauses (and the presumption therefore is that it was intended to apply to exclusion clauses), the requirement that a term has not been complied with will surely likely mean that the section will not apply to any exclusion clauses that come into effect on the happening of an identified event, as opposed to on a breach of a provision of the policy terms.
(iii) The requirement in s11(1) that the section applies to terms, compliance with which would tend to reduce risk, means that some provisions will not be eligible for assistance from the section: for example we have seen that the Insurance Act would be of no assistance to the assured in *Yorkshire Insurance Co v Campbell.*[121]

120 1991 2 Lloyd's Rep191 (HL).
121 [1917] AC 218.

Additionally it seems clear that neither s10 nor s11 apply to non-risk clauses: this is a further shortcoming.

(iv) The Insurance Act includes no right of termination in the event of a breach of warranty or other provision. In circumstances such as those in *The Good Luck* case, this would mean that the insurer is unable to terminate following a breach of warranty, even though he may be in a position where he would not have agreed to the risk if he had known the insured would breach the relevant warranty. Further the Insurance Act fails to take account of any prejudice suffered by the insurer.

(v) S11(3) is in effect a causal linkage provision. While this volume is a proponent of causal linkage as a tool for ameliorating the impact of breaches of warranties and other relevant provisions, s11(3) appears (by setting a test where the bar is that non-compliance *could* not have increased the risk of loss that actually occurred) to set a linkage test based on the *possibility* of the breach causing loss, rather than on the reality of this having occurred. This text argues that such an approach is imprecise and vague and unnecessarily tilts the playing field in favour of the insurer.

(vi) The relationship between s10 and s11. As discussed in Chapter 9, following the manner in which s11 was incorporated at the last minute into the Insurance Act, the relationship between s10 and s11 is, at best, not as clear as it could be. On balance this volume believes that, where there is any potential or real conflict between the sections, the intention was that s11 should take precedence over s10; accordingly this approach has been adopted in stress testing the Act. It may well be that the imprecision on this issue is simply a function of the manner in which s11 came into being. Nevertheless, it represents another example of lack of clarity in the Act.

(vii) S10 offers no possibility of relief in circumstances where a breach of warranty remains un-rectified, even in circumstances where it is clear that there is no causal link between breach and loss.

(viii) As discussed in Chapter 9, the application of the Insurance Act, and in particular s11, to conditions precedent is at best unclear.

CHAPTER 11

Issues

Problems with the law on warranties and potential solutions for resolving them

In defence of the law on warranties

11.1 In 1796 JA Park argued[1]

> and though the condition broken be not perhaps a material one, yet the justice of the law is evident from this consideration: that it is absolutely necessary to have one rule of decision, and that it is much better to say that warranties shall in all cases be strictly complied with, than to leave it in the breast of a judge or jury to say, that in one case it shall, and in another it shall not. The very meaning of a warranty is to preclude all inquiries into the materiality or the substantial performance of it, and although sometimes partial inconveniences may arise from such a rule, yet upon the whole, it will certainly produce public salutary effects.[2]

Have the arguments in favour of certainty now been replaced by other factors?

Intervention by the courts: is reform necessary?

11.2 Is legislative reform necessary? We have seen that in England and Wales efforts by the courts to ameliorate the worst aspects of the law on warranties have led to uncertainty.[3] However can a flexible approach by the courts be an alternate to legislative reform? In its Insurance Contract Law Issues Paper 2, Warranties,[4] the Law Commission observed that courts had found a number of methods of circumventing the harsher effects of warranties on insureds. These had included the following:

(i) That the warranty applies only to past or present facts, and not to the future.
In *Hussain v Brown* a statement covered by a basis clause stated that the insured property was fitted with an intruder alarm. The statement was true at the time the policy was entered into, but later the insured failed to make payment for the alarm service and it was suspended. The Court of Appeal held the provision was a statement of present facts only: 'if underwriters want such protection [of a continuing warranty] then it is up to them to stipulate for it in clear terms.'[5]
(ii) Interpreting the warranty as relevant to only some sections of the policy.

1 JA Park, *A System of Law of Marine Insurances,* Printed by A. Strahan for J. Butterworth, London, 1796, pg 318.
2 JA Park, *A System of Law of Marine Insurances,* Printed by A. Strahan for J. Butterworth, London, 1796.
3 See Chapter 3.
4 Law Commission Insurance Contract Law Issues Paper 2 Warranties, November 2006, part 4.
5 [1996] 1 Lloyd's Rep 627, per Saville LJ at p 630.

DOI: 10.4324/9781003031734-11

In *Printpak v AGF Insurance Ltd*[6] the policy contained a warranty that the insured would maintain a burglar alarm. Despite the wording of the warranty, the Court of Appeal held that the alarm warranty only applied to the risk of theft and not to the risk of fire: the policy was not a seamless document, but instead consisted of separate schedules, each concerned with a different type of risk.

(iii) That the clause was not a true warranty, but merely descriptive of the risk.
In *Farr v Motor Traders Mutual Insurance*, the Court of Appeal rejected the insurer's argument that a statement that taxis were to be driven for only one shift a day was a warranty. Rather, the court held it was descriptive of the risk. Accordingly cover was merely suspended when the taxi was used for two shifts in a day, and then re-instated.[7]

(iv) That the wording of the warranty did not apply to the facts in question.
In *Provincial Insurance Co v Morgan* the policy declared in a basis clause that the insured's lorry would be used for transporting coal. While at the time of the loss only coal was on the lorry, it had previously been used to move timber. The House of Lords held that on 'a strict but reasonable construction,' the clause only meant that transporting coal was to be the normal use.[8]

11.3 In *Kler Knitwear v Lombard General Insurance Co* the court arguably went further still, prima facie ignoring the wording of the policy to hold that a provision that a sprinkler system would be inspected 30 days after renewal was a suspensive condition and not a warranty.[9] This was despite the fact that the provision was clearly stated to be a warranty and the policy later went on to spell out the consequences, namely that non-compliance would bar any claim, 'whether it increases the risk or not.' Commenting on the decision Bird and Hill observed, 'It is difficult to see how the insurer could have stipulated this in any clearer terms. The term itself was called a warranty and was drafted in clear and intelligible language and the consequences of non-compliance were spelled out.'[10]

11.4 In Canada the courts have limited application of the law on warranties as contained in the Marine Insurance Act 1993[11] 'to situations where the warranty is material to the risk and the breach has a bearing on the loss.'[12] In *Century Insurance Company of Canada v Case Existological Laboratories Ltd. ('The Bamcell II')*[13] the policy included the following term: 'warranted that a watchman is stationed on board the *Bamcell II* each night from 2200 hours to 0600 hours with instructions for shutting down all equipment in an emergency.' In reality there was never a watchman on board. The loss occurred mid-afternoon, and as a result the breach had no bearing whatever on the loss. Ritchie J in the Supreme Court held:

6 [1999] Lloyd's Rep IR 542.
7 [1920] 3 KB 669.
8 [1933] AC 240.
9 [2000] Lloyd's Rep IR 47.
10 J Birds and NJ Hird, *Birds' Modern Insurance Law, Sweet and Maxwell,* London, 6th Edition, 2004, page 161.
11 Based closely on the English Marine Insurance Act 1906.
12 C Giaschi, Warranties in Marine Insurance, a paper to the Association of Marine Underwriters of British Columbia, Vancouver, 10 April 1997. www.admiraltylaw.com/papers/warranties.htm (24 May 2006).
13 *Century Insurance Company of Canada v Case Existological Laboratories Ltd. ('The BAMCELL II')* [1984] 1 WWR 97.

> The clause would only have been effective if the loss had occurred between 2200 hours and 0600 hours, and it was proved that there was no watchman stationed aboard during those hours. To this extent the condition contained in the clause constituted a limitation of the risk insured against, but it was not a warranty.[14]

11.5 Soyer suggests there was a clear intention in *The Bamcell II* that the term should be a warranty and that an English court would have regarded it as an express warranty.[15] Soyer has argued that subsequent to the *Bamcell* decision, Canadian insurers have sought to insert more unambiguous wording into policies in an attempt to overcome the kind of interpretation applied by the court in *Bamcell II.*[16] Such provisions have however yet to be considered by the courts, so their effectiveness is unclear. Nevertheless, the use of such clear language must be an improvement on the (pre Insurance Act) status quo.

11.6 While intervention by the courts may on occasion ameliorate some of the worst aspects of the law on warranties, this is surely not an adequate solution in itself. In the view of the Law Commission, the courts' efforts to dilute the negative impact of insurance warranties provided a partial solution to the problem, but did so at the 'cost of adding complexity and uncertainty to the law.'[17] While such decisions may act as a deterrent to insurers to deflect them from seeking unreasonably to enforce warranties, the Law Commission acknowledged that the problem that flowed from this approach was confusion and uncertainty.[18] Furthermore the Commission was of the view that the sort of approach adopted in *Kler Knitwear* would mean that each case would depend on the particular words used. In the Commission's view insurers would (as in Canada) likely respond to unfavourable decisions by attempting to achieve the desired effect with different words.

11.7 Far from providing clarity, a court driven approach is, at best, a charter for continuing uncertainty and uncertainty rarely does anyone any favours. Bennett has argued that business would prefer a clear rule that might operate harshly against their interests in particular circumstances, rather than an unclear rule designed to produce fair and equitable results, but that might require a lengthy and costly process to apply.[19] As long ago as 1776, Willes J observed in *Lockyer v Offley*:

> As in all commercial transactions the great object is certainty, it will be necessary for this court to lay down some rule, and it is of course of more consequence that the rule should be certain, than whether it is established one way or the other.[20]

---

14 *Century Insurance Company of Canada v Case Existological Laboratories Ltd. (The 'BAMCELL II')* [1984] 1 WWR 97, 104, per Ritchie J.

15 B Soyer, *Warranties in Marine Insurance,* Cavendish Publishing, London, 2nd Edition, 2006, page 45.

16 For example the following adopted by the British Columbia Builders' Risk Clauses:

> 'This policy contains warranties and general conditions none of which are to be interpreted as suspensive conditions. The Underwriters have agreed to accept the risk of insuring the Vessel on the condition precedent that the Assured will comply strictly and literally with these warranties and conditions. If the Assured breaches any of these warranties or conditions, the Underwriters at their option will not pay any claims arising thereafter, regardless of whether or not breach is causative or in any way connected to such claim.'

17 Law Commission Insurance Contract Law Issues Paper 2 Warranties, November 2006, para 4.18.

18 Law Commission Insurance Contract Law Issues Paper 2 Warranties, November 2006, para 4.9.

19 H Bennett, 'Reflections on Values: The Law Commissions' Proposals with Respect to Remedies for Breach of Promissory Warranty and Pre-Formation Non-Disclosure and Misrepresentation in Commercial Insurance' in *Reforming Marine and Commercial Insurance Law,* General Editor Dr Bariş Soyer, Informa, London, 2008 page 159.

20 (1776) 1 TR 252 at 259.

But this is not a rationale for seeking certainty at any cost. It will be argued[21] that it is possible to craft an approach that overcomes the most egregious elements of the law of warranties/other provisions, while at the same time providing sufficient flexibility and a degree of clarity and certainty.

Warranties: the key problems

11.8 Whatever the historic merits of the law on warranties, this book, like the vast majority of practitioners and academics in the insurance world, argues that, in the modern environment, the case for reform was overwhelming. The Law Commission in England and Wales has stated that in its view the most significant problem with the law of warranties was that it permitted the insurer to escape liability for technical breaches that had nothing to do with the loss in question.[22] Such an outcome 'defies logic and normal expectations, is inconsistent with good practice as recognised by the industry's own Statements of Practice and risks bringing the UK insurance industry into disrepute.'[23] The law was unjust.

11.9 We have seen that in its 2014 Report on Insurance Contracts, the Law Commission identified the following as key problems with the law on warranties:

(1) An insurer might refuse a claim as a result a trivial mistake that has no bearing on the risk.
(2) The insured could not use the defence that the breach has been remedied.
(3) The breach of warranty discharged the insurer from all liability, not just liability for the type of loss in question.
(4) A statement might be converted into a warranty using obscure words that few policyholders understood.[24]

11.10 However, identifying the problems with the traditional law on warranties is the easy bit. By analysing attempts to craft a solution in Australia, New Zealand and the UK, we have seen that developing a solution that fairly balances the interests of the insured and insurer, while at the same time being sufficiently flexible and adjustable such that the solution is capable of being applied to a myriad of differing circumstances, but which also provides parties with a clear framework, rather than unstructured uncertainty, is altogether more challenging. Building on the multi-jurisdictional experience to date, the primary objective of this book is to lay out the framework for just such a solution.

BILA's objectives for reform

11.11 In 2002, a BILA[25] report to the Law Commission in England, Wales and Scotland recommended a series of reforms to insurance contract law including warranties. The Report set out a series of key principles that, in the BILA's view, any reform of warranties should achieve:

21 See Chapter 12.

22 Law Commission Consultation Paper No. 182 Insurance Contract Law: Misrepresentation, Non-Disclosure and Breach of Warranty by the Insured, November 2007 para 8.21.

23 Law Commission Consultation Paper No. 182 Insurance Contract Law: Misrepresentation, Non-Disclosure and Breach of Warranty by the Insured, November 2007 para 8.22.

24 Law Commission Report on Insurance Contract Law: Business Disclosure; Warranties; Insurers' Remedies for Fraudulent Claims; and Late Payment, Law Com No 353 / Scot Law Com No 238, July 2014, para 12.4.

25 The British Insurance Law Association.

(i) Certainty. However, BILA also flagged the need to be cognisant of the move by courts away from a formalist approach: an indication of the courts' willingness to put other factors ahead of certainty.
(ii) Freedom of contract. BILA argued it was difficult to see any reason for a departure from this key principle.
(iii) Reasonable expectations of the assured. While these would differ across different commercial sectors, if assureds' reasonable expectations were not met, BILA suggested business would drift away from London/England and Wales to other markets with more assured friendly rules. BILA suggested this might require some sectors (e.g. SMEs?) to be carved out.
(iv) Reform, not revolution. BILA cautioned that sweeping reform was likely to unsettle the fine balance in the market.[26]

Are voluntary codes the answer?

11.12 In 2006 the Law Commission considered whether in practical terms there was a problem: had the voluntary action of insurers not removed the issue? In 1977 the Association of British Insurers issued a Statement of General Insurance Practice (SGIP), dealing with the perceived problems with warranties and stating:

> Except where fraud, deception or negligence is involved, an insurer will not unreasonably repudiate liability to indemnify a policyholder ... on grounds of a breach of warranty or condition, where the circumstances of the loss are unconnected with the breach.[27]

This was later (in 1986) amended to remove the reference to deception and negligence so as to restrict the right to repudiate to circumstances of fraud only. However, these statements applied only to consumer insurance and left significant discretion to the insurer (such that insurers were permitted to repudiate claims where they suspected, but could not prove, fraud). There was also no ability to enforce compliance with the code. These shortcomings remained with subsequent industry variations of these self-regulating codes.[28] In the Law Commission's view, if the industry felt that the Marine Insurance Act no longer represented fair principles and good industry practice, this was itself evidence of the need for reform.[29] This must be right: the industry has had more than ample time to introduce properly effective voluntary codes and has failed to meet the challenge.

The issues

(i) Basis clauses

11.13 The problems posed by the use of basis clauses have already been discussed in detail.[30] There is widespread agreement that it is difficult to justify the use of basis clauses. In 1927 Lord Wrenbury described their use to avoid liability as 'contemptible': 'Here, upon

26 British Insurance Law Association, Report to the Law Commission, Insurance Contract Law, 2002.
27 Association of British Insurers Statement of General Insurance Practice, 1977, Clause 2(b)(ii).
28 For example Insurance Conduct of Business rules 7.3.6.
29 Law Commission Insurance Contract Law Issues Paper 2 Warranties, November 2006, para 5.6.
30 See Chapter 3.

purely technical grounds, [the insurers], having in point of fact not been deceived in any material particular, avail themselves of what seems to me the contemptible defence that although they have taken the premiums, they are protected from paying.'[31] While regularly changing its position in relation to the detail of the reform of insurance warranties, the Law Commission has consistently recommended the abolition of basis clauses.[32] It cannot be right that assureds can be 'tricked' into providing warranties; transparency and clarity are essential and should underpin any insurance contract. There is no case for preserving basis clauses and abolishing basis clauses is the most obvious and straightforward aspect of the reform of the law on warranties. The merits of the case are such that they require no further debate.

(ii) Should reform apply only to warranties?

11.14 In both New Zealand and Australian legislative reform of the law took a purposive approach and applies not only to terms expressed as warranties, but also to other terms that have a similar effect in that they seek to exclude or limit liability. Merkin is surely right in arguing that attempts at reforming the law on warranties will be materially weakened if insurers are able to replicate the effect of warranties through other avenues, such as exclusion clauses or clauses describing risk.[33] The Law Commission in England and Wales suggested that the principal challenges in developing a causal connection test were deciding which types of clause the causal connection test should apply to, and defining the nature of the causal requirement.[34] In 1980 the Commission recommended that a causal connection test should only apply to warranties. Because of the ease in which insurers could draft around this, Birds and Hird argued that this was a major flaw with the 1980 recommendations: the reform would merely encourage insurers to find other means of achieving the same ends.[35] Section 10 of the Insurance Act 2015 only applies to warranties, but as we have seen, s11 applies to any term, express or implied, of a contract of insurance, other than a term defining risk as a whole, where compliance with the term would tend to reduce loss of a particular kind, at a particular location or at a particular time.[36]

11.15 The ALRC commented that its recommendations should apply

> not only to strict warranties and other terms imposing obligations on the insured, but also to exclusions from cover of certain risks. Were they not to extend to temporal exclusions, legislation based on the present recommendations might be avoided simply by re-phrasing an obligation ("the insured warrants that the car will be kept in a roadworthy condition") as a temporal exclusion ("the insurer will not be liable while the car is in an unroadworthy condition"). The legislation might also be avoided if obligations and exclusions were omitted

31 *Glicksman v Lancashire and General Assurance Co* [1927] AC 139 at pp 144–5.

32 See Chapters 5 and 8.

33 R Merkin and J Lowry, 'Reconstructing Insurance Law: The Law Commissions' Consultation Paper' (2008) 71 *Modern Law Review* 95, 110.

34 Law Commission Consultation Paper No. 182 Insurance Contract Law: Misrepresentation, Non-Disclosure and Breach of Warranty by the Insured, November 2007 para 8.24.

35 J Birds and NJ Hird, *Birds' Modern Insurance Law*, Sweet and Maxwell, London, 6th Edition, 2004, page 166, note 36.

36 S11(1) Insurance Act 2015.

and the cover itself stated in such a way as to achieve the same ends ("cover is granted in respect of the roadworthy car").[37]

11.16 The Insurance Act seeks to have wide-ranging coverage but, as has been demonstrated, there remain significant gaps. Having reflected on the experience in the UK and overseas, it is argued that a reform package needs to apply not only to warranties, but also to any other term that has the effect of enabling the insurer to escape liability where there has been a breach of the term by the insured. While no reform measure can be truly bulletproof, if reform measures are not to be exposed to potential abuse through drafting semantics, a wide-ranging approach is important, at least with regard to post-contractual obligations. In particular it is important the proposals should apply to exclusion clauses as well as non-risk clauses. Crucially however experience in Australia and elsewhere demonstrates that it is essential that care is taken to ensure that there is no intrusion into issues of scope. At the same time, as illustrated in relation to s11 of the New Zealand Insurance Law Reform Act, it is important that reforms do not swing too far in favour of the insured, such that, for example, he can brazenly breach key provisions of a policy without sanction provided there is no linkage between breach and loss.[38] Any solution must seek to balance these conflicting priorities.

(iii) Pre-contractual representations

11.17 If basis clauses are to be abolished, are insurers to be offered any alternate protection against misleading or fraudulent pre-contractual statements or undertakings by prospective insureds? We have seen that in New Zealand representations made in proposal forms or other pre-contractual documentation are covered by sections 5 and 6 of the Insurance Law Reform Act, which state that the insurer may avoid liability where the insurer has made representations that are substantially incorrect and material. Under s6(1) a statement is substantially incorrect only if the difference between what was stated and what was actually correct would have been considered material by a prudent insurer. S6(2) confirms that a statement is material only if that statement would have influenced the judgement of a prudent insurer in fixing the premium or in determining whether he would have taken or continued the risk upon substantially the same terms.

11.18 In *Preece v State Insurance General Manager* Thorpe J suggested that the purpose of ss5 and 6 was to alleviate

> the harshness and artificiality resulting from the common practice of insurers requiring proponents to warrant the complete accuracy of all answers to questions put by insurers, with the result that any inaccuracy, whether by way of positive misstatement or omission, and whether major or trivial, material or immaterial to risk or loss, voided the policy.[39]

11.19 Tarr and Kennedy observed:

> The combined effect of these sections meant that an insurer could only avoid a policy when the difference between what was stated in the proposal and what was actually correct would

37 ALRC 20, Insurance Contracts (1982) at para 229.

38 Detailed proposals are set out in Chapter 12.

39 (1982) 2 ANZ Ins Cas 60–493, Thorpe J at 77–807.

> have been considered material by a prudent insurer and would have influenced that insurer's judgment in fixing the premium or determining whether he or she would have taken or continued the risk upon substantially the same terms.[40]

11.20 In Australia, while s54 only applies to insurance contracts that have come into effect (and accordingly does not apply to pre-contractual non-disclosure or misrepresentation), s24 of the Insurance Contracts Act provides that

> A statement made in or in connection with a contract of insurance, being a statement made by or attributable to the insured, with respect to the existence of a state of affairs does not have effect as a warranty, but has effect as though it were a statement made to the insurer by the insured during the negotiations for the contract but before it was entered into.

This has the effect of meaning that basis of contract clauses are ineffective where the statement is about existing, as opposed to future, facts. It is argued that once basis clauses are abolished, insurers do need some protection against misleading or fraudulent statements by prospective insureds where the insurer has relied on such statements in deciding to offer cover. The approach adopted in New Zealand has much to commend it. This is discussed further later in this chapter.[41]

(iv) Conditions precedent

11.21 What if the term that is breached is one that is a present warranty or other term requiring compliance prior to the contract's effective date? Should any reform apply to such circumstances? It is argued that the approach should depend on whether or not the term is a condition precedent. The onus should be on the insurer to establish that a given term was a condition precedent to the attachment of risk.[42] If this hurdle is met and the term has not been complied with, then the contract would never come on risk and the insurer would have no liability. This would however be subject to the assured being able to establish that the term (which has not been complied with) related to a specific risk (only); if he is able to do so, then only liability relating to that specific risk should be suspended. Once the condition is met, the contract would come on risk in relation to that element. Conditions precedent to liability should be dealt with separately.

(v) Issues of scope

11.22 The inter-relationship between warranties and issues of the scope of the insurance policy is key. As has been pointed out, by definition, an event that is beyond the scope of an insurance policy should not be a breach of that policy: it is simply not covered by it.[43] However, in seeking to find an equitable balance between the interests of the insured and the insurer, experience has shown that the boundary between exclusion clauses (which are covered by s11 of the NZ Insurance Law Reform Act and s54 of the Insurance Contracts Act in Australia) and issues of scope, which fall outside the coverage of the statutory provisions, is sometimes hard to identify.

40 AA Tarr and JA Kennedy, *Insurance Law in New Zealand,* Law Book Co of Australasia, Pyrmont, 2nd Edition 1992, page 80.

41 See Chapter 12, Proposed Solution.

42 See Chapter 12 for a full explanation of how this author believes the approach should work.

43 See also *Sutton on Insurance Law,* eds Merkin, Kirby and Enright, 4th Edition, Lawbook Co., 2015.

11.23 We have seen that in *East End Real Estate Pty Ltd v CE Heath Casualty & General Insurance Ltd*[44] the court observed, 'It would hardly be consistent ... to construe the language of s54 in such a way as to make its operation depend upon the choice that is made between various available drafting techniques.' Does this open the door for the scope of a contract to be adjustable by the court? In this case the court observed that, while the insurer was prima facie entitled to reject the claim on grounds of scope, it was able to do so because of an omission by the insured (a failure to notify a claim in a timely fashion), as a result of which s54 (of the Insurance Contracts Act) became applicable. In such circumstances the insurer may be able to gain some protection by claiming prejudice, but the decision in *East End* nevertheless appears to have transformed a 'claims made and notified' policy into a 'claims made' policy with the failure to notify the insurer of submission of the claim, being seemingly viewed as essentially a procedural matter, as opposed to something that lay outside the scope of cover. In *FAI General Insurance Co Ltd v Australian Hospital Care Pty Ltd* the court observed that for the purposes of s54, no distinction could be made 'between provisions of a contract which define the scope of cover, and those provisions which are conditions affecting an entitlement to claim.'[45]

11.24 The Law Commission observed that

> the main difficulty [with s54] lay in the ALRC's desire to extend protection beyond clauses which impose obligations on policyholders, to those which limited the scope of the cover (as in the example where cover is granted only "in respect of the roadworthy car"). This has led to considerable debate about how far s54 could be used to extend policies to cover risks outside the scope of the policy the insurer had written.[46]

As discussed in Chapter 6, the structure of s54 means that the boundary between legitimate resort to s54 and the sanctity of scope will always be somewhat blurred and will often require judicial interpretation. While this, of itself, may not be a fatal flaw,[47] one of the main problems with s54 is its tendency to blur the definition of scope, with the result that it runs close to impinging on the parties' freedom to contract.

11.25 In New Zealand section 11 of the Insurance Law Reform Act (which has been examined in detail in Chapter 7) would apply to a clause stating that a car was only insured while it was roadworthy. Such a clause purports to exclude or limit the liability of the insurer in certain circumstances because when a car is unroadworthy, the risk of a loss increases. Under s11 an insurer would not be entitled to rely on this clause if the policyholder proves that the loss was unrelated to the unroadworthiness. In *Barnaby v South British Insurance Co*, Hardie Boys J explained the effect of the section as follows:

> The key to this section is to be found in the last words of para. (b): the section is designed to deal with those kinds of exclusion clauses that provide for circumstances likely to increase the risk of a loss which the policy actually covers. The most common examples are found in the field of motor vehicle insurance, such as driving a motor vehicle whilst under the influence of alcohol, or driving a motor vehicle while it is in an unsafe condition. The section is not

44 (1991) 25 NSWLR 400; 7 ANZ Ins Cas 61–092. See also Chapter 6.

45 [2001] HCA 38; (2001) 204 CLR 641 at 656 [33]. The interaction between s54 and issues of scope is discussed in detail in Chapter 5.

46 Law Commission Insurance Contract Law Issues Paper 2 Warranties, November 2006, para 6.28.

47 See Chapter 12 for further discussion of this issue.

> designed to deal with exclusion clauses which specify the kind of loss or the quantum of loss to which the cover does not apply at all.[48]

11.26 This is fair enough so far as it goes. The danger is that such an approach and the wording of (the NZ) s11 opens the door to drafting manipulation: the open-ended nature of the approach is a flaw in relation to s11. It is surely perverse that an insured can flagrantly breach a fundamental provision of the policy, one which arguably goes to the root of the risk being covered, and yet still be covered if, when loss is suffered, it turns out that this was not connected with the breach. This is a variant to the issues discussed in connection with the Australian s54 and illustrates the problems that can potentially arise with an unfettered causal linkage approach that is not limited to application only to warranties, but applies to a wide range of contractual provisions.

11.27 The New Zealand Law Reform Commission seemingly agreed with this analysis as in 1998 it proposed that s11 should not apply to a provision which:

(1) defined the age, identity, qualifications or experience of a driver of a vehicle, a pilot of an aircraft, or an operator of a chattel; or
(2) defined the geographical area in which a loss must occur if the insurer is to be liable to indemnify the insured; or
(3) excluded loss that occurs while a vehicle, aircraft or other chattel is being used for commercial purposes other than those permitted by the contract of insurance.[49]

Neither this proposed amendment, nor the variant contained in the 2019 NZ Review of Insurance Contract Law[50] has however yet been enacted.

11.28 It is surely essential that the parties be able to specify the scope of cover without the assured being, in effect, able to expand this by ignoring provisions in the contract that seek to specify the agreed limitations. While the intent of the legislature may be clear, the challenges arise at the margin. It is at the very least arguable that s11 of the New Zealand Insurance Law Reform Act has failed to achieve the right balance. Overcoming concerns regarding scope, while at the same time achieving an equitable balance between the interests of the insured and insurer is one of the main hurdles in finding a solution to the challenges of insurance warranties and breaches of other terms that prima facie enable the insurer to avoid liability.

(vi) Causal linkage

11.29 Causal linkage has long been seen as a possible answer to dealing with some of the harsher aspects of the law of warranties and related provisions. Soyer has argued that, while questions of causation are not easy to resolve, a causal linkage approach (as recommended by the Law Commission in 2007) was on balance a vital step in producing a fairer regime.[51] As we have seen, broadly the concept is that if the breach of warranty (or other relevant term) can be shown to have no causal linkage with the loss incurred, then the insurer should not be excused liability. In New Zealand s11 states the insured has a right to be indemnified if

48 (1980) 1 ANZ Ins Cas 60–401, 77,008.

49 NZ Law Reform Commission, Some Insurance Law Problems (1998) NZLC R46, p 25.

50 See Chapter 7 for details.

51 B Soyer, 'Reforming Insurance Warranties: Are We Finally Moving Forward?' in *Reforming Marine and Commercial Insurance Law,* General Editor Dr Bariş Soyer, Informa, London, 2008.

he can prove, on the balance of probabilities, that the loss was not 'caused or contributed to by the happening of such events or the existence of such circumstances.'

11.30 We have seen that in Australia s54(2) of the Insurance Contracts Act permits the insurer to refuse to pay a claim where the act or omission *could* reasonably be regarded as being *capable* of causing or contributing to a loss in respect of which insurance cover is provided by the contract.[52] This is subject to the proviso that if the assured proves that no part of the loss was caused by the breach, the insurer may not refuse to pay the claim by reason only of that act (ICA, s54(3)). Proportionality is also allowed,[53] permitting the insurer to reduce its liability 'by the amount that fairly represents the extent to which ... [its] interests were prejudiced.' It can be argued that, because of the '*could*' formulation, the s54 approach sets the bar low for insurers (and high for the insured), making it easier than it should be for the insurer to establish a causal link and thus escape liability.

11.31 As has been seen elsewhere,[54] the Law Commission in England and Wales has flirted with causal linkage over many years.[55] In 1980 the Commission proposed that an insurer could not rely on a breach of warranty if, inter alia, the breach could not have increased the risk that the event which gave rise to the claim would occur in the way that it did in fact occur.[56] In its 2007 report the Commission re-affirmed its support for a causal linkage approach[57] and suggested that the principal challenges in developing a causal connection test were deciding which types of clause the causal connection test should apply to, and defining the nature of the causal requirement.[58] In a subsequent critique of the Law Commission's 2007 proposals, the ALRC offered an example where a motor vehicle had been modified in breach of a warranty in a way that increased the risk that the brakes would malfunction. The vehicle was subsequently involved in an accident, but the brakes operated without impairment and did not contribute to the accident. Although the breach did not cause or contribute to the loss, the ALRC asserted that the insured would be unable to prove that the breach did not increase the risk that the loss would occur in the way it did in fact occur. It is respectively suggested that the ALRC's analysis is flawed: providing it could be established that the brakes operated perfectly and the insured was without fault with regard to the cause of the accident ('the way it did in fact occur'), then there is surely no reason why the assured would be unable to establish that the breach did not increase the risk that the loss would occur *in the way it did in fact occur.*

11.32 Perhaps surprisingly, in its final report prior to the enactment of the Insurance Act, the Law Commission purported to come out against a causal linkage approach.[59] However, as discussed elsewhere, the revised (and barely debated) s11 of the Insurance

52 Insurance Contracts Act s54(2), emphasis added.

53 S54(4) Insurance Contracts Act. Note that s54 is discussed in detail in Chapter 6.

54 See Chapter 5.

55 For a detailed consideration of the Commission's evolving thinking see Chapter 5.

56 Law Commission Report Insurance Law, Non-Disclosure and Breach of Warranty (1980) Law Com No 104.

57 Law Commission Consultation Paper No. 182 Insurance Contract Law: Misrepresentation, Non-Disclosure and Breach of Warranty by the Insured, November 2007 para 8.51–8.53.

58 Law Commission Consultation Paper No. 182 Insurance Contract Law: Misrepresentation, Non-Disclosure and Breach of Warranty by the Insured, November 2007 para 8.24.

59 Para 18.39, Law Commission and Scottish Law Commission, Insurance Contract Law: Business Disclosure; Warranties; Insurers' Remedies for Fraudulent Claims; and Late Payment Law Com No 353 / Scot Law Com No 238 Cm 8898 SG/2014/131 July 2014. Available at: http://lawcommission.justice.gov.uk/docs.

Act 2015 incorporates what amounts to a 'back door' causal linkage test.[60] S11(3) provides that the insurer may not avoid liability if the insured 'shows that the non-compliance with the term could not have increased the risk of the loss which actually occurred in the circumstances in which it occurred.'[61] Although the Commission claims this is not a causal linkage test, as is argued elsewhere[62] it is submitted that it is in effect one.

11.33 How should the law deal with a situation where a breach by the insured was only one of a number of factors contributing to the loss? In 2007 the Law Commission recommended, in relation to warranties as to future conduct, that if the insured could prove that a breach contributed only to part of the loss, the insurer would not be able to refuse to pay for the loss that was unrelated to the breach.[63] Questions that arise include: how closely connected does linkage need to be? Clarke argued[64] that the law does not have good track record in giving analytical rigour to issues of causation.[65] Aikens queried whether the Commission's proposed approach would represent an improvement for the parties, or would it in practice reduce certainty.[66]

11.34 In its review of the Australian Marine Insurance Act, the ALRC recommended that

> the amended MIA should permit the parties to include a term that the insurer is discharged from liability to indemnify the insured for loss proximately caused by a breach by the insured of an express term of the contract. An express term providing for the insurer's discharge from liability could be drafted to apply to the insured's obligations generally or only to particular breaches. In the absence of such a term, breach of the contract will entitle the insurer only to such relief as may be available under the general law of contract, which would generally be the award of damages.[67]

11.35 The Law Commission concluded that in both Australia and New Zealand there was a consensus that insurers should not be permitted to avoid liability for breaches of insurance terms that are unrelated to the loss[68] and that the industry was comfortable with provisions which provided that the policy should not be avoided where the breach did not in fact increase the risk, or cause the loss.[69] The Commission suggested however that problems arose where the legislation went wider than this, to cover acts or omissions that did not increase the risk of a loss occurring, such as notification clauses.[70]

60 See Chapter 9.

61 S11(3) Insurance Act 2015.

62 See Chapter 9.

63 Law Commission Consultation Paper No. 182 Insurance Contract Law: Misrepresentation, Non-Disclosure and Breach of Warranty by the Insured, November 2007 para 8.48.

64 Clarke, (2007) LMCLQ 474 at 477.

65 See Viscount Simond in *Overseas Tankships (UK) Ltd v Morts Docks and Engineering Co Ltd (The Wagon Mound)* [1961] AC 388 at 419 and 424.

66 Sir R Aikens, 'The Law Commission's Proposed Reforms of the Law of Warranties in Marine and Commercial Insurance: Will the Cure Be Better than the Disease?' in *Reforming Marine and Commercial Insurance Law,* General Editor Dr Bariş Soyer, Informa, London 2008.

67 ALRC, Review of the Marine Insurance Act 1909 (2001) No 91; www.austlii.edu.au/au/other/alrc/publications/reports/91/ch9.html, para 9.129.

68 Law Commission Insurance Contract Law Issues Paper 2 Warranties, November 2006, para 6.42.

69 Law Commission Insurance Contract Law Issues Paper 2 Warranties, November 2006, para 6.43.

70 Law Commission Insurance Contract Law Issues Paper 2 Warranties, November 2006, para 6.44.

(vii) Defining the limits of causation

11.36 Accepting a causal linkage approach to determining an insurer's liability is, of itself, only one step in determining an effective approach to addressing remedies for breaches of warranties and other terms. It is at least equally important to define what constitutes causal linkage for these purposes. In 2006 the Law Commission of England and Wales concluded that the policyholder should be entitled to be paid a claim if he could prove on the balance of probability that the event or circumstances constituting the breach of warranty did not contribute to the loss.[71] Although a causation linked approach has much to recommend it, under this specific approach the insured has to do more than merely show that the breach was not the main or dominant cause of the loss: he has to show the breach did not contribute to the loss. Accordingly the Commission's 2006 approach is rejected on the grounds that it results in an all or nothing approach which may well fail to deliver equitable outcomes.

Sole cause or dominant cause

11.37 Under a dominant cause approach, the insurer would remain liable in circumstances where the breach was not the dominant cause of the loss. The potential problem with a dominant cause approach can be illustrated by an example where a car insurance policy includes a warranty that the car should not be driven by someone aged under 25. Suppose the car was however being driven by a 20 year old when it was involved in an accident caused primarily by the negligence of an uninsured cyclist. In these circumstances under the dominant cause approach the insurer would likely still be liable, even if a more experienced driver might have avoided a collision[72] and even though the insurer might never have intended to take the risk posed by a 20-year-old driver. This illustrates the tightrope that any solution must seek to navigate and, it is submitted, argues for a flexible approach that facilitates bespoke outcomes.

Flexibility in approach

11.38 It is argued that a better, and more equitable, approach would be to allow the court to reach a view on the proportional contribution of a breach. Causation is often not a black and white equation, and a flexible approach allows the apportionment of liability to reflect that reality. Take for example the situation where the policy requires a particular form of lock to be fitted to the main entrance of a building. Suppose the insured fails to fit such a lock and the property is subsequently burgled. The intruders did not, however, access the property through the door, but via a window on which there were no special requirements specified in the policy. In this situation it could well be difficult for the insured to establish that the absence of the lock did not contribute (in any way) to the break-in, as inadequate security on the main entrance may have been a factor in attracting the intruder's attention to the property. Much better that the situation be appraised on the facts of the individual case, such that the court is free to decide to what, if any, extent the breach contributed in a causal sense to the loss. Based on the specific facts, the court would then apportion liability

71 Law Commission Insurance Contract Law Issues Paper 2 Warranties, November 2006, para 7.76.

72 However this amounts to a 'but for' argument similar to the one rejected in New Zealand in *New Zealand Insurance Co Ltd v Harris* [1990] 1 NZLR 10 (CA) at 16.

accordingly. Under a proportionate arrangement it is true that insurer's liability would be reduced, but the outcome would still be harsh on the insurer without the ability to either reflect any prejudice suffered by the insurer and/or the ability to terminate the policy. For example in the underage driver illustration earlier, had the insurer known that the vehicle was to be driven by a 20-year-old, the insurer may well not have agreed to the risk, or would have at least charged an additional premium.

11.39 It is surely appropriate that any approach reflects reality by, for example, applying the relevant percentage to the liability of the insurer, as determined by the proportion of contribution resulting from the breach, while at the same time retaining the flexibility to take account of prejudice and other issues such as questions of scope. While this approach may involve a greater degree of complexity and analysis, the law's priority should surely always be to seek the most just and equitable outcome, not simply the one that is easiest to administer.

(viii) Reasonable expectations: an alternate to causal linkage?

11.40 We have seen that the Law Commission considered whether to recommend extending sections 3 (which applies to England and Wales) and 17 (which applies to Scotland) of the Unfair Contract Terms Act (UCTA) 1977 to insurance contracts as an alternate to a wide causal connections test.[73] S3 of the UCTA subjects certain clauses to a requirement of reasonableness. It applies between contracting parties where one of them deals as a consumer or on the other's written standard terms of business. Section 3(2)(b)[74] prevents the party who wrote the standard terms of business from claiming to be entitled:

> (i) to render a contractual performance substantially different from that which was reasonably expected of him, or
> (ii) in respect of the whole or any part of his contractual obligation, to render no contractual performance at all,
>
> except in so far as ... the contract term satisfies the requirement of reasonableness.[75]

The Commission saw three advantages in extending s3 of the UCTA to insurance contracts:[76]

(i) It would only apply to standard term contracts, not those negotiated on an individual basis;

(ii) It would apply to any term that defined cover in a way that policyholders would not reasonably expect, and to any term that allowed the insurer not to pay a claim at all. The Commission asserted that this would avoid the 'semantic distinctions' that had been a feature of the interpretation of s54 of the Australian Insurance Contracts Act in distinguishing for example between 'omissions' and 'inactions'[77];

73 Law Commission Consultation Paper No. 182 Insurance Contract Law: Misrepresentation, Non-Disclosure and Breach of Warranty by the Insured, November 2007 para 8.54.

74 See also s62 of the Consumer Rights Act 2015.

75 S3(2)(b) Unfair Contract Terms Act 1977.

76 Law Commission Insurance Contract Law Issues Paper 2 Warranties, November 2006, para 8.16.

77 Law Commission Insurance Contract Law Issues Paper 2 Warranties, November 2006, para 8.16(2).

(iii) In examining whether a term was fair and reasonable, the court would need to take into account both the extent to which the term was transparent and its substance and effect. The Commission argued that the reform would provide a strong incentive to insurers to re-write their contractual documents in a way that policyholders understood.

11.41 As we saw in Chapter 5,[78] arguments against extending the Unfair Contract Terms legislation included:

(i) That it would impinge on the freedom of contract.
(ii) That such an approach would introduce unacceptable uncertainty into the law.

In the event the Commission stopped short of recommending an extension of the UCTA legislation to commercial insurance contracts.[79] On balance this seems a sensible decision.

Reasonable expectations and scope

11.42 But is there a place for a reasonable expectations approach to issues of scope, as suggested by the England and Wales Law Commission in their 2006[80] and 2007[81] reports? In its 2007 Report the Commission proposed that there should be safeguards to ensure that the relevant term did not make the cover substantially different from that which the insured reasonably expected in circumstances where a business insured contracted on the insurer's standard terms of business.[82] The Commission suggested that the causal connection test should not apply where the insurance related to one purpose, activity or place, and the loss arose from an entirely different purpose or activity or in another place.[83] The Commission went on to suggest that a court should ask what it was reasonable for the insured to expect, and that a court would need to ask whether, for example, the difference in use was such that a reasonable insured could have expected the loss to be covered.[84] The Commission further suggested that a distinction should be made between occasional and regular misuse (for example where a policy is restricted to the use of a vehicle for the insured's private use, a provision which the insured broke, but not on a regular basis).

11.43 As we have seen, the Commission's proposals came in for considerable criticism.[85] Aikens was amongst those who expressed concern at the Commission's proposal, suggesting that there was a danger that the parties' freedom to contract might be constrained. He argued that an approach based on reasonable expectations was a slippery slope that, in the extreme, could end with all rights given to one side and none to the other. Business parties

---

78 See Chapter 5, The Law Commission's Previous Reports and Recommendations on Warranties.

79 Further details and analysis of the Commission's recommendations in relation to 'reasonable expectations' can be found in Chapter 5.

80 Law Commission Insurance Contract Law Issues Paper 2 Warranties, November 2006, para 7.94.

81 Law Commission Consultation Paper No. 182 Insurance Contract Law: Misrepresentation, Non-Disclosure and Breach of Warranty by the Insured, November 2007 para 7.47.

82 Law Commission Consultation Paper No. 182 Insurance Contract Law: Misrepresentation, Non-Disclosure and Breach of Warranty by the Insured, November 2007 para 8.53.

83 Law Commission Insurance Contract Law Issues Paper 2 Warranties, November 2006, para 7.94.

84 Law Commission Insurance Contract Law Issues Paper 2 Warranties, November 2006, paras 7.94–6.

85 See Chapter 5 for a detailed analysis.

should instead make themselves aware of the consequences of their actions.[86] This author agrees with Aiken's assertion that an approach based solely on the reasonable expectations of the insured is too subjective and uncertain. If there were to be any role for a reasonable expectations approach in commercial insurance, would it not be equitable that it also applied to the insurer's expectations, such for example, that if the policy clearly states that it only insures vehicles driven by drivers over 25, might it not be at least arguable that it is reasonable for the insurer to expect not to be liable for a breach and loss involving a 19-year-old driver?

11.44 In the round, the concerns regarding a 'reasonable expectations' approach are credible and it is suggested that a better approach in commercial insurance where standard terms are being utilised would be for the parties to nevertheless specifically agree any provisions that give the insurer the right to avoid liability, such that these be separately identified in writing, drawn to the insured's attention and explained to him. This, it is submitted, would reduce the scope for uncertainty. The inherent lack of certainty in a reasonable expectations approach would likely encourage litigation and potential inconsistency in decisions, as well as, importantly, risking erosion of the parties freedom to contract. Surely it is not outrageous to assume that business parties do understand the terms on which they contract, especially where these have been specifically drawn to their attention and explained to them? As far as issues of scope are concerned, where these arise, it is submitted that they should be subject to separate consideration by the court. Further details of reform proposals in this regard are set out in Chapter 12. In 2012 the Law Commission accepted that their proposals had gone too far and dropped the reasonable expectations element of their recommendations.[87]

(ix) Should parties have the ability to contract out from any revisions to the law on insurance warranties?

11.45 We have seen that the Insurance Act 2015 contains provisions that, subject to certain conditions, enable parties to contract out of the statutory regime.[88] On the other hand contracting out of s54 of the Australian Insurance Contracts Act is prohibited: under s52 of the ICA any term that purports to limit or exclude the operation of s54 to the prejudice of a person other than the insurer is void.[89] Like its Australian counterpart, we have seen that it is also not possible to contract out of section 11 of the New Zealand Insurance Law Reform Act.[90] In contrast the Insurance Act 2015 ss16 and 17 allow contracting out, providing (in summary) that the disadvantageous terms are brought to the attention of the insured and are clear and unambiguous as to their effect.[91] If contracting out is to be permitted, it is surely important that there be sufficient flexibility to allow the courts to adapt their approach in the light of different insurance markets and differing levels

86 Sir R Aikens, 'The Law Commission's Proposed Reforms of the Law of Warranties in Marine and Commercial Insurance: Will the Cure Be Better than the Disease?' in *Reforming Marine and Commercial Insurance Law*, General Editor Dr Bariş Soyer, Informa, London 2008.

87 Law Commission Consultation Paper No. 204 Insurance Contract Law: Business Insured's Duty of Disclosure and the Law of Warranties, A Joint Consultation Paper, June 2012.

88 See Chapter 9.

89 S52 Insurance Contracts Act 1984.

90 S15 NZ Insurance Law Reform Act.

91 S17(3) Insurance Act 2015. See Chapter 9 for a detailed discussion of ss16 and 17 of the Insurance Act 2015.

of knowledge and expertise amongst the parties.[92] S17(4) of the Insurance Act does provide that 'in determining whether the requirements of subsections (2) and (3) have been met, the characteristics of the insured persons of the kind in question and the circumstances of the transaction, are to be taken into account.'[93] It has however been argued earlier that the contracting out provisions of the Insurance Act go too far in offering flexibility and interpretation: on balance they leave too much open for interpretation by the courts with the result that they are likely to lead to less, rather than greater, clarity.[94]

11.46 Surely the better, and indisputably more certain, approach is for it to be forbidden to contract out of the provisions that seek to address the worst failings of the law on warranties. Such an approach also minimises the scope for abuse and at a stroke adjusts the gradient of the playing field, which for too long has been stacked in the insurer's favour.

(x) Should there be a right of termination?

11.47 In 2007 the Law Commission in England and Wales recommended that a breach of warranty should give the insurer the right to terminate the contract, rather than automatically discharging it from liability, but (unless otherwise agreed) only if the breach had sufficiently serious consequences to justify termination under the general law of contract.[95] Once a breach came to light, the insurer could either decide to repudiate the contract or to affirm it and continue with the relationship. In its 2012 proposals however, the Law Commission, while continuing to support a right to cancel, felt that this was best left to the terms of the contract.[96] The Commission's proposals in 2014 maintained this position and there is no right of termination in the Insurance Act 2015.

11.48 There is no doubt that providing for a right of termination does raise a number of issues, as flagged in the Law Commission's 2006 Issues Paper,[97] in relation to, for example:

(i) Premium payment: should the insured continue to be liable to pay premiums after the contract is terminated?
(ii) Notice: should the insurer's right to repudiate be subject to a requirement to give reasonable notice?
(iii) Waiver: what effect would the right to terminate have on the law of waiver?

11.49 Historically the payment of premiums has not been regarded as divisible: Chadwick LJ commented in *Chapman v Kardirga*:

> The fact that the successive instalments are due and payable on dates which occur at three monthly intervals during the term of the policy does not, in my view, lead to the conclusion that the premium, which comprises the aggregate of those instalments, is itself divisible between successive three month intervals.[98]

92 G Leloudas, 'Contracting Out of the Insurance Act 2015' in *Commercial Insurance Contracts, The Insurance Act 2015, A New Regime for Commercial and Marine Insurance Law*, edited by M Clarke and B Soyer, Informa Law for Routledge, London, 2016.

93 S17(4) Insurance Act 2015.

94 See Chapter 9.

95 Law Commission Consultation Paper No. 182 Insurance Contract Law: Misrepresentation, Non-Disclosure and Breach of Warranty by the Insured, November 2007 para 8.89.

96 Law Commission Consultation Paper 204 para 15.33.

97 Law Commission Insurance Contract Law Issues Paper 2 Warranties, November 2006, para 7.137.

98 *JA Chapman v Kadirga and others* [1998] CLC 860.

However in 2006 the Law Commission concluded that the normal default rule should be that the insured would no longer be liable to pay premium instalments that fell due after the contract had been terminated.[99] This seems reasonable. But what if premiums have been paid in advance? The Commission was of the view that no refund would be payable in circumstance where the insurer terminated following a breach of warranty by the insured.[100] While, on the basis of historic precedent, this is probably correct, it is argued that such an approach may place some perverse incentives on the insured. If the insured feels it likely that the insurer will terminate if notified of a breach, the insured is hardly likely to notify, particularly if he anticipates being able to rectify the breach in the near future. If the assured keeps silent, he will soon be on cover again with no additional payment due (assuming that rectifying the breach will restore cover). If he notifies the insurer of the breach, he may find himself with no cover and the need to find, and pay, a new insurer.

11.50 It is this author's view that the merit of the argument supports a right to terminate and that, on balance, and not withstanding some attendant uncertainty, the best approach is for the right to trigger only if the breach had sufficiently serious consequences to justify termination under the general law of contract. The right to terminate should not be confined only to warranties, but should also apply to breaches of other provisions that result in the insurer having the right to avoid liability. It is further argued that if the insurer decides to terminate in circumstances where the premium has already been paid, he should be obliged to offer a pro rata refund of that premium.

Should termination be immediate once the insurer has notified the insured, or be subject to notice?

11.51 In Australia, the insurer cannot bring a contract to an end as a result of the breach, but it is entitled to terminate the contract using a cancellation clause. Under section 59 of the Insurance Contracts Act 1984, the insurer must give at least three days' notice in writing. In Norway the insurer must provide 14 days' notice of an intention to terminate.[101] In its 2006 report (when the Commission still supported a right to terminate), the Law Commission favoured imposing a requirement for a notice period. This seems sensible as such an approach would, inter alia, enable the insured to seek alternate cover prior to the existing cover coming to an end. However, in 2007 the Law Commission rejected a requirement to give notice of the intention to exercise an option to terminate on grounds that assured's predicament arose from his own fault. This surely falls short of a robust argument; for one thing, the breach may be inadvertent. A more sensible approach would be that a right to terminate on the provision of notice provides certainty for all parties and reduces the chances of unintended loss of cover.

11.52 If the insurer is given the right to terminate the contract following a breach of warranty/other term, should the insurer be precluded or estopped from exercising this right as a result of his conduct? In 2006 the Law Commission felt that this question could be left

99 Law Commission Insurance Contract Law Issues Paper 2 Warranties, November 2006, para 7.144.
100 Law Commission Insurance Contract Law Issues Paper 2 Warranties, November 2006, para 7.147.
101 Ss3–10 Norwegian Marine Insurance Plan 1996.

to the general law of contract, such that the insurer's conduct could indeed lead to him losing this right.[102] This seems a sensible approach.

(xi) Suspension: risk specific or policy wide?

11.53 Like the Law Commission of England and Wales,[103] this author believes that breaches of warranties (and other conditions that prima facie enable the insurer to escape liability in the event of a breach) should be treated as suspensive conditions, rather than terms that, on breach, automatically trigger the insurer's right to avoid liability. If warranties/ other terms are to become suspensive conditions, what happens in situations where the breach is incapable of remedy, for example in a marine policy, where there has been entry by the insured vessel into a prohibited zone? In its latest report, the Law Commission argued that in practical terms sailing out of the prohibited zone remedied the breach.[104] This seems sensible, subject to the exception that the Commission flagged: where, for example, undisclosed damage was incurred as a result of the vessel's incursion into the prohibited zone, but this only subsequently came to light (after the breach was 'rectified' by the vessel leaving the prohibited zone). As we have seen,[105] s10(2) and (4) of the Insurance Act 2015 make it clear that an insurer has no liability for losses that are 'attributable to something happening' while the insured is in breach, but which do not come to light until after the breach has been remedied. Again, this seems sensible.

11.54 But to what risks/liability should the suspension apply? Should it apply to the breadth of the insurer's liability, or just to specified risks? As far as the breadth of any 'temporary' suspension goes (i.e. one that is capable of rectification and is subsequently rectified), it is suggested that the sensible approach should be to address the issue on the following lines: a breach of warranty should prima facie result in suspension of liability across the contract, but this should be subject to the insured being able to establish that the warranty related to a specific risk or category of risk. For breaches of other terms that purport to trigger a right to avoid liability, suspension should be applied consistent with the terms of the right to avoid liability set out in that provision. Once again, where the provision provides a right to suspend liability across the contract as a whole, this should be subject to the insured's ability to establish that the term which has been breached in fact related to a specific risk or category of risk. Accordingly, if the insured is successful in establishing that the warranty (or other relevant term) relates to a specific risk, then suspension should be in relation to that risk only. This can be referred to as a 'tailored' approach to the suspension of insurer's liability.

11.55 So for example, if a policy for the insurance of a factory has a warranty concerning the fitting of a particular specification of fire alarm which the insured then fails to install, the onus will be on the insured to demonstrate that the warranty applied to a specific risk (fire) only. If the specified alarm is subsequently installed, cover for fire will take effect from the date the alarm is commissioned. In the meantime, assuming the insured has been

102 Law Commission Insurance Contract Law Issues Paper 2 Warranties, November 2006, para 7.161.

103 And now reflected in the Insurance Act 2105.

104 Para 17.25 Law Commission and Scottish Law Commission, Insurance Contract Law: Business Disclosure; Warranties; Insurers' Remedies for Fraudulent Claims; and Late Payment Law Com No 353 / Scot Law Com No 238 Cm 8898 SG/2014/131 July 2014 para 18.68. Available at: http://lawcommission.justice.gov.uk/docs.

105 See Chapter 9 for a discussion of the relevant provisions of the Insurance Act 2015.

successful in establishing the warranty applies only to fire risk, the insurer would remain liable in relation to other risks covered under the policy. But what if, prior to the specified the alarm being fitted, the factory had an old and outdated, but still functioning, fire alarm? Suppose further, that before the new alarm has been fitted, there is a loss from fire, but the insured is able to establish that there was no causal linkage between the absence of the specified alarm and the losses incurred as a result of the fire? If, like this author, one supports the logic of a causal linkage approach then, in circumstances like these, if the insured is able to establish that the absence of the specified fire alarm had no causal link with the loss then, notwithstanding the tailored nature of the suspension that would otherwise apply, the insurer would still be liable.

(xii) Termination and rectification of breach

11.56 Assuming a right to terminate as discussed earlier, if the insurer served notice to terminate, it would seem logical that he would remain on risk (for all risks under the policy, save those that are subject to the suspension) until the expiry of the termination notice period. But what if the breach of warranty (or other relevant term) was rectified prior to the expiry of the notice period for the notice to terminate? In such circumstances, it is argued that rectification should not affect the termination, but the insurer would briefly be back on risk for *all* the risks covered by the policy until such time as the termination became effective.

(xiii) Liability following a breach

11.57 Aiken queries that (assuming a causal linkage approach), as the burden of proving that a breach is not causative is on assured, would the insurer be 'off risk' until that is demonstrated?[106] In the event that it is demonstrated that there is no causal linkage, it would surely be perverse if the insurer were excused liability for any losses that had occurred between the breach and confirmation of the absence of causal linkage. If causal linkage *were* established then it seems equitable that the insurer should have no liability for any relevant (as in those subject to any suspension) losses arising prior to the breach being remedied.

(xiv) Should any reform apply to marine insurance?

11.58 Unlike the UK, Australia has maintained a separation between marine and non-marine insurance. Merkin has argued that there is no rationale for the maintenance of a parallel system.[107] In practice, although formally one system, it can be argued that the UK does in reality maintain a dual track system as there are provisions (of which implied warranties are the prime example) that apply only to marine insurance. In its report ALRC 91, the ALRC recommended the maintenance of the two separate regimes.[108] Merkin argues that repeal of the [Australian] Marine Insurance Act 1909 would have almost no consequences and that much of its provisions relating to warranties and implied warranties

---

106 Sir R Aikens, 'The Law Commission's Proposed Reforms of the Law of Warranties in Marine and Commercial Insurance: Will the Cure Be Better than the Disease?' in *Reforming Marine and Commercial Insurance Law*, General Editor Dr Bariş Soyer, Informa, London 2008.

107 R Merkin, 'Australia: Still a Nation of Chalmers?' (2011) 30(2) *University of Queensland Law Journal*, University of Queensland 189–224. The maintenance of separate systems in Australia is considered in more detail in Chapter 5.

108 ALRC 91, Review of the Marine Insurance Act 1909.

were now inconsistent with modern practice, obsolete or unnecessary.[109] In 2006 the England and Wales Law Commission recommended that its proposed causal connection test should also apply to marine insurance.[110] As recognised by the Commission, in the modern world, marine insurance is much more like other forms of insurance than was the case when the doctrine of marine warranties was first introduced. Insurers are less dependent on the good faith of the insured, and can verify the information given through a variety of surveys and audits. They are also more likely to be aware of technical breaches, even if those breaches did not result in any loss. For these reasons, it is argued that, unlike the position adopted in Australia in relation to the Insurance Contracts Act, any reform of the law on warranties should also apply to marine insurance.

(xv) Should implied warranties be preserved?

11.59 Should implied warranties continue to play a role in modern marine insurance? We have seen that with the dominant role of held covered clauses, the implied warranty of seaworthiness is little used in practice in today's world.[111] Is it helpful that marine insurance should continue to be treated differently from all other forms of commercial (and consumer) insurance by continuing to maintain implied warranties? The existing regime of implied warranties was left essentially unaltered by the Insurance Act 2015.[112] When the ALRC considered the merits of retaining a separate regime for marine insurance, some submissions to the Commission suggested that abolition of the implied warranties of seaworthiness and legality could result in personal safety and the environment being put at risk.[113] This contention is respectfully rejected. It is submitted that there is a strong case in favour of the abolition of implied warranties and other implied voyage conditions. If such a move were felt to be too radical, the existing provisions could be amended, such that in relation to the implied warranty of seaworthiness, the insurer would only be able to escape liability in circumstances where the assured had knowledge of the unseaworthy condition of the vessel and there was a causal link between the breach of the implied warranty and the loss. In line with the approach recommended by the ALRC,[114] it is proposed that this amended version of the implied seaworthy warranty should be a continuing warranty, rather than one that is applicable only at the commencement of the voyage.

11.60 Independent of the law on warranties, given the general doctrine of illegality, if a contract is illegal, the insured will not be able to enforce it. It would not matter that the loss was unconnected to the risks posed by the illegal conduct; the insured would have no redress. The operation of the law as it currently stands has already been discussed.[115] It is suggested that the implied warranty of legality adds nothing to that which can be achieved through other means, such as public policy avenues. This would mean that in line with Merkin's assertion, any recovery following an illegal act should depend upon ordinary

---

109 R Merkin, 'Australia: Still a Nation of Chalmers?' (2011) 30(2) *University of Queensland Law Journal*, University of Queensland 189–224.

110 Law Commission Insurance Contract Law Issues Paper 2 Warranties, November 2006, para 7.108.

111 See Chapter 4.

112 See Chapter 4 for a detailed analysis of implied warranties.

113 ALRC 91 para 9.36.

114 ALRC, Review of the Marine Insurance Act 1909 (2001) No 91, Recommendation 12.

115 See Chapter 4.

common law principles, rather than a statutory provision.[116] It is established that a contract that is tainted by illegality cannot be modified to give a benefit to a party involved in the illegality. As we have seen, the implied warranty of legality is left essentially untouched by the Law Commission's final proposals on warranties/the Insurance Act 2015.[117] In Australia the abolition of the implied warranty of legality has been recommended, albeit not implemented.[118] This failure to do away with the implied warranty of legality in England and Wales was a missed opportunity and it is proposed that the implied warranty of illegality should be abolished. However, if it were to remain, it should be made clear that if an adventure is carried out in an illegal manner with the knowledge of the insured, the insurer should be discharged from any liability under the policy, regardless of the absence of a causal linkage between breach and loss.[119]

(xvi) Implied voyage conditions

11.61 We have seen that s43 of the Marine Insurance Act has impact similar to that of a warranty:[120] 'Where the place of departure is specified in the policy, and the ship instead of sailing from that place sails from any other place, the risk does not attach.'[121] Is there a substantive justification for this provision in the modern era? In *Molinos Nacionales v Pohjola Insurance Company Ltd*, Coleman J described the provision as enabling the insurer to escape liability for 'trivial, entirely immaterial, deviations.'[122] Similarly under s44, the policy does not attach if the ship sails to the wrong destination. Under sections 45 and 46, if the destination is changed or there is a deviation, the insurer is discharged. Again these provisions were left untouched by the Insurance Act 2015. It is suggested that there is little justification for such provisions in the modern world and that the failure of the Insurance Act to repeal them was another missed opportunity.

116 R Merkin, Reforming Insurance Law: Is There a Case for Reverse Transportation?; A Report for the English and Scottish Law Commissioners on the Australian Experience of Insurance Law Reform; available at http://www.lawcom.gov.uk/app/uploads/2015/03/ICL_Merkin_report.pdf or at https://eprints.soton.ac.uk/27860/.

117 Recommendation 27, Law Commission and Scottish Law Commission, Insurance Contract Law: Business Disclosure; Warranties; Insurers' Remedies for Fraudulent Claims and Late Payment; Law Com No. 353/Scot Law Com No. 238 Cmd 8898 SG/2014/131 July 2014. Available at http://lawcommission.justice.go.uk/docs.

118 ALRC, Review of the Marine Insurance Act 1909 (2001) No 91.

119 B Soyer, *Warranties in Marine Insurance,* Cavendish Publishing, London, 2nd Edition, 2006, page 219.

120 See Chapter 4.

121 S43 Marine Insurance Act 1906.

122 (Unreported) High Court, 5 May 1998.

CHAPTER 12

A proposed solution

Metrics

12.1 Before discussing the solution proposed by this volume, it necessary first to consider what constitutes a merit-worthy solution. It has been demonstrated that no one approach of those adopted to date deals satisfactorily with all aspects of breaches of warranties and other conditions in commercial insurance contracts. In developing a scheme for the treatment of such breaches, this volume proposes that the approach adopted must seek to address the following criteria:

(i) Provide an equitable balance between the interests of the insured and the insurer. Any proposals for commercial insurance, like those contained in this volume, must recognise and take account of the fact that the insureds in this sphere range from sophisticated multinational corporates to the small, one man, owner operator enterprises.

(ii) Apply not only to warranties, but also to any other contractual condition that, if breached, purports to enable the insurer to avoid liability for losses under the policy.

(iii) Address breaches that occur, both prior to the policy coming on foot and those arising after the policy's inception.

(iv) Address failures to comply with condition precedents, enabling breaches to be forgiven but only where once rectified, the risk remains substantially as contemplated by the parties.

(v) Acknowledge and take account of any prejudice suffered by the insurer.

(vi) Abolish 'basis' clauses.

(vii) Provide for breaches of warranties/other conditions to result, where appropriate, in tailored suspension of the insurer's liability (with the balance of the policy remaining on risk) while the breach continues, with cover reverting once the breach has been 'cured.'

(viii) Ensure that causal linkage plays a central role in determining liability.

(ix) Provide the courts with a degree of flexibility, such that decisions can be tailored equitably to reflect the circumstances of as wide a range of individual cases as possible. The objective should be to ensure the courts are not constrained by an overly prescriptive statutory framework, while ensuring that any regime provides a reasonable degree of predictability, clarity and certainty to all participants.

(x) Ensure that issues of the scope of cover remain a matter for agreement between the parties with which the courts should not interfere. While decisions of the court may

DOI: 10.4324/9781003031734-12

legitimately clarify the scope of the policy, it is important that any reform does not erode the sanctity of scope as a matter for agreement by the parties.

(xi) Ensure that exclusion clauses are covered by the proposals.

(xii) Ensure that the proposals cannot be easily circumvented by, for example, drafting techniques.

(xiii) Heed the lessons of earlier attempts at reform of this area of the law, both at home and abroad, seeking to improve on the shortcomings of the current regimes in England and Wales, Australia and New Zealand as outlined and discussed in this volume.

(xiv) Demonstrate robustness by providing rational, equitable and consistent outcomes when 'stress tested' against the facts of well-known historic cases from various jurisdictions.

(xv) Address the question of whether a separate regime should be maintained for marine insurance.

(xvi) Determine the future of implied warranties.

Proposed solution

12.2 The approach proposed by this volume would apply to breaches of warranties and other terms where the contract specifies that the insurer's remedy is avoidance of liability for losses incurred by the insured.

(i) Prior to contract coming into effect

12.3 As in New Zealand, this volume proposes that an insurer should be able to avoid liability where the insured makes pre-contractual representations that are both substantially incorrect and material.[1] Under this volume's proposals a statement would be substantially incorrect only if the difference between what was stated to be the case by the insured and what was actually correct would have been considered material by a prudent insurer.[2] A statement would be material only if that statement would have influenced the judgement of a prudent insurer in fixing the premium or in determining whether he would have taken, or continued, the risk upon substantially the same terms.[3]

12.4 Conditions precedent and other terms requiring compliance prior to the contract's effective date. Like the Insurance Act 2015, the solution proposed in this volume is based on the premise that, subject to the earlier provisions regarding pre-contractual representations, breaches of warranties and other relevant conditions, (being those that would, when breached, otherwise entitle the insurer to avoid liability under the policy) result in suspension of risk, rather than (in the case of warranties) automatic termination of the insurer's liability.

12.5 The presumption in this volume is that when a term that is also a condition precedent to the attachment of risk[4] is breached/not complied with, the conditionality

1 Ss5 and 6 of the NZ Insurance Law Reform Act.

2 This mirrors the wording of s6(1) of the NZ Insurance Law Reform Act.

3 This mirrors the wording of s6(2) of the NZ Insurance Law Reform Act.

4 A distinction needs to be made between a condition precedent to the attachment of risk and a condition precedent to the liability of the insurer. The latter usually, although not always, relates to the claims process and imposes obligations on the insured (e.g. to provide notice) that must be satisfied before the insured is able to recover

applies to the whole risk and as a result the risk as a whole does not attach. The onus is on the insurer to establish that the term is a genuine condition precedent and that the parties intended it to be such. It is this volume's presumption that, in order to ensure that the proposals cannot be easily circumvented through drafting devices, a court would wish to satisfy itself that any provision is genuinely a condition precedent: it will not be sufficient for it simply to be described as a condition precedent in the contract. If the insurer is able to demonstrate that the term was a genuine condition precedent (to the attachment of risk) and that the insured had failed to meet the requirements of the condition precedent, the insurer will not be on risk and will face no liability under the contract. It would however be open to the insured to demonstrate that the intention was that the condition precedent related only to a specific risk under the contract, rather than all risk under the contract and/or that the non-compliance having been rectified, that the resultant risk exposure was the same/essentially the same as that originally contemplated by the parties (in this latter regard, this volume's proposals mirror section 10(5) and (6) of the Insurance Act). Where the court was persuaded that the condition precedent that had not been complied with related only to a specific risk, the contract would fail to come on risk in relation to that risk only, unless and until the breach was rectified. If the loss related to another risk under the contract, the insurer would prima facie remain liable. It may also be possible in exceptional circumstances where the CP relates to the attachment of risk generally for the insured to persuade the court that the risk remains essentially the same as originally contemplated once the non compliance is remedied. In these circumstances the risk would attach once the remedy was effected.

12.6 So for example, take the situation where a policy for the insurance of commercial premises includes a condition precedent that a particular specification of burglary alarm be installed in the premises prior to the commencement date of the policy, but the insured fails to install such an alarm by the due date. Under the proposals set out previously, if the insurer was able to demonstrate that the provision was a condition precedent, the policy would not come on risk, unless the insured was in turn able to establish that the parties' intent was that the provision be a CP only in relation to burglary risk. Assuming the insured is able to meet this hurdle then, prior to the specified alarm being fitted, the insured would only be able to claim for a loss arising after the contract came on risk if the CP was held to be specific to burglary risk *and* the loss incurred related to another part of the contract. Once the alarm was fitted the contract would (assuming the risk to be substantially the same as originally contemplated) be fully on risk, including for burglary risk.

(ii) After the contract has come into effect

12.7 As with the Insurance Act 2015,[5] basis clauses would be abolished under the solution advocated by this volume. This author is of the view that the provisions of s9 of

in relation to the claim. (A variant to this norm can be seen in *Ferrcom Pty Ltd v Commercial Union Assurance Co of Australia Ltd*, (1993) 176 CLR 332 where the policy for a mobile crane contained a condition precedent to the insurer's liability requiring notification 'as soon as possible ... of any change materially varying any of the facts and circumstances existing at the commencement of [the] policy.')

5 S9 of the Insurance Act 2015.

the Insurance Act[6] work well and it is proposed these would be incorporated into this volume's solution.

12.8 Under the proposals in this volume it would be a requirement that the parties specifically agree any provisions that give the insurer the right to avoid liability, such that these be separately identified in writing, drawn to the insured's attention and explained to him.

12.9 In these proposals the onus is on the insurer to establish a breach, whether of a warranty or other contractual provision. The proposals would apply to both risk and non-risk clauses.

12.10 As in the Insurance Act, the concept of any breach of warranty automatically discharging the insurer's liability under the policy would be abolished.

12.11 Where a breach of warranty (or other provision enabling the insurer to avoid liability under the policy) occurs after a policy has come on risk, the breach will prima facie suspend the insurer's liability to meet a loss until the breach is remedied. The assumption is that, where a warranty has been breached, suspension will apply to all liability under the contract except where

(i) The assured demonstrates that the provision which has not been met applies to a specific category of risk only, or to a specific location or time and that the insured's claim relates to a different element of the contract or category of risk (or to a different location or time); and/or
(ii) Where there is no causal linkage between the breach and the loss. Again the onus will be on the insured to establish the absence of such linkage.

12.12 Where the contract specifies that breach of another contract term, not being a warranty, will result in the insurer being able to avoid liability under the policy (in part or in whole), a breach of that term will prima facie result in suspension of the insurer's liability consistent with the terms of the right to avoid liability set out in that provision. Suspension would last until such time as the breach is remedied.

12.13 Notwithstanding the breach of a relevant contract term (whether warranty or otherwise), the Insurer will be obliged to meet the insured's claim if:

(i) The Assured is able to establish that the provision (whether warranty or other provision) which has not been met applied to a specific category of risk only, or to a specific location or time and that his claim relates to a different element of the contract or category of risk (or to a different location or time); or
(ii) The Assured is able to establish there is no causal linkage between the breach and the loss.

12.14 Where cover has been suspended, cover will be restored when, and if, the breach is remedied. If the breach is remedied, liability will be restored from the time of rectification. As identified in the Insurance Act 2015, certain conditions (whether warranties or other provisions), such as those that require something to be done by a specific deadline are, prima facie, incapable of remedy if not met by the deadline. As in the Insurance Act, this text proposes that such conditions be treated as remedied if, when the conditionality is met, the risk remains essentially the same as that originally contemplated by the parties. This

6 See Chapter 9 for a discussion of s9 of the Insurance Act.

approach mirrors that set out in s10 (5) and (6) of the Insurance Act 2015, but, unlike in the Act, would not be confined to warranties.[7]

12.15 Causal linkage: this is central to the proposals set out in this volume. If a breach of a warranty or other relevant condition is continuing at the time of loss, the insurer will be able to avoid liability (in relation to that risk or the contract as a whole, depending on the nature and/or terms of the relevant provision that has been breached) by reason of that breach, unless the insured is able to establish, on a balance of probabilities, that the loss in relation to which the insured seeks to be indemnified was not caused by the insured's breach.[8] For example, suppose a policy requires that a particular specification of lock be fitted to the main door of a factory, but the insured fails to fit such a lock. Following the recommendations set out in this volume, let us suppose the court holds that the condition is a warranty, but (following successful arguments from the insured) one relating to a particular risk, burglary, and that accordingly the policy be suspended in relation to this risk until such time as the breach is rectified. Under this volume's proposals, it would be open to the insured to argue that on the facts, the absence of the specified lock had no causal linkage with the loss as the intruders had used a JCB to smash a hole in the factory wall. This is very different from the way the Law Commission originally intended the Insurance Act 2015 to operate, although arguably not substantially different from the final wording of s11(3) of the Insurance Act.[9] This text submits that experience in overseas jurisdictions shows that determining issues of causal linkage is not unduly challenging. Under this volume's causal linkage test, subject to the court retaining flexibility in relation to proportionality (see later in this chapter), the insured would still be able to claim in circumstances where, on the balance of probabilities, he is able to show that the breach did not cause the loss incurred. Even where there is causal linkage, it is proposed the insurer would remain liable in circumstances where the action that resulted in the breach was taken to preserve life or property and/or could not reasonably have been avoided.

12.16 Proportionality will apply; accordingly if the assured were able to establish that, for example, the breach was responsible only for 40% of the loss incurred, the insurer would be obliged to meet 60% of the loss. A key element of this volume's proposals is that in addition the court would retain the flexibility of applying a measure of proportionality in circumstances where, although the breach did not, on the facts, cause the loss, it *could* have done so (see example provided later in this chapter).

12.17 Prejudice: if the insurer is able to establish that he has suffered prejudice as a result of the insured's breach, the quantum of prejudice suffered will reduce the amount for which the insurer would otherwise be liable. However, under these proposals, the insurer would need to demonstrate that it would actually have taken a different course of action and/or steps to avoid the prejudice, had it been aware of the breach, or known of the insured's intentions: this may prove to be a high bar.

7 The application of such provisions to conditions precedent has been discussed earlier in this chapter.

8 As already indicated, the insurer will also remain liable if the insured is able to establish that term that has been breached relates to a particular risk and the loss that has occurred relates to a different risk.

9 Law Com 353 Insurance Contract Law: Business Disclosure, Warranties, Insurers' Remedies for Fraudulent Claims and Late Payment, July 2014, para 18.48 (2). Under the Commission's original draft of the Insurance Act, if there was a break-in, liability would be suspended and the insurer would not be liable even if the specified lock would not have prevented the loss. Although somewhat unclear, the final version of s11(3) of the Insurance Act seems to reverse this, adopting what appears to be a causal linkage approach.

12.18 Right of termination: in the event of a breach of warranty or other relevant condition that would enable the insurer to avoid liability, or would have done so, save for these provisions, the insurer will have the right to terminate the policy on provision of 14 days' notice. The right of termination will however only trigger if the consequences are sufficient to justify termination under the general contract law. The right of termination ensures that the insurer is not required to take on a risk he might not otherwise have been comfortable with, enables the assured to maintain cover (by seeking cover from another party) and avoids the risk of inadvertent loss of coverage. As we have seen, the right of termination is absent from the Insurance Act 2015.[10] Following a relevant breach, the insurer would have 14 days from the date at which he becomes aware of the breach to serve notice of his intent to terminate. Termination will be effective 14 days after the service of such notice. The insurer will remain liable for past losses arising from events prior to the date of the breach. The insurer will also be liable for losses under any aspect of the policy not subject to suspension, up to the point at which termination becomes effective (and for losses in relation to the suspended risk from the point at which the relevant breach is rectified until termination takes effect). The treatment of premium payments on termination is considered later in this chapter.

12.19 Scope of cover: as discussed elsewhere[11] this volume believes the reference to the 'risk as a whole' in s11(1) of the Insurance Act 2015 to be a difficult and confusing concept. Despite the scope of the policy being a recognised legal concept, none of the relevant legislative schemes dealing with insurance warranties in England and Wales, Australia or New Zealand specifically mention the scope of cover. Under this volume's proposals the legislative provisions would explicitly state that an insurer has no liability in any circumstances for an event or loss that is outside of the scope of the policy. Under these proposals, in any dispute over liability for loss involving a breach, or alleged breach, of a relevant condition under a policy, the proposals would require that the first issue that should be determined by the court is whether the facts fall within the scope of the policy. Of course there will be questions over whether a particular provision is a clause defining risk (scope) e.g. in determining whether the policy provides cover (only) for a building with an operational burglar alarm, or alternatively is a policy covering all standard risks for a building policy, but includes a present fact warranty where risk is excluded (via, for example, an exclusion clause) in the event that the specified alarm is not fitted or is not operational.[12] It is this text's contention that such definitional questions will always be present in contract interpretation and should not therefore be seen as particularly problematical. What is important is that the question be specifically addressed by the court as a threshold issue. In the vast majority of cases, the scope of the policy will not be in dispute. The fact that this requirement is specified under these proposals would not result in any additional burden on the courts as it is a question that should anyway be addressed. Interpretation of the intent of parties to a contract is something with which the courts are well versed.[13] Explicitly addressing the issue of scope merely avoids the potential for confusion that can arise where it is not specifically referenced: for

10 See Chapter 9.

11 See Chapter 9.

12 A similar issue was raised in *Highway Hauliers v Maxwell* [2012] WASC 53 concerning the application of s54(1) of the Australian Insurance Contracts Act: see Chapter 6.

13 The observations of Lord Neuberger in *Arnold v Britton* [2015] UKSC 36 at para 126 summarise the courts' approach:

example see some of the cases determined under s54 of the Australian Insurance Contracts Act, as discussed in Chapter 6.

12.20 Exclusion clauses. The proposals in this volume would specifically apply to exclusion clauses where these purport to excuse the insurer from liability. In circumstances where the court holds that the circumstances of the loss fall within the terms of an exclusion clause (whether or not as a result of a breach of the policy terms by the insured), the insurer will have no liability for losses incurred by the insured, unless the insured is able to demonstrate that there is no causal linkage between the events that triggered the operation of the exclusion clause and the loss incurred by the insured. However, if the facts are such that the circumstances triggering the exclusion clause *could* have caused or contributed to the loss that occurred, the court would retain the option of applying an element of proportionality (see example next) when determining liability. In circumstances where a loss is attributable to something that occurred while the exclusion clause was in play, but where the loss does not come to light until after the exclusion clause ceases to operate, the insurer will have no liability. The fact that the loss is attributable to the breach will mean, by definition, that the insured will be unable to establish the absence of a causal linkage; proportionality would, however, apply where appropriate.

12.21 An illustration. An example will demonstrate how this volume's proposals on both causal linkage and exclusion clauses would work. Suppose a policy covering the operation of a fleet of haulage trucks contains a provision stating that the insurer will have no liability for any loss under the contract arising from the operation of the trucks by drivers under the age of 25. For the purpose of this example, it will be assumed that the policy has been drafted in a fashion that leads the court to conclude the relevant provision is properly interpreted as being an exclusion clause, rather than an event that is outside the scope of the policy. (In accordance with these proposals, scope would be the first issue to be addressed by the court.) Suppose in this instance there is an accident and the driver was under 25, but the court concludes that the underage driver's conduct did not, on a balance of probabilities, cause the loss that occurred. Accordingly the insurer would be liable for the loss, unless the court felt it appropriate to apply a measure of proportionality. The court would do so if it concluded that the circumstances resulting in the triggering of the exclusion clause (or breach of condition, where relevant) *could* have contributed to the loss. In circumstances such as this, where the driver is under 25, the risk for the insurer increases (in addition to triggering the exclusion clause); this is the prime reason that insurance policies for young, inexperienced drivers are more expensive than those for older, more experienced counterparts. As a result, this text would argue that it would be both appropriate and equitable for the court to have the flexibility to apply a measure of proportionality. The court would exercise its discretion if it felt this was appropriate, bearing in mind that, on the facts, the breach did not *in fact*

The court is concerned to identify the intention of the parties by reference to "what a reasonable person having all the background knowledge which would have been available to the parties would have understood them to be using the language in the contract to mean."

... And it

does so by focussing on the meaning of the relevant words, ... in their documentary, factual and commercial context. That meaning has to be assessed in the light of (i) the natural and ordinary meaning of the clause, (ii) any other relevant provisions of the lease, (iii) the overall purpose of the clause and the lease, (iv) the facts and circumstances known or assumed by the parties at the time that the document was executed, and (v) commercial common sense, but (vi) disregarding subjective evidence of any party's intentions.

contribute to the loss. We have seen that a review of insurance contract law in New Zealand has recognised the greater statistical likelihood of loss that can arise in certain circumstances (by way of example it cites the use of a vehicle for commercial purposes rather than private), even though such use may not have caused the loss in question.[14] In this example it may be that in the circumstances the court feels there are credible circumstances in which having an inexperienced driver *could* have contributed to the loss. As we have seen, it would also be open to the insurer to argue that it has suffered prejudice, at least to the extent of the premium that would have been charged for a driver aged under 25.[15] This text argues that an approach on the lines set out gives the court greater flexibility equitably to balance the interests of the insured and insurer, albeit arguably at the cost of some loss of certainty. It is this author's position that it surely cannot be acceptable for an insurer to be obliged (where on the facts there is no causal linkage) to meet the full measure of a claim where the insured has flagrantly and without any mitigating circumstances, breached a policy condition and increased the risk. The approach in this volume provides the court with the flexibility it needs to deliver an equitable outcome.

Implied warranties: is a separate regime necessary for marine insurance?

12.22 This author argues that the proposals set out in this volume should apply to all forms of commercial insurance including marine insurance. The existing regime of implied warranties was left untouched under the Law Commission's proposals. As we have seen, ss10(2) and 11(1) of the Insurance Act 2015 make it explicitly clear that ss10 and 11 apply to the implied warranties identified in the Marine Insurance Act 1906.[16] This author believes this to be a flawed approach and that ideally the implied warranty of seaworthiness should be abolished on the grounds that, inter alia, it is of little relevance in the modern world.[17] Instead it should be open to parties to make what provisions they felt appropriate for seaworthiness through express terms. Alternatively, if such abolition is viewed as too radical, then as a minimum, this author believes that the existing provisions relating to implied warranties should be amended such that the insurer would only be able to escape liability in circumstances where the insured had knowledge of the unseaworthy condition of the vessel and failed to take such steps as were reasonably available to render the vessel seaworthy. Even then the insurer would remain liable if the breach was remedied by the time of loss and/or if the insured were able to establish the absence of any causal linkage between the breach and loss. If abolition was rejected such amendments would significantly reduce the impact of the implied warranty and ensure that it more equitably reflected the interests of the insured. However, if this alternate approach was to be adopted then, in order to ensure that this did not result in tilting of the playing field too far in the favour of the insured, this

14 See www.mbie.govt.nz/business-and-employment/business/financial-markets-regulation/insurance-contract-law-review discussed in Chapter 7.

15 As discussed earlier in these proposals, where the insurer is able to establish prejudice, the extent of the insurer's liability would be reduced by the quantum of prejudice he has suffered.

16 Note that as observed in Chapter 4, s39(5) of the Marine Insurance Act 1906 provides that there is no implied warranty of seaworthiness in relation to time policies but that where, with the privity of the insured a vessel is sent to sea in an unseaworthy state the insurer is not liable for any loss attributable to unseaworthiness. As a result s11 of the Insurance Act 2015 applies to s39(5), but s10 does not.

17 See Chapter 4.

volume recommends that the amended implied seaworthy warranty should be a continuing warranty (rather than one that is only applicable at the commencement of the voyage), such that in circumstances where the insured becomes aware of a development during a voyage that renders the vessel unseaworthy and failed to take such steps as were reasonably available to render the vessel seaworthy, the insurer would have no liability. This reflects the approach discussed by the ALRC in ALRC 91.[18] In the words of the ALRC, this

> better recognises that with modern communications and technology an insured shipowner or management company may have knowledge of unseaworthiness that has arisen in the course of a voyage and may be in a position to take steps to remedy the deficiency.[19]

12.23 In circumstances where the insured was not aware of the unseaworthy condition his position will not be prejudiced.[20] This text agrees with the ALRC that such an approach would not compromise marine safety. The deterrent effect of the implied warranty of seaworthiness would be maintained and in circumstances where the unseaworthiness arose during a voyage, it will be more difficult for the insured to claim unless, where he was aware of such a development, he has acted reasonably to counter the effects of unseaworthiness where the circumstances allowed.[21]

12.24 This author emphasises that his preferred approach would be for the implied warranty of seaworthiness to be abolished. However, if this were rejected, it is submitted that a package of measures on the lines recommended earlier would result in the implied warranty creating less controversy, not least because its impact would be more evenly distributed between the interests of the insured and insurer. Although at first sight, extending the implied warranty to a continuous warranty may appear a radical step and one that increases the significance of the implied warranty, this text rejects such a view. Provided the extension is subject to the insured having knowledge of the unseaworthiness and failing to take reasonable steps to correct it, this author argues it would, when balanced by the other proposed changes, represent a reasonable and balanced approach and one that better reflects the realities of modern seafaring and communication technology.

12.25 In relation to time policies, it is clear that there is no implied warranty that the vessel be seaworthy at any stage of the adventure.[22] Consistent with its position in relation to the implied warranty of seaworthiness, this volume's preferred position is that s39(5) of the Marine Insurance Act be repealed and that it be left to the parties to incorporate an express term on similar lines, should they wish to do so. However, were this judged to be too radical

18 Note that the ALRC, while recommending that the implied warranty of seaworthiness should be abolished, proposed that parties should be at liberty to include an express term on similar lines to the implied warranty of seaworthiness and should be free to craft this as a continuing obligation, providing that where unseaworthiness developed during a voyage this would not generally prejudice an insured if the insured did not know and could not reasonably be expected to have known of the unseaworthiness, or if the insured did all it reasonably could to remedy the position (which might well be nothing). In such circumstances the insured would not have breached the contractual term and the insurer would have no grounds on which to avoid liability. ALRC 91, para 9.176 refers.

19 Australian Law Reform Commission Review of the Marine Insurance Act 1909 (ALRC Report 91), para 9.174.

20 Nor will he be liable if, in circumstance where he was aware of the unseaworthiness, he has taken all reasonable steps to combat it.

21 Australian Law Reform Commission Review of the Marine Insurance Act 1909 (ALRC Report 91), para 9.175.

22 S39(5) of the Marine Insurance Act 1906 refers, see Chapter 4.

an approach, this author would be comfortable with s39(5) being retained, consistent as it is with a causation approach to liability.[23]

12.26 As we have seen,[24] this author believes sections 43–46 of the Marine Insurance Act are of little significance in the modern era. It is submitted that failure to abolish them in the Insurance Act 2015 was a missed opportunity. Accordingly it is recommended that they be repealed. Once again, if this was felt to be too radical an approach, the provisions could be retained but linked to causation, such that the insurer would avoid liability only where there is a causal linkage between breach and loss.

12.27 This author believes that the implied warranty of legality adds nothing that cannot be achieved through other means such as public policy avenues. This text supports Merkin's assertion that any recovery following an illegal act should depend upon ordinary common law principles, rather than a statutory provision.[25] In this author's view, the implied warranty of legality should be abolished on the grounds that it is not necessary. However, if it is to remain, it should be made clear that if, for example, a voyage is carried out in an illegal manner with the consent of the assured, the insurer should be discharged from any liability under the policy, regardless of the absence of any causal link between the breach and loss.[26] As we have seen, it is already the case that a breach of safety regulations does not generally, of itself, constitute a breach of the implied warranty of legality. If the implied warranty of legality were to be retained, this text proposes that any transgression of such regulations would require the insured's specific approval prior to any consideration of whether it constituted a breach of the implied warranty.

Premium payments

12.28 What is the position in relation to premium payments under the proposals set out here? In the event of a relevant breach, as cover is only suspended, it seems logical that the assured should not be entitled to any refund of premium: as we have seen, cover will automatically be restored once the breach is remedied. This would change however in circumstances where the insurer chose to trigger his right to terminate following a breach. Where payment has been made in advance, a pro rata refund would be owed to the assured for the period of cancelled cover. Where a condition precedent that applies to the risk as a whole has not been honoured, such that the policy never comes on foot, it is likely that no premium would be payable. Where the CP is held to refer to a specific risk only[27] no refund of premium would be applicable.

Comparison with s54 ICA and s11 NZ Insurance Law Reform Act

12.29 As already described, the approach set out in this volume would apply where there has been a breach of warranty or other relevant condition, or where the terms of an

23 As discussed in Chapter 4, s39(5) provides that the insurer would escape liability where the vessel is sent to sea in an unseaworthy state with the privity of the assured and the loss incurred is attributable to unseaworthiness.

24 See Chapter 4.

25 R Merkin, Reforming Insurance Law: Is There a Case for Reverse Transportation?; A Report for the English and Scottish Law Commissioners on the Australian Experience of Insurance Law Reform; available at http://www.lawcom.gov.uk/app/uploads/2015/03/ICL_Merkin_report.pdf or at https://eprints.soton.ac.uk/27860/.

26 B Soyer, *Warranties in Marine Insurance,* Cavendish Publishing, London, 2nd Edition, 2006, page 219.

27 Such that the specific risk only is suspended as discussed earlier in this chapter.

exclusion clause have been triggered. Under s54 of the Insurance Contracts Act in Australia an act or omission that is not necessarily a breach of any contractual term can result in the application of that section. The formula under s54 can be unclear regarding its application to exclusion clauses: there must be a triggering act or omission. As we have seen,[28] there has been considerable debate in Australia over the concept of what amounts to an act or omission for the purposes of s54, and it is the view of this author that the concept of 'act or omission' is best avoided. The Insurance Act 2015 addresses breaches of warranties (s10) and 'non-compliance' (s11). This text argues that it is sometimes not possible to extend 'non-compliance' or 'breach' to include omissions: non-compliance requires an act that is inconsistent with the relevant provision of the contract, whereas an omission can be a failure to do something, while in no way being 'non-compliant' with the terms of the contract. Further, a triggering event for an exclusion clause will not necessarily be a 'breach' (or omission): whether or not the exclusion clause has been triggered will, instead, as we have seen, depend on the terms of the clause. This author submits that the way to deliver the highest degree of clarity is for the proposals to have a 'breach' (of a term of the policy) as their triggering event, but for exclusion clauses additionally to be specifically subject to the application of the proposals.

12.30 In practice the distinction between this volume's proposals and s54 of the Insurance Contracts Act may however not be as great as it seems. Take the situation in *Pantaenius Australia Pty Ltd v Watkins Syndicate 0457 at Lloyd's*;[29] as we have seen, in this case a marine policy covered the insured's yacht while within in a 250-nautical mile range of the Australian coast. However, the policy included an exclusion clause that triggered in circumstances where the vessel cleared Australian Customs with the purpose of leaving Australian waters. Under its terms, the exclusion clause remained in place until the vessel again cleared Australian Customs on its return. A key issue in the Australian court's deliberation was to determine the inherent restrictions or limitations of the policy (the scope of the policy in the words of this volume) and whether the exclusion clause on which the insurer sought to rely constituted such an inherent restriction or limitation: in other words was the loss incurred as a result of an activity which was outside the scope of the policy? The court held that the exclusion clause was not such a limitation and that accordingly s54 applied. In assessing causation, the court held that the correct approach was a 'with and without' test of causation and that the nature of the risk would have been precisely the same whether the vessel had cleared Australian Customs or not.[30] No causation had thus been established under s54(2) as the act of clearing customs on departure and sailing from Fremantle had not increased the risk that the vessel would run aground and no prejudice was established under s54(1). As a result the insurer was obliged to make a contribution to the payments made to the insured under a separate policy.

12.31 Although the proposals set out in this volume specifically apply to exclusion clauses, the first question the court would address is whether the facts fall within, or outside, the scope of the policy. Were the *Pantaenius* facts to be assessed under the approach proposed herein, it is argued that a court would, like the Australian court, likely hold that the circumstances were within the scope of the policy, but covered by the exclusion

28 See Chapter 6.
29 [2016] FCA 1.
30 [2016] FCA 1 at 96.

clause. In these circumstances the onus would be on the insured to establish that there was no causal linkage between the event(s) that triggered the exclusion clause and the loss. In the event that the insured was able to establish the absence of a causal linkage, the insurer would remain liable. Were the court to address causation in the same way as its Australian counterpart, it would likely hold that there was no causal linkage. Were it to do so, the insurer would not escape liability; however, the court might chose to apply a measure of proportionality to causation on the grounds that, although the facts leading to the triggering of the exclusion clause did not, in fact, cause or contribute to the loss, they *could* have done so. On the facts such a finding could well be seen as credible.

12.32 In a situation where a marine policy has an exclusion in relation to a prohibited geographical zone, this author would argue that it would potentially be open to the court to find that, while in the prohibited zone, the vessel was outside the scope of the policy (as opposed to being within scope, but subject to the provisions of an exclusion) and that accordingly the insured would be unable to claim/the insurer would have no liability for any losses incurred while in the zone. Whether or not the court made such a finding would depend on the facts. Where the facts result in a finding that the issue is outside the scope of the policy, causal linkage and proportionality have no part to play: the insurer will have no liability. Under this volume's proposals, where a loss occurs which, in the words of the Law Commission, is 'attributable to something happening'[31] while the vessel was in the prohibited zone (and was otherwise held to be within the scope of the policy), the insurer will similarly have no liability, notwithstanding that the loss does not come to light until after the vessel has left the prohibited zone (and the breach has thus been 'remedied'). This is, in effect, an application of causal linkage. As far as matters of scope are concerned, the approach recommended by this volume does not require the court to ask any different questions from those it would otherwise be expected to pursue; nor do the proposals open any additional avenues for the insurer to use drafting techniques to circumvent his obligations. A court will continue to look at substance over form. The proposals would, it is argued, simply make the process rather more transparent.

12.33 How would *New Zealand Insurance Co Ltd v Harris*[32] be decided applying the proposals set out in this volume? Here cover in relation to a tractor was confined to private use, but the loss occurred whilst the tractor was being used for commercial purposes. In accordance with these proposals, the court would first determine if commercial use was outside of the scope of the policy. Consistent with the finding in the New Zealand court, let us suppose that a court applying the proposals set out here would likely find the facts to be within the scope of the policy. It is argued that the court would further probably find that, on the facts, the breach did not contribute to the loss. Does this mean that, like s11 of the NZ Insurance Law Reform Act, the proposals in this volume can be criticised for being too unreasonably slanted in favour of the insured? The New Zealand Law Commission expressed concern that the courts had interpreted s11 in such a way as to impose liability on insurers even if the policyholder was in blatant breach of a term delimiting the risk.[33] It is submitted that the same could not be said of the proposals set out in this volume. Because it would potentially be open to the court to apply a measure

31 See also s10(4) of the Insurance Act 2015.

32 [1990] 1 NZLR 10 (CA).

33 NZ Law Reform Commission *Some Insurance Law Problems* (1998) NZLC R46, p 25.

of proportionality in circumstances where the breach *could* have contributed to the loss, it is argued that the proposals set out earlier are sufficiently flexible so as to overcome the perceived shortcomings of the New Zealand legislation. If, on the facts of *Harris*, the court held that the commercial use of the tractor *could* have contributed to the loss, the court could apply proportionality, thus reducing the extent to which the insurer was obliged to meet the insured's claim. Under this volume's proposals the insurer would also have the opportunity to demonstrate that it had suffered prejudice (for example to the extent of an additional premium not charged).

Contracting out

12.34 This author agrees with Soyer that the contracting out provisions for non-consumer contracts in the Insurance Act 2015[34] are likely to be one of the first areas to attract litigation.[35] The volume further agrees with Leloudas that the contracting out provisions were likely included in the Act as a sop to insurers to water down opposition to the Act that might otherwise have existed.[36] It is the view of this author that too often the lobbying power of large insurers has frustrated the introduction of legitimate reforms aimed at redressing the balance between insureds and insurers. Chapter 5 has reviewed the various proposals developed by the Law Commission for the reform of the law of warranties, many of which have floundered in the face of opposition from the insurance industry. As we have seen, the Act does forbid contracting out from the s9 abolition of basis clauses[37] so there is nothing remarkable in a prohibition on contracting out per se. Further we have seen that in both Australia and New Zealand, contracting out from the provisions governing insurance warranties (and similar terms) is prohibited,[38] demonstrating that insurance markets are perfectly capable of dealing with a prohibition on contracting out. This is perhaps particularly noteworthy in the context of New Zealand where the provisions of s11 are regarded by some, including this author, as unduly favouring insureds. In any event, the position under the Insurance Act represents something of a prevarication, given that while the Law Commission evidently felt that insurers would be keen to contract out of the Insurance Act provisions, the Government saw 'no pent up demand for widespread contracting out.'[39] In the light of this latter view, it is perhaps odd that the Act should contain comprehensive contracting out provisions. Against the background of this lack of clarity, the Government decided that a review of the merits of contracting out would be undertaken after five years' experience of the new statute. In the view of this author the final position, as represented by ss16 and 17 and the Government's intent to hold a review, amounts to something of a botched compromise. The Law Commission indicated that one of the aims of the Insurance Act was to ensure that the contracting out provisions were 'not

34 Ss16 and 17 of the Insurance Act 2015 refer.

35 B Soyer, 'Risk Control Clauses in Insurance Law, Law Reform and the Future' (2016) 109 CLJ 124.

36 G Leloudas, 'Contracting Out of the Insurance Act 2015' in *Commercial Insurance Contracts, The Insurance Act 2015, A New Regime for Commercial and Marine Insurance Law,* edited by M Clarke and B Soyer, Informa Law for Routledge, London, 2016.

37 S16(1) Insurance Act 2015 refers.

38 S52 of the Australian Insurance Contracts Act and s15 of the NZ Insurance Law Reform Act refer. See Chapters 6 and 7.

39 House of Lords debate 29 July 2014, col GC 629, see Chapter 8.

so onerous as to interfere with the smooth running of the insurance market.'[40] As discussed in Chapter 9, the risk is that this desire to accommodate the industry's preferences endangers the overarching intent of the Act to achieve a better balance between the interests of the insured and insurer. Experience in Australia and New Zealand suggests that markets rapidly adapt to a prohibition on contracting out, notwithstanding initial opposition. If measures for reform of this area of the law can be shown to strike a fair balance between the interests of the insured and insurer, it is hard to see why, over time, there would be serious objection to a prohibition on contracting out. This is perhaps particularly the case where the historic regime has long been criticised for providing a playing field that is clearly tilted unjustly in favour of the insurer. Although some might argue that the commercial particulars of some of the larger commercial entities seeking cover justify bespoke arrangements, this text would counter that if the contracting provisions are even handed, there is no reason why they should not be capable of applying equitably to any commercial situation. Even if a hidden agenda of reform is to protect the insurance industry in a given jurisdiction, it is hard to see how imposing a balanced regime can be seriously prejudicial to insurers in circumstances where (such as in the London market) insureds have been increasingly turning to alternate jurisdictions in search of a more balanced allocation of risk.

12.35 This author believes that the proposals set out herein offer a fair and transparent balance between the interests of the insurer and insured, as well as offering a reasonable degree of flexibility. Accordingly this author is of the view that parties should not be permitted to contract out from the proposals.

Further stress testing the proposed solution

12.36 In order to validate the solution set out in these pages, the proposals will be stress tested by applying them to the facts of a number of historic cases. This will also enable a comparison to be made with the methodology adopted in the original jurisdiction, the outcome achieved under that methodology, as well as with the outcomes this volume believes would have been achieved under the other regimes examined earlier. It is submitted that, taken together, this analysis demonstrates that the outcomes delivered under the proposals set out in this volume offer better, more rounded solutions than those offered by the Insurance Act 2015 or the approaches adopted in either Australia or New Zealand.

12.37 *Maxwell v Highway Hauliers*.[41] The facts of the *Highway Hauliers* case have been set out previously.[42] If the approach to breaches of warranties and other conditions recommended in this volume were applied, the first question that would need to be addressed by the court would be whether the facts fell within the scope of the policy. It is submitted it is likely that, as in Australia, the court would find that the circumstances did fall within the scope. This author submits that a court would either interpret the failure to provide drivers with adequate PAQS scores as a breach of the policy, or alternatively simply hold that the facts fell within the exclusion clause in the policy. In both circumstances the situation would fall

40 Law Commission and Scottish Law Commission, Insurance Contract Law: Business Disclosure; Warranties; Insurers' Remedies for Fraudulent Claims; and Late Payment Law Com No 353 / Scot Law Com No 238 Cm 8898 SG/2014/131 July 2014, para 29.29 (3). Available at: http://lawcommission.justice.gov.uk/docs.

41 [2014] HCA 33, 10 September 2014.

42 See Chapter 6.

within the parameters of the proposals set out in these pages. It is suggested that the insurer's liability has prima facie been suspended in accordance with the terms of the exclusion clause/as a result of a breach of the policy, with the consequence that the assured's ability to claim under the proposals in this volume would depend upon him being able to establish the absence of a causal linkage between the breach and loss. Given, on the facts of *Highway Hauliers*, the insurer acknowledged that there was no linkage between breach and loss, it is anticipated that, as in the original case, the assured would be able to recover under the regime proposed in these pages. Given the insurer's acknowledgement of the absence of a causal linkage, it is unlikely the court would exercise its discretion to apply proportionality, even if it was accepted that the breach *could* have had a causal linkage with the loss. As there was no suggestion that the insurer suffered prejudice as a result of the insured's breach, the proposals in this regard would have no application.

12.38 In *Ferrcom Pty Ltd v Commercial Union Insurance Co of Australia Ltd*,[43] it was accepted that the breach (failure to notify the insurer of a change of registration of a mobile crane) resulted in the insurer suffering prejudice as it was denied the opportunity to go off risk because of the insured's failure to notify. The quantum of prejudice was assessed as equal to the amount of liability that would otherwise have been imposed. Under the approach proposed in this volume, the policy as a whole would likely be suspended (it is difficult to see how the insured could argue that the breach related to a specific risk), however as it was accepted that there was no causal linkage between the breach and the loss, the insurer would prima facie become liable for the loss, but would likely avoid some or all liability as a result of having suffered prejudice, assuming that he was able to demonstrate that he would not have offered cover. This seems reasonable and is in line with the original decision in Australia.

12.39 In *FAI Insurance Limited v Australian Hospital Care Pty Ltd*[44] a failure to notify circumstances in a claims made and notified policy was held to constitute an omission for the purposes of s54,[45] because the effect of the contract was that the insurer could refuse to meet the claim by reason only of the fact that the insured did not give notice of the occurrence to the insurer. As a result the omission was cured by s54 and the insurer held liable. Under this volume's proposals, the first question to be addressed would again be whether the facts fall within the scope of the policy. It is argued that a court would likely find that the circumstances were outside the scope of the policy and as a result that the insurer would have no liability. If the court were of a different view, it is possible (although perhaps unlikely) that the failure to provide notice of the claim would be treated as a breach of the policy under the proposals in this volume; as a result it is likely that the policy as a whole would be treated as suspended. If the insured was successful in arguing that there was no causal linkage between the breach and the loss (as the loss in question was any damages the insured was required to pay as a result of the claim, as opposed to the failure of the insurance company to reimburse those damages), the insured would recover. A final alternative interpretation would be that there had been no breach of the contractual terms of the policy (merely a failure to comply with the claims procedure) and as a result the proposals would have no application. Under this interpretation the insured

43 [1993] 176 CLR 332 at 14–15.

44 [2001] HCA 38; 204 CLR 641; 75 ALJR 1236 (27 June 2001); described in more detail in Chapter 6.

45 Of the Australian Insurance Contracts Act.

would fail to recover. This author believes a court would most likely find that either that the facts were outside the scope of the policy or that there had been no breach of the policy terms. Either of these outcomes would have merit, given the controversy caused in Australia by the finding in favour of the insured.[46]

12.40 In *Kelly v New Zealand Insurance Co Ltd*[47] it was held that a failure to declare items of unique value under a property policy which, had there been such a declaration, would have extended the sum insured to cover those items, was not something to which s54 of the Insurance Contracts Act responded. The court held that the reason s54 did not apply was because the insured had not chosen to extend the scope of the policy under the provision allowing for this.[48] It is argued that the same outcome would be achieved under the proposals set out herein: in first considering the issue of scope, the court would likely find that the loss was outside the scope of the policy with the result that the insurer would have no liability for the loss. Again it is submitted that this is a sensible and equitable outcome.

12.41 In *Antico v Heath Fielding Australia Pty Ltd*[49] the court in Australia found in favour of the insured in circumstances where the insured had failed to obtain the consent of the insurer to defend a claim, the insured's omission being excused by s54. It is argued that under the proposals set out in this volume the court would (having first examined the question of scope, and it is assumed, concluding the claim was within the scope of the policy) likely view the failure to obtain permission as a breach of the terms of the policy. Assuming, as seems likely, the insured was able to establish the absence of a causal linkage between the breach and the loss, the court could be expected to find in the insured's favour: the insurer would be liable for the claim. This is consistent with the original finding and, it is submitted, seems sensible.

12.42 In *Greentree v FAI General Insurance Co Ltd*[50] the NSW Court of Appeal held that a failure by a third party to make a claim on the insured within the period of insurance cover under a claims made and notified policy was not an omission by some other party under s54. Although this rationale was later criticised in *Australian Hospital Care*, the same outcome would almost certainly be reached under the proposals in this volume: it would be an issue of scope and the court would likely hold that the insured would have no locus to claim under this volume's proposals on the grounds that the claim fell outside the agreed scope of the policy. Despite criticism of the result in Australia, this author would argue the outcome under this volume's proposals is sensible.

12.43 In *Gibbs Holdings Pty Ltd v Mercantile Mutual Insurance (Australia)*[51] a failure to notify a material alteration of risk (as required under the policy) arising from a plastics manufacturer taking occupancy of the insured premises was held to be an act that failed to satisfy s54(2)[52] and was therefore covered by s54(1). The court in Australia held that although s54(1) applied, the insurer had suffered prejudice equivalent to the quantum of the insured's

46 See Chapter 6.

47 (1993) 7 ANZ Ins Cas 61–197.

48 *Kelly v New Zealand Insurance* (1996) 9 ANZ Ins Cas 61–317 at 67,518. Merkin takes a similar view: R Merkin; Reforming Insurance Law: Is There a Case For Reverse Transportation?; A Report for the English and Scottish Law Commissioners on the Australian Experience of Insurance Law Reform; available at http://lawcommission.justice.gov.uk/docs/ICL_Merkin_report.pdf.

49 (1997) 188 CLR 652; 146 ALR 385; 71 ALJR 1210; BC9703412.

50 (1998) 44 NSWLR 706; 10 ANZ Ins Cas 61–423; 158 ALR 592 at 595, 601.

51 *Gibbs Holdings Pty Ltd v Mercantile Mutual Insurance (Australia)* (2002) 1 Qld R 17.

52 Of the Insurance Contracts Act.

claim. Under this volume's proposals, having confirmed the claim to be within the scope of the policy, it is likely that the court would find that the breach of contract in this instance (failure to notify the insurer of the change in risk) was one that would trigger suspension of the insurer's liability across the contract as a whole. That breach could not, of itself, be said to have a causal linkage with the loss incurred (the loss was caused by the assured permitting the change of use, rather than his failure to notify the insurer) and accordingly, the court would likely find that there were grounds for overturning the presumption that the insurer's liability was suspended. As a result the assured would prima facie be able to seek redress from the insurer. However, it is likely the court would find the insurer had suffered prejudice and might well assess this as equal to amount of the insurer's claim. Alternatively it is possible (though unlikely) that the court might overlook the slightly technical distinction in relation to causal linkage and find that there was a causal connection, in which case the insured's claim would fail. Whichever approach were adopted, it is submitted that the practical outcome would likely be the same as that under the Australian regime.

12.44 *East End Real Estate Pty Ltd v CE Heath Casualty & General Insurance Ltd.*[53] In a claims made and notified policy a demand was made on the insured by a third party, however the insured failed to notify the insurer until six weeks after the expiry of the period of cover. Under the terms of the policy, the insurer was entitled to deny liability based on the failure to notify. The court held that the insurer was able to deny cover because of an omission by the insured and as a result s54 applied. The insurer argued its interests had been prejudiced to the extent that it was required to pay the costs of the proceedings, but the court held there was no prejudice as the decision to bring proceedings had been the insurer's. Applying the proposals set out in this volume, it is suggested that a court might regard the failure to comply with the notification procedures as a breach of the policy for the purposes of the proposals, although arguably it would be open to the court to rule that the claim was outside the scope of the policy agreed by the parties on the grounds that failure to notify in the prescribed period took it outside scope. In these latter circumstances the insured would fail in his claim (this author would favour such an outcome). If the court viewed the action as a breach of the policy then, assuming that the insured would be able to establish the absence of a causal linkage, the insurer would likely be liable to meet the insured's loss. This is consistent with the result reached by the court applying s54, albeit for differing reasons. This author believes that such an outcome would be somewhat harsh on the insurer. If the insured had brought the case against the insurer, applying this volume's proposals, the court would likely find that the insurer had suffered prejudice. This author would argue that applying this volume's proposals to the original facts would produce a result that, at worst, could be argued to be at the margin in terms of equitable outcomes.

12.45 In *Gosford City Council v GIO General Ltd*[54] it was held that a claims made policy which attached only if a claim was made against the assured during the currency of the policy could not operate to allow the assured to seek indemnity for a claim made against him after the policy had expired as there was no relevant act or omission on the part of the assured. Applying this volume's proposals, it is likely a court would find that the claim lay

53 (1991) 25 NSWLR 400; 7 ANZ Ins Cas 61–092.

54 (2003) 56 NSWLR 542; 12 ANZ Ins Cas 61–566; [2003] NSWCA 34.

outside of the scope of the contract and as a result the insurer would escape liability. This seems reasonable.

12.46 In *Allianz Australia Insurance Ltd v Inglis*[55] it was held that a 'state of affairs' was not an act or omission for the purposes of s54. Under the proposals contained in this volume, it is likely that a court would find that, although there was no breach of the contract of insurance,[56] the proposals would apply as they specifically cover exclusion clauses.[57] As a result (and assuming a court would find that the circumstances were within scope, but covered by the exclusion clause), it is anticipated that for the court to hold Allianz liable, the insured would need to establish the absence of any causal linkage between the circumstances triggering the exclusion clause and the loss suffered. It is anticipated the insured would, on a balance of probabilities, be able to establish the absence of linkage, with the result that the insurer would be held liable. This would reverse the decision of the Australian court, which in the Australian context, this text welcomed as a victory for common sense. Does this represent a failing for the proposals set out here? This author would argue that it does not, given the additional flexibility offered to the court under this volume's proposals. As we have seen in relation to the application of these proposals to the facts of *New Zealand Insurance Co Ltd v Harris*[58] earlier, if the court were satisfied that the circumstances that triggered the exclusion clause *could* have contributed to the loss (and on the facts of *Inglis* it might well do so), the court would have the option of applying proportionality to its decision. It is argued that this would ensure that the court retains the flexibility to ensure the outcome is one that fairly balances the interests of both insurer and insured. Furthermore in obiter comments in the Australian hearing, McLure P indicated that had the circumstances of the daughter living with the insured constituted an 'act' for the purposes of s54, the increase in risk of financial loss might arguably have constituted prejudice for the purposes of s54(1).[59] Under this volume's proposals it would similarly be open to the court to find that the insurer had suffered prejudice and to reflect this in the court's findings.

12.47 *Bank of Nova Scotia v Hellenic Mutual War Risks, The Good Luck*[60]: as seen previously,[61] *The Good Luck* confirmed the automatic discharge of the insurer from liability following a breach of warranty. This can be especially harsh on the assured: the policyholder may well be unaware that it must either negotiate with the insurer to restore cover or take steps to find alternative cover.[62] In addition, the loss of insurance cover may also have serious consequences for third parties, such as assignees or mortgagees. They may be left without cover, even if they did not cause or contribute to the breach.[63] This has long been acknowledged as unduly harsh and, consistent with the approach in the Insurance Act 2015, the proposals set out in this volume would abolish the concept of an automatic, permanent

---

55 [2016] WASCA 25. A full description of the facts is provided in Chapter 6.

56 See Chapter 6 for a detailed summary of the facts.

57 The relevant clause excluded 'Injury to any person who normally lives with you, or damage to their property.'

58 [1990] 1 NZLR 10 (CA).

59 *Allianz Australia Insurance Ltd v Inglis* [2016] WASCA 25.

60 [1991] 3 All ER 1, 2 Lloyd's Rep 191.

61 See Chapter 3.

62 As pointed out by the Association of British Insurers in a submission to the Law Commission, cited in Law Commission and Scottish Law Commission, Insurance Contract Law: The Business Insured's Duty of Disclosure and the Law of Warranties (LCCP No 204; ScLCDP No 155: 2012).

63 See for example *Scottish Equitable Life Assurance Society v Buist & Ors* (1877) 4 R 1076.

discharge of the insurer's liability in the event of a breach of warranty. Instead cover would be suspended following a breach. On the specific facts that required the insurer to notify the bank if it ceased to provide insurance, it could be argued that the insurer would arguably not be obliged to give such notice: the insurer was (unless it chose to exercise its right to terminate under this volume's proposals) still offering insurance and the policy was still on foot, albeit suspended. However, as we have seen,[64] a more compelling argument may well be that the obligation to inform arose at the point suspension triggered as at that point the vessel was not insured.

12.48 In *Printpak v AGF Insurance Ltd*[65] the policy contained a warranty that the insured would maintain a burglar alarm. Despite the wording of the warranty, the Court of Appeal held that the alarm warranty only applied to the risk of theft and not to the risk of fire: the policy consisted of separate schedules, each concerned with a different type of risk. Under the approach set out in this volume it would fall to the insured to argue that the provision which had been breached related to a particular risk. It seems likely that the court would determine that the breached provision related only to the risk of theft, with the result that the insurer would remain liable for fire losses. Even if it was decided that the policy as a whole was suspended (because the insured failed to establish otherwise), it is submitted that the outcome would likely remain the same, assuming the insured could establish the absence of a causal link between the failure to maintain a burglar alarm and the fire losses.

12.49 In *Hing v Security & General Insurance Co (NZ) Ltd* the assured proposed to relocate his house and stated in the proposal that haulage would be performed by a particular firm of haulage contractors. This statement was in turn converted to a warranty by a basis clause. In fact, the haulage operation was conducted by the insured, together with others who were not qualified for the task and the house was damaged beyond repair. Assuming the policy contained an express warranty in the same terms (basis clauses are abolished under this volume's proposals), it is suggested that on these facts the insured would not be able to argue that the breached term related to a particular risk. Accordingly it is submitted that the court would likely find that the policy as a whole would be suspended. Assuming the insured was unable to establish the absence of a clear causal connection between the breach and loss, the insurer would escape liability. This seems sensible and is consistent with the original decision.

12.50 Applying the proposals in this volume to the classic case of *De Hahn v Hartley*,[66] it is suggested the first question for the court (having confirmed there was no issue of scope) would be whether the warranty that the vessel had sailed 'from Liverpool with 14 six-pounders, swivels, small arms and 50 hands or upwards' was a present fact warranty, constituting a condition precedent to cover.[67] It is submitted that, as we have seen elsewhere, unless the parties have made it explicitly clear that the intention was that the provision should be a condition precedent, it is unlikely that the court would find it to be one: otherwise the provisions could be easily bypassed simply through drafting techniques. If the

64 See Chapter 10.

65 [1999] Lloyd's Rep IR 542.

66 [1786] 1 TR 343.

67 The court would consider this before any issue of scope because if the condition precedent had not been met, the insurer would not have come on risk.

court did find that the provision was a condition precedent and assuming the insured did not argue that it was a provision that related to a specific risk, rather than the risk as a whole, then at first sight the policy would never have come on foot and the insurer would thus not be liable. If the provision was held not to be a condition precedent, nevertheless the clause did have a requirement that had to be met within a specific timeframe (by the time the vessel sailed) and with this conditionality having not been met, it is at least arguable that the breach was thus incapable of rectification. Even if this proposition is accepted, (it is submitted the alternate, more likely, argument would be that the term was not a CP and that the breach was rectified when the requisite manning levels were met, in which case the insurer would be liable) it is argued that this is precisely the sort of circumstance where the proposals in this volume (and s10(5) and (6) of the Insurance Act), that relate to breaches of provision that are prima facie incapable of remedy, would kick in. Under these proposals, such breaches are to be treated as remedied if when the conditionality is subsequently met, the risk remains essentially the same as that originally contemplated by the parties. It is submitted that, on the facts, once the manning levels had been met, the risk would likely be viewed as having been restored to that originally anticipated by the parties. As a result the court could well hold the breach to be rectified and the insurer would consequently be liable. This outcome is to be welcomed.

12.51 In *Agapitos v Agnew (The Aegeon) (No. 2)*[68] the insured vessel became a total loss as a result of fire. Although the vessel had the warranted London Salvage Association approval of firefighting arrangements at the commencement of the policy, this had been allowed to lapse and the insurer escaped liability. Under the proposals in this volume, this decision would likely remain unchanged. Even if the warranty was held to be specific to fire risk only (as opposed to applying to the policy as a whole), the cover would be suspended until such time as the breach was remedied and the assured would only be able to recover if he was able to establish the absence of a causal link between breach and loss. The breach had not been remedied by the time of loss, and it seems likely that the insured would be unable to establish the absence of a causal linkage between breach and loss. Again, this seems a reasonable outcome.

12.52 In *Hibbert v Pigou*[69] applying the Marine Insurance Act 1906, the court held that the fact that a ship was warranted to sail in convoy, but did not do so, was sufficient to absolve the insurers of any liability for the subsequent loss of the vessel in a storm. Under the proposals in this volume it is assumed liability would likely be suspended across the policy as whole,[70] but it would be open to the assured to seek to show that there was no causal linkage between breach and loss. As the loss resulted from storm damage, it seems likely that the assured would be able to establish the lack of any causal linkage and would thus be able to claim under the policy. This reflects a sensible outcome.

12.53 In *Forsakringsaktielselskapet Vesta v Butcher*[71] the failure of the assured to comply with a warranty to maintain a 24-hour watch on his fish farm was held to be fatal to his

68 [2002] EWHC 1558; [2003] Lloyd's Rep IR 154.

69 [1783] 3 Doug KB 213.

70 For the sake of argument it is assumed that it is unlikely the insured could successfully argue that the warranty applied to a particular risk only. In practice it might well be possible to argue that the convoy warranty applied only to the risk of loss through enemy action, in which case under the proposals in this volume the insurer would remain liable for the loss arising from the storm.

71 [1989] AC 852.

claim for loss from storm damage. Applying the proposals in this volume, let us assume that the insured would be unable to argue that the warranty related to a specific risk (such that the policy was only suspended in relation to that risk), with the result that prima facie liability across the policy as a whole would be suspended. Nevertheless, it is surely the case that the assured would be able to establish the absence of causal linkage between breach and loss and so be able to claim under the policy. In *Yorkshire Insurance Co Ltd v Campbell*[72] the pedigree of a horse was not as stated in a warranty (the latter having been established via a basis clause) in a policy insuring marine risks and mortality and the insurer was thus able to escape liability. Under this volume's proposals (and assuming an express warranty, rather than one established via a basis clause), assuming the assured was able to establish the absence of a causal linkage between the breach of warranty and the loss (and this author submits that he would), the insurer would be liable under the policy. The revised outcomes in both these cases are, it is submitted, to be welcomed.

12.54 In *Nelson Forests Ltd v Three Tuis Ltd.*[73] cover was provided for legal liability for accidents 'in connection with' the operation of a lifestyle farm business. There was a fire that arose in connection with tourism activities undertaken on the property by the assured. The court in New Zealand found that cover was restricted to farming operations and that, as a result, tourism was outside the scope of cover provided under the policy. The court rejected utilisation of s11 of the New Zealand Insurance Law Reform Act on the grounds that the section only applied to exclusions otherwise covered by the policy. Applying the approach proposed in this volume, the court would first consider issues of scope. This author sees no reason why a court would reach a different conclusion from that in the original hearing. Accordingly, as the loss lay outside the scope of the policy, the insurer would have no liability to meet the claim.

12.55 In *Barnaby v South British Insurance Co Ltd*[74] a policy on a building excluded liability for 'fault, defect, error or omission in design.' A wall collapsed in bad weather and was found to have been constructed with a defect. The question arose, did the policy cover a wall, but excluding the risk of its collapse due to a defect, or did it cover only a wall free of defects?[75] The NZ court found the loss to be outside the scope of the policy and as a result s11 of the NZ Insurance Law Reform Act had no application.[76] We have seen that this author has questioned this decision, given that it potentially opened up s11 of the New Zealand Insurance Law Reform Act to attempts to circumvent it through drafting semantics.[77] Applying this volume's proposals, it is argued a court would likely find that the facts lay within the scope of the policy, but were covered by the exclusion clause. As it seems unlikely that the insured would be successful in arguing the absence of a causal link,

72 [1917] AC 218.

73 HC Nelson CIV-2010-442-84, 9 December 2010.

74 (1980) 1 ANZ Ins Cas 60-401 (HC).

75 R Merkin and O Gurses, The Insurance Act 2015: Rebalancing the Interests of Insurer and Assured, (2015) 78(6) Modern Law Review 1004-1027.

76 *Barnaby v South British Insurance Co Ltd* (1980) 1 ANZ Ins Cas 60-401 (HC) at 77,008.

Hardie Boys J observed that 'the key to this section is to be found in the last words of paragraph (b): the section is designed to deal with those kinds of exclusion clauses which provide for circumstances likely to increase the risk of a loss which the policy actually covers ... the section is not designed to deal with exclusion clauses which specify the kind of loss or the quantum of loss to which cover does not apply at all.'

77 See Chapter 7.

the insurer would avoid liability. The fact is that the boundaries in issues of scope cannot, by definition, always be clear-cut and it must be acknowledged that this volume's solution may, like any other, lack a measure of precision in this regard. This author would argue however that, precisely because issues of scope are open to interpretation by the courts, the approach outlined in this volume's solution offers the best avenue for minimising abuse through drafting semantics.

12.56 We have seen that in *Sugar Hut v Great Lakes Reinsurance (UK) Plc*[78] the policy required installation of a burglar alarm that rang through to a central monitoring station. Instead, a non-specified alarm was fitted and the premises were subsequently damaged by fire. The court held that failure to comply with the burglar alarm provision was sufficient to release the insurers from liability under the policy. Under this volume's solution, it is submitted that the insured would likely be able to establish[79] that the provision that had been breached referred to a specific category of risk and that cover should be suspended only for losses in that category, with the result that the insurer would remain liable for fire losses. Even if the insured was unsuccessful in arguing that the term applied to a specific category of risk, there would seem to be a good chance that he would be able to establish that there was no causal linkage between the failure to fit the specified burglary alarm and the loss from fire. Were he successful in doing so, the insurer would be obliged to meet the loss. This seems equitable and an improvement on the original outcome.

12.57 In *Provincial Insurance Company Ltd v Morgan and Foxton*[80] coal merchants declared that their lorry would be used for coal and this statement was converted to a warranty through a basis clause. The lorry was damaged in an accident and had that same day been used for the transport of timber, although at the time of the accident only coal was on board. In the original case the House of Lords held that on a 'strict but reasonable construction' the clause meant only that transporting coal was to be the normal use and that accordingly transporting other material would not terminate liability under the policy. The approach proposed by this volume would see the abolition of basis clauses as in the Insurance Act 2015[81]; this would prima facie likely mean that the insurer remained liable to meet the loss. However, let us assume that, notwithstanding that the provision was not therefore a warranty, its wording gave the insurer a right to avoid liability in the event of a breach.[82] Under this volume's proposals it may be that the insured would not be successful in arguing that the provision applied to a specific category or risk. Nevertheless, it is submitted that the likelihood is that the insured would be able to establish that there was no causal linkage between the breach and the loss, with the result that the insurer would be liable for the loss. This matches the original outcome but, it is submitted, on sounder grounds.

12.58 In *Prepaid Services Pty Ltd v Atradius Credit Insurance NV*,[83] s54 of the Australian Insurance Contracts Act was held not to apply because the reason the insurer was able to refuse payment was because the insured's claim was in respect of a payment default which

78 [2010] EWHC 2636.

79 It having been confirmed that the facts lay within the scope of the policy.

80 [1933] AC 240.

81 S9 Insurance Act 2015.

82 Or alternatively that the policy contained an express warranty on identical terms.

83 (2013) 302 ALR 732; 17 ANZ Ins Cas 61–981; [2013] NSWCA 252. See Chapter 5 for a description of the facts.

was not covered by the policy: it was outside the scope of the policy. It is submitted that on the same facts, but applying this volume's proposals, the decision would be the same as that reached in Australia under the Insurance Contracts Act: the claim was for a loss outside the scope of the policy.

12.59 It seems unlikely that this volume's proposals would affect the judgements reached in cases where the court has strived hard to reach an outcome that favours the assured.[84] This of itself should not be of concern: the focus here is on providing an equitable balance between the interests of insureds and insurers. The following cases illustrate the point. In *Kler Knitwear Ltd v Lombard General Insurance Co Ltd*[85] Morland J held that a provision that 'warranted' that a sprinkler system would be inspected within 30 days of the policy renewal and that any necessary rectification work would be commissioned within 14 days of the inspection report being received was a suspensory provision, rather than a warranty. As the remedy for breaches of warranty under this volume's proposals is anyway suspension, there would be no impact on the decision, even assuming the term was held to be a warranty. Similarly, in *Case Existological Laboratories Ltd v Foremost Insurance Co et al (the Bamcell II)*,[86] despite apparently clear wording that the relevant condition (concerning the appointment of a nightwatchman) was a warranty, the court held it to be a suspensory provision. Even if, under this volume's proposals, the court held the provision to be a warranty, the outcome would be unaffected as the breach would be suspensory only.

12.60 Warranties would not be abolished by the proposals in this volume, nor is the definition of what amounts to a warranty changed. As a result, the proposals would not impact the decision in *HIH Casualty and General Insurance Co. Ltd. v New Hampshire Insurance Co.*[87] It would remain the case that a warranty 'must be exactly complied with, whether material to the risk or not.'[88] However, although this would mean that minor breaches of warranty would still be caught, a breach would only trigger suspension and liability would in most cases now be determined by causal linkage, rather than simply by the existence of the breach of warranty per se.

12.61 Under the proposals in this volume, even where there is a causal linkage between breach and loss, the insurer will remain liable if the action (that resulted in the breach) was taken in order to preserve life or property or could not have been reasonably avoided. This would mean, it is submitted, that in circumstances like those of *Allison Pty Ltd v Lumley General Insurance Ltd, The Pilbara Pilot*,[89] where a warranty concerning mooring was potentially breached in order to reduce the risk from an approaching cyclone, the assured would not be punished.[90] On the other hand, in 'normal' circumstances the proposals in this volume would not change the position in *Hore v Whitmore*[91] (where the breach of warranty was caused by an insured peril): it matters not what causes the breach, instead the assured's

84 See the examples provided in Chapter 3.

85 [2000] Lloyd's Rep IR 47.

86 [1983] 2 SCR 47.

87 [2001] EWCA Civ 735.

88 S33(3) Marine Insurance Act 1906.

89 [2006] WASC 104 cited in R Merkin, 'Australia: Still a Nation of Chalmers?' (2011) 30(2) *University of Queensland Law Journal*, University of Queensland 189–224.

90 The proposals in this volume would not affect the obligation on the insured under s78(4) of the Marine Insurance Act 1906, to take all reasonable steps in order to avert or minimise loss.

91 [1778] 2 Cowp 784 (see Chapter 2).

ability to claim would be dependent on whether the breach had been remedied and/or the existence of causal linkage between breach and loss.[92]

12.62 How would this volume's proposals operate in relation to a case involving implied warranties? As this volume proposes that implied warranty of legality be abolished,[93] this question is primarily relevant to the implied warranty of seaworthiness.[94] If this volume's preferred position (that the implied warranty of seaworthiness also be abolished) was not adopted, its proposed fallback position would require the assured to have knowledge of the unseaworthy condition. Thus, the decision in *Lee v Beach*,[95] where the innocence of the assured was held to be immaterial, would be overturned. In *Quebec Marine Insurance Co v Commercial Bank of Canada*[96] we have seen that although a defective boiler was repaired soon after the commencement of the voyage, the assured was unable to recover for the loss of the vessel in a storm because of the breach of the implied warranty. Under the fallback proposals in this volume, the insurer would only escape liability for the loss if (i) the assured had been aware of the breach of implied warranty and (ii) the breach had not been remedied and there was a causal link between breach and loss. As a result, on the facts, the insurer would be liable. On the other hand, unlike the current position, this author suggests that the revised implied warranty should apply throughout the voyage. This would mean that Lord Mansfield's ruling in *Berman v Woodbridge*,[97] that the implied warranty should only apply at the commencement of the voyage, would be overturned.

Summary

12.63 Despite the vast amount of time dedicated to the subject, to date no one solution has emerged that satisfactorily addresses breaches in insurance warranties and similar conditions. This volume has demonstrated the flaws in the regimes currently in existence in Australia, New Zealand and the UK. In Australia this volume has shown that, while s54 of the Insurance Contracts Act provides a well-respected solution, it has, in particular, led to uncertainties and difficulties with regard to the interface between the legislation and the freedom of the contractual parties to define the scope of cover. The New Zealand approach, set out in the Insurance Law Reform Act has, on the other hand, been criticised for tilting the balance too far in favour of the insured. As far as the Insurance Act 2015 is concerned, this volume has sought to demonstrate the problems this author perceives in relation, in particular, to s11 of the Act. As this volume has shown, these difficulties are likely to lead to enhanced uncertainty and litigation.

92 In practice the decision would likely change under this volume's proposals: the policy would prima facie be suspended (and by its nature be incapable of 'remedy'), but the likelihood is that the insured would be able to establish there was no causal link between the breach and subsequent loss and as a result the insurer would be liable.

93 The author's fallback position is that were the implied warranty of legality to be retained, then, if an adventure were to be carried out in an illegal manner with the consent of the insured, the insurer should be discharged from any liability under the policy, regardless of the absence of a causal linkage between breach and loss.

94 *De Hahn v Hartley* (see preceding) could be seen as a case concerning the implied warranty of seaworthiness, but this volume argues that as an explicit warranty was breached it is better considered in that context, rather than in the context of the implied warranty.

95 [1795] 91 ER 858.

96 [1870] LR 3 PC 234.

97 [1781] 2 Dougl 781, pg 788.

12.64 While the proposals developed in this volume will undoubtedly leave some areas of imprecision, it is argued that, for the commercial arena, they provide a more equitable and multi-purpose solution than any of the three attempts at reform that have currently been adopted in common law jurisdictions. While providing a clear framework for resolution, the proposals additionally provide sufficient flexibility to enable the courts to craft solutions that reflect the complexities of individual cases. The approach set out in this volume responds to all the metrics identified at the start of this chapter and enables courts to reach balanced and equitable decisions, without destabilising any of the key tenets of insurance law or infringing on the parties freedom to contract. The proposals leave more discretion in the hands of the court to flex solutions to the particular circumstances of the case, preserve the sanctity of the scope of contract and ensure that causal linkage plays a clear role in delivering a balanced outcome. The proposals do not unfairly impinge on the interests of the insurer, who remains adequately protected and is provided with an additional option to terminate cover in the event of a relevant breach by the assured. Any prejudice suffered by the insurer is also reflected under the proposals. The ability of the court to take proportionality into account in matters of causation provides further flexibility, enabling the courts to reach solutions that fairly balance the interests of both the insurer and the insured. Certainly there are areas where the courts will need to interpret the intentions of the parties, but the judiciary is well versed in so doing and the risk of arbitrary outcomes would be greatly reduced were the proposals adopted. Although the proposed approach may mean less certainty in advance regarding the outcome of litigation, this is balanced by increased confidence that the outcome will fairly reflect the interest of both the insured and the insurer. These two factors would in turn, it is suggested, likely result in less litigation in the long term.

CHAPTER 13

Conclusion

13.1 Although the need for reform of the law relating to insurance warranties and other terms has long been acknowledged and has been the subject of several reviews by the Law Commission, it was not until the Insurance Act 2015 that reform was finally implemented in the United Kingdom. Both New Zealand and Australia had previously implemented reform. Shortcomings have been identified with both the Australian and New Zealand approaches; these have been acknowledged in both jurisdictions, as well as overseas. Nevertheless, despite criticism and officially sanctioned reviews, practitioners in both jurisdictions have accepted the respective approaches and now view them as coping reasonably well with the challenges confronting them. Time will tell whether the same result is achieved by the Insurance Act 2015.

13.2 This volume has critically evaluated the reform measures enacted in all three jurisdictions. It is this author's position that the reforms enacted to date can be improved upon. Unfortunately in this author's view, the measures contained in the Insurance Act to reform the law of warranties represent a missed opportunity. This volume has demonstrated a number of crucial shortcomings that will result in both uncertainty and additional litigation. While a structure that is both entirely predictable and easily administrated is impossible to achieve, this volume, building on the lessons from the reform efforts to date, outlines an approach that, it is argued, offers tangible improvements over all of the reforms so far developed.

13.3 Through detailed analysis of s54 of the Insurance Contracts Act in Australia, relevant case law to date, as well as 'stress testing' of the s54 approach against the facts of several key historic cases, this volume has demonstrated that s54 has blurred the boundaries surrounding the sanctity of scope of contract and represents an unnecessarily complex, and ultimately flawed, approach. On the other hand, examination of the reforms in New Zealand (contained in the Insurance Law Reform Act) demonstrates that efforts to achieve greater balance between the interests of the insured and insurer have resulted in the pendulum swinging too far in favour of the insured. It is perhaps unsurprising that the Law Commission recommended that the approach to reform in the UK should plough its own furrow, rather than follow the path set by either Australia or New Zealand.

13.4 Drawing on the experience from Australia and New Zealand, as well as the Law Commission's reviews of the law in this area, this volume has undertaken an in-depth evaluation of the provisions in the Insurance Act 2015 dealing with breaches of warranties and other terms. Many of the reform measures contained in the Act are to be welcomed. This volume applauds the proposal to make a breach of warranty suspensory, together with provisions to abolish basis clauses; it also gives a guarded welcome to the proposal to limit suspension to a specific category of risk where the clause that has been breached relates to a particular kind of loss, or loss at a particular location or place. Nevertheless, the analysis

 DOI: 10.4324/9781003031734-13

undertaken by this volume has demonstrated a number of failings and shortcomings in the provisions contained in the Insurance Act. It is submitted that, at best, these failings will lead to increased uncertainty and litigation.

13.5 This volume has shown that the main flaw with the Insurance Act lies with s11. This author believes that this likely arises from the way in which, despite the balance of the provisions being the product of careful evolution over a number of years, in its final form s11 was a last minute addition to the statute, and was therefore subjected to very little in the way of parliamentary scrutiny. This volume has sought to demonstrate that, at best, s11 leaves the law facing an uncertain future. The analysis in this volume has shown that the concept of 'the risk as a whole'[1] is flawed, as well as being vague and unclear: it will likely result in increased uncertainty and litigation. The reach of s11, in terms of what provisions are subject to it, is also far from clear. It is this author's contention that an effective reform of the law in this area must, in addition to warranties, also address exclusion clauses, conditions precedent and other provisions that seek to release the insurer from liability under the policy. This volume has sought to demonstrate it is unlikely, for example, that all exclusion clauses are subject to s11. Analysis has shown that it can be argued that exclusion clauses by definition refer to the risk as whole (and are thus outside s11). Even if this is not correct, it is clear that s11 requires there to be a breach of (or 'non-compliance' with) a provision of the contract. Many exclusion clauses are not dependent upon there being a breach as a trigger for the exclusion to take effect and as a result would lie outside the ambit of s11. Similarly, the relationship between s11 and conditions precedent is also uncertain. This volume has shown that at least some conditions precedent will lie outside the reach of s11. This is regrettable. Although the Law Commission eventually positioned itself firmly against the concept of causal linkage, this author believes it is difficult to interpret s11(3) as anything other than a form of causal linkage introduced, effectively, via the back door. Yet the Commission suggested that the consequences of breach should not be considered in light of what actually happened. This volume argues that the outcome is confused and uncertain: far better to adopt a clear causal linkage approach.

13.6 Building on an analysis of the multitude of challenges facing a reform of the law in this area, as well as the lessons from the reform initiatives to date in the UK and overseas, this volume proposes a new approach for addressing breaches of insurance warranties and similar provisions. The analysis acknowledges that there is no perfect solution and that any attempt at reform in this area will come with some degree of uncertainty and a risk of litigation. To assist the development of the proposals and as a basis for assessing the extent to which the proposals adequately address the challenges, this volume has set out the substantial range of issues that any reform initiative in this area must attempt to address, or at least accommodate. It is argued that the approach set out in this volume represents a significant improvement on all previous attempts at reform and is successful in addressing the majority of these issues. This author believes it is essential that any reform does not erode the sanctity of the scope of contract agreed by the parties. In order to address this, the proposals provide explicitly for scope to be the first issue addressed by the court. If the subject matter is outside the scope of the policy, the proposals will not apply and the insured will have no claim.

1 S11(1) Insurance Act 2015.

13.7 This volume argues that causal linkage must lie at the heart of reform of the law of insurance warranties. Central to the proposals set out herein is the granting of sufficient flexibility and discretion to the court to enable solutions to be tailored to the specific circumstances of the particular case. The approach proposed in this volume combines elements of the solutions adopted in the Insurance Act and overseas, but crucially incorporates as a central tenet an evaluative approach based squarely on an assessment of whether or not there is a causal linkage between the breach and the loss incurred. The recommended approach applies not only to breaches of warranties, but also to non-compliance with any term that purports to give the insurer a right to avoid liability. Exclusion clauses are specifically within the ambit of the proposals (regardless of whether or not they are triggered by a 'breach' of provision). The mechanism set out in this volume also incorporates an assessment of any prejudice suffered by the insurer. It is further argued that the incorporation of a right of termination for the insurer offers advantages, not only to the insurer, but also to the insured. In order to ensure that the court has the flexibility to avoid decisions that might otherwise be harsh on the insurer, the proposals would give the court the flexibility to grant a measure of proportionality where it has been demonstrated that a breach *could* have contributed to the loss in a causal manner, even if, on the facts, it did not do so.

13.8 In order to test the approach set out in this volume, the proposals have been stress tested against the facts of a range of well-known cases, drawn from a number of jurisdictions. This analysis supports the contention that this volume's proposals offer more comprehensive and equitable, and in some respects certain, outcomes than those delivered to date by the reforms in Australia or New Zealand, or those likely to be offered under the Insurance Act 2015.

13.9 Although confident about the effectiveness of its proposals, this author is however realistic about the prospects for the proposals in this volume being utilised as the basis for further reform in the jurisdictions examined. There is little evidence of a current political appetite for further reform of the law in Australia. While in New Zealand there has recently been a further review of insurance contract law, the Review's proposals in relation to matters considered in this volume are relatively modest and have yet to be implemented.[2] In the UK, not only has the Insurance Act only relatively recently reached the statute book, but the backcloth of Brexit and the COVID-19 virus makes further examination of the law extremely unlikely in the foreseeable future. Nevertheless, the proposals developed in this volume, building as they do on the lessons from the three jurisdictions that have developed detailed reforms, could, post COVID, provide the basis for reform in common law jurisdictions that have yet to implement initiatives in this sphere of the law. It is submitted that any jurisdiction implementing such reforms would benefit from a regime that offered advantages over any of its counterparts.

2 www.mbie.govt.nz/business-and-employment/business/financial-markets-regulation/insurance-contract-law-review/ Chapter 7 refers.

APPENDIX 1

S54 INSURANCE CONTRACTS ACT 1984 (AUSTRALIA)

Insurer may not refuse to pay claims in certain circumstances

(1) Subject to this section, where the effect of a contract of insurance would, but for this section, be that the insurer may refuse to pay a claim, either in whole or in part, by reason of some act of the insured or of some other person, being an act that occurred after the contract was entered into but not being an act in respect of which subsection (2) applies, the insurer may not refuse to pay the claim by reason only of that act but the insurer's liability in respect of the claim is reduced by the amount that fairly represents the extent to which the insurer's interests were prejudiced as a result of that act.

(2) Subject to the succeeding provisions of this section, where the act could reasonably be regarded as being capable of causing or contributing to a loss in respect of which insurance cover is provided by the contract, the insurer may refuse to pay the claim.

(3) Where the insured proves that no part of the loss that gave rise to the claim was caused by the act, the insurer may not refuse to pay the claim by reason only of the act.

(4) Where the insured proves that some part of the loss that gave rise to the claim was not caused by the act, the insurer may not refuse to pay the claim, so far as it concerns that part of the loss, by reason only of the act.

(5) Where:

- (a) the act was necessary to protect the safety of a person or to preserve property; or
- (b) it was not reasonably possible for the insured or other person not to do the act; the insurer may not refuse to pay the claim by reason only of the act.

(6) A reference in this section to an act includes a reference to:

- (a) an omission; and
- (b) an act or omission that has the effect of altering the state or condition of the subject-matter of the contract or of allowing the state or condition of that subject-matter to alter.

APPENDIX 2

SECTIONS 5, 6, 9 AND 11 INSURANCE LAW REFORM ACT 1977 (NEW ZEALAND)

Section 5 Mis-statements in other contracts of insurance

(1) A contract of insurance shall not be avoided by reason only of any statement made in any proposal or other document on the faith of which the contract was entered into, reinstated, or renewed by the insurer unless the statement –
 (a) was substantially incorrect; and
 (b) was material.

(2) Nothing in this section shall –
 (a) apply in respect of any contract of insurance embodied in a life policy; or
 (b) limit the provisions of sections 4 and 7.

Section 6 Incorrectness and materiality defined

(1) For the purposes of sections 4 and 5, and notwithstanding any admission, term, condition, stipulation, warranty, or proviso in the application or proposal for insurance or in the life policy or contract of insurance, a statement is substantially incorrect only if the difference between what is stated and what is actually correct would have been considered material by a prudent insurer.

(2) For the purposes of sections 4 and 5, and notwithstanding any admission, term, condition, stipulation, warranty, or proviso in the application or proposal for insurance or in the life policy or contract of insurance, a statement is material only if that statement would have influenced the judgment of a prudent insurer in fixing the premium or in determining whether he would have taken or continued the risk upon substantially the same terms.

Section 9 Time limits on claims under contracts of insurance

(1) A provision of a contract of insurance prescribing any manner in which or any limit of time within which notice of any claim by the insured under such contract must be given or prescribing any limit of time within which any suit or action by the insured must be brought shall –
 (a) if that contract of insurance is embodied in a life policy and the claim, suit, or action relates to the death of the insured, not bind the insured; and
 (b) in any other case, bind the insured only if in the opinion of the arbitrator or court determining the claim the insurer has in the particular circumstances been so prejudiced by the failure of the insured to comply with such provision that it would be inequitable if such provision were not to bind the insured.

(2) Where –

(a) the insured under any contract of insurance to which subsection (1)(b) applies fails to give notice of any claim in any manner or within any limit of time prescribed by the contract; and

(b) the cost of repairing, replacing, or reinstating any property when it fails to be met is greater than that which would have applied if the notice had been given in the manner or within the time so prescribed, –

that greater cost shall not constitute prejudice to the insurer for the purposes of subsection (1)(b), but the insurer shall not be obliged to apply or pay in repairing, replacing, or reinstating the property a greater sum than that for which he would have been liable if the notice of claim had been given in the manner or within the time so prescribed.

Section 11 Certain exclusions forbidden

Where –

(a) by the provisions of a contract of insurance the circumstances in which the insurer is bound to indemnify the insured against loss are so defined as to exclude or limit the liability of the insurer to indemnify the insured on the happening of certain events or on the existence of certain circumstances; and

(b) in the view of the court or arbitrator determining the claim of the insured the liability of the insurer has been so defined because the happening of such events or the existence of such circumstances was in the view of the insurer likely to increase the risk of such loss occurring, –

the insured shall not be disentitled to be indemnified by the insurer by reason only of such provisions of the contract of insurance if the insured proves on the balance of probability that the loss in respect of which the insured seeks to be indemnified was not caused or contributed to by the happening of such events or the existence of such circumstances.

APPENDIX 3

INSURANCE ACT 2015 SECTIONS 9, 10, 11, 16 AND 17

Section 9 Warranties and representations

(1) This section applies to representations made by the insured in connection with –
   (a) a proposed non-consumer insurance contract, or
   (b) a proposed variation to a non-consumer insurance contract.

(2) Such a representation is not capable of being converted into a warranty by means of any provision of the non-consumer insurance contract (or of the terms of the variation), or of any other contract (and whether by declaring the representation to form the basis of the contract or otherwise).

Section 10 Breach of warranty

(1) Any rule of law that breach of a warranty (express or implied) in a contract of insurance results in the discharge of the insurer's liability under the contract is abolished.

(2) An insurer has no liability under a contract of insurance in respect of any loss occurring, or attributable to something happening, after a warranty (express or implied) in the contract has been breached but before the breach has been remedied.

(3) But subsection (2) does not apply if –
   (a) because of a change of circumstances, the warranty ceases to be applicable to the circumstances of the contract,
   (b) compliance with the warranty is rendered unlawful by any subsequent law, or
   (c) the insurer waives the breach of warranty.

(4) Subsection (2) does not affect the liability of the insurer in respect of losses occurring, or attributable to something happening –
   (a) before the breach of warranty, or
   (b) if the breach can be remedied, after it has been remedied.

(5) For the purposes of this section, a breach of warranty is to be taken as remedied –
   (a) in a case falling within subsection (6), if the risk to which the warranty relates later becomes essentially the same as that originally contemplated by the parties,
   (b) in any other case, if the insured ceases to be in breach of the warranty.

(6) A case falls within this subsection if –
   (a) the warranty in question requires that by an ascertainable time something is to be done (or not done), or a condition is to be fulfilled, or something is (or is not) to be the case, and

(b) that requirement is not complied with.

(7) In the Marine Insurance Act 1906 –

(a) in section 33 (nature of warranty), in subsection (3), the second sentence is omitted,

(b) section 34 (when breach of warranty excused) is omitted.

Section 11 Terms not relevant to the actual loss

(1) This section applies to a term (express or implied) of a contract of insurance, other than a term defining the risk as a whole, if compliance with it would tend to reduce the risk of one or more of the following –

(a) loss of a particular kind,

(b) loss at a particular location,

(c) loss at a particular time.

(2) If a loss occurs, and the term has not been complied with, the insurer may not rely on the non-compliance to exclude, limit or discharge its liability under the contract for the loss if the insured satisfies subsection (3).

(3) The insured satisfies this subsection if it shows that the non-compliance with the term could not have increased the risk of the loss which actually occurred in the circumstances in which it occurred.

(4) This section may apply in addition to section 10.

Section 16 Contracting out: non-consumer insurance contracts

(1) A term of a non-consumer insurance contract, or of any other contract, which would put the insured in a worse position as respects representations to which section 9 applies than the insured would be in by virtue of that section is to that extent of no effect.

(2) A term of a non-consumer insurance contract, or of any other contract, which would put the insured in a worse position as respects any of the other matters provided for in Part 2, 3 or 4 of this Act than the insured would be in by virtue of the provisions of those Parts (so far as relating to non-consumer insurance contracts) is to that extent of no effect, unless the requirements of section 17 have been satisfied in relation to the term.

(3) In this section references to a contract include a variation

(4) This section does not apply in relation to a contract for the settlement of a claim arising under a non-consumer insurance contract.

Section 17 The transparency requirements

(1) In this section, 'the disadvantageous term' means such a term as is mentioned in section 16(2).

(2) The insurer must take sufficient steps to draw the disadvantageous term to the insured's attention before the contract is entered into or the variation agreed.

(3) The disadvantageous term must be clear and unambiguous as to its effect.

(4) In determining whether the requirements of subsections (2) and (3) have been met, the characteristics of insured persons of the kind in question and the circumstances of the transaction are to be taken into account.

(5) The insured may not rely on any failure on the part of the insurer to meet the requirements of subsection (2), if the insured (or its agent) had actual knowledge of the disadvantageous term when the contract was entered into or the variation agreed.

APPENDIX 4

CLAUSES 9, 10 AND 11 OF DRAFT LEGISLATION ON WARRANTIES AND OTHER TERMS AS SET OUT IN LAW COMMISSION REPORT LAW COM NO 353, JULY 2014[1]

Warranties and representations

s9 (1) This section applies to representations made by the insured in connection with
(a) a proposed non-consumer insurance contract, or
(b) a proposed variation to a non-consumer insurance contract.

(2) Such a representation is not capable of being converted into a warranty by means of any provision of the non-consumer insurance contract (or of the terms of the variation), or of any other contract (and whether by declaring the representation to form the basis of the contract or otherwise).

Breach of warranty

S10 (1) Any rule of law that breach of a warranty (express or implied) in a contract of insurance results in the discharge of the insurer's liability under the contract is abolished.

(2) Subject to section 11, an insurer has no liability under a contract of insurance in respect of any loss occurring, or attributable to something happening, after a warranty (express or implied) in the contract has been breached but before the breach has been remedied.

(3) But subsection (2) does not apply if
(a) because of a change of circumstances, the warranty ceases to be applicable to the circumstances of the contract,
(b) compliance with the warranty is rendered unlawful by any subsequent law, or
(c) the insurer waives the breach of warranty.

(4) Subsection (2) does not affect the liability of the insurer in respect of losses occurring, or attributable to something happening
(a) before the breach of warranty, or
(b) if the breach can be remedied, after it has been remedied.

(5) For the purposes of this section, a breach of warranty is to be taken as remedied
(a) in a case falling within subsection (6), if the risk to which the warranty relates later becomes essentially the same as that originally contemplated by the parties,
(b) in any other case, if the insured ceases to be in breach of the warranty.

(6) A case falls within this subsection if

1 Available at http://lawcommission.justice.go.uk/docs.

(a) the warranty in question requires that by an ascertainable time something is to be done (or not done), or a condition is to be fulfilled, or something is (or is not) to be the case, and

(b) that requirement is not complied with.

(7) In the Marine Insurance Act 1906

(a) in section 33 (nature of warranty), in subsection (3), the second sentence is omitted,

(b) section 34 (when breach of warranty excused) is omitted.

Terms relevant to particular descriptions of loss

S11 (1) This section applies to any term (express or implied) of a contract of insurance compliance with which would tend to reduce the risk of one or more of the following

(a) loss of a particular kind,

(b) loss at a particular location,

(c) loss at a particular time.

(2) Breach of such a term may not be relied upon by the insurer to exclude, limit or discharge its liability for, respectively

(a) loss of a different kind,

(b) loss at a different location,

(c) loss at a different time.

This section may apply in addition to section 10.

APPENDIX 5

MARINE INSURANCE ACT 1906 SECTIONS 33 AND 35 (AS AMENDED BY THE INSURANCE ACT 2015)

Section 33 Nature of warranty

(1) A warranty, in the following sections relating to warranties, means a promissory warranty, that is to say, a warranty by which the assured undertakes that some particular thing shall or shall not be done, or that some condition shall be fulfilled, or whereby he affirms or negatives the existence of a particular state of facts.
(2) A warranty may be express or implied.
(3) A warranty, as above defined, is a condition which must be exactly complied with, whether it be material to the risk or not.

Section 35 Express warranties

(1) An express warranty may be in any form of words from which the intention to warrant is to be inferred.
(2) An express warranty must be included in, or written upon, the policy, or must be contained in some document incorporated by reference into the policy.
(3) An express warranty does not exclude an implied warranty, unless it be inconsistent therewith.

APPENDIX 6

MARINE INSURANCE ACT 1906: IMPLIED WARRANTIES AND SIMILAR PROVISIONS

S39 Warranty of seaworthiness of ship

(1) In a voyage policy there is an implied warranty that at the commencement of the voyage the ship shall be seaworthy for the purpose of the particular adventure insured.
(2) Where the policy attaches while the ship is in port, there is also an implied warranty that she shall, at the commencement of the risk, be reasonably fit to encounter the ordinary perils of the port.
(3) Where the policy relates to a voyage which is performed in different stages, during which the ship requires different kinds of or further preparation or equipment, there is an implied warranty that at the commencement of each stage the ship is seaworthy in respect of such preparation or equipment for the purposes of that stage.
(4) A ship is deemed to be seaworthy when she is reasonably fit in all respects to encounter the ordinary perils of the seas of the adventure insured.
(5) In a time policy there is no implied warranty that the ship shall be seaworthy at any stage of the adventure, but where, with the privity of the assured, the ship is sent to sea in an unseaworthy state, the insurer is not liable for any loss attributable to unseaworthiness.

S40 No implied warranty that goods are seaworthy

(1) In a policy on goods or other moveables there is no implied warranty that the goods or moveables are seaworthy.
(2) In a voyage policy on goods or other moveables there is an implied warranty that at the commencement of the voyage the ship is not only seaworthy as a ship, but also that she is reasonably fit to carry the goods or other moveables to the destination contemplated by the policy.

S41 Warranty of legality

There is an implied warranty that the adventure insured is a lawful one, and that, so far as the assured can control the matter, the adventure shall be carried out in a lawful manner.

S42 Implied condition as to commencement of risk

(1) Where the subject-matter is insured by a voyage policy 'at and from' or 'from' a particular place, it is not necessary that the ship should be at that place when the contract is concluded, but there is an implied condition that the adventure shall be commenced within a reasonable time, and that if the adventure be not so commenced the insurer may avoid the contract.

(2) The implied condition may be negatived by showing that the delay was caused by circumstances known to the insurer before the contract was concluded, or by showing that he waived the condition.

S43 Alteration of port of departure

Where the place of departure is specified by the policy, and the ship instead of sailing from that place sails from any other place, the risk does not attach.

S44 Sailing for different destination

Where the destination is specified in the policy, and the ship, instead of sailing for that destination, sails for any other destination, the risk does not attach.

S45 Change of voyage

(1) Where, after the commencement of the risk, the destination of the ship is voluntarily changed from the destination contemplated by the policy, there is said to be a change of voyage.

(2) Unless the policy otherwise provides, where there is a change of voyage, the insurer is discharged from liability as from the time of change, that is to say, as from the time when the determination to change it is manifested; and it is immaterial that the ship may not in fact have left the course of voyage contemplated by the policy when the loss occurs.

S46 Deviation

(1) Where a ship, without lawful excuse, deviates from the voyage contemplated by the policy, the insurer is discharged from liability as from the time of deviation, and it is immaterial that the ship may have regained her route before any loss occurs.

(2) There is a deviation from the voyage contemplated by the policy –
    (a) Where the course of the voyage is specifically designated by the policy, and that course is departed from; or
    (b) Where the course of the voyage is not specifically designated by the policy, but the usual and customary course is departed from.

(3) The intention to deviate is immaterial; there must be a deviation in fact to discharge the insurer from his liability under the contract.

S48 Delay in voyage

In the case of a voyage policy, the adventure insured must be prosecuted throughout its course with reasonable dispatch, and, if without lawful excuse it is not so prosecuted, the insurer is discharged from liability as from the time when the delay became unreasonable.

BIBLIOGRAPHY

Books and articles

Sir R Aikens, 'The Law Commission's Proposed Reforms of the Law of Warranties in Marine and Commercial Insurance: Will the Cure Be Better than the Disease?' in *Reforming Marine and Commercial Insurance Law,* General Editor Dr Bariş Soyer, Informa, London 2008.

Justice J Allsop and M Wells, Marine Insurance Act 1909, 100th Anniversary, speech delivered to the Maritime Law Association of Australia and New Zealand, 11 November 2009.

Arnould, *Law of Marine Insurance and Average,* eds J Gilman, Prof R Merkin, C Blanchard QC and M Templeman QC, Sweet and Maxwell, London, 18th Edition, 2013.

Association of British Insurers Statement of General Insurance Practice, 1977.

Association of British Insurers submission to the Law Commission, cited in Law Commission and Scottish Law Commission, Insurance Contract Law: The Business Insured's Duty of Disclosure and the Law of Warranties (LCCP No 204; ScLCDP No 155: 2012).

Association of Consulting Engineers Australia, The Impact of Changes in Professional Indemnity (PI) Insurance on Costs and Fees for Consulting Engineering Firms, May 2003.

Australian Insurance Law Association, Geoff Masel Memorial Lecture 2009, Directors' and Officers' Insurance and the Global Financial Crisis, Robert Merkin.

Australian Justice Dept Terms of Reference for a Review of the Marine Insurance Act 1909 by the ALRC.

H Bennett, 'Good Luck with Warranties' (1991) *Journal of Business Law* 592.

H Bennett, 'Reflections on Values: The Law Commissions' Proposals with Respect to Remedies for Breach of Promissory Warranty and Pre-Formation Non-Disclosure and Misrepresentation in Commercial Insurance,' in *Reforming Marine and Commercial Insurance Law,* General Editor Dr Bariş Soyer, Informa, London, 2008.

J Birds, 'Warranties in Insurance Proposal Forms' (1977) *Journal of Business Law* 231.

J Birds, 'The Effect of Breach of Warranty' (1991) *Law Quarterly Review* 540.

J Birds, *Birds' Modern Insurance Law,* Sweet and Maxwell, London, 8th Edition, 2010.

J Birds and NJ Hird, *Birds' Modern Insurance Law,* Sweet and Maxwell, London, 6th Edition, 2004.

A Borrowdale, 'Insurance Law Reform Acts in Practice (I)' (1987) *NZLJ* 30.

British Insurance Law Association, Insurance Contract Law Reform – Recommendations to the Law Commissions (2002).

Clark, 'The Marine Insurance System in Common Law Countries: Statutes and Problems, paper delivered at Marine Insurance Symposium' (1998) *Mar Ins* 242, pg 63.

J Clarke, 'After the Dust Settles on Antico: *FIA v Perry Lives*' (1997) 9 *Ins LJ* 29.

M Clarke, 'The Nature of Warranty in Contracts of Insurance' (1991) *Cambridge Law Journal* 393.

M Clarke, 'Insurance Warranties: The Absolute End?' (2007) *LMCLQ* 474.

Clayton Utz, Include Me Out: Exclusion Clauses, Reinsurance, and Section 18B of the Insurance Act, 10 October 2011 available at https://www.claytonutz.com/knowledge/2011/october/include-me-out-exclusion-clauses-reinsurance-and-section-18b-of-the-insurance-act

Colinvaux's Law of Insurance in New Zealand, Merkin and Nicholl, Brookers, Wellington, 2014.

Colinvaux's Law of Insurance (Insurance Practitioner's Library), ed Prof RM Merkin, Sweet and Maxwell, London, 11th Edition, 2016.

R Cooper, Australian Perspectives in Marine Insurance, paper to the Shipping in the New Millennium Conference MLAANZ Brisbane, 19 March 1999.

J Davey, 'Remedying the Remedies: the Shifting Shape of Insurance Contract Law' (2013) *LMCLQ* 478.

I Davis, Reform of the Marine Insurance Act: Options and Constrains, a paper presented at Maritime Law Association of Australia and New Zealand Annual Conference, August 2000 available at http://www5.austlii.edu.au/au/journals/ALRCRefJl/2000/29.html.

S Derrrington, The Law Relating to Non-disclosure, Misrepresentation and Breach of Warranty in Contracts of Marine Insurance: a Case for Reform? PhD thesis 1998, University of Queensland.

S Derrington, 'Marine Insurance Law in Australia: the Australian Law Reform Commission Proposals' (2002) *LMCLQ* 214.

S Derrington, The Law of Marine Insurance in Australia – Perspectives and Permutations in DR Thomas (ed) *The Modern Law of Marine Insurance*, Volume Two, LLP, 2002, 363–403.

Diamond A, 'The Law of Marine Insurance: Has it a Future?' (1986), *Lloyd's Maritime and Commercial Law Quarterly* 25.

DF Dugdale, 'Insurance Law: Sorting out Section 11' (1992) *NZLJ* 99 at 101.

P McDonald Eggers, The Marine Insurance Act 1906: Judicial Attitudes and Innovation – Time for Reform?, a paper presented at International Colloquium on Marine Insurance Law, Swansea University, 30 June 2005.

C Fawlk, 'The Meaning and Effect of S33 of the MIA of 1906' (1991) *Insurance Law and Practice* 98.

C Giaschi, Warranties in Marine Insurance, a paper to the Association of Marine Underwriters of British Columbia, Vancouver, 10 April 1997.

R Giblett and N Wiesener, The Long Haul: High Court Endorses Broad Application of S54 of the Insurance Contracts Act, Norton Rose Fulbright, September 2014.

S Goldman, 'Marine Insurance – the Literal Compliance Rule Applies to Breaches of Trading and Navigational Warranties', *Journal of Maritime Law and Commerce*, 1995, 315.

Goodacre SB, 'To Err is Human: An Appraisal of Some Possible Effects of ISM Code on English Marine Hull Policy' (1997), *International Maritime Law,* 263.

O Gurses, Section 11 of the Insurance Act 2015: When Does a Term Define the Risk as a Whole in an Insurance Contract? Balancing the Interest of the Assured and Insurer, (2020) 3 *Journal of Business Law* 184–201.

Hare, The Omnipotent Warranty, England v The World,' paper delivered at the International Marine Insurance Convention, Antwerp, 1999 available at www.uct.ac.za/depts/shiplaw/imic99.htm (24 February 2000).

J Hare, 'Report to the 38th Conference of the CMI Vancouver 2004, CMI Yearbook 2004, Part II, 255.

F Hawke, S54: 'Where to Draw the Line?' (2012) 23 *Insurance Law Journal* 223–244.

D Hertzell, 'Insurance Contract Law Reform in England Wales and Scotland,' in *Reforming Marine and Commercial Insurance Law,* General Editor Dr Bariş Soyer, Informa, London, 2008.

Hertzell and Burgoyne, The Law Commissions and Insurance Contract Law Reform, 114 (2013) 19 *JIML*.

Hjalmarsson, J. (2015). Insurance Act 2015 – a new beginning or business as usual? *Shipping & Trade Law, 15*(2), 4–5.

Hjalmarsson, J. (2014). Insurance contract law draft Bill. *Shipping & Trade Law, 14*(2), 4–5.

S Hodges, *Law of Marine Insurance,* Cavendish Publishing, London, 1996.

HB Hurd, *Marine Insurance,* Effingham Wilson, London, 1922.

M Huybrechts et al (eds), *Marine Insurance at the Turn of the Millennium,* Vol. 2, (2000).

N Jenkins, Forecasting Changes in the World of Marine Insurance Markets and Predicting London's Place in it in the Long Term, paper delivered at Marine Insurance Market Conference, 1996, organised by IIR Ltd London.

G Leloudas, Contracting Out of the Insurance Act 2015 in Commercial Insurance Contracts, *The Insurance Act 2015, A New Regime for Commercial and Marine Insurance Law,* edited by M Clarke and B Soyer, Informa Law for Routledge, London, 2016.

K Lewins, Marine Insurance Reform – Rocking the Boat?, (2001) 79 *Australian Law Reform Commission Reform Journal* 48.

Kate Lewins, Australia Proposes Marine Insurance Reform, JBL 2002, May, 292–303

Kate Lewins, 'Breach of Warranty in Marine Insurance: Allison Pty Ltd t/as PilbaraJiannan Lin, The Resounding Success of the Insurance Act 2015 with a Slight Blemish, *Legal Issues Journal* 5, no. 1 (January 2017): 41–74.

Sir Andrew Longmore, Good Faith and Breach of Warranty: Are We Moving Forwards or Backwards? (2004) *LMCLQ* 158.

Andrew Longmore, An Insurance Contracts Act for a New Century? (2001) *LMCLQ* 357–368.

Lowry PD, Perils of the Seas and Warranties: A Case for the Assured, paper delivered to the Third International Maritime Law Conference, 1986, Vancouver.

Derek Luxford, Reform or revolution? Maritime Advocate, Issue 16, September 2001.

P Mann, *Mann's Annotated Insurance Contracts Act,* Thompson Reuters, Sydney, 7th Edition, 2016.

F Marks and A Balla, *Guidebook to Insurance Law in Australia,* CCH, North Ryde, NSW, 3rd Edition, 1998.

G Masel, 'Taking Liberties with Claims Made Policies' (2000) 11(2) *Ins LJ* 104.

Marine Insurance: Hull Practice, Volume 3, 2nd Edition, (ed. RH Brown), London 1993.

McEven DF, Perils of the Seas and Warranties: the Underwriter's Perspective, paper delivered to the Third International Maritime Law Conference, 1986, Vancover.

Mead, The Effect of Section 54 of the Insurance Contracts Act 1984 and Proposals for Reform, (1997) 9 *Ins LJ* 1.

R Merkin, Reforming Insurance Law: Is There a Case for Reverse Transportation?; A Report for the English and Scottish Law Commissioners on the Australian Experience of Insurance Law Reform (2008) available at http://www.lawcom.gov.uk/app/uploads/2015/03/ICL_Merkin_report.pdf or at https://eprints.soton.ac.uk/27860/.

R Merkin, Australia: Still a Nation of Chalmers? (2011) 30(2) *University of Queensland Law Journal,* University of Queensland 189–224.

R Merkin, Foundations of Marine Insurance: Law, War and Trade, draft: not yet published.

R Merkin and C Croly, Doubts About Insurance Codes, (2001) *Journal of Business Law* Nov, 587–604.

R Merkin and O Gurses, The Insurance Act 2015: Rebalancing the Interests of Insurer and Assured, (2015) 78(6) *Modern Law Review* 1004–1027.

R Merkin and O Gurses, Insurance Contracts after the Insurance Act 2015, (2016) 132(3) *LQR* 445–469.

Merkin and Hemsworth, *The Law of Motor Insurance,* Sweet and Maxwell, London, 2nd Edition, 2016.

R Merkin and J Lowry, Reconstructing Insurance Law: The Law Commissions' Consultation Paper, (2008) 71 *Modern Law Review* 95, 110.

Merkin and Nicoll, Colinvaux's Law of Insurance in New Zealand, Thompson and Reuters NZ, Wellington, 2nd Edition, 2017.

M Muscillo, The Lesser of Two Evils: *FAI General Insurance Co Ltd v Australian Hospital Care Pty Ltd* (2001) 1(2) QUTLawJJl 20.

Jan Miller, Potential Pitfalls of Insurance Act – (2015) 165 *NLJ* 7666, p4 (1).

Lord Mustill, Fault and Marine Loss, (1988) *LMCLQ* 310.

C Nicoll, HIH litigation, *LQR* 2003 119 (Oct) 572, page 574.

P North, Law Reform: Process and Problem, (1985) 101 *LQR* 338.

NZILA Lecture Series 2018, Can the Assured's Conduct Defeat a Claim? *Dougal v BoatsRUs* 2018, Unreported, Professor Rob Merkin QC.

JA Park, *A System of Law of Marine Insurances,* Printed by A. Strahan for J. Butterworth, London, 1796.

G Pynt, *Australian Insurance Law: A First Reference,* Butterworths, Chatswood, Australia, 3rd Edition, 2015.

Report of International Financial Markets in the UK (May 2008).

Review of the Insurance Contracts Act 1984 (Cth), Report into the Operation of Section 54, Alan Cameron and Nancy Milne, October 2003, Commonwealth of Australia Department of Treasury.

TJ Schoenbaum, Warranties in the Law of Marine Insurance: Some Suggestions for Reform of English and American Law, (1999), *Tulane Maritime Law Journal,* 267.

TJ Schoenbaum, *Key Divergences Between English and American Law of Marine Insurance: A Comparative Study,* Maryland 1999.

Schoombee, Antico's Case and Other Recent Decisions on Notification of Claims and Circumstances: Sections 54 and 40 of the Insurance Contracts Act, (1997) 8 *Ins LJ* 167.

B Soyer, Potential Legal Implications of ISM Code for Marine Insurance, International, (1998) *Journal of Insurance Law,* 279.

B Soyer, A Survey of The New International Hull Clauses 2002, (2003) 256 *JIML.*

B Soyer, *Warranties in Marine Insurance,* Cavendish Publishing, London, 2nd Edition, 2006.

B Soyer, Reforming Insurance Warranties: Are We Finally Moving Forward? in *Reforming Marine and Commercial Insurance Law,* General Editor Dr Bariş Soyer, Informa, London, 2008.

B Soyer, Reforming Insurance Warranties: A Response to the Law Commissions, July 2008, paper presented at the symposium held by the Institute of International Shipping and Trade Law, held at Lloyd's of London.

B Soyer, Beginning of a New Era for Insurance Warranties? (2013) *LMCLQ* 3(Aug), 384–400.

B Soyer, Risk Control Clauses in Insurance Law, Law Reform and the Future (2016) 109 *CLJ*.

B Soyer, *Warranties in Marine Insurance,* Routledge, London, 3rd Edition, 2017.

Submissions to the ALRC referenced in ALRC 91 including P Grieve Submission 6; Law Society of WA Submission 7; K Carruthers Submission 9; Law Council of Australia Submission 10; Insurance Council of Australia Submission 11; MLAANZ Submission 12.

Sutton on Insurance Law, eds Merkin, Kirby and Enright, 4th Edition, Lawbook Co., 2015.

Sutton, The High Court Widens the 'Reach' of the Insurance Contracts Act (1998) 26 *Australian Business Law Review* 57.

AA Tarr and JA Kennedy, *Insurance Law in New Zealand,* Wellington, 2nd Edition, 1992.

DR Thomas, Held Covered Clauses in Marine Insurance, in *The Modern Law of Marine Insurance,* chapter 1, Vol. II, LLP, 2002.

DR Thomas, in Modern Law of Marine Insurance, (2002) 2 *LLP* at 1.141–1.152.

Waddell, Current Issues and Developments in Marine Insurance (1993) *University of San Francisco Maritime Law Journal* 185.

The Warranties in Your Marine Insurance Policy May No Longer Matter, Briefing note from Piper Alderman Quintin Rares, Association of Corporate Counsel 10 May 2012.

T Wilhelmsen, Duty of Disclosure, Duty of Good Faith, Alternation of Risk and Warranties: An Analysis of the Replies to the CMI Questionnaire, CMI Yearbook 2000.

JD Wright, Insurance Warranties Under Fire – (2018) 29 7 *Cons.Law* 30.

New Zealand, English and Australian Law Commission Reports

Australian Justice Dept Terms of Reference for a Review of the Marine Insurance Act 1909 by the ALRC.

Australian Law Reform Commission, Insurance Contracts, Report No 20, (1982). See also Australia, House of Representatives, Insurance Contracts Bill 1984.

Australian Law Reform Commission, Review of the Marine Insurance Act 1909 (ALRC Report 91) available at www.alrc.gov.au.

Contracts and Commercial Law Reform Committee (NZ) Aspects of Insurance Law (1 July 1975).

New Zealand Law Commission Report 46, Some Insurance Law Problems, (1998) available at https://www.lawcom.govt.nz/sites/default/files/projectAvailableFormats/NZLC%20R46.pdf.

Fifth Report of the Law Reform Committee (1957) Cmnd 62.

Insurance Law: Non-Disclosure and Breach of Warranty (1980) Law Com No 104 available at https://s3-eu-west-2.amazonaws.com/lawcom-prod-storage-11jsxou24uy7q/uploads/2016/08/LC.-104-INSURANCE-LAW-NON-DISCLOSURE-AND-BREACH-OF-WARRANTY-REPORT-ON-A-REFERENCE-UNDER-SECTION-3le-OF-THE-LAW-COMMISSIONS-ACT-1965.pdf.

Law Commission Issues Paper 2: Warranties (November 2006) available at http://lawcommission.justice.gov.uk.

Insurance Contract Law: Misrepresentation, Non-Disclosure and Breach of Warranty by the Insured (2007) LCCP 182/SLCDP 134 available at http://www.lawcom.gov.uk/app/uploads/2015/06/ICL2_Warranties.pdf.

Insurance Contract Law: The Business Insured's Duty of Disclosure and the Law of Warranties, the Law Commission and the Scottish Law Commission, LCCP 204 / SLCDP 155 (June 2012) available at https://www.lawcom.gov.uk/document/insurance-contract-law-misrepresentation-non-disclosure-and-breach-of-warranty-by-the-insured/.

Law Commission and Scottish Law Commission, Insurance Contract Law: Business Disclosure; Warranties; Insurers' Remedies for Fraudulent Claims; and Late Payment Law Com No 353 / Scot

Law Com No 238 Cm 8898 SG/2014/131 July 2014 available at: http://www.lawcom.gov.uk/app/uploads/2015/03/lc353_insurance-contract-law.pdf.

Law Reform Commission of Ireland, Consultation Paper LRC CP 65–2011, Insurance Contracts, December 2011.

The Draft Insurance Contracts Bill 2014 submitted by the Commission at the same time as their report available at http://www.lawcom.gov.uk/app/uploads/2015/03/lc353_insurance-contract-law.pdf.

Statutes (English and international)

Marine Insurance Act 1906

Marine Insurance Act 1909 (Australia)

The Consumer Insurance (Disclosure and Representations) Act 2012 (CIDRA)

Insurance Bill 2014–2015 available at http://services.parliament.uk/bills/

Explanatory Notes to the Insurance Bill 2014–2015 available at http://services.parliament.uk/bills/

Insurance Act 2015 available at http://services.parliament.uk/bills/

Insurance Act 2015 Explanatory Notes, Commentary on Sections, para 94, available at http://www.legislation.gov.uk

Special Public Bill Committee on the Insurance Bill [HL], Committee Stage, available at http://www.parliament.uk

Transcript of the Special Public Bill Committee on the Insurance Bill [HL], Committee Stage, 15 December 2014, pages 12–14, available at http://www.parliament.uk

Explanatory Memorandum to the Insurance Contracts Bill 1984, available at www5.austlii.edu.au/au/legis/cth/bill_em/icb1984230/memo_0.html

The Explanatory Notes to the Draft Insurance Contracts Bill 1982

Insurance Contracts Act 1984 (Australia)

New Zealand Insurance Law Reform Act 1977

Marine Insurance Codes

International Hull Clauses (IHC) 2003 available at https://www.google.com/search?client=safari&rls=en&q=International+Hull+Clauses+(IHC)+2003&ie=UTF-8&oe=UTF-8

Institute Time Clauses (Hull) (ITCH) available at www.medav.co.uk

Institute of Cargo Clauses available at https://www.lmalloyds.com/LMA/Underwriting/Marine/JCC/JCC_Clauses_Project/Cargo_Clauses.aspx

Norwegian Marine Insurance Plans, (NMIP) available at www.nordicplan.org

NMIP 2013 Part One, Rules Common to All Types of Insurance

The Norwegian Marine Insurance Plan of 1996, Version 2010 available at www.nordicplan.org

The Norwegian Marine Insurance Plan of 1996, Version 2013 available at www.nordicplan.org

Other sources

European Institute of Maritime and Transport Law

Association of British Insurers

Association of British Insurers, Insurance: Facts, Figures and Trends (1999)

Centre for Marine Law University of Queensland

Institute of London Underwriters

London International Insurance and Reinsurance Market Association

Lloyd's Insurance Broker's Committee

Comite Maritime International CMI

International Union of Marine Insurance

LIST OF WEBSITES

https://www.lawcom.gov.uk
www.alrc.gov.au
https://www.lawcom.govt.nz/home/welcome-law-commission
http://services.parliament.uk/bills/
http://www.lawcom.gov.uk/app/uploads/2015/03/ICL_Merkin_report.pdf or at https://eprints.soton.ac.uk/27860/
www.medav.co.uk
www.lloyds.com
www.nordicplan.org
www.alrc.gov.au
www.themaritimeadvocate.com
https://www.legislation.gov.uk
http://www.austlii.edu.au

INDEX

All references are to paragraph numbers.

For Product Safety Concerns and Information please contact our EU representative GPSR@taylorandfrancis.com
Taylor & Francis Verlag GmbH, Kaufingerstraße 24, 80331 München, Germany

www.ingramcontent.com/pod-product-compliance
Lightning Source LLC
LaVergne TN
LVHW080808011026
849160LV00015B/1566
* 9 7 8 1 0 3 2 0 1 7 3 6 5 *